Democracy's Feast

DEMOCRACY'S FEAST

Elections in America

edited by

Herbert F. Weisberg
The Ohio State University

Chatham House Publishers, Inc.
Chatham, New Jersey

DEMOCRACY'S FEAST: ELECTIONS IN AMERICA

Chatham House Publishers, Inc. / Post Office Box One / Chatham, New Jersey 07928

Publisher: Edward Artinian
Editor: Christopher J. Kelaher
Cover design: Lawrence Ratzkin
Composition: Bang, Motley, Olufsen
Printing and binding: R.R. Donnelley and Sons

LIBRARY OF CONGRESS CATALOGING-IN-PUBLICATION DATA

Democracy's Feast: Elections in America / edited by Herbert F.
   Weisberg.
      p.   cm.
   Includes bibliographical references and index.
   ISBN 1-56643-011-9
   1. Presidents—United States—Election—1992. 2. United States.
Congress—Elections, 1992. 3. Elections—United States.
I. Weisberg, Herbert F.
JK5261988m
324.973'0928—dc20   94-46140
                                                             CIP

Manufactured in the United States of America
10 9 8 7 6 5 4 3 2 1

To
Randall Ripley, Chair
Department of Political Science
The Ohio State University
1969–91

Contents

HERBERT F. WEISBERG
1. Democracy's Feast: The 1992 U.S. Election   1

Part I: The Presidential Election Outcome

STEPHEN M. NICHOLS AND PAUL ALLEN BECK
2. Reversing the Decline: Voter Turnout in the 1992 Election   29

HERBERT F. WEISBERG AND DAVID C. KIMBALL
3. Attitudinal Correlates of the 1992 Presidential Vote:
   Party Identification and Beyond   72

CHARLES E. SMITH, JR., AND JOHN H. KESSEL
4. The Partisan Choice: George Bush or Bill Clinton   112

ANTHONY MUGHAN AND BARRY C. BURDEN
5. The Candidates' Wives   136

HERB ASHER
6. The Perot Campaign   153

Part II: Group Voting in 1992

KATHERINE TATE
7. Structural Dependence or Group Loyalty?
   The Black Vote in 1992   179

ELIZABETH ADELL COOK AND CLYDE WILCOX
8. Women Voters in the "Year of the Woman"   195

HAROLD W. STANLEY AND RICHARD G. NIEMI
9. The Demise of the New Deal Coalition:
   Partisanship and Group Support, 1952–92   220

HERBERT F. WEISBERG, AUDREY A. HAYNES,
   AND JON A. KROSNICK
10. Social-Group Polarization in 1992   241

Part III: The Elections for Congress

SAMUEL C. PATTERSON AND MICHAEL K. BARR
11. Congress Bashing and the 1992 Congressional Election   263

JANET M. BOX-STEFFENSMEIER AND
   CHARLES H. FRANKLIN
12. The Long Campaign: Senate Elections in 1992   292

Appendix

BARRY C. BURDEN
Chronology of the 1992 Presidential Campaign   319

References   325
Index   337
Contributors   351

Figures and Tables

Figures

1.1. State Vote Map for the 1992 Presidential Election 22
2.1. Turnout in American Presidential Elections 31
2.2. Reported Turnout by SES 37–41
2.3. Reported Turnout by Race, Gender, and Age 42–43, 45
2.4. Reported Turnout by Region, Religion, Residential
Mobility, and Marital Status 46–49
2.5. Reported Turnout by Strength of Partisanship,
Political Efficacy, and Citizen Duty 50–52
2.6. Reported Turnout by Short-Term Political
Attitudes 53–55, 58
3.1. Changing Democratic Plurality 77
3.2. Party Thermometer Means 78
3.3. Growth of Political Independence 79
3.4. Trends in Democratic Lead 81
3.5. Trends in Presidential Approval and Economic
Variables 83
3.6. Trends in First Party Identification Question Series 84
3.7. Trends in Full Party Identification Question Series 86
3.8. Nominee Thermometer Means 100
8.1. Gender Differences in Partisanship 201
10.1. Correlation of Liberal and Conservative Factors 251
10.2. Loadings of Party and Ideology Groups 255
11.1. Retirements from the House 265
11.2. Congressional Fever Chart 272
11.3. Support for Term Limits in Fourteen States 274
11.4. House Election Margins 275
12.1. Stability of Roll-Call Record 298
12.2. Mean Liberal/Conservative Placement by Roll-Call
Voting Record 299
12.3. Stability of Mean Liberal/Conservative Placement 300
12.4. Prior Perception and Current Residuals 302

12.5. Challenger Spending by Incumbent Job Approval   304
12.6. Incumbent Vote by Long Campaign   311
12.7. Incumbent Vote by Short Campaign   311

Tables

1.1. 1992 Presidential Primary Results   14–16
1.2. 1992 Democratic Caucus Results   18
1.3. 1992 Presidential Vote by State   20–21
2.1. 1992 Reported Turnout by Race, Gender, and Age,
     Controlling on Education   44
2.2. Percentages Difference in the Probability of Voting be-
     tween Persons in High- versus Low-Turnout Cate-
     gories of Each Turnout Variable   56–57
2.3. Percentage of NES Sample Falling in Each Category
     of Turnout Variables   60–61
2.4. Percentage "Very" or "Somewhat" Interested in the
     Election by Age, Gender, Union Membership, Strength
     of Partisanship, Reading about the Campaign   63
2.5. Reported Turnout and Perot Support, by Education   64
2.6. Policy Preferences of Voters and Nonvoters   67–68
3.1. Party Identification by Year   76
3.2. Popularity of Parties by Year   78
3.3. Vote by Party Identification   80
3.4. Regression of Party Identification on Presidential
     Approval and Unemployment   87
3.5. Average Placement on Seven-Point Scales   91
3.6. Vote by Economic Issues   92
3.7. Presidential Vote by Race, Gender, Marriage,
     and Children   95
3.8. Vote by Issue Positions   97
3.9. Popularity of Nominees by Year   100
3.10. Candidate Images   101
3.11. Vote by Preelection Thermometer Ratings of Major-
      Party Candidates   105
3.12. Vote by Issue Positions   107
4.1. Probit Results from the Three-Variable Vote Model   118
4.2. Probit Results from the Sixteen-Variable Vote Model   118
4.3. Central Tendencies of the Independent Variables   119
4.4. Dispersion of the Independent Variables   123
4.5. Potency of the Predictors in the Three-Variable Model   124

4.6. Potency of the Predictors in the Sixteen-Variable
     Vote Model   125
5.1. Husband and Wife Thermometer Scores   139
5.2. Zero-Order Correlations between Individual
     Thermometer Scores   140
5.3. The Effect of Sociodemographic Variables and
     Husband and Wife Thermometer Scores on the
     Presidential Vote   142
5.4. Sources of Affect: Husbands and Wives Compared   144
5.5. Women's Issues, Candidates' Wives, and the
     Presidential Vote   147
6.1. The Standing of the Candidates during the 1992
     Campaign   155
6.2. The Relationship between Vote Choice and Party
     Identification   159
6.3. The Explained Variance in Thermometer Ratings of
     Bush, Clinton, and Perot Based on Four Models   166
6.4. The Statistically Significant Variables in Evaluations
     of Bush, Clinton, and Perot in Model 4   168
6.5. Citizens' 1988 and 1992 Presidential Votes   171
6.6. The Relationship between Preferred Candidates as
     Measured by Thermometer Rating and Actual
     Vote Choice   172
7.1. Percentage of Democratic Vote in Presidential
     Elections by Key Social and Political Groups   180
7.2. Voting and Registration by Race in Presidential
     Elections   184
7.3. Percentage of Registered Voters Who Did Not Vote, by
     Race and Hispanic Origin   186
7.4. Registered Black Voters Who Reported That They
     Did Not Vote in the 1992 Presidential Election   187
7.5. Percentage of Those Who Named the Democrats as Op-
     posed to the Republicans on Policy Matters, by Race 188
7.6. Percentage Who Said "Neither Party" or Had No
     Opinion on Policy Matters, by Race   189
7.7. Logit Analysis of Perception of Party Difference on
     Policy Matters (Republicans or Democrats vs.
     Neither Party or No Opinion)   190
7.8. WLS Confirmatory Factor Analysis of Perception of
     Party Difference on Policy Matters: Four-Factor
     Model   194

8.1. Partial Correlations between Sex and Issue Position
with Partisanship Controlled   202
8.2. Voting for Democratic Candidate in Senate
Elections   206–7
8.3. Gender Differences in Presidential Vote   210
8.4. Issue Salience in Vote Decisions, VRS Exit Polls   211
8.5. Sources of Candidate Evaluations for Men and Women   214
9.1. Mean and Incremental Probabilities of Democratic
Identification for Members of Each Group   224–25
9.2. Mean and Incremental Probabilities of Republican
Identification for Members of Each Group   227–28
9.3. Size and Composition of the Democratic Coalition   232–34
9.4. Size and Composition of the Republican Coalition   235
10.1. Social-Group Popularity in 1992   245
10.2. Social-Group Popularity by Ideology in 1992   246
10.3. Loadings of Attitudes toward Social Groups on
Latent Factors   248
10.4. Trends in Group Ratings   252
10.5. Social Group Popularity by Ideology in 1976   254
11.1. Evaluating and Voting for House Incumbents:
1992 Congressional Election   277
11.2. Strength of Partisan Congruence and Evaluations
of House Incumbents, 1992   279
11.3. Support for House Candidates in the
1992 Congressional Election   282–83
11.4. Predicting Voter Turnout in the
1992 Congressional Election   286–87
12.1. Development of Ideological Perceptions of
the Incumbent, 1992   301
12.2. Challenger Strength in 1992 as a
Function of Past Incumbent Approval   305
12.3. Median Incumbent Contributions and War Chests
over the Course of the Election Cycle   305
12.4. Incumbent Job Approval and Thermometer
History by 1992 Vote Outcome   306
12.5. Correlations of Senators' Perceived Ideology with
Mean Voter Ideology in 1990, by 1992 Vote
Outcome   307
12.6. Estimates of Long- and Short-Campaign Influences
on the 1992 Vote   310

Preface

Many books have already been written about the 1992 U.S. election, including journalistic accounts and several edited volumes. This book is distinctive in terms of pulling together the views of several election analysts based primarily on the National Election Study (NES) 1992 surveys. The books written immediately after the election have to rely on quick analyses of media polls and exit polls, both of which are much more limited in the questions they can ask about popular attitudes. Some voting behavior textbooks come out with new editions after each presidential election, incorporating the results of the latest election along with analysis of the NES surveys. But the texts tend to revisit the same topics in each edition, without being able to adapt fully to election-specific topics such as the Perot candidacy or the first lady competition in election 1992. By focusing on the NES survey in this book without needing to maintain continuity with earlier editions, we attempt to provide a comprehensive analysis of the forces influencing the voting decisions of 1992.

Books are always collective activities. This book certainly is. As editor, I owe a considerable debt to the authors of the several chapters who responded with considerable speed to many urgings and deadlines, and to Barry Burden and Mark Kemper, who gave me assistance while working on this book. Special appreciation is to be given to Ed Artinian, the publisher of Chatham House, for suggesting this project. I also want to give the standard acknowledgment to the National Election Studies for continuing to pursue an important electoral data collection, to Warren E. Miller, Donald R. Kinder, and Steven J. Rosenstone, who directed the 1992 NES surveys, to the National Science Foundation for funding those surveys, and to the Inter-University Consortium for Political and Social Research for making these data available to the larger community of election scholars; these studies are a valuable resource, and we are fortunate that these individuals and organizations continue to put so much effort into these surveys.

On behalf of the authors of these chapters, I want to thank those who reviewed parts of this book other than their own chapters, including Herb Asher, Paul Beck, Janet Box-Steffensmeier, Barry Burden, Elizabeth Adell Cook, Donald Green, Audrey Haynes, John Kessel, David Kimball, Anthony Mughan, Stephen Nichols, Samuel Patterson, Charles Smith, Harold Stanley, Katherine Tate, and Clyde Wilcox. Finally, a very heartfelt debt is to Randall Ripley, the long-time chair of the Department of Political Science at The Ohio State University and now Dean of the College of Social and Behavioral Sciences at Ohio State. Most of the authors of this book have or have had associations with the department, largely because Rip Ripley helped attract us to Columbus, Ohio, and helped create the collegial and congenial atmosphere that led to the writing of this book.

CHAPTER I

Democracy's Feast: The 1992 U.S. Election

HERBERT F. WEISBERG

H. G. Wells in 1927 wrote that "democracy's ceremonial, its feast, its great function, is the election." The idea of the election as "democracy's feast" is engaging, especially because "feast" has so many meanings at once. The most obvious is that of a banquet, and elections are reminiscent of banquets, with their many separate races corresponding to the many courses served at such an event. But the other important meaning of the term is a celebration, and elections are indeed the celebrations of democracy.

Celebrations have many facets: they can be part ceremony and part carnival. Elections are both of these: they are the rites of democracy, and they are accompanied by the revelry and diversion associated with carnivals. Speaking of elections as carnival is unusual, in that they are generally viewed more seriously. But an election is not merely a solemn occasion bereft of enjoyment; it is also the stuff of entertainment, providing enjoyable activities and new friends for campaign workers, as well as an occasion for the public to turn its attention from normal activities to the hoopla and excitement of a campaign.

Every election provides some combination of these different characteristics. Some seem so predictable in their outcomes that it is difficult to imagine them as occasions for carnival, though campaign workers generally find elements of enjoyment in even the most cut-and-dried elections. Other election campaigns possess so much color, so many unexpected twists and turns, and so much drama and melodrama that they capture the public's attention and imagination. This book is about such an election, the 1992 U.S. election.

The 1992 Election

One could debate whether it was a feast or a famine, but few would view the 1992 campaign as boring. There was George Bush at the highest point of popularity a president had ever achieved after the decisive victory of the Alliance forces in Desert Storm in early 1991 and then losing that popularity in record speed to become vulnerable by 1992. There were David Duke and Pat Buchanan trying to humiliate Bush in the Republican primaries, with Buchanan succeeding in drawing some blood. There was the wide-open race for the Democratic nomination, populated mainly by political unknowns when leading Democrats prematurely decided that 1992 was not the year to run against a popular Republican incumbent. There were Paul Tsongas and Jerry Brown, railing against politics as usual, catching public attention with such unlikely issues as deficit reduction and a flat-rate income tax. There was Bill Clinton, always on the defensive against charges both of marital infidelity and of draft evasion. There was Ross Perot, threatening to run a third-party race for the presidency and at times leading the public opinion polls, then dramatically dropping out of the race during the Democratic convention, and then returning to the race just in time to attract public attention in the presidential debates. Toss in Dan Quayle's focus on the family values issue as personified by television character Murphy Brown, Al Gore's attempt to make the environment into a sexy issue, and Admiral Stockdale's turning up his hearing aid during the vice-presidential debate, and 1992 could not be considered a boring election year.

The 1992 elections provided many diversions for the American public. Barbara Bush and Hillary Clinton offered two very different models for the nation's first lady. It was the "year of the woman" political candidate, after the Senate hearings on confirmation of Supreme Court nominee Clarence Thomas turned to the allegation that he sexually harassed Anita Hill and then to how fairly she was treated by the all-male Senate Judiciary Committee. It was a year of Congress bashing, after the House of Representatives was caught in scandal because many of its members had bounced checks at the House bank. It was perhaps predictable that the campaign would be fought out on television, but it was surprising when the specific venue turned out to be alternative television, such as *Larry King Live,* Ross Perot's infomercials, and Bill Clinton's town hall meetings. If elections are democracy's feast, then the 1992 election was reminiscent of eating to excess.

The 1992 election reminds one of the importance of the rituals of democracy. It showed again how even the most popular of presidents can be turned out of office by an electorate that becomes dissatisfied with unresolved national problems. It demonstrated how peaceful exchanges of power between competing political elites are the distinguishing features of democracies. It emphasized how new political leaders can emerge both within and outside the existing political party structure when the public feels there is need for change.

But the 1992 election was also a celebratory feast, marked by diversion and carnival. This was exemplified by the Clinton-Gore bus trip on the road through Middle America back to the land of nostalgia. The level of unreality was increased by the television character Murphy Brown's rebuttal to real-life vice-president Dan Quayle. The carnival element was highlighted by Ross Perot's entertaining the public with televised rallies in which he danced with his wife to his campaign theme, "Crazy." The campaign moved toward soap opera when the Clintons appeared on television on *60 Minutes* after the Super Bowl to deal with the marital infidelity issue.

Feasts sometimes mark the ending of a long preparation process; at other times they presage the beginning of a new cycle. In viewing an election as a feast, it is important not to view the election as an ending. It is not an ending as much as it is a turning point—whether as reaffirmation or as a point of change. Even the reelection of a president is often marked by large changes in his cabinet and/or staff, as was the Reagan reelection of 1984. Bush's election as president in 1988 was an instance of the White House staying in the control of one party, but it, too, was marked by changes, as epitomized by Bush's "kinder, gentler America." Ronald Reagan's 1980 defeat of incumbent president Jimmy Carter was certainly a case of change, a move toward the political right on economic and social issues; Bill Clinton's 1992 defeat of incumbent president George Bush was similarly a case of change, a move toward the political left, especially on social issues. Furthermore, politics continues after the election, though with newly reconstructed issues and themes. Thus, on the night that George Bush was going down to his electoral defeat, Bob Dole appeared on television to take over the mantle of Republican leadership in Washington in a manner that suggested that he was going to be a leading contender for the Republican presidential nomination of 1996.

Every presidential election is a transition in some sense. The 1992 election was a transition in many ways. It was the first post–Cold War presidential election for the United States, with worries about the Communist threat and the resulting possibility of nuclear war lessened. Yet regardless of U.S. victories in the Cold War and in Desert Storm, the 1992 election was largely focused on domestic issues, particularly the economy. As the legendary sign in Bill Clinton's campaign headquarters in Little Rock, Arkansas, reminded his forces, "It's the economy, stupid!" The economy was the Democrats' issue, with unemployment relatively high and the country unable fully to shake off the recession that had started in 1990.

The 1992 election also marked a generational transition, as the candidate who fought in World War II lost to the candidate who avoided military service in Vietnam. More important, it was a transition in campaign technology, as many of the key campaign events were fought out on cable television rather than on network TV. The new information technology permitted users of computer networks to read campaign news on-line and to communicate with the candidates' campaign staffs. And the Clinton candidacy became the first "postmodern" candidacy. Bill Clinton epitomized the contradictions of postmodern society, as he was both a Rhodes Scholar and the running target of tabloid journalism trying to uncover scandal about his supposed affairs with Gennifer Flowers and others.

Feasts are often large gatherings, pulling together many different groups. The 1992 election involved the activity of many groups, several of which were new to presidential campaigns. Women's groups participated actively, especially EMILY'S List, which helped channel early campaign money to promising female candidates. Homosexual groups participated more actively in the campaigns, especially when Clinton promised to permit gays to serve in the military. The Perot forces developed a new campaign group, United We Stand, throughout the fifty states.

Describing an election as a feast has an extra normative connotation, implying that the citizens viewed the election in a favorable manner. Without carrying this metaphor too far, one has to admit that the American public did not necessarily find the 1992 election so very delectable. Indeed, many citizens and commentators viewed the election (and most recent elections) as more famine than feast. They did not consider the choices available in the election to be the best possible choices for the nation's highest office.

There was also a general distrust of politicians in 1992. Such distrust was certainly nothing new in American politics, but it had intensified as a result of the scandal over checks bounced by members of Congress at the House bank. Add to that questions about whether Bill Clinton could be trusted, based on rumors of marital infidelity plus his inability to put aside questions about his past. Meanwhile, President Bush remained dogged by questions about his truthfulness in the Iran-*contra* affair of the mid-1980s. These questions intensified in the last week of the campaign when Special Prosecutor Lawrence Walsh indicted Reagan's Secretary of Defense Caspar Weinberger on the basis of Weinberger's diaries. Those diaries cast doubt on Bush's denial of his involvement as vice-president in the decision-making loop on the arms sales to Iran.

The distrust of politicians boiled over to fuel H. Ross Perot's campaign for the presidency. Promising a "government you can trust" and telling voters that they are the "owners" of the country for whom the politicians merely work, Perot managed to keep the election year in perpetual ferment. Perot dominated the political headlines of 1992 so that the major-party candidates had to keep responding to his initiatives. Perot's withdrawal from the campaign in mid-July gave Clinton his opportunity to speak directly to the American public and zoom ahead in the polls, just as Perot's return to the campaign in October muddied the waters of the presidential debates and took away Bush's sole remaining opportunity to capture the attention of the public. Yet the Perot candidacy raised at least as many questions as it answered. He was the billionaire running as outsider, although he had gained considerable money over the years from government contracts for his firm. Many people viewed him as a quitter after his initial withdrawal, while others were bemused by his later explanation that the withdrawal was intended to frustrate GOP attempts to wreck his daughter's wedding. As a result, most citizens did not find Perot to be an acceptable solution to the perceived lack of quality presidential candidates.

While it is fun to think of the 1992 election in terms of the "feast" metaphor, it is important to go further in order to understand the results of the election. Why did voter turnout increase in 1992? Were party ties stable during the election? What explains Clinton's victory over Bush? Did the first ladies affect the result? How is the Perot vote to be understood? Were gender voting differences important in the "Year of the Woman"? What motivated the black vote? Did the Clinton victory represent a return to power of the old New Deal coalition that had long been the basis of Democratic support? What was the effect of Congress bashing in the end in the congressional election? And how should the Senate elections of 1992 be understood? These are important questions that can best be answered through a careful analysis of surveys of the 1992 voting public.

The 1992 National Election Study

The analysis in this book relies very heavily on the American National Election Study (NES) of 1992, a survey conducted by the University of Michigan's Survey Research Center with funding by the National Science Foundation. Scholars based at the University of Michigan started taking surveys of the electorate on a regular basis in the 1950s. Responsibility for the surveys was turned over to the "National Election Studies" (NES) in the 1970s when the National Science Foundation assumed responsibility for regular funding.

The main elements of the presidential election studies in this series are a preelection survey in September–October of the election year followed by a postelection interview with the same respondents in November–December. The 1992 study consisted of interviews with 2,462 respondents in their homes.[1] The sampling frame for the study was all U.S. citizens who were age eighteen by election day and who lived in housing units. Residents of Hawaii and Alaska were excluded, as were people who lived on military reservations. The pre- and postelection surveys were both lengthy interviews, typically lasting an hour.

In some presidential election years the NES surveys have been "panel studies" with the same respondents being interviewed across a series of elections (such as 1956–58–60 and 1972–74–76). The 1992 NES survey was partly of this type. Half of the respondents were new, while the other half were the third wave of a panel study that had first been conducted after the 1990 congressional election and continued with reinterviews in summer 1991 after the Alliance victory in Desert Storm.

Additionally, the NES has conducted several important studies of legislative elections. The number of questions on voting for the House of Representatives was increased considerably starting in 1978, and has remained high since. Further, in 1988 NES started a special Senate election study, interviewing a sample of respondents in every state. Only a third of the Senate is up for election in any election year, so it takes three election years for every Senate seat to be up for election. Therefore, the NES Senate study continued in 1990, and it ended with another survey in 1992. Taken together, these three studies permit an analysis of changing attitudes toward senators across a full election cycle. Chapter 12 of this book, by Janet Box-Steffensmeier and Charles Franklin, takes advantage of this unique study design to discuss voting in Senate elections.

Returning to the main NES presidential election surveys, there has been considerable continuity over time in the questions asked in these studies. This continuity is both an advantage and a disadvantage. The lengthy time series permits the analysis of change over time on a number of questions. Yet the need to re-ask many of the same questions from election year to election year has meant that the surveys do not have enough time to introduce many new questions. Actually the 1992 survey included more new questions (on such diverse matters as gays in the military and feelings toward the candidates' wives) than most previous NES studies, but this meant that some traditional questions were dropped and cannot be followed through 1992.

The Perot candidacy proved to be as considerable a challenge for the NES survey as for candidates Bush and Clinton. The first draft of the NES questionnaire included a large number of Perot questions, but they were dropped when he left the race. The preelection study was already half completed when Perot reentered, and there was no opportunity to reinsert the Perot questions. As a result, the NES study has relatively few questions about Perot. This makes it more difficult to assess the nature of the Perot candidacy, though Herb Asher, in chapter 6 of this book, argues that this does not materially affect our understanding of that candidacy. In any case, the minimal number of questions about Perot should be recognized from the outset.[2]

Note that the decision to interview 1,500 to 2,500 people in the NES surveys has a particular implication for statistical generalizations. There are many sources of error in polls, such as the interviewer misreading a question, poor question wording, or an answer being recorded incorrectly. One important source of error in polls is related to the sampling. "Sampling error" results from interviewing only a sample of people rather than the full population of interest. For example, the level of sampling error for the 1992 study has been estimated to be 3.2 percent. That means that results are accurate to about 3 percent. Finding that 45 percent of the sample has some attitude thus really means that the proportion of the population with that attitude is probably between 42 (45 − 3) and 48 (45 + 3). The NES surveys generally take about 1,500 to 2,500 interviews, since a 3 or 4 percent sampling error is usually considered reasonable. Note that this does not include those nonsampling errors mentioned at the beginning of this paragraph, as it is impossible to estimate statistically the degree of error from misreading questions or biased question wording. In any event, it is appropriate to keep in mind this 3 percent margin of error in reading the results in the following chapters (and to recognize that the margin of error increases when dealing with smaller subsamples of the population).

Many different question formats can be used in surveys. The most basic distinction is between precoded (or "closed-ended") questions in which respondents are given the choice between a few answers versus "open-ended" questions to which respondents can freely answer anything on their minds. Asking whether the respondent is a Republican, a Democrat, or an independent is an example of a closed-ended question, while asking what the person likes and dislikes about the Democratic Party is an example of an open-ended question. Open-ended questions can take more time during a survey and are more expensive to analyze, so commercial polls tend to rely on closed-ended questions.

The NES surveys are known for using many open-ended questions and for developing some unusual closed-ended question formats. Their open-ended questions about the 1992 presidential contest are particularly valuable in that they allow an investigation of what was on the minds of people who voted for different candidates. These open-ended questions are analyzed extensively in chapter 4 by Charles Smith and John Kessel in order to obtain an understanding of the relative importance of different factors in the 1992 race. One of the more unusual closed-ended formats in this study is the "thermometer" question, which asks people to rate on a scale of 0 to 100 how "warm" they feel toward particular political personalities and social groups. The thermometer question on the political personalities is examined in several chapters of this book, while the social group thermometers are used as the basis for studying the role of ideology in 1992 in chapter 10. Another unusual closed-ended format in the study is the "seven-point scale," in which respondents are asked to locate their position (and often where they believe the parties or candidates stand) on ideological scales ranging typically from 1 for a liberal position to 7 for a conservative position. Responses to the seven-point-scale questions are analyzed in chapter 3 as part of seeing how issues affected the 1992 election.

In stressing the NES data, it is important to recognize that several other high-quality studies of voter attitudes in 1992 exist, including exit polls, government surveys, and media polls, each of which are used on occasion in this book. Voter Research and Surveys (VRS) conducts the exit polls used extensively by television networks for election night projections of which states went for which candidates. These are very large surveys that, because of their size, give very precise statements about the voting of many demographic groups; however, they do not include as many attitudinal questions as do the NES surveys. The Census Bureau conducts a large postelection survey of who voted and did not vote because of the need for statistics to monitor compliance with the Voting Rights Act. Because of its size, this study gives very precise statements about the turnout of particular demographic groups, but the usefulness of these data are limited by the fact that the Census Bureau is not permitted to ask attitudinal or vote-direction questions. Finally, the media conduct several surveys, such as the prestigious CBS News/*New York Times* polls. These surveys tend to be about the same size as the NES survey. Their principal advantage is that they are conducted many times between elections, making it possible to trace the nature of opinion change from 1988 through 1992. They tend to focus on topical matters that can be analyzed quickly, however, rather than on issues that lead to complicated, over-time comparisons. Each of these surveys has its own advantages and disadvantages. Later chapters make some use of these polls, as appropriate, while emphasizing mainly the NES data.

Use of the NES data also carries some implications as to the type of analysis that can be conducted. Just as the choice of questions in the VRS, Census Bureau, and media polls reflects particular orientations, the same is true in academic surveys. The American National Election Studies have been conducted since the middle of the twentieth century, with a considerable continuity of questions based mainly on one particular view of voting.

The Framework for Studying Voting

The approach to looking at the 1992 presidential election in this book follows the main framework of voting behavior studies in the United States. The dominant paradigm since the writing of *The American Voter* (Campbell, Converse, Miller, and Stokes 1960) has been a social-psychological emphasis on attitudes. Three main classes of relevant attitudes are distinguished in studying voting direction: attitudes toward the political parties, attitudes toward the issues, and attitudes toward the candidates. While there is some controversy on this point (Niemi and Weisberg 1993b, chap. 16; Weisberg and Kimball, chap. 3 in this volume), most studies treat attitudes toward the parties as long-term aspects of voting that affect the shorter-term attitudes toward the issues and the candidates. Some studies have tried to disentangle the extent to which attitudes on the issues and the candidates affect one another (see particularly Markus and Converse 1979; Page and Jones 1979), but these attempts have not led to definitive conclusions. In any event, party identification is generally treated as a long-term component—most Republicans vote Republican in presidential elections and most Democrats vote Democratic; short-term issue and candidate factors can cause partisans to defect to the opposite party and influence the voting behavior of independents. Issues and candidates vary more between elections, and the advantage they give one side or the other also varies between elections. The early social-psychological work emphasized more the importance of partisanship in voting, whereas "revisionists" have given more emphasis to the importance of issues.

Several chapters in this book focus on these aspects of the 1992 election. David Kimball and I examine the nature of party identification in considerable detail in chapter 3, and John Kessel and Charles Smith consider the relative importance of issues and candidates in the presidential election in chapter 4. In chapter 5 Anthony Mughan and Barry Burden provide an analysis of an intriguing short-term effect: the role of the prospective first ladies.

It is more difficult to use this framework to understand voting for third-party candidates. The emphasis on party identification is less relevant for such candidacies. Some findings do apply, such as the greater loyalty of strong partisans to their party, and so third-party candidates would receive more of their vote from independents and weak partisans. Additionally, the usual finding is that older people have stronger partisan ties than younger people, so third-party candidates would receive more of their vote from younger citizens. Issues can be particularly important for third-party candidates, and obviously the candidate factor is likely to be particularly important. Chapter 6 by Herb Asher examines the Perot candidacy, applying these ideas and testing the extent to which the Perot vote can be understood from this perspective.

In addition to vote direction, it is important to understand voting turnout and its determinants. Turnout can also be considered from both long-term and short-term perspectives. In chapter 2 Stephen Nichols and Paul Allen Beck examine voting turnout in 1992, with special attention to the short-term effect of the Perot candidacy on turnout.

Although the approach described here emphasizes the role of parties, issues, and candidates, it also recognizes that these attitudes have their own antecedents. Citizens develop stands on parties, issues, and candidates because of their own background, their demographics, and their learning about politics from their parents ("political socialization"). This leads to an interest in how different social groups develop different views on parties, issues, and candidates and hence vote differently. The chapters in part II of this book apply this perspective. Katherine Tate (chapter 7) analyzes the important black vote in 1992. In chapter 8 Elizabeth Adell Cook and Clyde Wilcox turn to the role of gender in the election in the "year of the woman." In chapter 9 Harold Stanley and Richard Niemi extend their analysis of social-group differences in partisanship (Stanley and Niemi 1993) to the 1992 contest, testing whether the return of a Democrat to the White House represents the reemergence of the New Deal coalition. The social-group topic is continued in chapter 10, in which Audrey Haynes, Jon Krosnick, and I examine the structure of attitudes toward social groups as a means of understanding the nature of ideological conflict and polarization in the 1992 campaign.

While the emphasis so far has been on presidential elections, the general framework described in this section has also been used to study congressional elections, but some further factors must be taken into account. In the 1980s the typical election was marked by 90+ percent of incumbent members of the House of Representatives who were running for reelection being returned to Congress. As a result, the literature on congressional elections has emphasized the importance of incumbency. Many studies have sought to understand the nature of the incumbency advantage (Jacobson 1987). These explanations have focused on the ways in which incumbents can use their office to build future campaign support by helping individual constituents with their problems with government ("casework"), as well as by helping get federal projects that create jobs ("pork") to the district.

Two further factors must be considered in analyzing recent congressional elections. First, scandals have affected individual races (Peters and Welch 1980), as well as public evaluations of Congress as a whole. Second, the development of attitudes toward U.S. senators over their full six-year terms should be taken into account. The chapters in part III of this book focus on these permutations. In the aftermath of a serious scandal involving the U.S. House of Representatives, chapter 11 by Samuel Patterson and Michael Barr examines Congress bashing in the 1992 House elections. Chapter 12 by Janet Box-Steffensmeier and Charles Franklin turns to the Senate elections of 1992 in the context of citizen attitudes toward these same senators in 1990 and 1988.

It should be added that other frameworks are used to analyze voting. These frameworks give less attention to party identification than does the approach described above, but give more attention to such elements as issues, candidates, or social groups. The rational-choice approach treats voters as rational actors choosing between parties and candidates on the basis of their utility calculations; this leads to a greater emphasis on the issue side of voting. The NES surveys have generally included enough issue questions to permit some analysis of this approach as well, though, unfortunately, there were fewer issue questions in the necessary format in the 1992 study. Meanwhile, the "political psychology" approach tries to model how voters think through political choices when they have to make decisions with limited information on the basis of stored knowledge and new information; this approach leads to greater attention to political candidates and to how voters process information about those candidates (Rahn, Aldrich, Borgida, and Sullivan 1990). Recent NES surveys ask many candidate-related questions that can be used in applying this approach, though, again unfortunately, such questions were not asked about Perot in 1992 because of his temporary withdrawal from the race. Additionally, the sociological approach examines social groups and their voting behavior. This approach was the basis of some of the earliest voting surveys (Lazarsfeld, Berelson, and Gaudet 1944; Berelson, Lazarsfeld, and McPhee 1954) and remains important today. It underlies much of the attention to the group basis of the 1992 vote in part II of this book.

While the chapters in this book emphasize the social-psychological framework for understanding voting, it is important to admit that there is no attempt to proclaim a single model of voting in the chapters that follow. There is considerable variety in the exact models used in understanding voting in the broader voting behavior literature, so it is appropriate for that variety to be reflected in the chapters in this book. The chapters tend to follow a similar framework, but the models employed vary somewhat from chapter to chapter in accord with what is most appropriate for the topics of those chapters.

The 1992 Presidential Contest

It may be useful to provide a quick recounting of the 1992 presidential contest. Later chapters fill in several details, but it is important to understand the main stories of the election year.[3]

THE NOMINATIONS

Understanding a general election often requires understanding how the candidates were nominated by their parties. Technically, party presidential nominees are selected by national party conventions that meet in the summer of the election year. Delegates to those conventions are chosen from each state in the preceding half-year. Some states choose their delegates to these national conventions by caucuses (public meetings in which any citizen in the community can participate), but since 1972 most states have chosen their delegates by voting in presidential primaries.

The incumbent president generally hopes for a free ride in the primaries so that all his resources can be saved for the general election in the fall; however, incumbents are often not that lucky. For example, Jimmy Carter was challenged in the 1980 Democratic primaries by Edward Kennedy. Carter was able to withstand the challenge and win the nomination, but by then he was sufficiently weakened that he lost the general election to Ronald Reagan. Sometimes a strong early challenge can actually help make an incumbent decide against running for reelection, as happened when Eugene McCarthy's success in the early 1968 Democratic primaries and Robert Kennedy's imminent entry into the race helped lead to Lyndon Johnson's decision against running for reelection that year.

President Bush looked like a shoo-in for renomination and reelection in March of 1991, when the victory of Alliance forces in the Persian Gulf propelled him to record popularity in public opinion polls. Nevertheless, his candidacy faced two problems. First, the country was in an economic recession that seemed about to end after the war, but instead continued. Second, Bush had taken a "no new taxes" pledge in the 1988 New Hampshire primary and then had accepted a 1990 budget that included a large tax increase. These problems made him potentially vulnerable in the primaries, especially from the political right.

George Bush did face competition in the 1992 Republican primaries, but not from Republican senators or governors. David Duke, a state legislator in Louisiana, was his first announced opponent. State legislators running for president would not normally receive much press attention, but Duke received considerable media coverage because he was an ex-wizard of the Ku Klux Klan. At that point, Pat Buchanan, a political commentator and former aide to President Reagan, jumped into the race on the conservative side.

In the end, Bush won the Republican nomination with relative ease. Buchanan took attention away from Duke. There was likely to be a protest vote against Bush, but with Buchanan on the ballot, this protest vote did not have to go to the extremist Duke. Buchanan's best showing turned out to be in the first primary, the New Hampshire contest in mid-February, where he won 37 percent of the vote and Bush obtained 53 percent. If Bush looked weak at that point in the campaign, he quickly improved his performance, scoring from 60 to 83 percent of the vote in later state primaries. The primary results are recounted in table 1.1A and summarized in table 1.1B.

Buchanan's candidacy probably helped the Bush campaign in some respects. Not only did it draw attention away from David Duke, but it forced the Bush campaign team to start work earlier than it might otherwise have done. Had Bush won the nomination without any contested primaries, Democratic challengers could have attacked him for months without his having the opportunity to practice his campaign pitches. Instead, Bush got press attention by campaigning actively for his party's nomination, while Buchanan's 22 percent of the primary

TABLE 1.1. 1992 PRESIDENTIAL PRIMARY RESULTS

		Republican Primary			Democratic Primary			
		Bush vote	Second		Clinton vote	Clinton position	First or Second	
Date	State	(%)	(%)	Candidate	(%)		(%)	Candidate
18 Feb	New Hampshire	53	37	Buchanan	25	2	33	Tsongas
25 Feb	South Dakota	69	31	Uncommitted	19	3	40	Kerrey
3 Mar	Colorado	68	30	Buchanan	27	2	29	Brown
	Georgia	64	36	Buchanan	57	1	24	Tsongas
	Maryland	70	30	Buchanan	34	2	41	Tsongas
7 Mar	South Carolina	67	26	Buchanan	63	1	18	Tsongas
10 Mar	Florida	68	32	Buchanan	51	1	34	Tsongas
	Louisiana	62	27	Buchanan	70	1	11	Tsongas
	Massachusetts	66	28	Buchanan	11	3	66	Tsongas
	Mississippi	72	17	Buchanan	73	1	10	Brown
	Oklahoma	70	27	Buchanan	70	1	17	Brown
	Rhode Island	63	32	Buchanan	21	2	53	Tsongas
	Tennessee	72	22	Buchanan	67	1	19	Tsongas
	Texas	70	24	Buchanan	66	1	19	Tsongas
17 Mar	Illinois	60	22	Buchanan	52	1	26	Tsongas
	Michigan	67	25	Buchanan	51	1	26	Brown
24 Mar	Connecticut	67	22	Buchanan	36	2	37	Brown
5 Apr	Puerto Rico	99	0.4	Buchanan	96	1	2	Brown
7 Apr	Kansas	62	17	Uncommitted	51	1	15	Tsongas
	Minnesota*	64	24	Buchanan	31	1	31	Brown

	New York	—	—		41	1	29	Tsongas
	Wisconsin	76	16	Buchanan	37	1	34	Brown
28 Apr	Pennsylvania	77	23	Buchanan	56	1	26	Brown
5 May	District of Columbia	82	18	Buchanan	74	1	10	Tsongas
12 May	Indiana	80	20	Buchanan	63	1	22	Brown
	North Carolina	71	20	Buchanan	64	1	15	Uncommitted
	Nebraska	81	14	Buchanan	46	1	21	Brown
	West Virginia	81	15	Buchanan	74	1	12	Brown
19 May	Oregon	67	19	Buchanan	45	1	31	Brown
	Washington*	67	20	Perot	42	1	23	Brown
26 May	Arkansas	83	12	Buchanan	68	1	18	Uncommitted
	Idaho*	64	23	Uncommitted	49	1	29	Uncommitted
	Kentucky	74	26	Uncommitted	56	1	28	Uncommitted
2 Jun	Alabama	74	18	Uncommitted	68	1	20	Uncommitted
	California	74	26	Buchanan	48	1	40	Brown
	Montana	72	17	Uncommitted	47	1	24	Uncommitted
	New Jersey	78	15	Buchanan	59	1	20	Brown
	New Mexico	64	27	Uncommitted	53	1	17	Brown
	Ohio	83	17	Buchanan	61	1	19	Brown
9 Jun	North Dakota*	83	8	Perot				Brown

SOURCES: *Congressional Quarterly's Guide to the 1992 Democratic National Convention*, 4 July 1992, 69; and *Congressional Quarterly's Guide to the 1992 Republican National Convention*, 8 August 1992, 63.

NOTE: "Position" shows Clinton's position in the primary (1 = winner, 2 = second, etc.). "First or Second" shows the winner's percentage if Clinton lost the primary or the second-place candidate's percentage if Clinton won the primary.

* Nonbinding "beauty contest" primary.

TABLE 1.1B
SUMMARY OF 1992 PRESIDENTIAL PRIMARY RESULTS

Republican Primary Totals (%)		Democratic Primary Totals (%)	
73	Bush	52	Clinton
22	Buchanan	20	Brown
2	Uncommitted	18	Tsongas
1	Duke	4	Uncommitted
.4	Perot	2	Kerrey
1	Other	1	Harkin
		.2	Perot
		3	Other

votes was not enough to cause serious injury to Bush's reelection chances. Still, much of Bush's press attention was negative, and he had to recover from this in the fall campaign.

Contests for the nomination are to be expected for the opposition party. Several well-known Democrats decided against running in 1992, partly because of Bush's strong standing in the early 1991 polls. In particular, House Majority Leader Dick Gephardt (Missouri), Senators Bill Bradley (New Jersey), Al Gore (Tennessee), Sam Nunn (Georgia), and Jay Rockefeller (West Virginia), the Reverend Jesse Jackson, and Governor Mario Cuomo of New York all decided against running. Still, it was a lively race, with two senators (Tom Harkin of Iowa and Bob Kerrey of Nebraska), one ex-senator (Paul Tsongas of Massachusetts), two governors (Bill Clinton of Arkansas and Doug Wilder of Virginia), and one former governor (Jerry Brown of California). The "six-pack" of Democratic candidates held several early debates, until the early primaries winnowed the pack.

Wilder, the only African American in the race, dropped out early because of the need to pay more attention to governing his state. Harkin did well in the early caucuses in his home state of Iowa (see table 1.2) but never did well in primaries. Kerrey won the little-noticed South Dakota primary (see table 1.1A) but did poorly elsewhere.

By Super Tuesday, 10 March, when eight states held primaries, the race had narrowed down to three contenders: Paul Tsongas, who had won the New Hampshire and Maryland primaries and was trying to tell the American public how to deal more responsibly with the large budget deficit; Jerry Brown, who had won the Colorado primary and was campaigning for a simplified flat-rate income tax; and Bill Clinton, who had won the Georgia primary and had managed to stay in the race despite stories about his evading the draft in the Vietnam war, marital infidelity, and trying marijuana.

The Super Tuesday primaries were concentrated in the South. Southerner Clinton won six of the eight primaries. Tsongas won the primary in his home state of Massachusetts that day, along with the Rhode Island primary, but he suspended his race after poor showings the following week in the Michigan and Illinois primaries. Brown stayed in the race until the end, but his only other victory was in the mid-March Connecticut primary. Meanwhile, Clinton racked up delegates from presidential primary states (table 1.1A) and caucus states (table 1.2), and after the last primary on 2 June had amassed enough delegates to claim the nomination.

What is missing from this account of the 1992 primary season is a proper appreciation of the role of Ross Perot (see chapter 6 by Herb Asher). Perot stepped onto the national scene just after the New Hampshire primary. He received considerable press play throughout the spring, culminating on 2 June when he chose Hamilton Jordan, formerly a leading adviser to President Jimmy Carter, and Ed Rollins, onetime adviser to President Reagan, as his campaign managers. Bush had the lead over Clinton in early polls, and Clinton needed public attention if he was going to catch up with Bush. Perot, however, was the one getting the press attention, and he was doing well in the national polls.

The one remaining point of suspense in the preconvention season was the choice of vice-presidential candidates. Bill Clinton chose fellow southerner Al Gore to be his running mate, and this proved to be a popular selection in the media. Meanwhile, Vice-President Dan Quayle had become the object of many jokes, mainly questioning his intelligence. Still, he was popular with Republican conservatives, who often distrusted the strength of Bush's commitment to their positions. In the end, Bush decided to stick with Quayle.

There were few surprises at the party conventions. The Democratic convention in mid-July and the Republican convention in mid-August followed their scripts fairly exactly. The big surprise occurred the day Clinton was to give his speech formally accepting the Democratic nomination. Ross Perot unexpectedly pulled out of the race, saying that the unified Democratic campaign made it unnecessary for him to run. The result was a large audience for Clinton's acceptance speech. This speech and the accompanying biographical film on "The Man from Hope" (Arkansas) were effective. As a result, Clinton took a lead over Bush in the polls at that point, with most of Perot's support migrating to him. The Republicans hoped for a bounce in the polls after the Republican convention, but it did not occur. Thus, after trailing Bush in the polls

TABLE 1.2
1992 DEMOCRATIC CAUCUS RESULTS

Date	State	Clinton vote %	Clinton position	First or Second %	First or Second Candidate
10 Feb	Iowa	3	4	76	Harkin
23 Feb	Maine	15	4	30	Brown
3 Mar	American Samoa	4	3	87	Uncommitted
	Idaho*	11	4	30	Harkin
	Minnesota*	10	4	27	Harkin
	Utah	18	3	33	Tsongas
	Washington*	13	4	32	Tsongas
5–19 Mar	North Dakota*	46	1	26	Uncommitted
7 Mar	Arizona	29	2	34	Tsongas
	Wyoming	28	1	23	Brown
7–9 Mar	Democrats Abroad	27	2	37	Tsongas
8 Mar	Nevada	27	2	34	Brown
10 Mar	Delaware	21	3	30	Tsongas
	Hawaii	52	1	14	Tsongas
	Missouri	45	1	39	Uncommitted
28 Mar	Virgin Islands	40	2	56	Uncommitted
31 Mar	Vermont	17	3	47	Brown
2 Apr	Alaska	31	3	35	Uncommitted
11–13 Apr	Virginia	52	1	36	Uncommitted
3 May	Guam	49	1	31	Uncommitted

SOURCE: *Congressional Quarterly's Guide to the 1992 Democratic National Convention,* 4 July 1992, 70.

NOTE: "Position" shows Clinton's position in the caucus (1 = winner, 2 = second, etc.). "First or Second" shows the winner's percentage if Clinton lost the caucus or the second-place candidate's percentage if Clinton won the caucus.

* Also held nonbinding primary.

throughout the primary season, Clinton took the lead at convention time and that was the standing when the fall campaign started.

THE CAMPAIGN

Election campaigns are fought, in part, on the issues. Many issues were raised in the 1992 campaign, but the issue that dominated was the economy. The economy had grown rapidly during the Reagan years, but that growth slowed during the Bush administration. Not only was there a recession, but it became a "double dip" recession when the initial recovery faltered, and some claim it became a "triple dip" recession when the second recovery slowed. The Clinton campaign viewed the economy as *the* issue, their issue. Perot, when he reentered the race in October, emphasized a different issue—the need to tame the budget deficit that had skyrocketed through the 1980s.

Election campaigns are also fought, in part, on the basis of the candidates and their stories. The country was already used to George Bush. Bill Clinton was a new personality on the national political scene. If his team wanted to paint him as the candidate of hope, the Bush people wanted to damage him by emphasizing the "trust" issue. They portrayed Clinton as someone the public could not trust as president. Whenever the trust issue was raised, the public was expected to remember Clinton's "Slick Willie" nickname as well as the marital infidelity claims.

Recent U.S. presidential election campaigns have been fought partly in televised debates. The debates were the prime events of the 1992 campaign season. After the usual preliminary haggling over the number, timing, and format of the debates, there were three presidential debates (plus one vice-presidential debate). By then, Ross Perot had reentered the race, although his poll standings were meager at that time. George Bush had to accept debates as his best chance for catching up with Bill Clinton. The debates (along with his televised infomercials) permitted Perot to reestablish himself as a serious political personality. Perot's presence took away Bush's ability to confront poll-leader Clinton directly; instead, Bush's record was attacked on two sides. The debates led to reaffirmation of voter support for Clinton. Clinton was able to solidify his standing, based on his ability to project empathy for the public.

THE ELECTION RESULTS

The polls throughout the 1992 fall campaign showed Clinton with a lead. The Bush campaign was buoyed in the final week of the campaign when *USA Today* published a poll showing Bush's standing improving. But careful inspection showed that the change partly reflected a redefinition of the base of the numbers, looking at probable voters rather than all respondents in the sample. Bush's standing seemed to go down again a couple of days later when the special prosecutor's indictment of Caspar Weinberger brought the Iran-*contra* scandal of the 1980s back into the headlines. Still, these developments led to some uncertainty as to what to expect in the final election results.

The election results contained their share of surprises. In 1988 George Bush became the first sitting vice-president in more than a cen-

TABLE 1.3
1992 PRESIDENTIAL VOTE BY STATE

	Popular Vote Percentage			Electoral Votes [a]	
	Clinton (Democrat)	Bush (Republican)	Perot (Independent)	Clinton (Democrat)	Bush (Republican)
Alabama	41	48	11		9
Alaska	32	41	27		3
Arizona	37	39	24		8
Arkansas	54	36	11	6	
California	47	32	21	54	
Colorado	40	36	23	8	
Connecticut	42	36	22	8	
Delaware	44	36	21	3	
District of Columbia	86	9	4	3	
Florida	39	41	20		25
Georgia	44	43	13	13	
Hawaii	49	37	14	4	
Idaho	29	43	28		4
Illinois	48	35	17	22	
Indiana	37	43	20		12
Iowa	44	38	19	7	
Kansas	34	39	27		6
Kentucky	45	42	14	8	
Louisiana	46	42	12	9	
Maine	39	31	30	4	
Maryland	50	36	14	10	
Massachusetts	48	29	23	12	
Michigan	44	37	19	18	
Minnesota	44	32	24	10	
Mississippi	41	50	9		7
Missouri	44	34	22	11	
Montana	38	36	26	3	

Continued ...

tury to win the presidency. Yet President Bush managed to snatch defeat from the jaws of victory in 1992. Indeed, his lower-than-expected 37.7 percent of the popular vote fell between the levels of two recent landslide defeats: Goldwater's 38.5 percent in 1964 and McGovern's 37.5 percent in 1972. The result continued the trend since William Howard Taft of presidents who succeed incumbent presidents of the same party not winning more than one term on their own.

Bill Clinton won the presidency despite Republican attempts to focus on the trust issue, but with a surprisingly weak 43.2 percent of the

TABLE 1.3 – *Continued*
1992 PRESIDENTIAL VOTE BY STATE

	Popular Vote Percentage			Electoral Votes[a]	
	Clinton (Democrat)	Bush (Republican)	Perot (Independent)	Clinton (Democrat)	Bush (Republican)
Nebraska	30	47	24		5
Nevada	38	35	27	4	
New Hampshire	39	38	23	4	
New Jersey	43	41	16	15	
New Mexico	46	38	16	5	
New York	50	34	16	33	
North Carolina	43	44	14		14
North Dakota	32	44	23		3
Ohio	40	39	21	21	
Oklahoma	34	43	23		8
Oregon	43	32	25	7	
Pennsylvania	45	36	18	23	
Rhode Island	48	29	23	4	
South Carolina	40	48	12		8
South Dakota	37	41	22		3
Tennessee	47	43	10	11	
Texas	37	40	22		32
Utah	26	46	29		5
Vermont	46	31	23	3	
Virginia	41	45	14		13
Washington	44	31	24	11	
West Virginia	49	36	16	5	
Wisconsin	41	37	22	11	
Wyoming	34	40	26		3
Total	43	38	19	370	168

a. Perot won no electoral votes.

vote, maintaining a string of limited mandates for nonincumbent presidents. (The last victory of a nonincumbent president by as much as 55 percent was Eisenhower in 1952, followed by Bush's 53 percent in 1988, Reagan's 51 percent in 1980, Carter's 50+ percent in 1976, Kennedy's 50– percent in 1960, and Nixon's 43 percent in 1968.) Clinton's weak victory left him vulnerable to later attacks on his ethics in the Whitewater investigation of 1994.

Clinton's victory in the Electoral College was more decisive than his popular vote margin; he won 370 electoral votes compared to Bush's 168 (see table 1.3). As the map in figure 1.1 shows, Clinton was

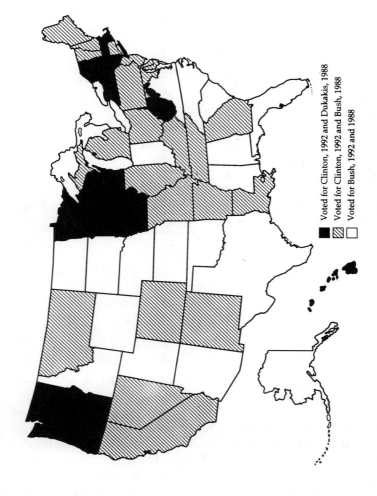

Voted for Clinton, 1992 and Dukakis, 1988

Voted for Clinton, 1992 and Bush, 1988

Voted for Bush, 1992 and 1988

FIGURE 1.1. STATE VOTE MAP FOR THE 1992 PRESIDENTIAL ELECTION.

able to win states in each region, from New England and the large eastern industrial states, to the South, the Midwest, the Mountain states, and the Pacific coast. Clinton won the two largest states, New York and California, whereas Bush won the next two most populous states, Texas and Florida. Ross Perot came in second in two states (Maine and Utah) but won no electors.

The most distinctive aspect of the 1992 election was the Ross Perot candidacy (see Herb Asher's chapter 6). Perot ended up with 19 percent of the vote, the highest non-major-party vote since Teddy Roosevelt in 1912. This vote was much higher than preelection polls had forecast.

Another unexpected result of the election was the increase in turnout (see chapter 2 by Nichols and Beck). The drop in turnout since 1960 was dramatically reversed, with a climb from a 50 percent rate in 1988 to 55 percent in 1992. The higher level calmed fears of having the first presidential election since the 1920s in which less than half of the eligible citizens chose to vote.

On the congressional election side, the Democrats retained control of the House and the Senate. The House scandals led to a bumper crop of freshmen representatives, but little partisan change. The new House contained only ten fewer Democrats than before. The party totals in the Senate were completely unchanged. What did change was the representation of women and minorities. The number of women in the Senate increased from two to six (with a seventh elected a few months later). There were considerable increases in the numbers of women, African Americans, and Hispanics elected to the House. Additionally, term limits on legislators were enacted by ballot measures in fourteen states.

These trends were modified in the 1994 midterm elections in ways that were severe on Democratic incumbents. As usual, 90 percent of House incumbents were reelected in 1994, but the changes that occurred were virtually unidirectional toward the Republicans. The Republicans gained over fifty seats in the House and eight in the Senate (plus a ninth when Senator Richard Shelby of Alabama switched parties and became a Republican). As a result, the Republicans gained control of the Congress—the first time since 1953–54 for the House and since 1981–86 for the Senate. At least 87 freshmen were elected to the House in 1994, but the representation of women and minorities changed less than in 1992—the number of women in each chamber went up by just one, while the numbers of African Americans and Hispanics held steady. As another sign of the anti-incumbent mood of the 1994 electorate, six more states enacted term limits on legislators, so that 22 of the 23 states that permit citizen initiatives have adopted term limits.

Conclusions

Opinion surveys are very useful in assessing the shape of popular attitudes as well as in understanding elections. The surveys of 1992 repeat many results that are familiar from polls taken in earlier election years, while they show some elements of change—such as the attention to the candidates' wives, the discontent that led to the vote for Perot, and the high level of Congress bashing. The 1992 surveys also show how easily trends can be reversed, such as the increase in Republican partisanship throughout the 1980s, which led many election analysts to think they were witnessing a long-term partisan realignment.

Nevertheless, election polls at best reflect the political present and are much less useful in predicting the political future. Thus, emphasizing the crucial role that the economy played in the 1992 election just serves to remind us how fickle the voting public can be: voters are likely to turn to other voting issues when the economy improves, but the public can throw out the incumbent party if the economy worsens before the next election. Similarly, Ross Perot could draw a large vote and influence voting turnout in an election in which the country was uneasy about politics-as-usual, but it would take little to draw the public's attention to different themes by the 1996 election, at which point Perot might find himself a historical irrelevancy (just as Harold Stassen became a national laughingstock in the 1960s when he was seen as a perennial presidential candidate). The unusual dynamics of the Clarence Thomas nomination for the Supreme Court and the charges that Anita Hill aired against him in the Senate Judiciary Committee resulted in gender and race factors having particular poignancy in the 1992 election, but a different unpredictable event could galvanize other voting groups by the next presidential election.

This does not mean that the 1992 elections are lacking in lessons for the country or for the study of voting. We learn that the decline in voting turnout that started in 1960 is neither inevitable nor irreversible. We learn that the public can pay a lot of attention to an election when the economic situation and the candidates are interesting enough to attract that attention. We learn that social groups can take advantage of circumstances to increase their representation in Congress. These are important lessons, for they remind us of the vitality of American democracy.

The 1992 findings also have implications for major themes in voting behavior research. For example, there has been controversy as to the importance of issues in elections, but one common claim is that the public is most likely to vote on the basis of economic issues. The important role of the economy in the 1992 election reinforces the image of rational voters who make economic judgments when the situation warrants. Similarly, there has been controversy as to whether short-term developments can affect party identification, with particular focus on the effects of the economy on partisanship (MacKuen, Erikson, and Stimson 1989; Weisberg and Smith 1991; Abramson and Ostrom 1991; Miller 1991). The reversal in direction of partisan change from 1988 to 1992 correlates sufficiently with economic changes to bolster the view that partisanship is changeable, especially with respect to economic changes.

The NES surveys are ideal in some respects but less useful in others. One of the most important stories of 1992 cannot be studied well from the 1992 NES survey: the role of the media. The media constantly change, and skilled politicians know how to take advantage of that change. Thus television became an important part of elections by 1960, and John Kennedy was the early master of appealing to the public through that medium. By the 1980s it was possible to obtain quick measurements of public opinion and plan media strategies on the basis of those measurements, and Ronald Reagan became known as the "great communicator" because he took effective advantage of those possibilities. By 1992 the importance of the traditional media slipped as alternative media became important, and Ross Perot and Bill Clinton, each in his own way, knew how to use alternative media to his advantage. There is a debate in the communications literature as to whether the media have minimal effects on politics or have larger effects, but the Perot and Clinton handlers knew with certainty that the media can have large effects. The importance of the alternative media will not be lost on contenders in future presidential elections, though some may be too busy learning the lessons of 1992 to notice what further changes occur in the media.

If there is a continuing theme to voting behavior studies of the last several decades, it is the increased volatility of the electorate. By most academic accounts, there was a major change in voting in the 1930s, with the nation switching from a Republican majority to a Democratic majority because of the Great Depression. Once this "New Deal realignment" took full effect, voting trends seem to have been very stable in the late 1930s and 1940s. Defection from party ties became more prominent in the 1950s, but there was little sign of another lasting realignment. Instead, many analysts argue that the real change since then has been a dealignment—a movement away from the parties—starting in the middle of the 1960s and accelerating in the 1970s. Another interpretation of voting change over these years is that voting volatility has been on the increase, with the electorate less willing to remain stable in their political views than they were in the 1930s and 1940s. This volatility was temporarily stilled in the 1980s when the Republicans managed to keep the White House in their hands, but it resumed with a vengeance in 1992 with the Clinton victory, the large Perot vote, and the increased voter turnout. Politicians and their handlers used the new political media to create voting change in 1992, and this may be the election's enduring legacy. The election of 1992 showed that the feast of democracy can be served on the newest platters of telecommunications. We look forward with relish to the next serving.

Notes

1. There were actually 2,485 interviews; however, standard practice is to "weight" interviews to correct for any unusual aspects of the sampling process, and the weighted number of cases for this survey was 2,462.

2. A more serious problem with the Perot candidacy is the difficulty in statistical analysis of a three-candidate race. Classical statistical procedures (such as "linear regression analysis") for assessing the relative importance of different causal factors assume that the variable being studied (the "dependent variable") is continuous. Common dependent variables in the study of voting behavior are just dichotomous, however, including the decision whether or not to vote and vote direction in a two-party contest. Analogs to regression analysis have been developed for such situations, in particular the probit analysis and the related logit analysis technique used in some later chapters.

The situation becomes even more dicey when dealing with a three-candidate election. Some exotic solutions have been proposed, mainly a multivariate logit procedure and more recently a multivariate probit estimator (Alvarez and Nagler 1993), but these are more complicated techniques than are appropriate to use in this book. The third candidate can be disregarded in the analysis, but it was easier to ignore the 8 percent of the vote that John Anderson received in 1980 or the 14 percent that George Wallace won in 1968 than to ignore Ross Perot's 19 percent. The situation would be especially problematic if there were reasons to feel that the third candidate received his vote disproportionately from one candidate, but at least most analyses of 1992 agree that Perot's vote came from both Clinton and Bush. The analysis in this book focuses on the Bush-Clinton race (or on Perot specifically in the Asher chapter); one hopes that the estimates of effects provided here will be relatively close to those of more complicated three-candidate analyses.

3. A full chronology of election 1992 by Barry Burden appears in the appendix to this book.

PART I

The Presidential Election Outcome

Reversing the Decline:
Voter Turnout in the
1992 Election

STEPHEN M. NICHOLS AND PAUL ALLEN BECK

For close to thirty years, in a ritual as inevitably a part of the presidential election aftermath as victory speeches and inaugurations, scholars and pundits alike have spoken in solemn tones about the decline of voter participation in the United States. Warnings of the dire consequences of the decline were especially pronounced after the 1988 election, when turnout fell to a modern low of 50.1 percent. Although there is nothing magical about the 50 percent level, many wondered if 1992 would mark the first time in the contemporary political era that nonvoters would outnumber voters in the most important U.S. election. Some voiced concern for the quality of democracy in a country wherein virtually a majority of citizens fail to participate in this most fundamental way.

For the time being at least, these fears were not realized. Voter participation climbed to an official level of 55.2 percent in 1992, the first significant increase since 1960. Turnout rose in forty-nine of fifty states[1] as over 100 million Americans (the highest number in U.S. history) went to the polls.

The underlying causes of the turnout upswing are as important as the magnitude of the increase. If 1992 witnessed significant and enduring changes in the traits and attributes associated with voting, we might then view the election as the beginning of an era of growing electoral involvement in the United States. The evidence to be presented in this chapter, however, supports a different conclusion. Our findings point to short-term factors specific to 1992—in particular, heightened interest in the election, concern over the outcome, and expectations of a close race, all perhaps intertwined with the presence of the popular independent candidate, Ross Perot—as the sources of the turnout increase. Unless short-term factors emerge again to enhance voter turnout in future years, 1992 will have been merely a brief respite from the long trend of declining political participation, rather than the onset of a new era of high turnout.

As we lay out the evidence for this interpretation of the turnout increase, we address a number of interesting topics. First, who voted in 1992, and how did their behavior differ from preceding years? We examine turnout across various groups in the electorate, comparing 1992 turnout with voting rates in other recent elections. These comparisons shed light on our effort to account for the 5 percent turnout rise from 1988, and to ascertain what the presence of Perot might have contributed to the increase. Finally, we address the consequences of low U.S. voter turnout for the 1992 election specifically and, more generally, for the quality of American democracy. Before examining these questions, however, we should first place contemporary American turnout into a broader perspective.

Recent American Voter Turnout in Broad Perspective

With only slightly over half the potential electorate participating in the most important election, voter turnout in the United States today is quite low by historical standards. Throughout much of the 1800s voting rates were markedly higher than they have been in recent years. From 1828 to 1900, turnout never fell below 56 percent of the voting-age population;[2] in fact, from 1840 to 1900, turnout *averaged* better than 74 percent (see figure 2.1).

The high points of voter participation in the 1800s appear to coincide with especially riveting electoral periods. The 1830s and 1840s marked a period of unusually competitive partisan battles between the Whig and Democratic parties. Unlike the recently defunct Federalist Party, neither the Whigs nor the Democrats were reluctant to pursue popular support, and their mobilization efforts stimulated turnout in specific elections during this period.[3] High turnout between 1856 and 1876 was no doubt linked to the nation's battle over slavery and Reconstruction, some of which was waged in the voting booth. Participa-

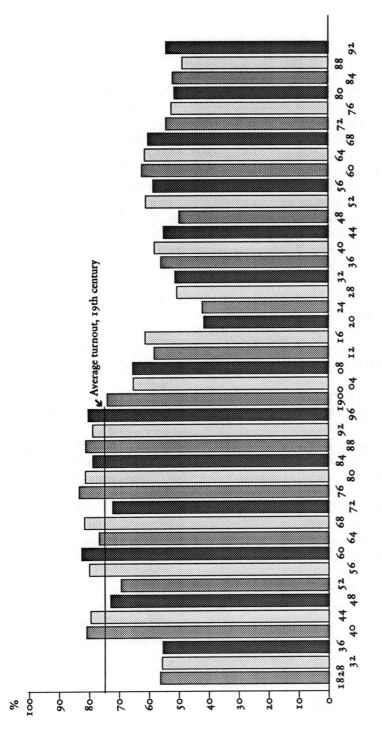

FIGURE 2.1. TURNOUT IN AMERICAN PRESIDENTIAL ELECTIONS, 1828–1992.

SOURCES: 1828–1984: Eric W. Austin, *Political Facts of the United States Since 1789* (New York: Columbia University Press, 1987), table 3.12. 1988: *Statistical Abstract of the United States* (Washington, D.C.: U.S. Bureau of the Census, 1990), 265. 1992: Richard M. Scammon and Alice V. McGillivray, *America Votes* (Washington, D.C.: Elections Research Center, Congressional Quarterly, 1993), 9.

tion declined somewhat after 1880, largely as a result of the effective disenfranchisement of blacks and poor whites in the South after federal troops left the region at the end of Reconstruction. Turnout peaked again in 1896 when William Jennings Bryan, a Populist who captured the Democratic presidential nomination, lost to Republican William McKinley in an election cited by scholars as one of a handful of "realigning" elections that have reshaped the country's political landscape.

While the peaks and valleys of nineteenth-century turnout may be easily understood, the reasons for the general participatory decline after 1896 are the subject of spirited debate. Turnout fell from nearly 80 percent in 1896 to under 50 percent by 1920. Poor turnout among women is one obvious factor in the low 1920 rate. The Nineteenth Amendment (passed shortly before the 1920 election) granted women in all states the right to vote, but overall turnout levels waned as this newly enfranchised portion of the electorate did not immediately exercise their voting rights in large numbers.

Nonetheless, the post-1896 participation decline was well under way before women gained the franchise, and the trend continued even as turnout differences between the genders narrowed. Thus, other factors must account for the decline in voting turnout in the 1900s. But considerable disagreement remains over the nature of these "other factors."

Walter Dean Burnham contends that the American party system became much less competitive after the 1896 election, as single parties came to monopolize local and state politics across the land. The effect (and even, he suggests, the cause) was that industrial elites were able to insulate themselves from the pressures of participatory democracy during the critical early years of the twentieth century. Lacking the workers' or socialist party alternatives that existed in European democracies, many Americans grew increasingly disinterested in politics, and turnout fell as a result (Burnham 1965).

Others prefer a less apocalyptic and conspiratorial explanation. Philip Converse (1972) hypothesizes that most if not all of the decline in turnout after 1896 may be accounted for by concurrent changes in voting laws—in particular, the introduction of voter registration. Stiff registration requirements, enacted across the country between 1890 and 1910, were aimed at reducing vote fraud, and fewer fraudulent votes would obviously lessen the overall vote tally. Registration also depressed turnout by placing a greater burden on honest citizens: whereas they could once simply show up at the polls on election day, they now faced the additional hurdle of registration.

Another reform designed to lessen vote fraud, and likely affecting turnout in the process, was the secret ("Australian") ballot adopted throughout the states in the 1890s.[4] This secret ballot, and the governmental control over elections it entailed, replaced a system in which citizens cast votes on ballots prepared by the political parties. Each party had used a ballot of a different color, which contained only *its* candidates for office, and distributed the ballot outside the polling booth. In their public choice of a party ballot, voters' preferences were obvious, and vote buying was common. Once voting became secret, candidates could no longer be sure they were getting a return on their investment. As vote buying declined, some citizens may have lost the incentive to vote. Government control over the voting process also made it more difficult (although hardly impossible) for dishonest politicians to stuff the ballot box. Turnout surely waned too as a result of the move to the Australian ballot.

The extent to which the post-1896 turnout decline should be attributed to institutional change versus decreased electoral competition is uncertain. What is clear is that voter turnout in this century is considerably lower than in the 1800s. This is not the only benchmark against which contemporary U.S. turnout appears low: citizens in other democracies vote at much higher rates than do Americans. Turnout routinely exceeds 80 percent in such countries as Germany, Norway, Denmark, New Zealand, the Netherlands, Greece, Portugal, Sweden, Belgium, and Austria; in Australia and Italy, where voting is compulsory, turnout of over 90 percent is common. Among advanced Western democracies, no nation regularly has lower turnout in its most important elections than the United States.

That Americans' turnout is so comparatively low is particularly puzzling because U.S. citizens enjoy a considerable advantage in terms of the attitudinal traits and sociodemographic factors—particularly overall education levels—most conducive to voter turnout. G. Bingham Powell (1986) contends that given their much higher levels of education and stronger feelings of citizen duty and partisanship, Americans ought to vote at a higher rate than their counterparts abroad. These sociodemographic and attitudinal advantages, however, are more than offset by the unusual legal and institutional barriers confronting the American electorate.

The highest of these barriers, voter registration, encompasses a package of rules, including residency requirements, deadlines for registration well before election day, location and availability of registrars, and rules for purging names from registration lists after a period of nonvoting.[5] Voting in the United States is essentially a two-step process, and the first step, registering, in many ways requires more initiative than the voting act itself. Moreover, this initiative must be taken at least one month before an election in most states, often before interest in the contest has been aroused. Voter registration is thus a far more difficult act in the United States than elsewhere; in nearly every other democracy, the burden of registration in fact is placed on the shoulders of the government rather than the citizen. Powell estimates that roughly 10 percent of the difference in turnout between the United States and other democracies may be attributed to the impact of U.S. voter registration laws alone. The registration task became somewhat easier in the United States with the recent passage of the "motor voter" bill, enabling citizens to register to vote as they apply for driver's licenses and for services at some governmental agencies. Though this legislation was not passed in time to affect turnout in 1992, it may well have an impact on future voting rates (Weisberg 1994).

Powell notes that other American institutional and political features contribute to its low turnout. For example, in systems with multiple parties contesting elections (the norm in other democracies), parties are able to appeal to smaller and more homogeneous segments of the electorate; the electoral appeals of the two American "catchall" parties are necessarily much broader. Parties elsewhere are therefore better able to represent group differences in society, resulting in stronger party-group ties and greater success in turning out the vote. Additionally, proportional representation, common in multiparty systems, produces more competitive elections. Citizens supporting a party with little chance of outright victory still have an incentive to vote because even a second- or third-place showing may earn their party seats in the legislature and a role in forming a government. The "winner-take-all" nature of plurality elections and single-member districts in the United States affords citizens supporting a likely loser little reason to vote.[6]

Still other factors underlie the comparatively low voter turnout. Elections are commonplace in the United States. Counting general presidential contests, primary elections, off-year congressional races, local elections, and referendums and initiatives, Americans may vote as many as eight times in a four-year period. British voters, by comparison, may participate only two or three times over the same span.[7] Electoral participation may thus seem less of a privilege to American citizens than to citizens of other countries. Additionally, elections abroad are often held on weekends—in some countries election days are national holidays[8]—and absentee voting is easier elsewhere than in the United States. In short, less effort is required for voters in other democracies to make it to the polls on election day.

Thus it seems that institutional and legal arrangements, as much as the nature of politics, account for low American voter turnout relative to other democratic nations and, where they have changed, even to U.S. turnout in the 1800s. These same factors, however, cannot explain why U.S. turnout steadily waned after 1960. The fact of the matter is that voting has become easier in this country since that time, as registration requirements have been relaxed and, in the South, discriminatory practices aimed at depressing turnout among poor whites and especially blacks (such as poll taxes and literacy tests) have been eliminated. The post-1960 turnout decline is even more curious because aggregate education levels in the United States have risen steadily over this period—and, as we later see, education is one of the strongest correlates of voter turnout.

Against this backdrop, the sudden reversal of the thirty-year trend of participatory decline that began after the 1960 Kennedy-Nixon contest is noteworthy, even if it does not come near to lifting turnout to historical or comparative levels. The questions are, why did it happen and what does it mean for the future of American electoral politics? As we turn to examine voter turnout in 1992, these twin questions motivate our inquiry. Before dealing directly with them, though, we first need to identify the factors that account for variations in turnout levels among Americans across recent presidential elections—to specify, in short, who votes and who does not.

Who Votes in American Elections?

Before the advent of survey research, analysts had to rely on aggregate voting records to study electoral participation. While useful for constructing overall turnout figures and estimates for various regions of the country, these documents reveal little about the factors that account for turnout differences among citizens in any single place. To examine the forces associated with turnout at the individual level, information on individuals—collected through surveys rather than large aggregations within local or state voting districts—is necessary.

The most useful of these surveys, and the ones scholars studying elections rely on most, are the National Election Study (NES) series conducted by the University of Michigan's Center for Political Studies in every presidential election since 1952. The data presented in the remainder of this chapter are from these NES surveys.

Before turning to the survey results, however, we should point out that turnout estimates from surveys are invariably higher than actual turnout rates, in part because some survey respondents claim to have voted when they have not.[9] The NES frequently checks voter registration records in order to validate their respondents' reported turnout, but this validation was not done for the 1992 survey. We must therefore base our analysis on reported turnout. Because the 1992 turnout figures presented here are thereby inflated, when we compare these to past elections we use reported rather than validated vote for the earlier periods as well. Assuming that vote overreporting was no greater in 1992 than in past years (and this strikes us as a reasonable assumption), the relative comparisons made in this chapter between 1992 and previous elections will be valid. We should also note that even validated vote figures from surveys exceed actual turnout levels, in part because survey samples tend to underrepresent certain social categories having very low turnout (e.g., the homeless and persons who travel extensively) and because inclusion in a survey about politics tends to increase political awareness, thus producing higher turnout among survey respondents.

The interesting aspects of voter turnout in 1992 are best illuminated through a comparison with participation levels in other recent presidential contests. To this end we have identified two "turnout eras" in modern American elections.[10] The first is the high turnout period from 1952 to 1960, during which an average of better than 61 percent of the voting-age population went to the polls. Average turnout from 1964 to 1988, by contrast, fell to around 55 percent, and, for contests after 1968, this figure dips to 53 percent. This was an era of relatively lower and steadily declining turnout that culminated in the 50.1 percent figure for 1988.

Examining individual differences in turnout across different electoral eras serves two valuable purposes. First, it enables us to establish the factors most strongly related to turnout year in and year out. The factors we study are the conventional ones: socioeconomic attributes, sociodemographic traits, long-term political attitudes, and election-specific attitudes. By showing that the relationships found for 1992 are replicated in earlier years, we can have more confidence that we have uncovered enduring patterns of turnout differentials among Americans.

Second, a comparison of these relationships in 1992 with those in the earlier eras helps to account for the *changes* in turnout since 1952. Different turnout levels in the three eras may be the result of changing relationships between individual attributes and attitudes and participation. This, however, may tell only part of the story. We must also consider shifts over time in the *composition* of the electorate, that is, in changes in the proportion of the electorate within the various categories of these turnout correlates. Evidence on both fronts is needed to explain the 1992 turnout rise.

SOCIOECONOMIC ATTRIBUTES

Perhaps the most striking feature of American turnout patterns is that persons of higher socioeconomic status (SES) vote at significantly higher rates than those below them on the SES totem pole; similar patterns are conspicuously absent in many of the world's democracies.[11] Citizens in the upper socioeconomic brackets—those with a college education, those holding white-collar jobs and earning above-average incomes, those who deem themselves "middle class"—are much more likely to vote than persons in lower education, income, occupation, and social-class categories. As figure 2.2A-E indicates, this has consistently been the case for the turnout eras studied here, including 1992.

The SES attribute most closely related to turnout is education. The association is particularly evident in 1992, when more than 90 percent of the college-educated electorate went to the polls; among persons who

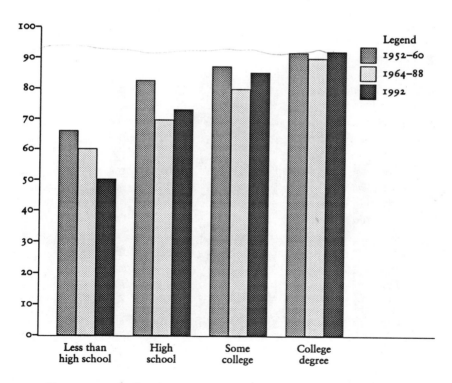

FIGURE 2.2A. REPORTED TURNOUT (IN PERCENT) BY SES: EDUCATION.

SOURCE: National Election Studies, 1952–92.

had not completed high school, barely half reported having voted. Wolfinger and Rosenstone (1980, 35–36) argue that an individual who has successfully navigated the bureaucratic terrain of higher education should have relatively little difficulty dealing with the obstacles (particularly registration) confronting a potential voter. Additionally, advanced education should provide the cognitive skills helpful in dealing with the often abstract world of politics, as well as a larger store of political knowledge. Finally, education promotes a stronger sense of citizen duty, suggesting that educated citizens derive more gratification than the undereducated from voting.

Beyond its direct link to turnout, education is tightly intertwined with other SES variables and thus indirectly influences participation. For example, white-collar occupations, held primarily by the college educated, typically involve more complex mental activity and greater cog-

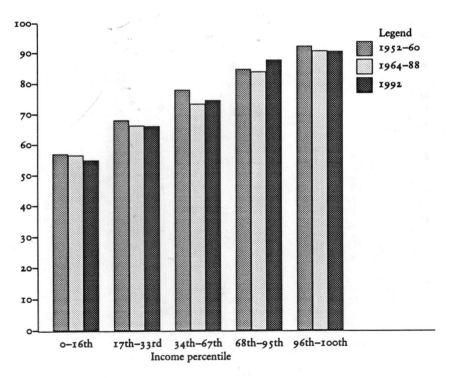

FIGURE 2.2B. REPORTED TURNOUT (IN PERCENT) BY SES: INCOME.

SOURCE: National Election Studies, 1952–92.

nitive effort than do blue-collar jobs. They may be linked to higher turnout, then, for many of the same reasons as advanced education. Belonging to the middle class and enjoying higher income—again, largely the province of the educated—may be associated with turnout in much the same way. In short, persons in the upper SES categories are better able to cope with the procedural and informational demands of voting. Additionally, higher turnout among upper-income persons may be tied to the perception of a greater stake in the socioeconomic system. Ruy Teixeira (1987, 22) views SES variables as turnout "facilitators," a term that nicely captures the link between socioeconomic status and electoral participation.

One other factor, labor union membership, deserves mention here. Other things being equal, households in which a union member resides tend to have higher turnout than other households, undoubtedly because of their involvement in an organization that stimulates political

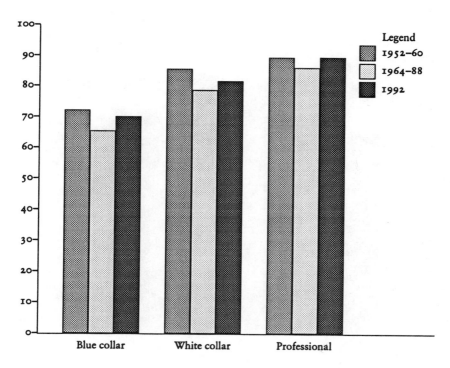

FIGURE 2.2C. REPORTED TURNOUT (IN PERCENT) BY SES: OCCUPATION.

SOURCE: National Election Studies, 1952–92.

awareness. One lesson we have learned about turnout from studying
other nations and other times is that the existence of organizations ded-
icated to mobilizing particular groups in political action, especially
lower SES groups that might not ordinarily participate at high rates,
can boost their turnout. Unions are the best example of such mobilizing
groups in the United States. As figure 2.2A-E suggests, however, the
"boost" they can achieve is neither as powerful nor as consistent as that
of the SES traits and turnout. This is probably because "other things"
are *not* equal: union members tend to have relatively low levels of education and thus are less likely to vote than one might guess based on
their group affiliation. Nonetheless, among those with a high school diploma or less, belonging to a union adds nearly 20 percent to turnout
levels over those who do not belong.

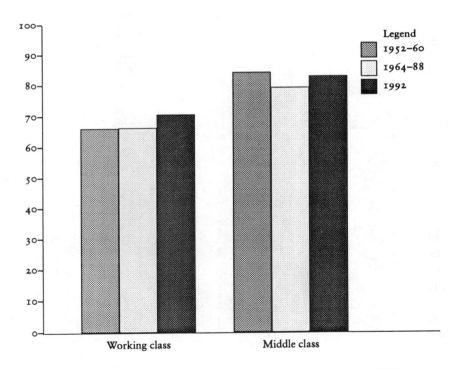

FIGURE 2.2D. REPORTED TURNOUT (IN PERCENT) BY SES:
SOCIAL CLASS.

SOURCE: National Election Studies, 1952–92.

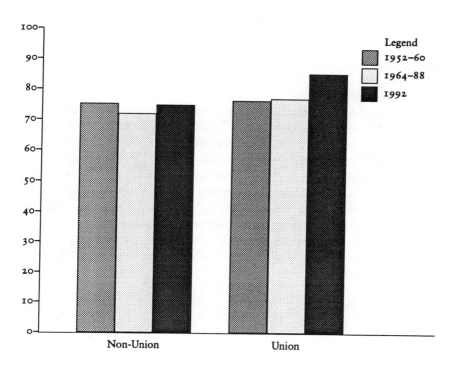

FIGURE 2.2E. REPORTED TURNOUT (IN PERCENT) BY SES:
UNION MEMBER IN HOUSEHOLD.

SOURCE: National Election Studies, 1952–92.

SOCIODEMOGRAPHIC TRAITS

Voter turnout also varies considerably across a number of sociodemo-graphic categories commonly used to describe people. The most impor-tant of these are race, gender, age, region, religion, residential mobility, and marital status (see figures 2.3A-C and 2.4A-D).

Whites evince higher turnout rates than blacks,[12] although the dif-ferences, once large, have narrowed considerably in recent years. In fact, in view of the institutional and legal (not to mention extralegal and blatantly illegal) electoral roadblocks that have confronted black voters in the United States, the rise in black turnout since the 1950s is nothing short of remarkable. We have more to say on this topic shortly (see also Katherine Tate's discussion of the black vote in 1992, chapter 7 in this volume); here we simply note that the post-1960 turnout decline would have been even larger were it not for the rising participation among black voters.

Similarly, there once was a sizable turnout disparity between men and women. Traces of it turn up in the gender differences for 1952–60 and 1964–88; it is even larger among the older generations of women, who have had difficulty adjusting to the changing norms governing women's suffrage. The gender gap in turnout appears to have closed completely by the end of the 1980s. In 1992, gender-related turnout differences were so small as to be undetectable in the NES survey.[13]

The relationship between age and voter turnout, by contrast, seems to have changed little over time. The youngest members of the electorate have the lowest turnout rates. Voting among those under age thirty was high in 1992 relative to earlier years, but nonetheless remained considerably lower than turnout among older voters. Young people tend to have less-well-developed political orientations and have yet to cultivate the social and political "roots" associated with high turnout.

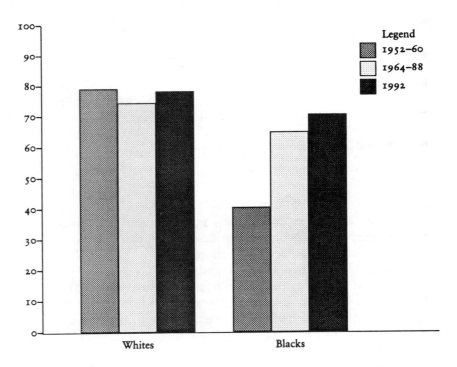

FIGURE 2.3A. REPORTED TURNOUT (IN PERCENT) BY RACE.

SOURCE: National Election Studies, 1952–92.

Turnout rates are highest for voters in the "middle-aged" group, here generously defined as ages thirty to sixty-nine. Among older citizens there is a slight turnout decline, commonly attributed to the physical infirmities associated with aging and to the lack of sociopolitical stimulation for the many elderly who live alone. Still, the elderly participate far more regularly than young people.

The relationships between race, gender, age, and turnout cannot be fully understood without taking education into consideration, because educational disparities may underlie racial, gender, or age differences. Table 2.1 presents 1992 turnout levels for these sociodemographic groups at various levels of educational attainment.

These results demonstrate the importance of looking behind demographic group differences for the effects of education. Once the different educational achievement rates of blacks and whites and men and women are taken into account, the group turnout differentials in 1992

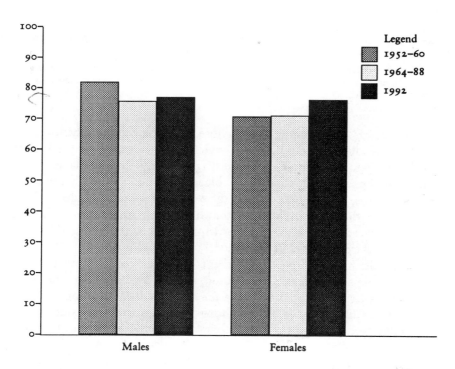

FIGURE 2.3B. REPORTED TURNOUT (IN PERCENT) BY GENDER.

SOURCE: National Election Studies, 1952–92.

TABLE 2.1

1992 REPORTED TURNOUT (BY PERCENTAGE) BY RACE,
GENDER, AND AGE, CONTROLLING
ON EDUCATION

	Less than high school		High school diploma		Some college		College degree	
	%	(N)	%	(N)	%	(N)	%	(N)
Race								
Black	48.7	(38)	65.8*	(67)	87.8	(51)	95.5	(43)
White	51.0	(147)	74.5*	(471)	85.4	(385)	92.4	(423)
Gender								
Male	50.0	(86)	70.6	(234)	84.7	(203)	90.7	(276)
Female	50.4	(114)	74.9	(317)	85.5	(246)	93.9	(207)
Age								
18 to 29	25.0*	(15)	54.4*	(109)	75.2*	(110)	87.4	(66)
30 to 69	49.6*	(114)	79.1*	(386)	88.4*	(299)	92.7	(390)
70 and over	66.8*	(66)	84.7*	(56)	93.9*	(40)	94.5	(28)

SOURCE: 1992 National Election Study.

NOTE: Numbers in parentheses are the number of respondents on which percentages are based.

* Turnout differences between these groups are statistically significant at $p = .05$ or below. In other words, the likelihood of occurrence merely by chance is no more than 5 percent.

mostly vanish. Only among those whose highest level of educational attainment is a high school diploma, which not incidentally is the largest single group in the sample, do whites significantly outvote blacks. Elsewhere, at the same education levels, blacks turn out at roughly the same rate as whites, and women vote at the same rate as men. (Indeed, there is a hint in these data, although the differences are unreliably small, that blacks and women may outparticipate their white and male counterparts at the same level of education.)

The situation for age is different. Middle-aged citizens outvote young people at each level of education, though by diminishing margins (note also that the difference among the college educated is too small to be consequential). But the elderly show the highest turnout rates within each educational grouping. This provides an excellent illustration of a so-called *compositional effect:* The previously cited downturn in voting participation after age sixty-nine is the result of the low educational composition of the elderly group. If their education levels had matched those of middle-aged voters, the elderly would have outparticipated them.

Voter turnout also varies across different regions of the country. A state-by-state examination reveals considerable differences (compare, for example, Hawaii's 49 percent turnout with Maine's 72 percent) but perhaps the most meaningful regional disparity is that between the South and the rest of the nation (see figure 2.4A). The South is politically unique in many respects, and turnout is no exception. We have already mentioned the barriers erected in the South to discourage participation among blacks and poor whites for nearly a century; in addition, the South trails the rest of the nation in terms of overall education levels. It is no surprise, then, that participation rates are noticeably lower in the South than elsewhere. Like the gender and race voting gaps, however, the regional turnout discrepancy has narrowed over time, as education levels in the South have slowly climbed and the disenfranchisement of large segments of the voting population has ended. Although southern turnout rates have trailed the rest of the country throughout the contemporary political era, voter participation in the South actually

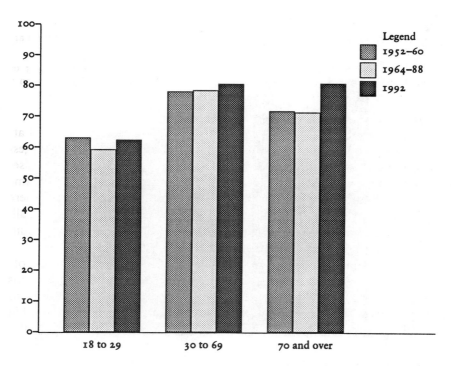

FIGURE 2.3C. REPORTED TURNOUT (IN PERCENT) BY AGE.

SOURCE: National Election Studies, 1952–92.

rose from 1964 to 1988, while turnout in the rest of the nation was in decline.

Turnout disparities across religious denominations also have emerged fairly consistently over time (figure 2.4B), although the differences tend to be small. Catholics vote at a somewhat higher rate than Protestants, in part because "Protestant" encompasses numerous denominations whose members often fall into other low-turnout sociodemographic categories. It is likely, for example, that educational differences account for some portion of the religious voting disparity. Turnout among Jews appears to be very high—no surprise, given the high percentage of Jews with advanced educations—and those who claim no religious affiliation seem to vote at below the national average. For both these latter groups, however, the number of people included in the NES sample is too small to warrant firm conclusions.

Ruy Teixeira, author of one of the more thorough investigations of the post-1960 turnout decline, argues that two additional sociodemo-

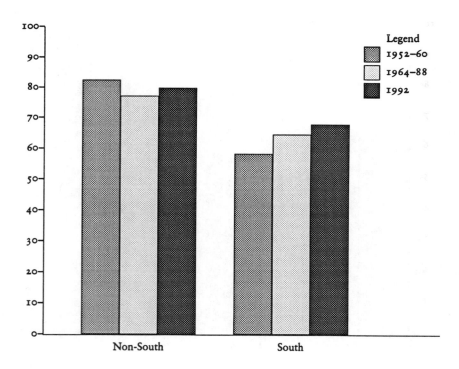

FIGURE 2.4A. REPORTED TURNOUT (IN PERCENT) BY REGION.

SOURCE: National Election Studies, 1952–92.

graphic factors—residential mobility and marital status—merit attention. He contends that persons who have lived in the same area for a long period of time[14] and those who are married and live with their spouses have established strong ties to the social structure and political system and are thus more likely to vote (Teixeira 1987, 23). As figures 2.4C and D reveal, such individuals do participate with greater frequency than their more socially and residentially mobile counterparts. These two factors may well underlie poor turnout among young people, given that the young make up a relatively large share of the single, mobile population.

LONG-TERM POLITICAL ATTITUDES

Although ascribed traits and social location certainly influence a person's decision to participate, in the end the voting act falls to individual choice. It is hardly surprising, then, that individual political attitudes loom large as determinants of turnout.

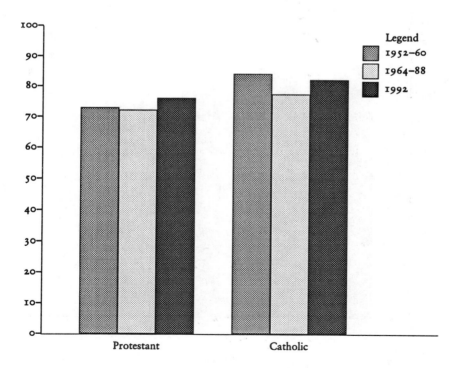

FIGURE 2.4B. REPORTED TURNOUT (IN PERCENT) BY RELIGION.

SOURCE: National Election Studies, 1952–92.

Scholars have identified several attitudes that might be character-ized as long-standing political orientations. In particular, two of these —the strength of one's attachment to a political party and the extent to which a citizen feels politically efficacious—have been cited by many as the principal forces behind the post-1960 turnout decline. Special atten-tion to them is also in order in trying to account for the 1992 turnout increase.

Citizens who feel strong allegiance to a political party[15] are far more likely to vote than are persons with weak party ties—and the lat-ter turn out with greater regularity than do political independents (see figure 2.5A). Because party loyalty involves a sense of attachment to a political party, persons who feel this attachment strongly are more likely to care about the outcome of an election and are more likely to vote, in hopes of bringing about the preferred partisan outcome. The sharp contrast in turnout among strong partisans, weak party identifi-ers, and independents is clear for all three turnout periods. Especially

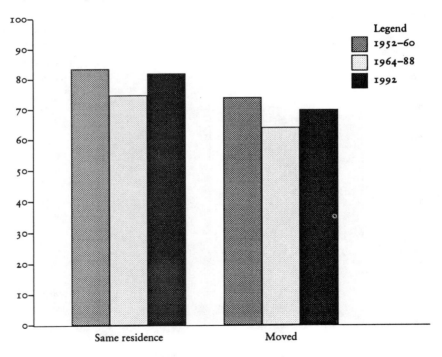

FIGURE 2.4C. REPORTED TURNOUT (IN PERCENT) BY RESIDENTIAL MOBILITY (LAST FOUR YEARS).

SOURCE: National Election Studies, 1952–92.

noteworthy, considering the hallowed position of political independence in the American political culture, is the fact that independents
participate at far lower levels than partisans in presidential elections.[16]

"Political efficacy" refers to attitudes about government responsiveness to citizens;[17] persons with a high sense of political efficacy
believe that the government is responsive to what citizens think. The
argument in anticipation of a link between efficacy and turnout is
straightforward: Voting makes sense if one believes the government is
responsive to the wishes of the electorate. Individuals who feel politically inefficacious believe their vote does not matter and thus are less
likely to cast it. As figures 2.5B indicates, people with low levels of political efficacy do turn out at the lowest rates; surprisingly, though, the
turnout differences between the high, medium, and low efficacy categories are not large. Still, citizens with the highest levels of efficacy have
exhibited the highest levels of participation.

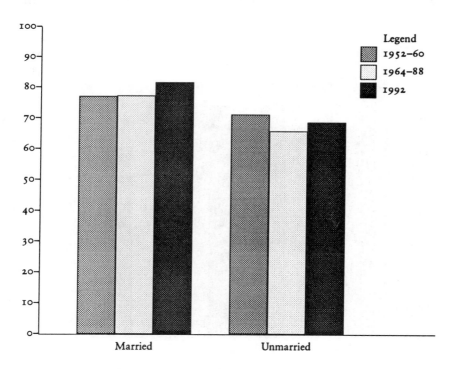

FIGURE 2.4D. REPORTED TURNOUT (IN PERCENT) BY
MARITAL STATUS.

SOURCE: National Election Studies, 1952–92.

A sense of one's obligations as a citizen is also associated with electoral participation.[18] Voting is typically believed to be the hallmark of good citizenship, and those with a well-developed sense of citizen duty turn out at higher rates than others by a substantial margin (figure 2.5C).

ELECTION-SPECIFIC ATTITUDES

Partisanship, efficacy, and citizen duty represent general orientations toward the political world. Another set of political attitudes is short term by contrast, stimulated by and relevant to a specific electoral context. Because of their sensitivity to the immediate electoral context, election-specific factors per se seldom can be pointed to as sources of long-term trends of turnout increase or decline; nonetheless, a number of these election-specific attitudes are often strongly associated with voter turnout in a particular contest (sees figure 2.6A-D).

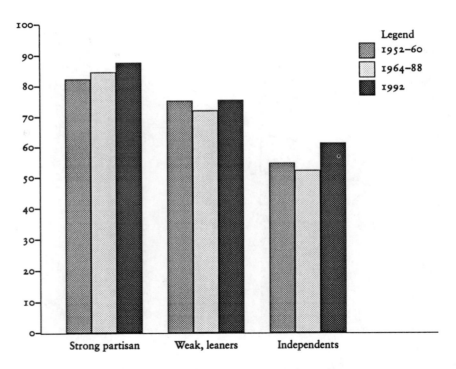

FIGURE 2.5A. REPORTED TURNOUT (IN PERCENT) BY STRENGTH OF PARTISANSHIP.

SOURCE: National Election Studies, 1952–92.

Perhaps the most obvious of these is whether or not a person is interested in the election. As expected, those professing interest vote more frequently than those less interested. The turnout gulf between the "very interested" and the "not much interested" portions of the electorate, though, is surprisingly large. NES results suggest that in 1992 participation among the former exceeded that of the latter by nearly 50 percent; the differences in past years have been smaller, but sizable nonetheless.

Another election-specific variable—reading about the campaign in the newspaper—is more of an act than an attitude, but we address it here because the act is said to reflect attitudes about the campaign. Specifically, persons who follow a given election in the newspaper, a more intellectually demanding medium than television or radio, are thought to be more psychologically involved in the campaign. They are more aware of the candidates and issues of the contest, and the election is

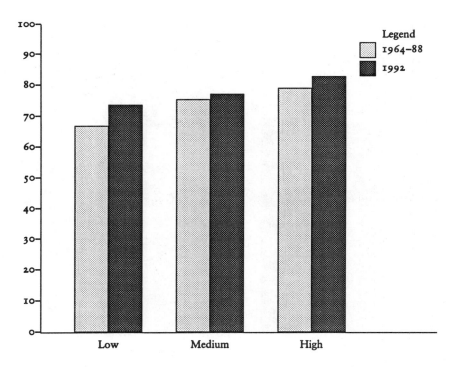

FIGURE 2.5B. REPORTED TURNOUT (IN PERCENT) BY
POLITICAL EFFICACY.

SOURCE: National Election Studies, 1952–92.

thereby more meaningful to them. Additionally, because newspapers convey more information than other media, regular readers are likely to know more about the contest, and thus for them the informational costs of voting are fairly low. Despite the relatively high turnout in 1992 among nonreaders, those who follow the campaign through the newspaper vote at a significantly higher rate than those who do not.

It seems hardly a revelation to learn that persons concerned about the outcome of an election are more likely to vote in it. This association was certainly evident in 1992: turnout among survey respondents claiming to "care a good deal" about the outcome of the contest was more than 40 percent higher than among those who said they "don't much care" who won. It also seems reasonable to expect a close, competitive election to generate higher turnout levels than a landslide. Surprisingly, though, 1992 turnout was only minimally higher among those who believed the race would be close. This suggests that the forces con-

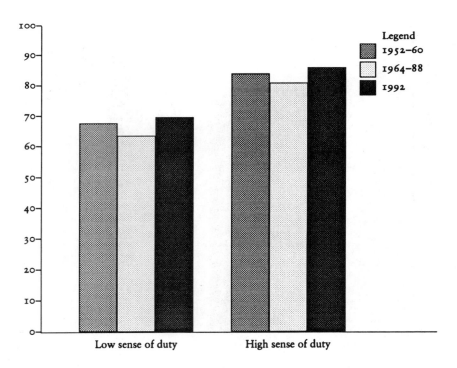

FIGURE 2.5C. REPORTED TURNOUT (IN PERCENT) BY SENSE
OF CITIZEN DUTY.

SOURCE: National Election Studies, 1952–92.

ducive to voting are strong enough to overpower the voters' sense that their vote would make little difference in an already decided outcome; voting may be less instrumental than is commonly supposed.

JOINT EFFECTS OF THE CORRELATES OF TURNOUT

To this point we have examined the correlates of turnout mostly one at a time. Yet, as we have seen in looking at the joint effects of education and race, gender, and age, the effects of these variables are often intertwined, and there is certainly some explanatory overlap among many of them. For example, low turnout among young people is undoubtedly linked to other turnout factors, such as marital status and social mobility; in fact, it is possible that age alone has little impact on turnout after marital status and mobility are taken into consideration.

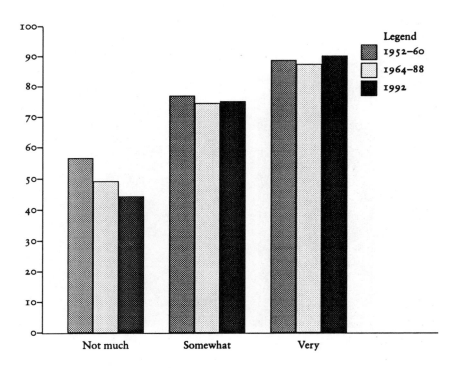

FIGURE 2.6A. REPORTED TURNOUT (IN PERCENT) BY SHORT-TERM POLITICAL ATTITUDES: "INTERESTED IN THE ELECTION?"

SOURCE: National Election Studies, 1952–92.

To test this requires the use of an analytical procedure enabling us to examine the impact of each turnout variable discussed here, while taking into account the effects of all the other variables. Such multivariable techniques are common in political analysis, and we make use of one of them here.[19] The results of this analysis are presented in table 2.2 (page 56) as the differences in the likelihood (or probability) of voting between persons in the high and low turnout category of each variable after all the dissimilarities between these categories on other factors have been accounted for. For example, the first entry in table 2.2 indicates that, all other turnout factors being equal, in 1992 a college graduate was 27 percent more likely to vote than a person who had not completed high school.

Predictably, the turnout disparity between the high and low ends of the educational spectrum suggests that education had the largest independent impact on voter participation in 1992. Strength of party ties,

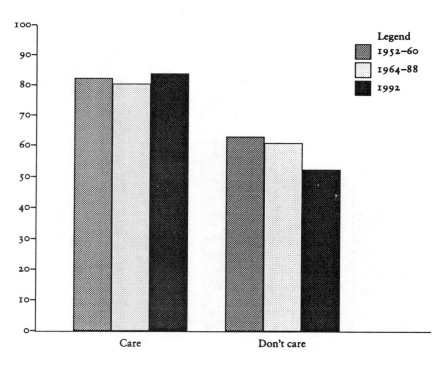

FIGURE 2.6B. REPORTED TURNOUT (IN PERCENT) BY SHORT-TERM POLITICAL ATTITUDES: "DO YOU CARE WHO WINS?"

SOURCE: National Election Studies, 1952–92.

income, residential mobility, interest in the election, reading about the campaign in the newspaper, and assorted other variables all had a noticeable impact on turnout as well. By controlling on all these other factors, a turnout gender gap emerges as well: other things being equal, women are *more* likely to vote than men.

We also see that several previously prominent factors proved inconsequential; among these are occupation, class, race, age, region, religion, marital status, and political efficacy.[20] This does not imply that the turnout disparities observed earlier across the different categories of these variables are not real. Instead, it suggests that the link between these variables and turnout hinges on other factors. For example, young people have much lower turnout than middle-aged citizens, but this difference is probably attributable to the fact that older adults tend to have stronger ties to a political party, are more likely to be married, and are less apt to have recently moved. Once these other factors are taken

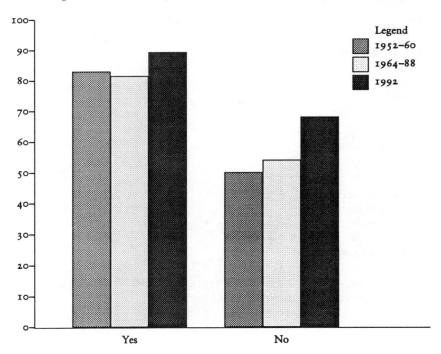

FIGURE 2.6C. REPORTED TURNOUT (IN PERCENT) BY SHORT-TERM
POLITICAL ATTITUDES: "DO YOU FOLLOW THE
CAMPAIGN IN THE NEWSPAPER?"

SOURCE: National Election Studies, 1952–92.

TABLE 2.2
PERCENTAGES DIFFERENCE IN THE PROBABILITY OF
VOTING BETWEEN PERSONS IN HIGH- VERSUS
LOW-TURNOUT CATEGORIES OF
EACH TURNOUT VARIABLE

	1992	1964–88	Difference
SES variables			
Education			
College degree vs. less than high school	27	33	–6*
Income			
96th–100th vs. 0–16th percentile	24	16	+8*
Occupation			
Professional vs. blue collar	n.s.	10	–10*
Social class			
Middle vs. working	n.s.	n.s.	0
Union member in household			
Yes vs. no	5	7	–2
Sociodemographic variables			
Race			
White vs. black	n.s.	6	–6*
Gender			
Female vs. male	12	n.s.	+12*
Age			
30–69 vs. 18–29	n.s.	3	–3
Region			
Non-South vs. South	n.s.	9	–9*
Religion			
Catholic vs. Protestant	n.s.	n.s.	0
Residential mobility			
Same residence vs. moved	17	17	0
Marital status			
Married vs. unmarried	n.s.	8	–8*

into account, as they are in a multivariate statistical test, age in and of itself retains little explanatory power.

Reversing the Turnout Decline: Some Initial Explanations

To begin to address the question of why turnout suddenly increased in 1992 after nearly thirty years of decline, we need to consider the data presented in figures 2.2 though 2.5 and tables 2.1 and 2.2 from a differ-

TABLE 2.2 — *Continued*
PERCENTAGES DIFFERENCE IN THE PROBABILITY OF
VOTING BETWEEN PERSONS IN HIGH- VERSUS
LOW-TURNOUT CATEGORIES OF
EACH TURNOUT VARIABLE

	1992	*1964–88*	*Difference*
Long-term political attitudes			
Strength of partisanship			
Strong partisans vs. independents	26	24	+2
Political efficacy			
High vs. low	n.s.	n.s.	0
Sense of citizen duty			
High vs. low	12	12	0
Election-specific political attitudes			
Interest in election			
"Very" vs. "not much"	15	36	–21*
Concern about outcome			
"Great deal" vs. "not much"	8	7	+1
Read about campaign in newspaper			
Yes vs. no	14	12	+2
Perceived closeness of election			
Close vs. not close	n.s.	n.s.	0

SOURCE: National Election Studies, 1964–92.

NOTE: n.s. = variable was not statistically significant in multivariate analysis.

* Difference between 1964–88 and 1992 is statistically significant at $p = .05$ or below.

ent vantage point. How did the influence of the various socioeconomic, sociodemographic, and attitudinal factors differ in 1992 from the preceding era?

The most obvious conclusion is that there is no simple answer to this question, no "smoking gun" that can be credited with the change. Turnout increased from 1964–88 to 1992 almost across the board; virtually all categories of the factors identified as important correlates of turnout exhibited higher levels of voting in 1992 than in the previous era. In some instances, this increase even brought turnout for that category to 1952–60 levels. There is a strong suggestion here that the period from 1964 to 1988 was an aberration where turnout was concerned and that 1992 was a return to normality. No single factor, though, stands out as responsible for the 1992 surge.

There are a few groups within which the increase was particularly noticeable. The turnout surge among voters seventy years of age and older, for one thing, was over twice that for the younger age groups and totally erased the long-standing downturn in participation among the elderly. Women, union members, political independents, and non-newspaper readers also exhibited greater turnout increases than the average. These results provide hints of where one should look for persuasive explanations of the 1992 phenomenon—to a mobilization of disgruntled independents by the Perot movement, worries about the economy that might have led to an anti-Bush surge among previously nonvoting workers, perhaps even to a swell of women's involvement over moral concerns. But the data in hand are insufficient to test these explanations.

An alternative approach to accounting for the 1992 turnout increase is to look for shifts in the *proportion* of the electorate falling within the various categories of the turnout correlates. As the composi-

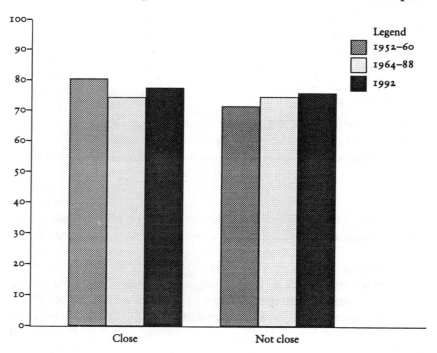

FIGURE 2.6D. REPORTED TURNOUT (IN PERCENT) BY
SHORT-TERM POLITICAL ATTITUDES:
"WILL THE RACE BE CLOSE?"

SOURCE: National Election Studies, 1952–92.

tion of the eligible voting population changes and a higher percentage of citizens fall into categories where turnout is high, we would expect an increase in overall voting rates. Not all these variables are equally likely sources of a compositional change explanation for 1992 turnout increases. To account for a sudden rise, it seems most reasonable to look to factors that themselves can change quickly, rather than to those, such as education, that may change steadily across a number of years. The percentages of the NES sample falling into the various categories of our turnout correlates are presented in table 2.3.

Looking first at the SES variables, we see that a growing proportion of the electorate is in fact well educated, highly paid, and of higher occupational and social status. The increases for 1992 are minor, but nonetheless they are in the direction that stimulate higher turnout. The most notable shift is in education: the percentage of college graduates is considerably greater in 1992 than for the 1964–88 period (although this gain is tempered somewhat by a decline among persons having attended some college), and the proportion of citizens with less than a high school education has fallen noticeably. We should note, though, that education levels rose even more dramatically from 1964 to 1988, and yet turnout declined during that time. This does not mean that turnout is *not* related to education after all; instead, it suggests that the post-1960 decline occurred *in spite of* the rise in education. The drop would have been far greater had it not been for the increase in aggregate education levels.

Changes in the sociodemographic composition of a population occur very slowly; not surprisingly, then, the breakdown of the electorate in terms of race, gender, religion, region, and age was much the same in 1992 as in the previous turnout era. As for residential mobility and marital status, we remain a highly mobile and increasingly single nation, but there is no evidence here of a sociodemographic shift of the magnitude needed to account for a 5 percent increase in voting in a single election.

The decline of party attachments and political efficacy is often cited as the primary reason for the post-1960 turnout decline. Our data support this claim (although we are unable to assess efficacy levels for the 1950s because NES survey questions tapping this concept were not asked before 1964). There was a clear decline in the proportion of persons professing strong attachment to a political party, and the rise of independents after 1964 has been well documented.[21] But there was not much change in the population distribution across these two variables (or for the citizen duty variable) from the low turnout era to 1992—nor would we expect there to have been, given that these are relatively

TABLE 2.3
PERCENTAGE OF NES SAMPLE FALLING IN EACH
CATEGORY OF TURNOUT VARIABLES

	1952–60	1964–88	1992
SES variables			
Education			
College degree	8.3	15.9	24.0
Some college	19.8	30.8	24.0
High school diploma	18.3	22.1	34.4
Less than high school	53.6	31.1	17.6
Occupation			
Professional, managerial	26.2	30.6	29.8
Other white collar	19.6	23.3	28.2
Blue collar	54.2	46.1	41.9
Social class			
Middle class	37.1	47.3	48.6
Working class	62.9	52.6	51.1
Union member in household			
Yes	27.2	23.3	17.5
No	72.8	76.7	82.5
Sociodemographics			
Race			
White	90.7	87.8	84.5
Black	8.8	10.4	12.9
Gender			
Male	45.3	43.1	47.3
Female	54.7	56.9	52.7
Age			
70 and over	8.1	24.2	21.7
30–69	75.7	65.0	67.5
18–29	16.2	10.8	10.8
Region			
Non-South	69.7	66.8	72.8
South	30.3	33.2	27.2
Religion			
Catholic	20.9	23.7	27.2
Protestant	73.2	66.8	69.0
Jewish	3.3	2.2	2.1

TABLE 2.3 — *Continued*
PERCENTAGE OF NES SAMPLE FALLING IN EACH
CATEGORY OF TURNOUT VARIABLES

	1952–60	*1964–88*	*1992*
Sociodemographics — CONTINUED			
Residential mobility			
Same residence	43.0	44.9	43.6
Moved within last four years	57.0	55.1	56.4
Marital status			
Married	85.2	64.2	61.9
Unmarried	14.8	35.8	38.1
Long-term political attitudes			
Strength of partisanship			
Strong partisans	35.8	28.6	28.7
Weak partisans, leaners	53.2	58.8	59.8
Independents	11.0	12.6	11.5
Political efficacy			
High	n.a.	17.3	12.4
Medium	n.a.	52.6	61.6
Low	n.a.	30.1	25.9
Sense of citizen duty			
High	52.0	51.0	45.8
Low	48.0	49.0	54.2
Election-specific political attitudes			
Interest in the election			
Very interested	35.3	33.9	39.5
Somewhat interested	37.4	43.2	44.9
Not much interested	27.3	23.0	15.6
Care about election outcome			
Care a good deal	65.5	61.7	76.8
Don't much care	34.5	38.3	23.2
Read about campaign in newspaper			
Yes	75.9	71.9	66.2
No	24.1	28.1	33.8
Perceived closeness of the election			
Close	76.4	63.3	82.0
Not close	23.6	36.7	18.0

SOURCE: National Election Studies, 1952–92.

stable, long-term political orientations. Moreover, the small shifts that did occur here were in the direction of lower, not higher, turnout; thus we may not credit these as sources of the turnout increase.

The most promising place to look for compositional sources of turnout increases is in the election-specific political attitudes associated with voting. Here we observe some important compositional change in 1992. A large percentage of individuals believed the 1992 election would be close, and the proportion of people who cared about the outcome of the election rose by 15 percent, propelling many more Americans to an orientation that is highly conducive to participation. Additionally, there was an 8 percent rise in the percentage of persons who were either somewhat or very interested in the contest. Of the election-specific variables, the continuing decline in newspaper readership is the only one for which we observe a compositional shift working against higher turnout.

It seems, then, that election-specific attitudinal variables played the largest role in the 1992 turnout increase. The 1992 presidential election—with its anti-incumbent flavor, the presence of a colorful Ross Perot, and ultimately its closely contested three-candidate race—captured the interest of an unusually large number of Americans. A voting population whose interest has been piqued will likely care more about the outcome of the race and pay more attention to it. The increase in interest alone, at 1964–88 rates of turnout for the different interest categories, adds over 2 percent to the turnout rate. That this increase occurs disproportionately among four of the five groups whose turnout was identified earlier as well exceeding the average in 1992 (table 2.4)—the elderly, union members, independents, and non-newspaper readers—lends even more credence to this account of the rise in voting in 1992.

The Perot Factor

It seems reasonable also to look to Ross Perot's candidacy for at least some of the heightened interest in the 1992 election. Support for this notion may be found at the aggregate level: across the fifty states and the District of Columbia, higher turnout at the state level appears to have been linked in some degree to higher levels of support for Perot.[22]

The NES also provides individual-level evidence corroborating a general link between increased turnout and support for Perot. First, note (table 2.5) that respondents who at some point during the campaign viewed Perot as their first choice for president turned out to vote

TABLE 2.4

PERCENTAGE "VERY" OR "SOMEWHAT" INTERESTED IN THE
ELECTION BY AGE, GENDER, UNION MEMBERSHIP,
STRENGTH OF PARTISANSHIP, READING
ABOUT THE CAMPAIGN

	1964–88		1992		
	%	N	%	N	*Change*
Age					
18–29	73.2	(2,594)	78.8	(423)	+5.3
30–69	77.5	(7,221)	85.2	(1,420)	+7.7
70 and over	69.8	(1,113)	81.6	(223)	+11.8
Gender					
Male	78.1	(4,902)	86.1	(1,020)	+8.0
Female	73.8	(6,081)	80.9	(1,046)	+7.1
Union member					
Yes	76.2	(2,568)	87.7	(380)	+11.5
No	75.5	(8,344)	82.5	(1,678)	+7.0
Strength of partisanship					
Strong partisans	86.1	(3,514)	92.5	(647)	+6.4
Weak partisans, leaners	74.5	(6,292)	83.1	(1,211)	+8.6
Independents	59.2	(1,131)	71.7	(204)	+12.5
Read about campaign					
Yes	85.4	(6,806)	93.7	(1,078)	+8.3
No	58.8	(1,854)	72.6	(426)	+13.8

SOURCE: National Election Studies, 1964–92.

NOTE: Numbers in parentheses are the number of respondents on which percentages are based.

at a rate nearly 10 percent higher than those who never considered voting for Perot. This is the result of the sizable turnout differential between sometime Perot supporters and nonsupporters among people with a high school diploma or less.

At the individual level, though, what might underlie a relationship between Perot and turnout? One possibility is that Perot may have served as an outlet for disaffected Americans. For example, voters who perceived little difference between the major parties and their presidential candidates in how they would address the most important problems facing the country were more likely to vote for Perot (by a margin of 24 percent to 14 percent) and to turn out (by a margin of 85 percent to 73 percent) if they were Perot supporters at one point during the campaign. This supports the notion that Perot stimulated turnout by serving as a plausible alternative to "politics as usual."

TABLE 2.5

REPORTED TURNOUT AND PEROT SUPPORT, BY EDUCATION

"Was Ross Perot ever your first choice for president?"

	High school or less*		Some college		College degree		Total*	
	%	N	%	N	%	N	%	N
Yes	79.3	(183)	88.9	(115)	90.7	(129)	85.2	(427)
No	63.8	(835)	86.6	(348)	93.7	(365)	76.0	(1,548)

SOURCE: 1992 National Election Study.

NOTE: Numbers in parentheses are the number of respondents on which percentages are based.

* Turnout difference is statistically significant at p = .001 or below.

There may also have been a link between support for Perot and interest in the election; given the strong association between interest and turnout, Perot may have indirectly stimulated turnout by arousing interest in the campaign. Respondents who considered Perot as their first choice at some time during the campaign were slightly more likely (by 6 percent) to be "very interested" or "somewhat interested" in the campaign than those who never preferred him. One must be cautious here, though, because the difference is small. Moreover, the causal relationship is unclear: did consideration of Perot generate interest in the election, or were the more politically interested portions of the electorate also more likely to have at some point considered Perot? But the Perot candidacy's impact went beyond a heightening of interest. Perot supporters among those with low interest in the campaign also turned out at substantially higher levels than nonsupporters (58 percent to 43 percent).

Thus, for three groups in the sample—those with lower education levels, those perceiving no difference between the parties, and those with little interest in the election—we see a turnout increase associated with Perot among unlikely voters. A similar story emerged when we added a Perot variable to a multifactor turnout model composed solely of the short-term political attitude variables. While the inclusion of the Perot variable left virtually unchanged the probability of voting associated with the other turnout variables in the model, the results suggest that Perot supporters were roughly 2 percent more likely to have voted than nonsupporters, other things being equal. Additionally, the model containing the Perot variable is more accurate in predicting turnout for each individual in the sample than the model without it.

None of this evidence establishes a definite link between Ross Perot and turnout, however plausible it seems to be on other grounds. Nor does it permit us to determine precisely how much of the 1992 increase may be credited to Perot's candidacy. All evidence, however—at both the aggregate and individual levels—points in the same direction: the presence of Perot in the 1992 presidential contest had a positive effect on turnout. Whether it was the stimulation provided by Perot himself or the tighter race his presence produced, turnout in 1992 benefited from the candidacy of Ross Perot.

The Consequences of Changes in Voter Turnout

While 1992 witnessed a significant rise in voter participation, the increase appears largely attributable to short-term, election-specific forces rather than enduring causes. Unless presidential politics continues to be highly competitive and perhaps even continues to attract viable third-party or independent candidates, the increase seems likely to prove to be only a temporary reversal of the trend of declining electoral involvement rather than the beginning of an era of increased participation. Moreover, while a 5 percent rise is noteworthy, American voter turnout remains low by most historical, comparative, and normative standards. With the nation apparently locked into current ranges of turnout, a final question remains: does low voter turnout matter?

Some view low turnout as inconsequential because it is difficult to construct a realistic scenario in which heightened participation would have changed the outcome of the election. A look at the presidential preferences of nonvoters reveals that they very much resembled those of voters. As is normally the case, nonvoters displayed a slight tendency to favor the election winner (in this case, both Clinton and Perot appear to have benefited from nonvoters' shift away from Bush). In general, though, voter and nonvoter preferences are so similar that it is hard to argue that Clinton's victory margin would have been noticeably different, let alone that the outcome would have changed, had turnout been substantially higher.

Although their candidate preferences are comparable, voters and nonvoters may differ in other meaningful ways. For example, are their political views alike? The NES attempts to assess respondents' political priorities by asking if federal spending on various national concerns should be increased, kept the same, or decreased. A comparison of voters and nonvoters on this score (see table 2.6) indicates that there are indeed some differences between citizens who participate and those who do not; these are fairly predictable, given what we know about the socioeconomic status disparities between voters and nonvoters. Nonvoters place substantially greater emphasis on aid for persons on social security, the unemployed, child care, and the poor; voters attach greater weight to federal spending on science and technology and in general are more willing to reduce spending in nearly all these areas. Nonvoters differ from voters in other issue spheres as well. At least in the NES survey, they lean more toward the pro-life side of the abortion debate than do voters. Nonvoters also favor greater effort on the part of the federal government to provide individuals with jobs and a guaranteed standard of living.

Thus, while higher turnout probably would not have changed the election outcome in 1992, the changes in the distributions of policy preferences produced by a larger electorate might have been conducive to somewhat different policy outcomes. To the extent that governmental policy reflects the input of electoral participants, one would expect policies to favor the preferences of voters.[23] In this sense, low voter turnout does matter.

A strong argument can be made that poor turnout is consequential in a more fundamental sense. Citizen participation is a cornerstone of democracy; is a nation in which only about half the eligible citizenry vote therefore only half a democracy? Some deny this, suggesting that the option not to vote is a *choice* democratic citizens can make and that low turnout may reflect contentment with the status quo. The difficulty with this argument is that the citizens least likely to vote are also those with the least reason to be satisfied with their situation.

More common is the worry that low levels of electoral participation weaken the nation's democratic system. Winners of low-turnout elections find the legitimacy of their victory undermined by the fact that they typically received a small majority—in Clinton's case, a mere plurality—from barely half the eligible electorate. With less legitimacy to draw on, it is more difficult for political leaders to deal successfully with the nation's problems.

Some have argued that low voter participation actually improves the governing process because it provides elected officials with the flexibility they need to make the many decisions and policy compromises that are a part of effective political leadership (Berelson, Lazarsfeld, and McPhee 1954, chap. 14). Others contend that high levels of nonvoting may imperil democracy by leaving large numbers of potential voters

TABLE 2.6

POLICY PREFERENCES OF VOTERS AND NONVOTERS
(IN PERCENTAGES)

"Should federal spending on [   ] be increased, kept the same,
or decreased?"

	Voters (1,652)	Nonvoters (504)
Social security*		
Increase	44.5	59.9
Same	50.9	36.9
Decrease	4.6	3.2
Science and technology*		
Increase	44.8	35.0
Same	44.4	46.6
Decrease	10.8	18.4
Child care*		
Increase	48.4	56.2
Same	41.2	37.2
Decrease	10.4	6.5
Dealing with crime		
Increase	69.8	73.7
Same	27.1	22.5
Decrease	3.2	3.8
Environment*		
Increase	60.2	65.6
Same	35.3	31.4
Decrease	4.5	3.0

Continued ...

outside the political mainstream, where they are available for mobilization by antisystem candidates. Inexperienced in the "give and take" of politics in a pluralistic democracy, these candidates have the potential to raise the stakes of political conflict to a point where it cannot be contained through the political process. Moreover, as the rise of Hitler in post–World War I Germany and the experiences of the former communist states in recent years illustrate, nonmainstream candidates, once elected, may repudiate democracy in favor of more decisive—albeit less solicitous of individual rights—forms of government (Converse 1964; Lipset 1981, chap. 5).

The debate over the consequences of nonvoting will not end because of the increase in turnout in the 1992 presidential contest. Even if 1992 marks the beginning of a return to higher levels of turnout, and turnout did edge up slightly over earlier midterm levels in 1994, Ameri-

TABLE 2.6 — *Continued*
POLICY PREFERENCES OF VOTERS AND NONVOTERS
(IN PERCENTAGES)

"Should federal spending on [   ] be increased, kept the same,
or decreased?"

	Voters (1,652)	Nonvoters (504)
Unemployment*		
Increase	36.4	47.0
Same	49.2	43.0
Decrease	14.4	9.9
Helping the poor*		
Increase	51.9	63.9
Same	40.6	31.3
Decrease	7.4	4.8
Helping big cities		
Increase	20.5	18.7
Same	49.8	52.2
Decrease	29.8	29.1
Public schools*		
Increase	64.0	69.4
Same	31.3	28.4
Decrease	4.7	2.2

SOURCE: 1992 National Election Study.

NOTE: Numbers in parentheses are the minimum number of respondents on which percentages are based.

* Voter/nonvoter differences on these issues are statistically significant at $p = .05$ or below.

can levels of voting will remain modest by any measure. This permits substantial differences in turnout among social, political, and economic groups in society—differences that have shown striking consistency for almost half a century. The story of participation in the 1992 presidential contest, for all the relief over increasing turnout, in the end is only another installment on a familiar theme.

Notes

1. Only in Hawaii did turnout decline, and since the polls closed there well after the election had been decided, this state may not be comparable to others. In any event, the turnout decrease in Hawaii was a mere 1.1 percent.

2. Calculating voter turnout is a surprisingly difficult task; there are several ways of doing it, each yielding somewhat different estimates of the extent

of voter participation. The numerator of the turnout fraction, the number of votes cast, is reasonably straightforward. Each state, however, keeps its own individual vote tally. Although generally accurate, there is some underestimation of the total vote: invalidated votes are not counted and, because turnout is based on the total vote for president, the ballots of those who vote for lower offices but not for president are not included in turnout figures. The real difficulty in the turnout fraction lies in the denominator, which stipulates the pool of potential voters for whom the turnout estimate is to be calculated. Typically—and we follow this convention here—this figure is based on Census Bureau estimates of the number of voting-age residents. Because many persons of voting age are ineligible to vote for other reasons (mental illness, a criminal conviction, etc.), this overestimates the size of the eligible voting population, thereby underestimating voter turnout. Even after taking this underestimation into consideration, however, we find that turnout in the United States today remains comparatively low.

3. For an interesting account of party efforts in specific campaigns during this era, see Bibby (1992, chap. 2).

4. In addition to its effect on turnout, the introduction of the Australian ballot also contributed to a sharp increase in split-ticket voting. On this point, see Rusk (1970).

5. For an analysis of the impact of registration on turnout, see Rosenstone and Wolfinger (1978).

6. For an insightful discussion of the source and consequences of two-party politics in America, see Riker (1982).

7. Richard Boyd (1986) suggests that voter participation in this country is underestimated because turnout figures are based on voting in presidential elections only: it may be that citizens are voting at a higher rate than we realize, but not always in presidential contests. The problem with this argument is that turnout has declined steadily in virtually all elections; in fact, the drop has been especially precipitous in subpresidential contests, particularly for state and local offices.

8. U.S. Representative Ron Wyden (D-Ore.) sponsored a 1992 House bill that would have made election day an unpaid federal holiday. The legislation (H.R. 3681) never made it out of committee, due in part to opposition from the Bush administration. Officials from the Justice Department and the Office of Personnel Management argued that the bill could evolve into another costly paid holiday and might pressure the private sector to give their workers the day off as well. See the *1992 Congressional Quarterly Almanac*, p. 224.

9. Interestingly, it appears that those who are most likely to vote—the highly educated, in particular—are also the most likely to overreport their turnout; see Silver, Anderson, and Abramson (1986).

10. By collapsing the nine presidential elections from 1952 to 1988 into two general turnout eras, we undoubtedly lose some of the flavor of individual elections during those periods. To ensure that we did not lose too much information in this process, we replicated parts of our analysis on each individual election from 1952 to 1988. We are confident that the general trends seen in the collapsed turnout eras accurately reflect the important turnout relationships in the individual years of the periods.

11. For a seven-nation comparative study of political participation, see Verba, Nie, and Kim (1978).

12. Turnout among those of Hispanic origin is very low, according to Census Bureau estimates and survey findings. The number of Hispanics included in NES surveys, however, is too small to permit firm conclusions about their electoral behavior. We simply note that while they are a sizable (and growing) segment of the electorate—and thus the target of voter registration efforts by both major parties—Hispanics have yet to turn out in sufficient numbers to realize their potential political clout.

13. Because the NES surveys use a sample of the population to estimate attributes of the entire population, small differences in a sample—such as those in turnout between men and women in the 1992 NES data—are likely to reflect no differences at all in the population. The probability that this may occur can actually be measured, and analysts take this into account by distinguishing between "statistically significant" versus "insignificant" relationships: the former *are* likely to appear in the population, while the latter are not. We dwell on relationships that achieve conventional levels of statistical significance; smaller relationships are ignored as insignificant.

14. Teixeira defines the residentially mobile population as those who have moved within the past two years. In our analysis we use a different cut-off point—four years—in order to maintain comparability in question wording between 1992 and previous NES surveys. This difference in the measurement of mobility seems to have little substantive impact, however; we find, as did Teixeira, that residential mobility has a strong negative effect on turnout.

15. The NES surveys assess strength of partisanship by asking respondents which party they feel closer to, followed with a question on the strength of this association. The result is a seven-point partisanship continuum: strong Democrat, weak Democrat, independent but leaning toward the Democrats, pure independent, independent but leaning toward the Republicans, weak Republican, and strong Republican.

16. For a recent look at political independents, see Keith et al. (1992).

17. The NES surveys include a series of items designed to tap feelings of political efficacy; unfortunately, there is variation in the questions used over the years, raising concerns about the validity of over-time comparisons of efficacy measured using different questions. Two items, however—"Do elections make government responsive to the people?" and "Government officials don't care what I think"—have been asked in every NES survey since 1964. We used these two questions to construct an index of political efficacy.

18. There has been some inconsistency in the NES measures of citizen duty. Here we rely on a question, included in all surveys since 1952, asking citizens whether someone who does not care about an election should nonetheless vote in it. An affirmative response suggests a high sense of citizen duty.

19. The specific statistical technique used here is logistic regression, or logit. Logit coefficients are not directly interpretable; they must first be converted into probabilities, which in this case represent the change in the probability of voting associated with the different values of the independent variables (holding constant the effects of the other independent variables). Of course, estimates of change in the likelihood of voting require some baseline

for comparison; here we have used the mean reported turnout values for our samples (69 percent for 1992, and 63 percent for 1964–88) as our starting turnout probability. We arrived at the entries in table 2.2 by first computing the change in the probability of voting associated with a single unit change in each of the turnout correlates and then calculating the difference in the probability of voting between individuals in the high turnout category of the variable versus those in the low turnout category. Information about the actual logit coefficients and the procedure used to convert these into probabilities is available from the authors. Inquiries should be addressed to The Ohio State University, Department of Political Science, 2140 Derby Hall, 154 North Oval Mall, Columbus, OH 43210–1373.

20. Careful analysis has shown that efficacy levels, along with turnout, have fallen precipitously since the 1960s. For evidence of the role of efficacy and partisanship in the post-1960 turnout decline, see Abramson and Aldrich (1982). For a persuasive argument that Abramson and Aldrich overstated the link between partisanship, efficacy, and turnout, see Cassel and Luskin (1988). What we have found here is that at any one specific time point, the power of the relationship between efficacy and turnout may be undercut by other variables in our turnout model.

21. See, for example, Wattenberg (1990).

22. The specific statistic used to measure this was Pearson's r, a correlation coefficient measuring the strength of a relationship between two variables—in this case, between turnout and Perot's share of the popular vote from state to state. It ranges from 1.0 (a perfect positive relationship) to −1.0 (a perfect negative association); Pearson's $r = 0$ indicates no association between the variables. The coefficient obtained for Perot and turnout, $r = .22$, suggests a modest connection between Perot's vote percentage and turnout. The correlations between turnout and the percentage of the vote in each state for Bush ($r = -.03$) and Clinton ($r = -.12$) were also computed. Note that these values are much smaller than the Perot coefficient and that, interestingly, they are negative. Data for the state-level turnout analysis were obtained from Duncan (1993) and from Scammon and McGillivray (1993).

23. Perhaps the best examination of the link between participation and policy may be found in Verba and Nie (1972).

CHAPTER 3

Attitudinal Correlates of the 1992 Presidential Vote: Party Identification and Beyond

HERBERT F. WEISBERG AND DAVID C. KIMBALL

Democrats and Republicans; the economy, foreign policy, abortion, and family values; George Bush, Bill Clinton, and Ross Perot. Elections involve a complicated interplay of political parties, issues, and candidates. The purpose of this chapter is to provide a broad overview of the role of these three factors in voting in 1992. Some of these themes are revisited in greater detail in later chapters, but a preliminary view helps place them in the proper context.

The perspective taken in this chapter on analyzing the election result is somewhat unusual. It is common in the political science literature to attempt to decompose the vote statistically; instead, we examine the factors affecting the election in a sequential sense. The distribution of party identification and any changes in it since the last election are treated as setting the slope of the playing field for the election. For example, finding that an overwhelming proportion of the electorate consider themselves Democrats would mean that the Republicans would need a large advantage on the issues and candidates in order to win an uphill battle for the presidency, while finding a more even balance between Democrats and Republicans would mean that whichever side was advantaged on the issues and candidates would win the election.

Once the playing field has thus been set, what matters next are the dominant issues. The status quo positions on these issues establish the terrain of the electoral contest. If the public is very satisfied with the status quo, then the incumbent party should be riding high. If the public is very dissatisfied with the status quo on the issues, then the incumbent party would be at a real disadvantage. Together, the distributions of party identification and issue positions set the contours for the competition.

The final elements, then, are the images that the candidates are able to project to the electorate. An incumbent usually has a well-developed image, whereas a challenger is more dimly perceived. The challenger tries to establish a positive image, while the opposition seeks to besmirch that image. Still, the candidate factor operates within the context established by the partisan playing field and the issue terrain. In the end, even a weak candidate may be able to win if most of the electorate identify with his or her party and if the public blames the other party for the status quo on such issues as a recession, whereas only a strong candidate can win if most of the electorate identify with the other party and if the public blames that candidate's party for not handling important national problems well.

In the 1992 election, we see that the partisan distribution of the voting public shifted somewhat to the Democratic side, but not enough to determine the election result all by itself. When one looks past party identification in 1992, one quickly finds that the economic recession badly weakened President Bush. There were other issues, but people were being hurt by the economy, and this was related to voting against Bush. If the economy put the Bush presidency in jeopardy, the outcome of the election still depended on the candidates. The images of Bush and Clinton both had points of strength but also enough vulnerabilities to permit a strong independent candidacy by Ross Perot. In the end, however, Perot was not a sufficiently attractive candidate to be more than a distraction from the main event, and a distraction who repeatedly worked to George Bush's disadvantage.

The Republicans might still have pulled out the election if most of the public thought of themselves as Republican, but the Republican gains of the 1980s had largely disappeared. The slightly pro-Democratic tilt of the party balance in 1992 thus helped keep George Bush from being able to ride to victory with the aid of partisan appeals. Still, understanding the voting result requires a careful analysis of partisanship in 1992 along with the issue and candidate factors.

The presentation in this chapter is at a general overview level. The distributions of attitudes on party, issue, and candidate factors are presented, along with some of the relationships with vote. More comprehensive analyses of the relative importance of these three factors in determining the vote are presented in following chapters.

Party Identification

Surveys dating back to the 1950s ask people if they consider themselves Republicans, Democrats, or independents. A Democratic lead in party identification that had been evident since those early surveys had eroded over the years to the point that the numbers of Democratic identifiers and Republican identifiers among voters in 1988 were quite balanced. This change led not only to discussion of realignment but to detailed discussions of which groups had realigned at what points during the Reagan presidency. When the Democratic lead in party identification was reestablished in 1992, discussion of realignment stopped. This could be a temporary reversal of a Republican realignment, or it could signify a more permanent return to a Democratic majority in this country. The evidence provided by one, two, or even three elections is too slim to make conclusions about realignment—as analysts in the 1980s should have remembered.

What complicates the party identification story is that there are now alternative claims as to its stability. The view of voting established in the literature of the 1960s was that party identification was highly stable, the most stable of political attitudes. The aggregate-level fluctuation between elections in party identification readings seemed to be of the order of sampling error. The few studies that hinted at larger shifts in party identification could be explained away in terms of the less politically involved part of the citizenry responding to short-term news, which seemed to matter little, because these were the people least likely to vote (Converse 1976, chap. 5).

The only real party identification change admitted in that early literature was the rare occurrence of party realignment—a lasting change in the party balance, such as the one that occurred during the Great Depression in the 1930s when the "New Deal realignment" resulted in a shift from a Republican majority held since the 1890s (as seen in control of Congress most of those years, as well as the presidency when the Republican Party was not split) to a Democratic majority. Since the 1950s, political scientists have interpreted elections in terms of their potential for realignment. The 1964 election looked like the beginning of a pro-Democratic realignment, until the Vietnam war and racial unrest at home undid the Democratic administration. The 1968 election appeared to be the beginning of a pro-Republican realignment, until the Watergate affair and the Nixon pardon undid the Republican administration. The 1976 election seemed to reestablish the old Democratic alignment, but the Iran hostage crisis and inflation at home caused Carter's defeat in 1980. None of these changes achieved the level of permanency required for realignment. Then the Reagan election in

1980 ushered in a twelve-year period of Republican rule with changes in party identification that seemed real even to analysts who had previously scoffed at claims of such changes. The result was a detailed analysis of the specifics of party realignment in the 1980s (Miller 1990).

The 1980s literature, however, provided another interpretation of party identification change: systematic responsiveness to political and economic changes. Studies found changes in party identification (Brody and Rothenberg 1988; Allsop and Weisberg 1988) that could be tied to presidential approval and/or economic indicators (MacKuen, Erikson, and Stimson 1989; Weisberg and Smith 1991). Changes in party identification were limited in size, but the claim was that these changes were real. Of course, some methodologists could make enough assumptions about the nature of error terms to claim that party identification should still be viewed as an "unmoved mover" (Green and Palmquist 1990), but with sufficient assumptions any change can be viewed as artifactual.

Realignment or systematic responsiveness? Which is the cause of party identification change? The answer may reveal more about who is responding to the question than about party identification itself. Both explanations can fit. The realignment answer focuses on the long term, though many recent judgments about realignment have not waited for the long term. The systematic responsiveness answer focuses on the short term, though this can trivialize the matter as change is found between elections, then between years, then between months, and then between days.

Added to this debate as to the cause of party identification change is a debate as to the nature of political independence. The usual set of party identification questions distinguish between strong partisans, weak partisans, independents who lean toward a party, and pure independents. The problem becomes what to make of the leaners—are they really independents (in which case independence grew in size considerably in the 1960s and 1970s) or are they closet partisans who behave a lot like weak partisans (in which case independence mattered not much more in the 1980s than in the 1950s)? The strongest argument for treating leaners like weak partisans was provided in a book arguing that party identification had not weakened over the years (Keith et al. 1992), a book published, ironically, just before the 1992 election brought a very high level of support for a third-party candidate.

PARTY IDENTIFICATION IN 1992

Table 3.1 and figure 3.1 show the distribution of party identification in 1992, with comparisons to earlier presidential election years. The Democrats were advantaged by partisanship in 1992. Note the Democratic

TABLE 3.1
PARTY IDENTIFICATION BY YEAR, 1952–92 (IN PERCENTAGES)

	1952	1956	1960	1964	1968	1972	1976	1980	1984	1988	1992
Democrat	47.2	43.6	45.3	51.7	45.4	40.4	39.7	40.8	37.0	35.2	35.4
Independent	22.6	23.4	22.8	22.8	29.1	34.7	36.1	34.5	34.2	35.7	38.0
Republican	27.2	29.1	29.4	24.5	24.2	23.4	23.2	22.4	27.1	27.5	25.7
Democratic plurality 1	20.0	14.5	15.9	27.2	21.2	17.0	16.5	18.4	9.9	7.7	9.7
Democrats plus leaners	56.8	49.9	51.6	61.0	55.2	51.5	51.5	52.3	47.8	47.0	49.3
Pure independents	5.8	8.8	9.8	7.8	10.5	13.1	14.6	12.9	11.0	10.6	11.5
Republicans plus leaners	34.3	37.4	36.1	30.2	32.9	33.9	32.9	32.6	39.5	40.8	38.3
Democratic plurality 2	22.5	12.5	15.5	30.8	22.3	17.6	18.6	19.7	8.3	6.2	11.0

SOURCE: 1952–92 National Election Studies.

NOTE: Leaners are treated as independents in the top half of the table and as partisans in the bottom half.

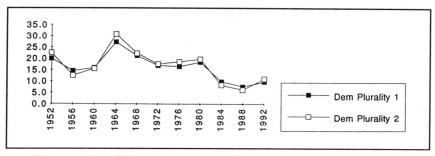

FIGURE 3.1. CHANGING DEMOCRATIC PLURALITY, 1952–92.

lead over Republicans by 11 percent when leaners are treated as partisans (49.3 percent Democrat versus 38.3 percent Republican and 11.5 percent pure independent), as well as the 10 percent lead when leaners are treated as independents (35.4 percent Democratic as opposed to 25.7 percent Republican and 38 percent independents). Democrats vote at lower rates than Republicans, but the Democratic lead remains intact when looking just at voters: a 10 percent edge when leaners are treated as partisans (50.7 percent Democrat versus 40.5 percent Republican and 8.6 percent pure independents) and a 9 percent edge when they were treated as independents (37.1 percent Democrat versus 28.2 percent Republican and 34.5 percent independents). The Democratic lead is enhanced by their considerable advantage among African Americans, but the Democrats also have a small advantage among whites—3 percent whether leaners are treated as partisans (45.1 to 42.3 percent with 11.6 percent independents) or as independents (31.1 to 28.6 percent with 39.3 percent independents).

These values do not match the robust Democratic advantage of the 1950s and 1960s, but they show that the Democrats have regained any post-1984 losses. The 1992 figures are also similar to the 1956 ones. The Democratic lead is lower now than in the 1970s, but that difference is less than the change between 1964 and the 1970s. Seen from the perspective of change since 1964, the trend may appear to be one of dramatic Democratic losses. Seen from the perspective of changes from the 1950s, the pattern is more one of oscillating with popular moods, along with an erosion of an average of just over 1 percent in the Democratic lead from one election year to the next.[1]

The Democratic lead in partisanship in 1992 is echoed in the party thermometers. The thermometer question asked people to rate the parties on a zero to 100 scale according to how cold or warm they felt toward the parties. The mean score for the Democratic Party (table 3.2

TABLE 3.2
POPULARITY OF PARTIES BY YEAR, 1964–92
(BASED ON THERMOMETERS)

Party	1964	1968	1972	1976	1980	1984	1988	1992
Democrats	71.5	65.3	66.1	62.7	61.1	62.1	61.5	58.5
Republicans	59.4	62.1	62.9	57.4	56.9	57.9	59.2	51.7
Correlation	–0.28	–0.18	0.02	0.01	–0.23	–0.40	–0.39	–0.27

SOURCE: 1964–92 National Election Studies.

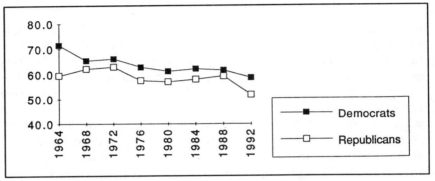

FIGURE 3.2. PARTY THERMOMETER MEANS, 1964–92.

and figure 3.2) was 58.5, compared to 51.7 for Republicans. While the Democratic edge is clear in these data, it is also important to notice that both parties received their lowest mean ratings ever in a presidential election year. Furthermore, the Republican rating of 51.7 marks the first time that either party received an average value below 56.

The Democrats had a clear edge with the public on other questions in the 1992 NES survey. Open-ended comments toward the Democratic Party tended to be favorable (an average of 2.09 likes compared to 1.88 dislikes), while comments toward the Republican Party tended to be unfavorable (an average of 1.87 likes versus 2.08 dislikes). Only half the sample felt that there would be much difference between the parties in dealing with what the respondent considered the most important problem facing the country, but by a 3–1 margin that half of the electorate thought the Democrats would do a better job on that issue.

Another important aspect of partisanship is the extent of partisan polarization. That is, to what extent are people who rate one party highly more likely to rate the other party low? One crude check of this is the correlation of the two-party thermometers (see table 3.2). A zero correlation would indicate little polarization, whereas a −1.0 correlation would represent maximal polarization. The correlation was −.28 in 1964, but became near zero in the 1970s. Polarization was evident in 1984 (−.40) and 1988 (−.39). The 1992 value for this correlation fell back to −.27, close to its 1964 starting point. Party polarization was intermediate in 1992 between the lows of the 1970s and the highs of the mid- to late 1980s.

The other important trend in party identification to note (table 3.1 and figure 3.3) is growth in political independence. When leaners are treated as independents, the proportion of independents reached a post-1940s high in 1992, with 38 percent of the sample considering themselves independents. The proportion of independents was steady through the 1950s and early 1960s, but increased steadily from 1968 through 1976. It fell slightly in 1980 and 1984 but went back up a little more in 1988 and even more in 1992. The 1992 value is slightly higher than the previous high in 1976. Differences between specific years might not be statistically significant, but 1992 seems to have as high a rate of political independence as in any year since national surveys began.[2] Perot's third-party candidacy with its inherent attacks on both parties would lead to an expectation of an increase in independents, but any increase was clearly slight.

Table 3.3 shows the relationship between party identification and vote.[3] The patterns are generally familiar. Strong partisans strongly supported their party's candidate, although, for a change, Republicans were less loyal than were Democrats. Independent leaners were more likely to support the candidate of their favored party than were weak supporters of that same party, the intransitive pattern that has appeared in many previous election studies (Petrocik 1974). Perot's greatest support was from pure independents, but he received substantial support

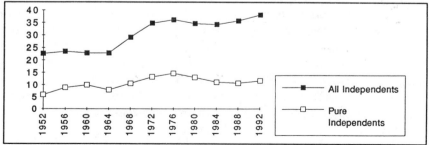

FIGURE 3.3. GROWTH OF POLITICAL INDEPENDENCE, 1952–92.

TABLE 3.3
VOTE BY PARTY IDENTIFICATION, 1992 (IN PERCENTAGES)

Vote	Strong Dem	Weak Dem	Ind Dem	Pure Ind	Ind Rep	Weak Rep	Strong Rep	Total
Bush	3.1	13.4	6.1	22.2	61.9	60.1	86.9	33.8
Perot	4.1	18.1	23.3	37.0	27.3	25.0	10.8	18.9
Clinton	92.8	68.5	70.6	40.8	10.8	14.9	2.3	47.3

SOURCE: 1992 National Election Study.

from independent leaners and from weak partisans. Indeed, Perot's support among strong partisans was much higher than the usual vote percentage that third-party candidates get from the electorate as a whole (see chapter 6 for a more complete discussion of the Perot support).

Overall, party identification had less effect on the vote than usual in 1992. For one thing, the large Perot vote meant that an unusually high proportion of voters did not vote their party identification. Combining Perot voters, pure independents, and defectors, only 65.7 percent of the electorate voted their party identification, compared to figures in the 80 percent range in other elections since the 1950s.[4] This diminished role of party identification is one of the most striking aspects of the 1992 election.

PARTY IDENTIFICATION DURING THE
BUSH ADMINISTRATION

While the analysis so far has concentrated on stability of readings of party identification in presidential election years, this approach may be deceptive. As argued by Weisberg and Smith (1991), change is understated when fewer readings are examined. Short-term change is more evident the more frequent measurements are taken. In this instance, party identification looks more stable when only change between presidential election years is examined than when change is studied at more frequent intervals. Previous analysis (MacKuen, Erikson, and Stimson 1989) has shown considerable change in aggregate "macropartisanship" from 1945 to 1988, during the 1984 presidential election campaign season (Allsop and Weisberg 1988), and through the Reagan years (Weisberg and Smith 1991). Change was also evident during the Bush term.

Figure 3.4 shows the pattern of change in party identification in CBS News/*New York Times* polls through the Bush administration,

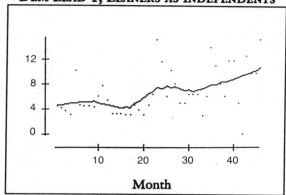

DEM LEAD 1, LEANERS AS INDEPENDENTS

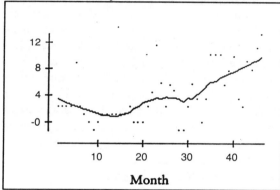

DEM LEAD 2, LEANERS AS PARTISANS

FIGURE 3.4. TRENDS IN DEMOCRATIC LEAD, 1989–92.

SOURCE: CBS News/*New York Times* Polls.

NOTE: Month 1 is January 1989; month 46 is October 1992. Lowess smoothing curves are shown.

from January 1989 through October 1992.[5] The time series graphed is the Democratic lead in identification, measured as

$$\text{Dem Lead}_t = \frac{100 \times (D_t - R_t)}{(D_t + R_t)}.$$

This gives the Democratic lead as a proportion of all partisan identifiers (Weisberg and Smith 1991, 1081–82). Two versions are shown in figure 3.4, DemLead1, which includes only strong and weak partisans (as advocated by Miller 1991), and DemLead2, which also includes independent leaners as partisans (as recommended by Keith et al. 1992). The curves shown in the figure employ a smoothing algorithm that emphasizes the main trends in the data.[6]

The changes over time are not drastic, but changes are evident. The overall pattern is one of increasing Democratic strength during the Bush years. The Republicans may have gained a little strength during the first year and a half of the Bush administration (particularly if leaners are counted as partisans), but they lost that gain before the 1990 midterm election. By the second half of 1990, problems in the economy became evident. There was a large drop in the stock market, a real estate slump hit homeowners, oil prices climbed with the Iraqi invasion of Kuwait, and the budget deficit seemed to be spiraling out of control. As Congress worked through a budget resolution, President Bush went back on his 1988 "no new taxes" pledge and accepted a tax increase. This led to considerable criticism and a drop in Bush's approval ratings (see figure 3.5). At the same time, unemployment was creeping upward (also in figure 3.5) and consumer confidence was dipping, leading the mainstream press to report on a developing recession. These factors helped the Democrats in the 1990 congressional elections and probably account for the slight jump in Democratic identifiers at the end of that year.

The economic story was soon trumped by the Gulf War, with the Alliance forces bombing Baghdad starting mid-January 1991. Public approval of Bush soon soared to record levels. If the Democrats had a large margin over the Republicans in readings of party identification in November 1990, that margin went back to more usual levels as Desert Storm progressed. Thus the smoothed values of figure 3.4 show only the slight increase in Democratic strength followed by a leveling off. Democrats again gained as the nomination campaign began toward the end of 1991 and then accelerated further by the end of the fall campaign. Figure 3.4 and table 3.1 are fairly consistent in finding about a 5 percent increase in the Democratic lead through the Bush term.[7]

Previous analysis of change in macropartisanship has used a composite score as above instead of disaggregating to examine change for each party separately. This has led to uncertainty as to how large claimed changes in partisanship actually are. Therefore it is useful to document separately the patterns for Democrats, Republicans, and independents. Once again, this can be done for either treatment of independent leaners. Figure 3.6 shows that Republican strength on the first party identification question fell in a fairly steady manner throughout the period; the correlation of Republican strength with time was −.59. The change was in the magnitude of about 4 percent. Democratic strength changed less, falling in the first year and a half and then recovering most of that loss by the end of the Republican administration. Independents increased over the period, particularly during the first year of Bush's presidency.

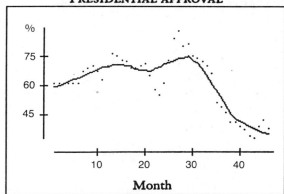

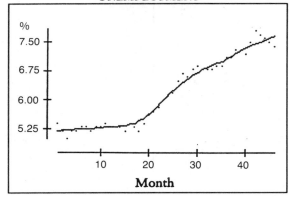

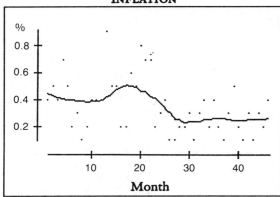

FIGURE 3.5. TRENDS IN PRESIDENTIAL APPROVAL AND ECONOMIC VARIABLES, 1989–92.

SOURCE: CBS News/*New York Times* Polls.

NOTE: Month 1 is January 1989; month 46 is October 1992. Lowess smoothing curves are shown.

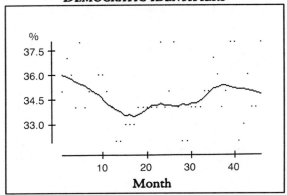

DEMOCRATIC IDENTIFIERS

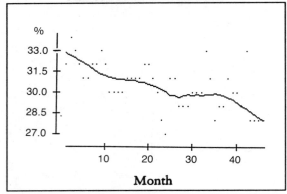

REPUBLICAN IDENTIFIERS

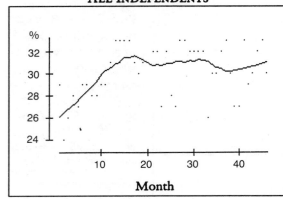

ALL INDEPENDENTS

FIGURE 3.6. TRENDS IN FIRST PARTY IDENTIFICATION QUESTION SERIES, 1989–92.

SOURCE: CBS News/*New York Times* Polls.

NOTE: Month 1 is January 1989; month 46 is October 1992. Lowess smoothing curves are shown.

When leaners are combined with partisans (see figure 3.7), the patterns for the two parties necessarily become more nearly reciprocals of one another, especially in the second half of Bush's term. Republican strength fell and Democratic strength increased. The Republican trend remains highly correlated with time (−.58), while the Democratic trend becomes more correlated with time (.46). The number of pure independents went up about 2 percent over the first half of Bush's term and went back down that 2 percent in the second half. Figures 3.6 and 3.7 show similar patterns for Republicans. In the second half of Bush's term, however, there was an increase in Democratic identification (including leaners) and a corresponding decrease in pure independents in figure 3.7 that are not fully echoed in figure 3.6 (which counts leaners as independents). This suggests that the drop in pure independents was to the Democratic-leaning category.

In line with the research literature of the past few years, it is important to examine the trends over this period in presidential approval, unemployment, and inflation. As shown in figure 3.5, presidential approval increased slightly for the first two and a half years of the Bush administration, but fell sharply thereafter. The zero-order correlations of Bush approval with partisanship are −.44 for DemLead1 (leaners as independents) and −.65 for DemLead2 (leaners as partisans), showing that Democrats gained in strength as President Bush became less popular. Unemployment (as measured by the seasonally adjusted monthly unemployment rate for all civilian workers) increased fairly steadily throughout the Bush term, the correlation of unemployment with time being a very high .96. As would be expected, there are substantial correlations between unemployment rates and partisanship: .47 with DemLead1 and .58 with DemLead2, showing Democrats gained in strength as the recession grew. Inflation (as measured by the percentage change from the previous month in the seasonally adjusted consumer price index for all items) fell in late 1990 and early 1991, but there was relatively little variance on this variable. As a result, its correlations with partisanship are meeker: −.28 with DemLead1 and −.27 with DemLead2. Generally one would expect that a president's party would gain as inflation is whipped, but these signs show the opposite: the Democrats gained in strength as inflation diminished. Unfortunately for the Republicans, the major economic story of this period was the increase in unemployment, and so they did not get the benefit they should have expected from cutting inflation.

Multiple regression confirms these impressions. Regression analysis seeks the best straight-line prediction equation for estimating the dependent variable, here party identification, from the predictors, in this

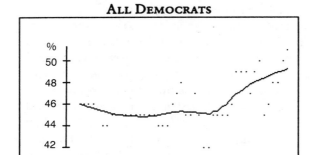

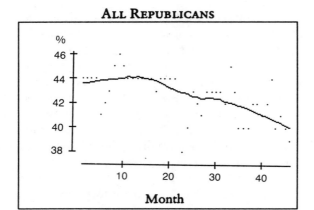

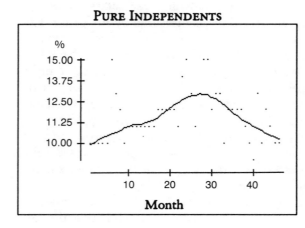

FIGURE 3.7. TRENDS IN FULL PARTY IDENTIFICATION QUESTION SERIES, 1989–92.

SOURCE: CBS News/*New York Times* Polls.

NOTE: Month 1 is January 1989; month 46 is October 1992. Lowess smoothing curves are shown.

case presidential approval and unemployment. Inflation was not included because of its small amount of variation.[8] Depending on exact model specification, presidential approval and/or unemployment have significant effects. The first equation in table 3.4 uses DemLead2 as the dependent variable—the Democratic lead with independent leaners treated as partisans. Approval had a very significant effect on party identification, with unemployment having a more marginal effect. The equation predicts that as presidential approval increased by 10 percent, the Democratic lead would decrease by 1.4 percent. As unemployment increased by 1 percent, the Democratic lead would increase by 1.2 percent.[9] The adjusted R^2 value for this equation is .52,[10] so that just over half the variance in the Democratic lead is being explained by the predictors. A similar analysis of DemLead1, in which leaners are treated as independents (as advocated by Miller 1991), finds unemployment having a very significant effect and presidential popularity also having an impact, with the adjusted R^2 value being .23. A comparison of the R^2 values in these equations implies that the partisanship of leaners is particularly responsive to changes in unemployment and presidential popularity, a result that is important in its own right.

TABLE 3.4

REGRESSION OF PARTY IDENTIFICATION ON PRESIDENTIAL
APPROVAL AND UNEMPLOYMENT, 1989–92

	DemLead2 [a]			DemLead1		
	Coefficient	Standard Error	t-ratio	Coefficient	Standard Error	t-ratio
Constant	5.1875	6.9627	0.745	2.7772	5.6852	0.488
Pres. approval	−.1430	.0481	−2.971***	−.0647	.0398	−1.624*
Unemployment	1.2228	.7847	1.558*	1.2616	.6291	2.005**
R^2, adjusted		0.522			0.228	
Number of cases		46			46	

SOURCE: 1992 National Election Study.

NOTE: DemLead2 treats leaners as partisans, whereas DemLead1 treats them as independents.

a. Corrected for first-order autocorrelation.

* $p < .1$; ** $p < .05$; *** $p < .005$, one-tailed.

CONCLUSIONS

The argument being made in this section is somewhat unusual. Previous examinations of party-identification change at the time of presidential election years focused on the question of realignment. That question is not being addressed here. The reason is definitional: Realignment entails enduring change in partisanship, and enough time has not yet elapsed to judge whether partisan change has been enduring. A glance at table 3.1 does suggest that partisanship was different in 1984 and 1988 than earlier, with the 1992 reading being intermediate, but this does not tell us what history will judge as enduring.

If realignment is not the concern, what then does one make of party identification in the 1992 election? Changes in party identification were found. Clearly these changes were not of mammoth proportions, but they were large enough to undo much of the Republican gains of the 1980s and to reinforce the image of partisanship as partly short term. The electorate moved in the Democratic direction, with that move occurring around the 1990 midterm election. The likely cause of the change was the economy. The recession was hitting by this time, and it hurt the Republicans. It did not hurt them enough to restore the Democratic advantage of the years leading up to 1980, but it did cause them to lose a good part of their gains in the 1980s. Yet viewing party change as partially short term recognizes that further changes in the economy could yield more shifts in these patterns. Economic gains under Clinton could bolster the Democratic gains that are evident in the data, while another failed recovery would shift party identification at least back to the equality level of 1988. So much depends on the nature of the economy during the Clinton years that speculation about the enduring nature of the changes in partisan strength found here would be futile.

What may be more important is the renewed growth in political independence. The low ratings of both parties on the thermometer questions suggests that there remains an opportunity for Ross Perot and other nontraditional candidates. Dealignment continues, with all the implications of such dealignment for political volatility.

What is required, then, is to move beyond party identification, as many Americans did in their 1992 voting. Party identification provides an interesting beginning to the study of elections, but it is not the end. The slope of the partisan playing field had a slight tilt to the Democratic side in 1992, but the tilt was still small enough that the issues and candidates could play a major role in the election result. Furthermore, party identification is partly dependent on the forces of the election itself, and so we must look past party identification to understand the election. The remainder of this chapter does so, looking at both the issue and candidate sides of the 1992 race.

Issues

The paradox of political campaigns in the United States is that presidential candidates give many speeches on the issues, but press attention focuses more on the candidates themselves. Many political scientists have argued that issues are important in elections, but that importance is not always visible in election surveys. The convenient explanation is that the NES surveys often focus on the wrong issues. The NES surveys have tended to emphasize continuity in issue questions over time rather than to focus on the issues of the particular campaign (though partly this just reflects the inability to predict in advance what issues will matter in a campaign). As a result, the NES surveys often seem to miss the issues over which the election was fought. Finding issues to be of minimal importance thus reflects as much on the question writers as on the electorate.

The 1992 NES questionnaire departed more radically from the usual issue questions than has been the case in other years, and it included more questions on new issues (e.g., gays in the military). Still, it largely missed some of the issues that became important over the course of the campaign (e.g., the environment). At the same time, the changes in the questionnaire meant that fewer over-time comparisons can be made for issues than in previous election years. In particular, there were many fewer "seven-point scale" questions in which respondents were asked to place themselves, the parties, and the nominees on seven-point issue scales.

Another way to examine the role of issues in the election is to focus on what issues people raise spontaneously. The NES questionnaires ask people what they like and dislike about each party and candidate. Some of the open-ended responses to these questions involve issues. Smith and Kessel analyze these open-ended issue references in the next chapter, supplementing the analysis of closed-ended issue questions in this section.

IDEOLOGICAL PROXIMITY

The 1992 campaign did not play in the press as a great ideological campaign. The 1988 campaign became focused on ideology when Bush attached the "L word" to his opponent, Michael Dukakis. The Bush campaign also tried to portray Bill Clinton as a liberal, but it was harder to make that tag stick to an Arkansas governor than to a Massachusetts governor. As a result, one would expect the ideological differences to have seemed less severe in 1992 than in 1988.

Table 3.5 shows the average placement of respondents and candidates on the seven-point issue scales. In each case the respondent has been shown a scale in which the liberal position is denoted by the number 1 and the conservative position is marked by the number 7. Respondents are asked to position themselves on these scales according to their views and to locate the candidates on these same scales.

There is a discernible tendency for the public to become less conservative in terms of overall ideology during the years shown. The average placement of respondents was 4.2, slightly to the conservative end (4 being the midpoint of the scale). Bush was seen as more conservative than the average person (5) and Clinton as more liberal (3.2), with Perot (4.3) being nearer the average respondent. In many recent elections the Democrats were seen as much farther away than the Republicans from the average citizen on ideology. The differences in 1992 were smaller.

There was also movement away from the conservative position on several of the issues in table 3.5, including desired amount of defense spending, government-guaranteed jobs and standard of living, government health insurance, and equal role for women in society. Full candidate placement questions were asked on only three issue scales in 1992: the tradeoff between cutting government services or spending, the desired size of defense spending, and government-guaranteed jobs and standard of living. The proximity difference between the average respondent and the candidates moved to a position less favorable to the Republican candidate on all three of these issues. These were not necessarily the most important issues of the election year, but the improved positioning of the Democrats on these issues helps show how a Democrat was able to recapture the White House in 1992.

While the 1992 NES survey did not ask for candidate placement on many issue scales, it did ask several questions about which candidate would handle particular issues better. Clinton had the edge on most of these issues. By margins in the range of 2–1, he was seen as likely to do better in making health care more affordable, in solving the problem of poverty, in handling the problem of pollution and protecting the environment, and, probably most important, in handling the economy. Bush was seen as better in handling foreign affairs (by more than a 2–1 margin). In the case of reducing the budget deficit, Clinton was seen as better by a wide margin, but more people saw no difference between the major-party candidates on that issue. Incidentally, only about 1 percent

TABLE 3.5
AVERAGE PLACEMENT ON SEVEN-POINT SCALES, 1984–92

Issue	1992				1988				1984			
	Average issue position			Proximity difference[a]	Average issue position			Proximity difference[a]	Average issue position			Proximity difference[a]
	Respondent	Bush	Clinton		Respondent	Bush	Dukakis		Respondent	Reagan	Mondale	
General ideology	4.22	5.03	3.17	−0.24	4.37	5.12	3.24	−0.38	4.44	5.31	3.16	−0.41
Cut services or spending	3.88	4.69	2.98	−0.09	3.85	4.45	2.90	−0.35	2.96	4.11	2.00	0.19
Size of defense spending	3.52	4.82	3.32	1.10	3.93	5.28	3.31	0.73	3.99	5.67	3.39	1.08
Gov't.-guaranteed job	4.28	5.14	3.49	0.07	4.41	5.04	3.38	−0.40	4.13	5.00	3.28	0.02
Gov't. health insurance	3.41				3.84							
Gov't. should help blacks	4.69				4.68							
Equal role for women	2.23				2.60							
Handling urban unrest	3.39											

SOURCE: 1984–92 National Election Studies.

NOTE: Scores are average scores on seven-point issue scales, where 1 is the liberal response.

a. Scores indicate how much closer the average respondent is to the Democratic candidate than to the Republican candidate; positive values show the average person is closer to the Democratic candidate.

of respondents volunteered that Perot would do better on these issues, the high being 1.6 percent on the deficit and the low being .3 percent on foreign affairs.

THE ECONOMY AND FOREIGN POLICY

The economy was clearly the key issue in 1992 because many people were hurting financially. Just over half the respondents had put off purchases during the prior year, and 43 percent looked for a job (or second job or extra hours at their present job). Overall, 73 percent felt the economy had gotten worse over the past year. There was some recognition that the economy was no longer getting worse, with only a third of the public feeling it had gotten worse in the past few months, but 82 percent felt it had gotten worse in the past four years. These economic variables are correlated with major-party vote at about .20 to .30, with a lower Bush vote among those who felt worse off or who felt the economy had gotten worse (see questions A and B in table 3.6). One of the most distinctive results of the survey was that most Americans thought the country had fairly seriously gotten off on the wrong track (83 percent), with only 17 percent feeling things were generally going in the right direction.

The Republicans sometimes have been behind on domestic policy concerns but have had the advantage on foreign policy. There was less

TABLE 3.6
VOTE BY ECONOMIC ISSUES (IN PERCENTAGES THAT ADD TO 100 IN EACH ROW)

Question Answer	Bush	Clinton	Perot	Total
A: Are you better off or worse off financially than a year ago?				
Better off	42.6	37.3	20.2	31%
Same	38.1	46.8	15.1	35%
Worse off	21.4	57.3	21.3	35%
B: Over the past year, the nation's economy has ...				
Gotten better	75.1	11.9	13.0	5%
Stayed the same	50.7	31.1	18.3	22%
Gotten worse	25.9	54.7	19.4	73%

SOURCE: 1992 National Election Study.

of this in 1992. People tended to feel that the U.S. position in the world had grown weaker in the past year rather than stronger. They saw little difference as to which party would best keep the country out of war in the next four years (20 percent Republican versus 18 percent Democrats). People overwhelmingly felt the country did the right thing in sending U.S. troops to the Persian Gulf in 1991 (77 to 20 percent), with more than two-thirds approving of George Bush's handling of the war. Still, only half felt that something good had come out of the war or that the war was worth its cost. Indeed, 61 percent felt that we should have continued to fight Iraq until Saddam Hussein was driven from power. All in all, the Republicans did not gain much advantage on foreign policy concerns, and certainly not enough to offset the disquiet about their handling of the economy.

SOCIAL ISSUES

One of the more unusual episodes of campaign 1992 involved what became known as the "family values" issue. A variety of social issues have been raised in elections since the late 1960s, issues from school prayer and abortion to homosexuality and feminism. These issues came together in a new way in 1992 when Vice-President Dan Quayle made a speech raising several moral issues. While this speech did not differ much from several of his earlier speeches, it received considerable attention when he attacked a television character, Murphy Brown, for becoming a single mother. This family values debate raged in the press for a few weeks, with many people making the point that the traditional family structure had changed in the United States so that Quayle's image of family values did not fit contemporary society. Meanwhile, the Democrats pushed a "family leave" bill to show their commitment to families, and Bush vetoed this bill, which sharpened the divisions. The family values debate eventually subsided, but it remains interesting to examine the demographics of voting in the light of that debate.

There are many usual demographic correlates of voting. Exact details change from year to year, but race, religion, region, and social-class cleavages have long affected both party identification (Stanley and Niemi 1992) and presidential voting (Erikson, Lancaster, and Romero 1989). The well-known gender gap emerged in 1980, with women less supportive of Republican presidential candidates than men. Additionally, there has been a "marital gap" in voting since 1972, with married people more supportive of Republican presidential candidates than unmarried people (Weisberg 1987; Kingston and Finkel 1987; Plutzer and McBurnett 1991). The marriage gap can be explained away statistically when controls are instituted on race and income, but nonetheless it constitutes another basis that politicians can use in their play for votes. As Weisberg (1987, 342) forecast, "party leaders who now find that their traditional racial and income appeals have led to a marriage gap in voting may choose to focus their appeals more directly on family issues that would increase this division." The family values issue is particularly interesting because it plays directly to this marital division.

Table 3.7 shows the 1992 vote by race, gender, marital status, and children. The black vote was extremely cohesive for Clinton (see chapter 7), a smaller majority of Hispanics voted for Clinton, and those of other races tended to favor Bush. Among whites, a gender effect is apparent, with Clinton getting 9–13 percent more support and Perot getting 6–15 percent less support from women than men within each demographic category. Comparing unmarried people (all categories combined) with married people who have no children at home under age six, with gender controlled, the unmarried gave Clinton more support by 10 percent and Bush less support by 8–16 percent. In addition to this marriage gap, there was a gap in voting associated with having young children in the house. Comparing married people with young children at home against those who do not have children under age six at home, again with gender controlled, those without children at home supported Clinton more and Bush less by 12–16 percent. The top rows of the table show that Bush received a majority of the vote of married white males with young children at home and nearly half the vote of married white females with young children at home. If these were the groups that the GOP was targeting with the family values issue, they were successful in their appeals. Yet the far-right column of the table reminds us that there are relatively few American families of this sort, with only 12 percent of the sample falling into these two categories combined. The Republicans had strong appeal to white married people with young kids in their houses, especially to men of this type, but they were less effective in appealing to families of different shapes. (For further analysis of this effect, see Arnold and Weisberg 1994.)

The NES survey also included several fascinating new questions on social issues. As an example of such an issue, sexual harassment in the workplace was seen as a very important problem by nearly a third of respondents, somewhat serious by nearly half, and not too serious by the remaining people. As question A in table 3.8 indicates, those who felt that sexual harassment was very serious were nearly twice as likely to vote for Clinton as were those who believed it was not too serious. In a series of questions about homosexuals, three out of five people favored laws to protect gays against job discrimination and a similar proportion felt gays should be allowed to serve in the armed forces, but

TABLE 3.7
PRESIDENTIAL VOTE BY RACE, GENDER, MARRIAGE, AND CHILDREN, 1992

Characteristics	Vote (in percentages)				Number (N)	Proportion
	Bush	Clinton	Perot	Total		
White, male, married, children [a]	55.7	19.9	24.4	100.0	101	6.2%
White, female, married, children [a]	49.0	32.7	18.2	99.9	98	6.0%
White, male, married, no children [a]	39.5	35.3	25.2	100.0	342	20.9%
White, female, married, no children [a]	37.3	44.9	17.8	100.0	320	19.5%
White, male, unmarried	23.5	46.0	30.5	100.0	183	11.2%
White, female, unmarried	29.7	54.8	15.5	100.0	267	16.3%
Black	5.5	92.0	2.5	100.0	193	11.8%
Hispanic	31.6	58.6	9.8	100.0	103	6.3%
Other	56.2	28.1	15.6	99.9	32	2.0%

SOURCE: 1992 National Election Study.

a. Under age 6.

only 28 percent felt they should be allowed to adopt children. These issues were quite powerful in separating Bush voters from Clinton voters (see chapter 6, table 6.4). When asked about English as an official language, 65 percent of respondents supported such a law, with Bush getting a greater vote among those supporters (see question B in table 3.8). On a related issue, only a fifth felt that immigrants should be eligible immediately for government services such as Medicaid, food stamps, and welfare. But it appears that this issue was not used by voters to differentiate between the candidates (question C in table 3.8).

The one social issue on which candidate placements were obtained was abortion. The public tended to favor the pro-choice position over a pro-life position by roughly a 3–2 split. Bush and Clinton were perceived fairly accurately on abortion on a four-point scale, with about 80 percent putting Bush on one of the two more pro-life positions and about 80 percent putting Clinton on one of the two more pro-choice positions (though 13 percent opted out of describing Bush's position and 18 percent did not attempt to describe Clinton's). Bush ended up getting a 22 percent greater share of the vote from those supporting a pro-life position than from those favoring a pro-choice position, with Clinton getting a 16 percent greater vote from those supporting a pro-choice position (table 3.8, question D).

THE FEDERAL GOVERNMENT

Dissatisfaction with the federal government and its size at first glance seems to have been at a high level in 1992. This was particularly the case with Congress, in the aftermath of the check-writing scandal at the House bank. Only 31 percent of the public approved of how Congress had been handling its job. Most people with opinions (69 percent) felt that the government in Washington was getting too powerful. The Democrats were seen as more likely to favor a powerful government in Washington, but only by a 28–19 percent edge, so the issue was less a partisan issue than one that could hurt both parties.

More complicated questions showed less dissatisfaction with the government. When asked about the size of government, 63 percent felt there were more things that government should be doing, instead of agreeing that the less government the better. Similarly, 70 percent of the public felt that we need a strong government to handle today's complex economic problems, instead of feeling that the free market can handle these problems without government's being involved. Also, 58 percent felt that government has become bigger because the problems we face have become bigger, whereas 38 percent felt that government has become bigger over the years because it has gotten involved in things that

TABLE 3.8
VOTE BY ISSUE POSITIONS (IN PERCENTAGES THAT ADD TO 100 IN EACH ROW)

Question Answer	Bush	Clinton	Perot	Total
A: How serious is sexual harassment in the workplace?				
Very serious	24.7	61.2	14.1	31%
Somewhat serious	34.7	46.0	19.4	47%
Not too serious	42.1	32.5	25.3	22%
B: Making English the official language of the United States.				
Favor	37.7	42.6	19.7	65%
Oppose	24.3	58.7	17.0	28%
C: Immigrants should be immediately eligible for government services.				
Yes	33.4	47.7	19.0	20%
No, wait a year	33.9	47.6	18.5	80%
D: Abortion position.				
Pro-life	47.3	37.5	15.3	39%
Pro-choice	25.6	53.5	20.8	61%
E: What is the proper role of government?				
The less the better	51.6	25.0	23.4	34%
Should be doing more	21.5	62.3	16.3	63%
F: How should economic problems be handled?				
Strong government	25.1	58.0	16.9	70%
Free market	51.9	24.4	23.7	25%
G: Why has the government grown? Doing things people should do				
for themselves	44.8	30.6	24.6	38%
Problems have become bigger	24.4	61.1	14.5	58%
H: Approval of George Bush's handling of his job as president.				
Approve	68.5	15.6	15.8	43%
Disapprove	8.4	70.4	21.2	57%

SOURCE: 1992 National Election Study.

people should do for themselves. Given all of the Washington bashing in the press and by candidate Perot, the willingness of the public to accept governmental solutions on these questions is remarkable. Public dissatisfaction with the role of government could lead to large-scale support of a nonparty candidate, like Perot, but these results show very real limitations to the success of such an approach. In fact, these three questions were all related to the vote (table 3.8, questions *E, F,* and *G*) with Clinton doing better among those who accepted a more expansive role for government and Bush and Perot both doing better among those who favored a less expansive role.

CONCLUSIONS

Clearly the U.S. public was uneasy about many issues during the 1992 campaign. Ideology per se may have mattered less as a campaign issue than in 1988, but the economy mattered a great deal. The president's performance was judged negatively by many voters, and this extended past the economy even to parts of the foreign relations realm. Social issues provided an opening for the Republican campaign, but efforts to appeal to voters on the basis of family values were limited by the changing nature of the American family. Distrust of the federal government provided another opening, but one that could be played most effectively by a candidate not associated with the major parties.

The issue terrain in general and the economy in particular put the Bush presidency in jeopardy. Nevertheless, what matter are not only the issues but whether there is a strong opponent who can make effective use of those issues. Such an opponent must project a positive image and at the same time withstand campaign attacks that attempt to divert public attention from issues to matters of character. The economy may have established the lay of the land for the 1992 election, but the campaign focused on the candidates as well.

Candidates

Many political analysts feel that U.S. politics is increasingly candidate centered. If the voting behavior literature of the early 1960s emphasized partisanship in understanding voting while the revisionist literature emphasized issues, the most recent literature emphasizes candidates. Perot's strong showing should make the 1992 election the high point of candidate-centered politics. But the NES survey was finalized at a point when Perot was not in the race, so there are few questions about him. Furthermore, his movement in and out of the race complicates interpretations. After his July withdrawal made him look like a quitter, Perot was not taken seriously again as a candidate until after the first debate. Reactions to the candidates therefore are likely to depend to an unusual degree on exactly when the interviews were taken. As with the issues discussion earlier, this section is limited to an analysis of closed-ended questions in the NES survey; open-ended comments about the candidates are examined in the next chapter.

THE MAJOR-PARTY NOMINEES

The candidate factor worked to Bush's disadvantage in 1992. It should be remembered at the outset that Bush was not a very popular candidate even in 1988. In fact, analyses of that election have focused on the contribution to his victory of a presidential succession effect resulting from the Reagan legacy (Weisberg 1989; Mattei and Weisberg 1994; Shanks and Miller 1991). With that succession effect no longer relevant in 1992, Bush's reelection chances depended on his building a record of performance that the public would approve.

The clearest indications of Bush's image as a candidate come from the job-approval questions. Asked to evaluate the president's performance in office, only 43 percent of the sample approved of Bush's handling of his job as president. This is obviously a low level of satisfaction for a president seeking reelection. As shown earlier in figure 3.5, Bush's approval rating was high through summer 1991, but fell considerably thereafter. Bush was viewed most positively on foreign affairs, with 62 percent approving his handling of our relations with foreign countries generally and 66 percent approving his handling of the crisis in the Persian Gulf. The recession took a heavy toll on Bush, however, with only 20 percent of respondents approving his handling of the economy.

Bush's weakness is also apparent in the candidate thermometers (see table 3.9 and figure 3.8). Clinton's preelection thermometer average of 55.7 was the lowest for any winning presidential candidate in the period, with the only other winning candidate with a mean rating below 60 degrees being Ronald Reagan in 1980. While reactions to Clinton were thus not very positive, reactions to President Bush were even less so. Bush's 52.3 rating was the lowest of all major-party presidential candidates since 1968, with the sole exception of George McGovern in 1972.[11] Another comparison to make is that Bush's popularity level was 60.6 as the 1988 Republican candidate, so he fell by 8 points in popularity over the years. By contrast, Reagan had gone up 5 points in popularity during his first four years in office, Nixon fell just 1 point in his first four years, and Carter lost only 6 points in going down to defeat in 1980. Perot's preelection rating was lower than Bush's, with a mean of

TABLE 3.9
POPULARITY OF NOMINEES BY YEAR, 1968–92
(BASED ON THERMOMETERS)

Nominee	1968	1972	1976	1980	1984	1988	1992
Democratic	61.7	48.9	62.7	56.6	57.4	56.8	55.7
Republican	66.5	65.5	60.5	56.1	61.2	60.6	52.3
Independent	31.4			52.0			45.4
D–R correlation	–0.18	–0.42	–0.31	–0.29	–0.54	–0.38	–0.39

SOURCE: 1968–92 National Election Studies.

NOTE: The postelection thermometer for Perot was 52.8.

45.4, but this low figure is deceptive because it combines ratings when he was out of the race in September and after he returned in October.[12]

In terms of comments about the candidates on the open-ended likes-and-dislikes questions, not only was Clinton viewed favorably, but Republican attempts to increase his negatives were not successful. The mean number of favorable comments on Clinton was 2.60 compared to .86 unfavorable. By contrast, Bush was viewed negatively, with 2.35 favorable comments on average compared to 2.60 unfavorable. Perot was in between, with 2.39 favorable and only 1.55 unfavorable on average.

The survey provides more detailed reactions to the major-party candidates, as summarized in table 3.10. This table shows not only how the public viewed the nominees but also how successful the candidates were in projecting the images they desired and in attaching negative labels to their opponents. For example, the Bush campaign emphasized

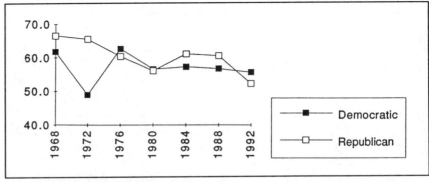

FIGURE 3.8. NOMINEE THERMOMETER MEANS, 1968–92.

TABLE 3.10
CANDIDATE IMAGES, 1984–92 (IN PERCENTAGES)

| | 1992 | | 1988 | | 1984 | | |
	Bush	Clin-ton	Bush	Duka-kis	Rea-gan	Mon-dale	Bush
Emotion							
Positive							
Proud	57	24	33	29	55	30	
Hopeful	48	51	39	42	60	41	
Negative							
Angry	52	26	25	29	48	30	
Afraid	41	24	15	21	24	17	
Trait							
Leadership							
Strong leader	56	62	54	57	71	49	55
Inspiring	39	59	39	49	59	44	48
Gets things done	41	68					
Competence							
Knowledgeable	83	83	83	82	77	81	82
Intelligent	82	87	78	88	83	86	
Integrity							
Moral	80	48	78	80	82	85	80
Honest	59	51	67	78			
Empathy							
Cares about people	35	66	50	65	47	64	46
Compassionate	59	79	62	73	60	79	66

SOURCE: 1984–92 National Election Studies.

NOTE: The top half of the table represents responses to questions asking whether the candidate "even made you feel" proud, etc. The bottom half summarizes reactions as to whether the candidate can be described as a strong leader, etc.

the "trust" issue as a means of discrediting candidate Clinton, so the results test the extent to which the character issue was made to work to Bush's advantage in the election.

The top part of table 3.10 summarizes the emotions that the candidates elicited, in answer to a series of questions asking whether each candidate ever made the respondent feel proud, hopeful, angry, or afraid. The reactions toward Bush had been relatively tepid in 1988, especially when compared to the strong emotions toward Reagan in 1984. By 1992, Bush also elicited strong emotions, with a majority of the public having felt proud of him and nearly half the public feeling hopeful about him, but about half the public felt angry toward him and 41 percent felt afraid. The Bush image had strengthened, but not fully in a positive manner. Clinton was less likely to make people feel proud, angry, or afraid, but half the public felt hopeful about him. Clinton's showing on the hopeful affect question was the highest of the Democratic nominees of this period. Clinton's biographical advertisement film in 1992 was entitled "The Man from Hope" (Arkansas), so the association between Clinton and hopeful may partly reflect the coincidence of this advertising theme with the survey item wording. Still, the results do show that the Democrats succeeded in associating Clinton with upbeat, positive affect.

The bottom half of table 3.10 summarizes the traits associated with the candidates, in answer to another series of questions asking whether each candidate was seen as a strong leader, inspiring, and so on. Bush's image in 1992 was very similar to his 1988 image except on two traits: honesty, where he fell by 8 percentage points, and caring about people, where he fell by 15. When the Bush campaign tried using the character issue against Clinton, the Clinton people responded by challenging Bush's honesty on such matters as the Iran-*contra* affair, breaking his "no new taxes" pledge, and searching Clinton's passport file. The decline in perceptions of Bush as honest suggests some success for the Democratic negative image building. Bush's decline on caring about people might be traced to voter reactions to the recession, an image emphasized in the debates when Clinton came off as more empathic to people hurt by the economy than did Bush. Note too that the one place where Bush came off much worse than Reagan did in 1984 was on the leadership questions. Reagan showed in 1984 how a president can win reelection by projecting an image of strong leadership combined with being inspiring, but Bush was not able to project such an image.

According to table 3.10, Clinton was successful in making citizens view him as competent and empathic, with ratings on these traits similar to those for Dukakis in 1988 and Mondale in 1984. He also was perceived well on leadership, here outscoring both Dukakis and Mondale. The weak point of Clinton's image was integrity; only half the public viewed him as moral or honest. The Democratic primaries focused much attention on Clinton's character, morality, and honesty, and the Republican campaign attacked further on these points. Clinton's low ratings on integrity in table 3.10 show that these charges had effects on the public, though half the respondents still viewed him positively in these regards.

Comparing the Bush and Clinton images, both were regarded as highly competent, Bush was perceived as better on integrity, and Clinton was viewed as better on leadership and empathy. Bush scored some important successes as president, especially in the Persian Gulf War against Iraq, but he was not able to convert these successes into a more positive image than he had had in 1988. Instead, Saddam Hussein's continued survival in Iraq and the prolonged recession at home hurt Bush's image in terms of leadership and empathy. Clinton did not look good on the integrity dimension, but this deficit was not enough to counter his advantage on the leadership and empathy factors.

A natural question at this point is whether Bush or Clinton was the stronger candidate. Unfortunately, the results in table 3.10 do not permit an answer to this question. They show the strengths and weaknesses of the images of the two candidates, but they do not show which of these factors mattered more to voters or how they affected the vote. Thus there is no indication in the table as to whether voters prefer a candidate who scores high on empathy or one who scores high on integrity. The analysis by Smith and Kessel in chapter 4 of open-ended reactions to the candidates is better able to answer this question. Still, this analysis shows weaknesses in both the Bush and Clinton images, weaknesses that help explain how both candidates could be kept to under 45 percent of the popular vote.

The overall weakness of Bush's image and particularly his ratings on the economy, leadership, and empathy made him vulnerable in 1992. Clinton's positives on empathy and leadership were balanced off by his negatives on integrity, so his image was not positive enough to make his election certain. Instead, it had sufficient deficiencies to allow a serious three-candidate race. It is now time to turn directly to that third candidate.

THE PEROT VOTE

The nature of the Perot vote is a topic that will be debated for years. He was one of the most successful third-party candidates in U.S. history, but the nature of his support remains elusive. He actually led some of the election polls in spring 1992, but then stunned the nation by withdrawing from the race during the Democratic convention. He became a national laughingstock during the early fall, particularly when he claimed he had dropped out of the race because of White House dirty tricks. When everyone was certain that his support had fallen so sharply that his return to the race would be irrelevant, he reentered the race, scored well in the debates and with his television infomercials, and ended up with a fairly high proportion of the popular vote. According to the postelection survey, 44 percent of voters either voted for him or said that they had thought of voting for him, showing that his candidacy had a very large potential impact, even if it was not fully realized. The Perot candidacy is considered in more detail by Herb Asher in chapter 6.

One obvious and important question is whether the Perot vote came mainly at the expense of Clinton or Bush. It is difficult to engage in this type of "what if" analysis, because the entire race would have been different had Perot never entered the presidential contest, had he not withdrawn, and/or had he not reentered. Still, it is worth looking for indications of the effect of the Perot candidacy.

There are several ways to examine which candidate Perot hurt the most. One is to look at the net Bush-Clinton thermometer difference for Perot voters. According to this test, Perot voters on average liked Bush more than Clinton by 1 degree, showing that their net ratings of the two candidates were fairly similar. A second comparison is to see the preelection preferences of Perot voters on the candidate thermometers. This test shows that 45 percent of the Perot voters liked Bush more in the preelection poll, 39 percent liked Clinton more, and the remaining 16 percent liked the two equally. These tests find marginally greater support for Bush than Clinton among Perot voters, with the differences never being very large.

Nor did Perot draw disproportionately from one party. Attitudes toward Perot varied not by partisanship but by strength of partisanship. In the preelection study, pure independents liked Perot the most (average thermometer of 52), leaners liked him next best (48), then weak partisans (46), and strong partisans least (40).[13] Partisan differences turn out to be minor, with Democrats and Republicans at the same level of partisan strength liking Perot about the same amount. In the postelection study, strong partisans liked him least (46 for strong Republicans and 49 for strong Democrats), with trivial differences between the other partisan categories (54 for weak partisans, 56 for partisan leaners, and 55 for pure independents).

A further question is the source of the movement to Perot over the course of the campaign. At the time of the preelection survey, 8 percent of respondents were planning to vote for Perot, but in the end he received 19 percent of the vote. Table 3.11 examines the source of this change by comparing preelection thermometer ratings of Bush and Clinton with actual vote. Some of the preelection interviews were taken when Perot was not in the race and others when he was in the race, but that should not have affected Bush-Clinton preferences. The table shows that most respondents voted for the candidate they initially favored. Being behind, Bush had to shake loose the Clinton support, but

TABLE 3.11
VOTE BY PREELECTION THERMOMETER RATINGS OF
MAJOR-PARTY CANDIDATES (IN PERCENTAGES)

	Favored Clinton	Neutral	Favored Bush
Vote			
Clinton	83.8	39.5	4.3
Perot	14.7	33.4	20.8
Bush	1.6	27.0	75.0
Total	100.1	99.9	100.1
N	837	150	679
Percentage	50.2	9.0	40.8

SOURCE: 1992 National Election Study.

that strategy did not succeed. Particularly important in the table is the comparison between the bottom left and the top right corners: 16 percent of respondents who liked Clinton more than Bush at the time of the first interview ended up voting for Perot or Bush, compared to 25 percent of respondents who liked Bush more at the time of the first interview but ended up voting for Perot or Clinton. Given that fewer people liked Bush than Clinton according to the thermometers, Bush could not afford to lose the vote of 25 percent of those who liked him more than Clinton. Additionally, the middle column shows that citizens who were neutral between the major-party candidates broke in favor of Clinton, in nearly a 3–2 ratio. Indeed, Perot received a somewhat greater proportion of the vote of these neutrals than did Bush.

This analysis of change across the campaign season is useful in considering which candidate was most harmed by Perot. Bush was behind during the preelection period. Winning reelection would have required Bush to keep his own support, win over the neutrals, and attract some Clinton support. Perot's candidacy muddied the waters. The press paid attention to Perot, distracting the public from the main Bush-Clinton race. Bush would probably have lost the election even if Perot had not reentered, but his reentry took away Bush's best chance.[14]

It is difficult to use the NES survey to probe the Perot vote in great detail. The designers of the study originally planned to include a large number of questions about Perot, but they naturally decided to drop those questions when he withdrew from the race in July. It was too late to add those questions to the preelection survey when he returned to the race at the beginning of October. As a result, questions about Perot's traits and affect toward him are missing from the survey.

It is tempting to probe the issue basis of his support from the survey; however, few variables are strongly correlated with the Perot vote. Dissatisfaction with the choice among the presidential candidates had a .25 correlation with voting for Perot over the major-party candidates. As shown in table 3.12, question B, Bush support was steady across levels of satisfaction with the candidate choice, but Clinton received 58 percent of the vote among those very satisfied with the choice but fell to a 24 percent vote from those not at all satisfied with that 30+ percent of the vote flowing to Perot. Of course this survey item only begs another question—people less satisfied with the choices were more likely to vote for Perot, so the next question becomes why they were less satisfied with the choices. Several NES questions ask respondents which party (or candidate) would do a better job of handling particular problems, with respondents also being given the alternative that there would not be any difference between them. These were correlated with the vote, such as a moderate .17 correlation between whether or not the respondent saw a difference on the economy and voting for Perot (see table 3.12, questions C, D, E, and F).

Voting for Perot had a 0.18 correlation with the feeling thermometer toward the federal government—the mean rating of the federal government by Clinton voters was 50 degrees, compared to 46 degrees for Bush voters and 39 degrees for Perot voters. Also, Perot received a greater portion of the vote from people who were more cynical about politics (see table 3.12, question G).

The variables involved in these correlations seem to make perfect sense. The larger lesson is how few variables had an effect on the Perot vote (see also chapter 6). The lack of strong effects is important in its own right. It contrasts sharply with the Wallace candidacy of 1968, which has been cited as an example of issue voting (Converse, Miller, Rusk, and Wolfe 1969). Third-party candidates are often identified with issues, but there is very little distinctive about the issue basis of Perot's considerable success as a third-party candidate beyond rejection of the major parties.[15] Studying the Perot vote is surprisingly similar to explaining turnout in presidential elections: there are different causes for different people, with less powerful explanatory success than with analyzing the determinants of major-party voting.

Conclusions

This chapter began by arguing that party identification, issues, and candidates can operate in a sequential manner in affecting election results.

TABLE 3.12
VOTE BY ISSUE POSITIONS (IN PERCENTAGES
THAT ADD TO 100 IN EACH ROW)

Question Answer	Bush	Clinton	Perot	Total
A: Strength of partisanship.				
Strong	36.4	56.8	6.8	33%
Weak	35.1	43.6	21.3	33%
Leaner	32.6	42.2	25.2	26%
Pure independent	22.2	40.8	37.0	9%
B: How satisfied are you with the presidential candidates?				
Very satisfied	33.7	58.5	7.9	14%
Somewhat	33.7	53.6	12.7	49%
Not very	33.7	37.0	29.4	29%
Not at all	35.8	24.1	40.1	7%
C: Which party would better handle the economy?				
Dem/Rep	31.9	54.6	13.5	62%
No difference	36.7	36.4	26.9	38%
D: Which candidate would better handle the budget deficit?				
Bush/Clinton	31.8	54.2	14.0	59%
No difference	36.2	39.0	24.8	41%
E: Which party would best handle the most important problem?				
Rep/Dem	26.6	59.2	14.2	55%
Not much difference	42.0	33.7	24.3	45%
F: Are there important party differences?				
Yes	34.2	49.9	15.9	70%
No	32.7	41.8	25.5	30%
G: How much of the time can you trust government?				
Just about always	42.2	51.2	6.6	3%
Most of the time	36.8	48.2	15.0	27%
Some of the time	31.9	47.0	21.1	68%
None (volunteered)	42.0	40.3	17.6	2%

SOURCE: 1992 National Election Study.

The partisan playing field tilted slightly to the Democrats in 1992. Mainly because of the economic recession, the issue terrain also favored the Democrats. The president's popularity was low by election time, but both major candidates had their share of strengths and weaknesses in their public images. Ross Perot sought to take advantage of the low level of partisanship, the dissatisfaction with politics as usual, and the weaknesses of the party nominees. Perot obtained a higher vote than most election analysts had expected, and he succeeded in gathering a lot of publicity for his campaign. His support seems to have come in fairly equal numbers from both camps, however, rather than at the expense of one side. In the end, the Democratic tilt to the partisanship, the economy, and the president's weak popularity combined to defeat George Bush and elect Bill Clinton. As 1976 and 1980 also showed, it is difficult for the incumbent to win reelection by managing party identification, issue, and candidate factors when the economy is weak.

Most presidential elections seem exciting and important when they occur, though few stand out as important from the perspective of history. If the 1992 election attains importance in the history books, it will be for reversing a series of Republican presidential victories and for the success of its third-party candidacy. How important this is will depend mainly on what happens in the next few years. If the Republicans regain control of the White House in 1996, the election will seem to have been only a minor blip, like 1976. If Clinton is able to tame the economy, produce the changes his candidacy promised, and get reelected in 1996, then 1992 may be regarded as a turning point of the magnitude of 1980. If trust issues prove to be Clinton's ultimate undoing as president but another Democrat wins the presidency in 1996, then the 1992 election will be seen as transitional. If Perot's large vote total encourages other nontraditional candidacies to take advantage of the modern media, then 1992 will be seen as a key stage in the demise of the two-party system. Other prospective nonparty candidates might not be millionaires who can fund their own campaigns, but might be ex-military leaders or other well-known personalities who can command media attention to speak directly to the American public.

Control of the White House changed in 1992 when a president could not maintain the level of popularity required for reelection. Party identification moved back in the Democratic direction a few points as a result of economic distress, with warmth toward Republicans falling sharply. Of greater importance, partisan dealignment continued when a significant fraction of the American public showed that it was willing to look past party identification.

Notes

1. Incidentally, the extent of Democratic lead does not depend on the handling of independent leaners. The pattern is virtually identical regardless of whether leaners are treated as independents or as partisans.

2. As table 3.1 shows, the proportion of pure independents was unremarkable in 1992 if leaners are included with partisans.

3. The row marginals in the table show that the NES sample understated the Bush vote and overstated the Clinton vote by 4 percent; the Perot vote is estimated accurately.

4. In 1992, 8.7 percent were pure independents who could not vote party, 17.7 percent were partisans who voted for Perot, and 8 percent were major-party defectors.

5. These polls are an especially good source for checking the stability of partisanship as their wording is virtually identical to that used in the NES surveys. While CBS News/*New York Times* polls took frequent readings of public opinion during the Bush administration, they did not take surveys every month. Missing months were filled in by linear interpolation. When they took multiple surveys in a single month, the monthly average was used. Similar procedures were used in dealing with their readings of presidential popularity used below.

6. The smoothing approach used in these figures is the Lowess technique implemented in DataDesk, with the smoothing parameter set for a tension of .20 (meaning that 20 percent of the data points are used in smoothing each curve value). Similar smoothing results were obtained using the Spline procedure in JMP (from SAS Institute) with the smoothing parameter lambda set at 250.

7. The NES 1990 postelection measurement picks up an atypical peak of Democratic strength before Desert Storm began, so NES data actually show a decrease in Democratic strength from 1990 to 1992. Thus relying only on NES readings of party identification suggests little pattern to the 1988–92 change, while the more frequent CBS News/*New York Times* poll readings show a clear trend toward the Democrats.

8. The only change in inflation was a drop when unemployment rose. The simultaneity of these changes would make it difficult to distinguish the separate effects of inflation and unemployment. Rather than being rewarded for the improvement in inflation numbers, however, the president and his party were punished by the electorate for the worsening in employment figures. As a result, it seems more appropriate to include unemployment than inflation in the regression analysis.

9. In fact, the range of presidential approval ratings during the Bush years was 55 percent, while the range of unemployment levels was 3 percent.

10. The equations in table 3.4 treat all effects as direct, but the literature on presidential popularity finds that the economy affects presidential approval ratings too, so much of the presidential approval effect found in table 3.4 may amount to an indirect effect of unemployment.

11. The candidate ratings were also less polarized than in some recent years. There was a negative correlation of −.39 between ratings of Bush and Clinton, less extreme than the record −.54 between Reagan and Mondale in 1984. Attitudes toward Perot were, incidentally, fairly independent of attitudes toward the major-party candidates, but with attitudes toward Clinton being more tied to views of Perot than attitudes toward Bush (correlations of .02 with Bush and .09 with Clinton in the preelection survey and .03 with Bush and .14 with Clinton in the postelection study).

12. By the postelection interviews, Perot had climbed to a mean thermometer rating of 52.8, below Bush's 55.8 and Clinton's 62.5. Bandwagon and sympathy effects make postelection thermometers hard to interpret, but Perot's postelection rating was actually on a par with Bush's preelection popularity.

The NES survey inexplicably did not include thermometer questions on Jerry Brown and Paul Tsongas, the major competitors for the Democratic nomination. Ignoring their assessments of the popularity of prospective first ladies, the only other politician viewed favorably by respondents was vice-presidential candidate Al Gore (mean = 57). Tom Foley received an average rating of 47.9, Jesse Jackson 46.9, Pat Buchanan 42.4, and Dan Quayle 42.2.

13. Recall that Perot had not reentered the race when the early preelection surveys took place.

14. This interpretation should be compared to those of other analysts. Pomper (1993, 142) concludes that the Perot vote would have been split evenly between the major-party candidates. In a sophisticated methodological analysis of the 1992 NES data, Alvarez and Nagler (1993) find that Perot's vote drew more from Clinton than Bush, but Perot supporters were more pro-Bush than the rest of the population, so Clinton would have received a smaller proportion of the major-party vote had Perot not run.

15. In a preliminary attempt to explore the Perot vote more systematically, a logit analysis was performed on the dichotomous choice between voting for a major-party candidate or Perot. The predictors included several of the variables discussed in this section, including strength of partisanship, seeing differences between the parties, being satisfied with presidential choices, seeing a difference between the parties or candidates on some issues such as health care and the deficit, approval of government institutions, economic variables, abortion, and ideology plus demographic variables such as race, gender, education, and age. With a total of eighteen predictors, the logit analysis was significant, with significant effects for most variables (with the exception of seeing differences between the parties on the economy and foreign policy, a pair of economic variables, and education). The analysis shows that strength of partisanship had a .11 impact on the probability of voting for Perot for those who were satisfied with the presidential candidates versus a .20 impact for those who were not. The model yields an 81 percent level of correct vote prediction, which seems very respectable until one notes that a similar level of prediction would have been obtained by just predicting that everyone voted against Perot. Further, 49 percent of those predicted by the model to vote for Perot actually voted for a major-party candidate.

Technically the Bush, Clinton, and Perot votes should be predicted separately as a single categorical dependent variable. We have employed discriminant analysis in this vein. With thirteen predictors, including many of those employed in the logit analysis, it was possible to predict 71 percent of the votes correctly, which is much more difficult with the trichotomous dependent variable than in the analysis described in the preceding paragraph. The model predicts correctly 53 percent of the actual Perot votes, but 59 percent of those predicted to vote for Perot instead voted for a major-party candidate. According to this analysis, Perot obtained more of the vote predicted to go for Bush (16 percent) than the vote predicted to go for Clinton (10 percent). What is most interesting about this analysis, though, is that the prediction pattern for actual Perot voters is very similar to that for nonvoters, except that a few more of the nonvoters would be predicted on the basis of the discriminant analysis to vote for Clinton and a few more of the actual Perot voters would be predicted to vote for Bush. This similarity between Perot voters and nonvoters merits further attention. We expect to work more on these models, but our feeling is that they aptly illustrate the difficulty of modeling the Perot vote successfully.

Alvarez and Nagler (1993) have developed a multinomial probit estimator for this purpose. Their best model predicts 77 percent of the votes correctly. Their analysis does well in replicating the national vote shares, but they do not show the proportion of people they predict to vote for Perot who actually did so.

CHAPTER 4

The Partisan Choice:
George Bush or Bill Clinton

CHARLES E. SMITH, JR., AND JOHN H. KESSEL

In most presidential elections, most Americans make a partisan choice. They vote for a Republican or a Democrat. Even when there is a serious third-party candidate—as in 1912, 1924, 1948, 1968, 1980, and 1992 —the principal choice is between the major-party candidates. In each of those years, substantial majorities (65, 83, 95, 86, 92, and 80 percent, respectively) cast ballots for one of the major candidates.[1] And in the elections since 1950 without a serious third-party candidate, the average major party vote has been over 99 percent.

Scholars, too, have focused on partisan conflict; the result is that we clearly know more about partisan choice than we do about voter reactions to third-party candidacies. The emergence of this focus can be traced to the classic studies of presidential voting, all of which focused on dichotomous, partisan choices and two-party conflict. For example, *The People's Choice* (Lazarsfeld, Berelson, and Gaudet 1944), the first major voting study, analyzed the 1940 election between Franklin Roosevelt and Wendell Willkie. *The American Voter* (Campbell, Converse, Miller, and Stokes 1960), the book that shaped the thinking of a whole generation of electoral analysts, focused on the Dwight Eisenhower–Adlai Stevenson elections of 1952 and 1956. John Jackson's 1975 *American Journal of Political Science* article explicating the relation between issues and party identification focused on the 1964 choice between Lyndon Johnson and Barry Goldwater. And the presidential elections interpreted by Morris Fiorina in his rational-choice analysis, *Ret-*

rospective Voting in American National Elections (1981), were the 1960 John Kennedy–Richard Nixon and 1976 Jimmy Carter–Gerald Ford contests.

Following these traditional lines of inquiry, we present a statistical model of the 1992 two-party vote divided between Bill Clinton and George Bush. Our aim is to identify and explore the underpinnings of the 1992 two-party vote cross-sectionally and at the same time bring evidence from past presidential elections to bear on our interpretations of 1992 voting. The model we use was designed to compare presidential elections and the wellsprings of vote choice across time. It has correctly predicted between 85 and 90 percent of the voters' presidential choices in every election since 1952 (Kessel 1980, 1992). Our data are based on the NES open-ended questions that allow survey respondents to volunteer what they like and dislike about the parties and candidates in the election. (Since we use open-ended questions to analyze the Clinton-Bush choice, our findings should be compared with those of Herbert Weisberg and David Kimball in chapter 3 of this book. They employ the NES precoded questions as the basis of their analysis.)

The model performed quite well with the 1992 NES data, correctly predicting the partisan direction of 91 percent of the votes cast for Clinton and Bush. Substantively, it confirmed that economic circumstances were the major factor in determining the outcome. The many commentators who said this were quite correct. But much more happened, and it was not all one-sided. Bill Clinton profited from his pro-choice stand, while George Bush gained votes as the guardian of traditional morality. Between the candidates themselves, Governor Clinton was seen as more intelligent and more likely to bring change, but President Bush was better trusted and more highly regarded for his diplomatic and military experience. In fact, on candidate attributes alone, George Bush was narrowly preferred over Bill Clinton. So there is much to be told here, and we start by reviewing our model.

The Contours of the Model

THE CONTENT OF THE INDEPENDENT VARIABLES

Since the 1960 publication of *The American Voter,* researchers modeling partisan choice have typically offered an accounting of voter attitudes toward the nominees, the parties, and the policy positions with which citizens associate them; and this trifold focus on candidates, parties, and issues lies at the heart of our modeling effort. We employ two versions of our model: a three-component version that uses just the three traditional categories, and a sixteen-component version that decomposes candidates, parties, and issues to permit a more fine-grained analysis.

Within the broad divisions of candidates, parties, and issues, the discrete attitude categories in the sixteen-component model were chosen in order to be specific enough to permit concrete statements yet inclusive enough so that statements falling into each will occur over a series of elections. The largest category of candidate references is a *general* category. This includes three classes of comments: those that are too general to be assigned to one of the specific categories ("He's a good [or bad] man" or "He's good [or bad] for the country"); statements on such topics as the candidate's age or wealth or family or campaign tactics that did not occur often enough to justify the creation of separate, specific categories; and comments that occur relatively frequently in a single campaign but are absent in other elections.

Two categories deal with attitudes about the candidates' experience. *Record and incumbency* concerns perceptions about the candidates' records in office. These are likely to relate to an incumbent running for reelection. *Experience* is a shortened name for more specific experience: military experience, diplomatic background, campaign ability. Sometimes the comments (e.g., "He's experienced in foreign affairs") refer directly to a presidential skill.

Two more categories are also office related. *Management* deals with executive capacity: how the candidate would be likely to run the government if elected, as well as more general references to leadership. *Intelligence* is given a broad enough definition to include comments about the candidate's education and willingness to accept new ideas, as well as cognitive skill in a general sense. The other specific candidate categories relate more to judgments about the individual than about executive ability. *Trust* touches on confidence, honesty, and any specific comments bearing on the candidate's integrity. *Personality* includes any comments about image and mannerisms, such as warmth, aloofness, and dignity.

Party comments were so infrequent that they were divided into only two classes. Attitudes about *people in the party* concern all party members named by the respondents: presidential and vice-presidential candidates, incumbent presidents not running for reelection, prominent senators and governors, party workers, and so on. All other party comments were categorized as *party affect*. These included trust of one party or the other, references to party factions, and the importance of achieving or preventing a party victory.

The determination of the seven issue categories rested on a bit more than the simple frequency of comments; they were discerned in separate studies of congressional roll-call votes and presidential State of the Union messages (Clausen 1973; Kessel 1974). The first, *international involvement,* concerns the traditional diplomacy of negotiation, the newer diplomacy of foreign aid, arms sales, information exchange, and presidential travel, as well as the military power that supports U.S. foreign policy. *Economic management* deals with attempts by the federal government to direct the national economy: the use of economic controls, adjustments in the level of federal spending, tax policy, and so forth.

The next two policy areas usually have less impact than foreign policy and economics. *Social benefits* includes programs that help individuals: education, health care, veterans' programs, and the like. *Civil liberties* embraces the great guarantees of individual liberty against government oppression, the protection of rights of classes of citizens by the government, and a willingness to tolerate various lifestyles.

The last two specific categories are distinctive, but rarely elicit many comments. Both may be conceptualized as special cases of other areas. The first, *natural resources,* may be thought of as a special case of economic management in which regulatory policy is used in the areas of the environment and energy. The second, *agriculture policy,* may be viewed as a special case of social benefits in which farmers are the beneficiaries.[2]

Finally, as with the candidate comments, there is a general issue category composed of comments too broad to fit into any specific class. These include references to the policy stands of the parties, liberalism or conservatism, and comments about "domestic policy" with no mention of specifics. Although this general issue category is vague, it has proven to be a very sensitive barometer of electoral sentiment. Indeed, since the advent of the data record in 1952, no party has won an election without an advantage on the positive-negative sum of these general policy attitudes.

MEASUREMENT

Vote choice is the binary dependent variable (0 = Republican, 1 = Democrat). Each of the independent variables was constructed from responses to open-ended questions about the parties and the two candidates (these questions are known familiarly as "like-dislike" questions). The sequence of questions about the parties asks respondents first if there is anything in particular they like about the Democratic Party, then if there is anything they dislike about the party. Identical questions about the Republican Party follow; in all four cases, up to five responses are coded for each respondent.

The sequence of questions about the candidates is similar, though perhaps less aptly characterized by the "like-dislike" terminology. The candidate series begins by asking respondents if there is anything in particular about the Democratic nominee (in 1992, Bill Clinton) that would make them want to vote for him. Then respondents are asked if there is anything in particular that would make them want to vote against him. This pair is then repeated for the Republican candidate; again, up to five responses to each question are coded in all four cases.[3]

The independent variables are constructed from these responses by summing the number of comments within each category that are pro-Democratic (Clinton) and pro-Republican (Bush) respectively, then taking the simple difference between these sums. The pro-Democratic (Clinton) sum is computed by taking the difference between the number of comments that were positive toward Clinton and the Democrats in the category and the number that were negative, and likewise for the Republicans. The resulting variables thus possess both sign (reflecting a partisan advantage) and extremity (reflecting the degree to which an advantage exists). If the sign is positive, it denotes a Democratic advantage; if the sign is negative, it denotes a Republican advantage.

PROBIT ANALYSIS

The relative importance of each of the independent variables in determining vote choice is estimated by means of *probit analysis*. This technique was first developed in biology and was introduced into political science thirty years ago (Kramer 1965). Probit analysis was developed to deal with dichotomous dependent variables such as vote. It has since been extended to dependent variables having more than two values, but its capacity to handle dichotomous dependent variables makes it particularly appropriate for the analysis of choice between two candidates.[4]

A probit model has some very useful properties.[5] First, it is curvilinear. This gives it the capacity to analyze the dichotomous dependent variables we just referred to. Second, it is a multivariate procedure. This means that when we estimate, for example, the effect of issues on vote choice in the three-component version of our model, it controls for the effects of candidates and parties. When we estimate for the effects of, say, international involvement on vote choice in the sixteen-component version of our model, the effects of the other fifteen independent variables are statistically controlled.[6] Third, the probit coefficients can be given a probabilistic interpretation. In our case we can predict the probability of a Democratic vote. (This also reveals the probability of a

Republican vote.) We rely heavily on these probabilities in interpreting the results of the analysis and in speculating about the relative influence the different classes of variables had in determining the outcome of the election. We also utilize them in the course of interpreting the 1992 outcome in longitudinal perspective, with specific comparisons to the 1980 election where, in stark contrast to 1992, an incumbent Democrat was defeated.

Analysis

Beyond giving attention to the existence of statistically relevant relationships between explanatory variables and vote, analysts studying attitudinal models of voting choice typically focus on two specific concerns: the partisan advantage that might result from the preponderant feeling on a given attitude favoring one party over the other, and the apparent potency of particular attitudes in leading a voter to cast a ballot for Candidate A or Candidate B. The aim of the analysis section is to examine these two topics. In the first subsection, we briefly report the basic results of the probit models for 1992. The subsections that follow broach each of the two more specific topics (partisan advantages and the potency of the predictors) in turn, describing the analytic strategies we see as most appropriate for each task. Then, in a discussion that integrates the issues of advantage and potency, we outline the "electoral verdict" from 1992, focusing on results derived from the strategies outlined earlier. There, we speculate about the relative importance of the various attitudes in determining the election outcome.

THE BASIC PROBIT RESULTS

Results of the two probit runs for 1992 appear in tables 4.1 and 4.2. Table 4.1 reports results from the three-variable model. It is clear from these estimates that each of the three summary regressors (i.e., candidate attitudes, partisan attitudes, and issue attitudes) has a statistically discernible relationship to the vote. And the results reported in table 4.2 show a similar pattern for the more atomized model. Fourteen of the sixteen independent variables are significantly related to vote choice.[7] Only the effects of *people in the party* and *agriculture* can be discounted.

PARTISAN ADVANTAGES ON THE INDEPENDENT VARIABLES

Identifying the statistical relevance of the attitude measures as predictors of vote provides us with very little detail about how the election

TABLE 4.1
PROBIT RESULTS FROM THE THREE-VARIABLE
VOTE MODEL

Independent variables	Probit coefficient	Standard error
Candidate attitudes	0.35*	0.03
Partisan attitudes	0.36*	0.07
Issue attitudes	0.32*	0.02
Constant	−0.13*	0.06
N = 1,336		

SOURCE: 1992 National Election Study.

*p > .05.

TABLE 4.2
PROBIT RESULTS FROM THE SIXTEEN-VARIABLE
VOTE MODEL

Independent variables	Probit coefficient	Standard error
Candidates		
General	0.35*	0.06
Record-incumbency	0.52*	0.09
Experience	0.39*	0.11
Management	0.26*	0.08
Intelligence	0.40*	0.11
Trust	0.44*	0.09
Personality	0.22*	0.11
Parties		
People in the party	0.23	0.13
Party affect	0.41*	0.09
Issues		
General	0.47*	0.08
International involvement	0.35*	0.07
Economic management	0.36*	0.04
Social benefits	0.11*	0.05
Civil liberties	0.44*	0.06
Natural resources	0.46*	0.19
Agriculture	−0.69	0.41
Constant	−0.06	0.08
N = 1,336		

SOURCE: 1992 National Election Study.

* p < .05.

was decided; all we know from the basic results is that most of these attitudes appeared to play a role in the decision making. So, we turn to the first of the specific questions, asking which party the public preferred on each of the relevant attitudes. We present two statistics about this in table 4.3.

The relevant data are found in the two columns of the table; the first reports the simple arithmetic means of independent variables in the probit equations; the second reports something we call the "partisan valence" associated with each of the variables. In different ways, each column of statistics is useful in understanding the predisposition of public opinion to favor one side or the other.

TABLE 4.3
CENTRAL TENDENCIES OF THE INDEPENDENT VARIABLES

Variable	Mean	Partisan valence
Candidates		
General	+.27	+.14
Record-incumbency	−.07	−.08
Experience	−.26	−.42
Management	+.06	+.06
Intelligence	+.12	+.18
Trust	−.12	−.13
Personality	−.08	−.13
Parties		
People in the party	+.04	+.08
Party affect	+.09	+.08
Issues		
General	+.03	+.02
International involvement	−.02	−.01
Economic management	+1.01	+.21
Social benefits	+.07	+.33
Civil liberties	+.18	+.08
Natural resources	+.09	+.34
Agriculture	+.01	+.10

$N = 1,336$

SOURCE: 1992 National Election Study.

NOTE: A positive sign means a Democratic advantage; a negative sign means a Republican advantage.

The first column—the mean scores of the independent variables —is the most straightforward: negative scores on a variable indicate a Republican advantage, while positive scores indicate a Democratic advantage. Note, first, that the preponderance of means favor the Democratic ticket—a near-split on the candidate-oriented attitudes, a modest advantage for challenger Clinton in the partisan realm, and then an overwhelming advantage on the issue-based attitudes. Most of these advantages are rather slight, with the notable exception of *economic management*. Indeed, it is here that we first see the potency of the Clinton decision to structure the campaign message around economic issues: the mean for the *economic management* variable is more one-sided (and in a Democratic direction) than any of the other independent variables.

The candidate-oriented variables show more of a mix. Remarks in the *general* comments category are on average more favorable to the Democrats, but *record-incumbency*, and in particular, *experience*, show an advantage for Bush. *Trust*, and to a lesser extent, *personality*, also appear in President Bush's favor, while the *intelligence* and *management* variables favor Governor Clinton.

The second column of data in table 4.3—"partisan valences"— warrants some explanation before interpretation. Most simply, partisan valences are, like the means, measures of partisan advantage on the independent variables from the probit equation. The valences, however, tap partisan advantage as a ratio of pro-Democratic comments to all comments about both parties, and do so across all voters rather than for individual voters. Therefore, the partisan valences represent the overall electoral advantage a party has because of a given attitude.

In the process of generating the valences, we begin by classifying all comments falling within a given category as pro-Democratic or pro-Republican. The original expression of a pro-Democratic attitude may be a positive comment about the Democratic candidate or party or a negative comment about the Republican candidate or party; that makes no difference. Since either a pro-Democratic attitude or an anti-Republican attitude would lead the voter to cast a Democratic vote, both comments are coded as pro-Democratic. Correspondingly, both pro-Republican and anti-Democratic comments are coded pro-Republican.

We then divide the pro-Democratic comments by the total number of comments in that attitude category to determine the *proportion* of the comments that are pro-Democratic. (Again, notice that this gives us information on the proportion that is pro-Republican. If 60 percent of the responses are pro-Democratic, 40 percent are pro-Republican.) In the unusual circumstance in which the proportion was exactly half, neither party would have any advantage. Therefore we adjusted this neu-

tral point so it has a value of zero. By doing so, the signs correspond to
the signs of the means in table 4.3. If the partisan valence is negative,
the Republicans have an advantage in that attitude category, and if it is
positive, the Democrats have an advantage. The values of the partisan
valences correspond to the percentage advantage the party enjoys because of the attitude. A −.12 indicates a 12 percent advantage for the
Republicans on that attitude, and a +.05 denotes a 5 percent advantage
for the Democrats.[8]

Now, what are the crucial differences between the means and partisan valences in table 4.3? As noted, the signs give identical information: a positive sign indicates a Democratic advantage, and a negative
sign indicates a Republican advantage. This is not true of the values,
however. In half a dozen cases, the values of the means and partisan
valences are the same or nearly so. But in the other cases, sometimes
the mean has a higher value, and more frequently the partisan valence
does. What is happening is that the mean, a simple difference between
the number of pro-Democratic and pro-Republican comments, is more
sensitive to the volume of comments. Its value is therefore more easily
inflated or depressed by respondents who give a larger overall number
of responses. The value of the partisan valence, however, reflects the
pro-Democratic comments as a proportion of all comments in that attitude category and is therefore a more dependable guide to partisan advantage.

Economic management provides one clear example of these dis-
tinctions. Because of the sheer volume of comments about the economy
in 1992, and because so many of them were pro-Democratic, the mean
had a very high value. When the pro-Democratic comments were
viewed as a proportion of all comments on the economy in the partisan
valence, one sees a very solid Democratic advantage, but no longer one
that is abnormally inflated. In the experience category, the Republican
advantage is more extreme when interpreted through the partisan valence. This suggests that the scores of a relatively small number of respondents who favored Governor Clinton's experience over President
Bush's worked to mask, in the mean value, the larger number of voters
who found President Bush's experience preferable.

THE POTENCY OF THE PREDICTORS
IN THE MODEL

It is important to look beyond the partisan advantages enjoyed on the
relevant attitudes. This is so because, most simply, a partisan advantage
on a given attitude is rather meaningless unless that attitude played a
key role in the voting calculus. The basic probit results—which include

statistical tests distinguishing the coefficients from zero, or "no effect"—provide the first hints on this topic. It is clear, for example, that our inability to distinguish the effects of *agriculture* policy attitudes and attitudes toward *people in the party* casts doubt on the purchase of these attitudes in the voting calculus.

But of course the issue of "potency" refers to a good deal more than the existence of differences from "no effect." The most obvious issue is related to the relative magnitudes of the coefficients associated with the variables. Less obvious is the importance of considering the dispersion of observations on the independent variables around their central tendencies. In the probit specification—which is nonlinear and thus posits a priori that all the independent variables interact in determining the outcome on the dependent variable—these issues are intimately related, and both must be considered together in the process of speculating about the relative influences of the variables in the model.

Typically, researchers interpreting estimated coefficients from a probit model rely on predictions of the probability the dependent variable would take one of its two values as it is derived from some set of established, "ordinary" values (typically the means) on the independent variables.[9] But in exploring the "potency" of the predictors, we wish, too, to incorporate some information about the likelihood of a unit shift on a given variable—that is, to focus not just on the ordinary value (mean) but also the magnitude of an "ordinary" shift—and here we must consider the dispersion of observations on the variables. Put most simply, it is critical to recognize that to speak of a single unit shift on one of the variables may be more or less plausible than to speak of a single unit shift on another.

If, for example (as in our case), some variables have substantial variances and ranges and others do not, it may be quite plausible, given the observed data, to describe the effects of a single unit shift of the variable with the larger variance but equally implausible to draw inferences from a similar exercise with the less-variant term. In the case of the variable with the substantial variance, we would likely be describing something that is quite realistic given the measured differences between individuals on that item. But in interpreting the results of an attitude with confined variance, we might risk making the proverbial mountain out of the proverbial mole hill. The perfect example lies in dispersion statistics reported in table 4.4. Note the values for *economic management* as compared to those for *agriculture*. On *economic management*, where the range is -9 to +13 and the standard deviation is 2.5, single unit differences (and even larger differences) between individuals are strikingly ordinary. By contrast, on the *agriculture* variable, where the range is a paltry -2 to +2 and the standard deviation a paltry 0.11, single unit differences between individuals are exceedingly rare. Thus, to speak of and interpret the result of a full unit "shift" on the *agriculture* variable, even if the variable was associated with a large and statistically significant coefficient, would involve describing an extraordinary event.

TABLE 4.4

DISPERSION OF THE INDEPENDENT VARIABLES

Variable	Standard deviation	Range
Candidates		
General	1.25	−5 to 6
Record-incumbency	0.73	−3 to 3
Experience	0.60	−4 to 1
Management	0.87	−5 to 5
Intelligence	0.62	−3 to 4
Trust	0.80	−4 to 3
Personality	0.63	−3 to 3
Parties		
People in the party	0.57	−4 to 4
Party affect	0.79	−4 to 4
Issues		
General	1.09	−6 to 5
International involvement	0.97	−5 to 4
Economic management	2.50	−9 to 13
Social benefits	1.44	−5 to 10
Civil liberties	1.89	−12 to 10
Natural resources	0.45	−2 to 4
Agriculture	0.11	−2 to 2

$N = 1,336$

SOURCE: 1992 National Election Study.

Therefore, in the following section, where we describe "the electoral verdict" with speculations about how potent the individual attitudes are in the determination of vote choice, we introduce a more appropriate method of interpreting the probit coefficients. We rely on the estimated differences in the predicted probabilities of a Democratic vote that result from shifting each independent variable *one standard deviation* from its mean (with the other regressors held constant at their mean values).

TABLE 4.5
POTENCY OF THE PREDICTORS IN THE THREE-VARIABLE VOTE MODEL

Independent variables	Predicted changes
Candidate attitudes	.32
Partisan attitudes	.25
Issue attitudes	.39

N = 1,336

SOURCE: 1992 National Election Study.

NOTE: Cell entries are predicted changes in the probability of a Democratic vote that result from shifting each independent variable one standard deviation from its mean, holding all others constant at their mean values.

This provides a more plausible strategy for interpreting coefficients than customary one-unit change system would provide; and it produces numbers (probabilities) that we are willing to interpret, if only loosely, as indicators of the potency of the individual attitude categories in the calculus of 1992 voters. These probability changes appear in table 4.5 (for the three-predictor, summary model) and table 4.6 (for the sixteen-predictor model).

THE ELECTORAL VERDICT

ISSUE ATTITUDES. Issues are ordinarily the most prominent components in voters' decisions.[10] They had greater consequence in the 1980s than in any previous decade, and they continued to dominate vote choices in 1992. The numbers in table 4.6 testify to this; issues account for the three largest predicted probability shifts. The three most potent attitudinal categories were *economic management, civil liberties,* and the *general* issues category (see table 4.6). The first two of these, which generate probability shifts of .23 and .22 respectively, are easily distinguishable from all else. And overall, issues taken together clearly had the greatest probability of affecting votes of any of the three major divisions.

Clinton campaign manager James Carville posted a sign in campaign headquarters: "It's the economy, stupid!" This was right on the mark. *Economic management* was the category where attitudinal changes had the greatest likelihood of changing the outcome of the election. As it happened, Democrats enjoyed an unusually strong advantage (the partisan valence for economics was +.21). In part, this is because many respondents linked Bush to the bad times, and almost all their comments were negative toward the sitting president. Other economic attitudes exhibited this same pattern. Five out of eight references to economic policies concerned President Bush, and only a third of the Bush comments were favorable, compared to three-quarters of the Clinton responses. George Bush thus joined Gerald Ford and Jimmy Carter among those whose reelection bids were scuttled by an adverse economy.

Interestingly, the recession itself was not the most salient economic topic. Indeed, the most frequent comments concerned the association between the Bush administration and big business. Eighty-seven percent of the respondents who mentioned this were critical of the Republicans.

TABLE 4.6
POTENCY OF THE PREDICTORS IN THE SIXTEEN-VARIABLE
VOTE MODEL

Independent variables	Predicted changes
Candidates	
General	0.13
Record-incumbency	0.12
Experience	0.07
Management	0.07
Intelligence	0.08
Trust	0.11
Personality	0.05
Parties	
People in the party	—
Party affect	0.10
Issues	
General	0.15
International involvement	0.11
Economic management	0.23
Social benefits	0.05
Civil liberties	0.22
Natural resources	0.07
Agriculture	—
$N = 1,336$	

SOURCE: 1992 National Election Study.

NOTE: Cell entries are predicted changes in the probability of a Democratic vote that result from shifting each independent variable one standard deviation from its mean, holding all others constant at their mean values.

Being seen as too closely tied to big business is rarely popular with the general public, but it can be an even heavier political burden when the economy turns sour.

There were fewer comments about the common man, but almost all of them were positive remarks about Clinton. Somewhat more surprising was a positive link between Clinton and white-collar workers. It is quite common for Republicans to be identified with big business and for Democrats to be seen as closer to the less well-to-do, but in 1992, the Democratic candidate was seen as better for the middle class as well.

Civil liberties, normally in the middle ranks of election-related attitudes, was the second most important category in 1992. Different topics were salient, too. This time they dealt more with lifestyle issues than with minority rights or crime. The attitudes were too mixed to speak of a simple advantage for one party or another, but on balance they produced a partisan valence (+.08) favorable to the Democrats. The most conspicuous attitudes concerned abortion. Bill Clinton's pro-choice stand was approved by a small majority, while George Bush's opposition to abortion was criticized by a somewhat larger majority.

The second most prominent topic in this category was morality. Republicans gained by being seen as the guardians of traditional morality, and a smaller number of respondents were critical of the Democrats as being too permissive.

The *general* issue category finishes a solid (if distant) third as a potential source of votes, as the change in the predicted probability of a Democratic vote associated with a standard deviation shift is a very substantial .15, but the Democratic advantage in partisan valence is only slight, +.03. In terms of the category's substantive content, roughly equal numbers of persons commented on the conservatism of Bush and the Republicans and on the liberalism of Clinton and the Democrats. Neither candidacy was buoyed much by ideology, but it appears that President Bush suffered substantially less than Governor Clinton. There were equal numbers of positive comments about Bush's conservatism and negative comments about Bush being too conservative, whereas for every voter who liked Clinton's liberalism, two criticized the Democrat as being too liberal.

Clinton did better with respondents who gave other general opinions on the issues, for the majority of them expressed positive views about the Democrat's positions. Moreover, those who commented on general domestic issues were quite likely to make negative remarks about the Bush administration's policies. To be sure, these general comments were vague, but there were enough of them to give this attitude category a Democratic tilt.

International involvement leaned very slightly in a Bush direction, but had less potency than usual and was less Republican than usual. Like the international category as a whole, the comments about the candidates' foreign policies were essentially a dead heat. Just over half the statements concerning Bush were favorable, and just under half of those concerning Clinton were positive. But there were almost five comments about Bush's foreign policies to every one about Clinton's, so it is clear that the reaction to President Bush's foreign policy largely defined this category.

The general assessments about his foreign policy, and feelings that he was strong and decisive in that area, elicited praise. The critical comments were that the sitting president was too internationalist, too much in favor of economic aid, and too much in favor of free trade. On balance, then, President Bush was aided by his foreign policy record. International involvement was the only issue attitude to produce a Republican advantage, but the boost was so slight (a partisan valence of −.01) that it was almost no help to Bush.

There is no need to give much attention to the other issues. As we noted earlier, *social benefits*—aid to the unemployed, national health care, and aid to education—produced an even more lopsided Democratic advantage than usual, but it held much less potential as a vote producer than any of the four attitudes discussed previously. *Natural resources* was also pro-Democratic, but these attitudes were no more than a trace element in the amalgam of Clinton's victory. Finally, attitudes toward agriculture were not significantly related to vote choice.[11]

CANDIDATE ATTITUDES. Three candidate attitudes had relatively visible impacts on presidential choice: *general* attitudes, *trust* in the two men, and the Bush and Clinton records in office. Looking at the probability change scores in table 4.6, each appears to have had as much or a little more potential than international involvement, but not nearly as much as the attitudes about economic management or civil liberties. The other four candidate attitudes—those relating to more specific *experience, intelligence, personality,* and *management* capacity—had detectable effects, and Bush had an advantage in two of these.

The partisan valence for the general candidate category was a pro-Democratic +.14. Three items seemed to go together. A large number of respondents repeated the standard election injunction, "it's time for a change." Five out of six said so because they were positively attracted to the Clinton candidacy, whereas only one in six said a change was needed to get President Bush out of office. There were also many positive references to Governor Clinton's youth, and the likelihood that he could lead the country in a new direction. The most salient attitudes were even more general (e.g., responses suggesting that one or the other candidate would be "good" or "bad" for the country). Bill Clinton did well with these responses, too, and it may be that these were echoes of the "youth" and "change" themes mentioned by others more specifically. In other words, voters may well have been saying that in the circumstances of 1992, new policies were needed, and the younger challenger was more likely to bring about such change.

President Bush was also hurt by his campaigning. Bill Clinton's speeches and tactics elicited an equal number of positive and negative reactions, whereas the references to George Bush's campaigning were almost completely negative. Indeed, Bush could take comfort in only two kinds of mentions in this area: affective comments and opinions about family. On the former, those who evaluated the candidates themselves as "good" or "bad" were more likely to make positive comments about George Bush and negative comments about Bill Clinton. And as Anthony Mughan and Barry Burden explain in chapter 5 on the candidates' wives, Barbara Bush was widely admired, while voters were a little more likely to have negative attitudes than positive attitudes about Hillary Clinton.

President Bush also profited substantially (partisan valence = −.13) on the trust-related attitudes, primarily because he was less distrusted than his challenger. On *trust,* there were only a few more negative than positive comments about Bush compared to three out of four negative comments about Clinton. The most frequently expressed attitudes concerned honesty and sincerity. The balance here was the same as in the overall trust category; the reaction to Bush's honesty was about even, while many more found Clinton to be dishonest or insincere. Moreover, voters thought Bush dependable by about a 2–1 margin, whereas Clinton was perceived as untrustworthy by a whopping 6–1. The probability shift associated with a one standard deviation shift on this variable is a substantial .11, so it is clear not only that President Bush enjoyed an advantage with these attitudes but also that these feelings were an important source of his electoral support.

Mr. Bush also gained from a third important class of candidate attitudes, those concerning the candidates' records in office. *Record-incumbency* had a pro-Republican valence, −.08. Yet this was not because of what George Bush had done in office. In fact, comments about the Bush and Clinton records in public service were a little more favorable to Clinton than they were to Bush. There were about equal numbers of compliments to Bush for presidential accomplishments as complaints that he had not produced results. What hurt President Bush was the larger number who assailed him for not having fulfilled his promises. But the source of President Bush's strength in *record-incumbency* was not found in these specific references. It was simply that he had been in the White House, whereas Governor Clinton had not.

Comments in the *experience* category produced the most lopsided advantage (a partisan valence of −.42) of any of our independent variables. The dominant attitudes in this category concerned two specific qualifications: military experience and proficiency in the conduct of foreign policy. In both aspects, voters were worried about Clinton's lack of experience and believed that Bush had demonstrated his competence. The balance of attitudes was different, though, for these two attributes. Most of the comments about military experience dealt with Clinton, while most of those on statesmanship were about Bush. Unfortunately for President Bush, the impact on vote choices of the skewed pro-Republican *experience* valence was limited. The meager .07 probability prediction reveals little room for this variable to affect vote choice. Concerns for military and diplomatic experience held less electoral potential than the *trust* or even *general* candidate attitudes.

The second of the medium-impact attitudes dealt with *intelligence*,[12] and the +.18 valence here reflected a positive evaluation of Governor Clinton's reasoning. The most frequently expressed view provides another reminder that the voters welcomed Bill Clinton's youth. There were many positive comments about the Arkansan's embrace of change, together with a less salient, but related, criticism of President Bush's resistance to change. A second theme was that Clinton understood the nation's problems while Bush did not. This also favored Clinton, but not to the same extent as the change theme. Neither candidate was thought to have a well-defined philosophy, but there was more criticism of Clinton than of Bush in this area. The relatively small number who spoke about intelligence itself were much more likely to say that Clinton was smarter. Still, this—and the Democrat's overall advantage in the *intelligence* category—held less electoral potential than it might have given the relatively meager variation in the category's responses. The probability shift associated with the variable is .08, a modest figure similar to *experience*.

Attitudes about *management* ability were mixed, but tilted moderately in a Democratic direction with a partisan valence of +.06. As with intelligence, though, the modest probability shift associated with the variable (.07) means that we should not overinterpret the effect of the advantage. Within the category, the dominant attitude was criticism resulting from perceptions of inefficiency regarding both of the candidates. Complaints of this sort were reported in about the same proportions about both men. By contrast, those who made general assessments about management ability were likely to see both in a positive light. Bill Clinton had a better ratio of positive to negative comments and derived some measure of his overall advantage in the category as a result of this. Finally, there were criticisms of President Bush for being unwilling to take on hard issues together with some feeling that Governor Clinton might do so. This last set of attitudes was most responsible for tipping this category in a Democratic direction.

A summary of the candidate effects thus shows that Bill Clinton was advantaged in three candidate categories, George Bush in four. Clinton was favored in the crucial *general* category and in two middle-impact categories, *intelligence* and *management* ability. George Bush did better in the relatively important categories of *trust* and *record-incumbency,* as well as in diplomatic and military *experience,* and in the category with the least potential to affect the vote, *personality.* Taking all of these candidate attitudes together, President Bush had a slight advantage.

PARTY ATTITUDES. The partisan attitudes tilted toward the Democrats. As has been true for decades, however, attitudes about the Republican and Democratic parties appeared to be much less consequential than those concerning issues and candidates.[13] Looking at the probability changes associated with standard deviation shifts, *party affect* appears to rank behind the four most potent issue attitudes and three of the candidate attitudes in determining vote choice. Attitudes toward *people in the parties* had no discernible effect.[14]

Party affect is similar to the *general* issue and *general* candidate categories in being an amalgam. In the 1992 mix, comments about Bill Clinton as being a good Democrat or a typical Democrat were more numerous and much more favorable than similar responses about George Bush in relation to the Republican Party. But perceptions of the parties as parties gave each one a distinctive advantage. Republicans were seen as more organized and the Democrats as disorganized. And the Democratic Party was thought to be more representative of the country, the Republican Party less so. Voters did not trust either party to keep their promises, but they were a little more skeptical about the Republicans.

Concluding Comments

Voters reached a mixed verdict in 1992. As we have seen, there were both pro-Democratic and pro-Republican attitudes. Bill Clinton had the upper hand on the economy, civil liberties, general attitudes about issues, and general attitudes about the candidates. George Bush had the advantage on international involvement, trust, and experience. Unhappily for Bush's reelection prospects,[15] though, each of the four pro-Clinton attitudes was more important in determining vote choice than any of the pro-Bush attitudes. In the immediate aftermath of the election, there were some optimistic claims by Democrats that there had been a sea change in American politics, that the years of conservatism were over. President-elect Clinton was closer to the mark on election night when he refused to claim more than "the American people have voted to make a new beginning."

Nowhere was the call for this "new beginning" more pronounced than it was on matters related to the status and management of the U.S. economy. Casting ballots on the heels of a recession and in the midst of an unusually slow economic rebound, the 1992 voting public turned away from incumbent Bush in favor of challenger Clinton in a manner not at all unlike the 1980 electorate did when it abandoned incumbent Carter for challenger Reagan. The customary signals of economic distress were more pronounced in 1980 than in 1992 (e.g., double-digit inflation), and the independent candidacy of 1980 (John Anderson) was less well funded than its 1992 counterpart, but the end result was strikingly similar: U.S. voters made a partisan change rooted very substantially in dissatisfaction with the economy.

But similarities between 1992 and 1980 end at this summary level of analysis, for at the individual level where partisan advantages in attitudinal categories are evident and the potency of the connections between voting and various attitudes can be compared, these two elections were perhaps as different as any pair since 1952. One source of difference is ongoing: the crispness of the associations between issue-based attitudes and vote choice has been on the increase since.[16] Other sources of differences include the distribution of attitudes, both between the summary categories and across the more specific categories. But of course the key difference lies in the partisan advantages associated with the attitudes. In 1980, as we have seen, the Democrats were in a very unfavorable position, particularly with respect to international involvement, and had actually lost their long-standing advantage in economic management. In 1992, by contrast, the Democrats had a much more even standing on international matters, and the tables had completely turned regarding the economy. With this perspective, and with the clear indication from the cross-sectional analysis presented here, it is difficult to avoid the conclusion that the economy largely determined the election.

There were, of course, clear Democratic advantages in 1992 beyond those derived from dissatisfaction over the economy. In particular, close ties between the Republicans and big business and restrictive policies regarding abortion left the Democrats in a favorable light, so it is clear that there was a reasonably broad desire for change. At the same time, conservatism remained more popular than liberalism, and Republican support for traditional values was better liked by voters than Democratic permissiveness. In another year when these sources of Republican strength are not swamped by economic adversity, the GOP might build on these pro-Republican attitudes to reclaim the White House.

Attitudes about the candidates were also mixed. Bill Clinton's youth and intelligence were sources of strength. Voters thought that new approaches were called for and that Clinton was more oriented to change. But Governor Clinton failed to win the trust of the voters. This distrust could signal trouble for the Clinton presidency, for having entered the White House when the public was skeptical about government, it might be difficult for Clinton to gain their confidence. What ultimately happens, of course, will depend far more on what President Clinton accomplishes in office than on any residue of 1992 attitudes. But it seems clear that the manner of his election offered him only an opportunity to demonstrate his capacity for leadership; the omens were not auspicious enough to signal certain success.

Acknowledgment

We wish to thank Peter Radcliffe of The Ohio State University for his able assistance with data management and analysis.

Notes

1. These figures (65, 83, 95, 86, 92, and 80 percent, respectively) reflect the differences between the total vote cast for president and the votes cast for all minor candidates, not just the difference between the total vote and the vote for the major third-party candidate. In 1992, for example, 19,741,048 votes were cast for Ross Perot, but another 669,332 votes were cast for the other minor candidates. Thus, Bush and Clinton together received 80.97 percent of the three-candidate vote, but only 80.45 percent of the total vote.

2. We should point out that all comments about groups are assigned to the appropriate issue category. This practice assumes that respondents use references to groups as a way to discuss policy. Thus, for example, when there is

a reference to African Americans, the response is grouped with those under the heading of civil rights. When farmers are mentioned, since the probable topic is agricultural policy, these responses are grouped under that issue heading; and so forth.

3. NES studies typically include both preelection and postelection interviews. The candidate and the party like-dislike questions were asked in the preelection wave of interviewing. Vote choice, of course, is measured in the postelection wave.

4. In an excellent survey of the assumptions and appropriateness of the application of various statistical models to voting data, Alvarez and Nagler (1993) have recently outlined some potential pitfalls associated with several techniques, ours in particular. The statistical criticism is derived from the classical "selection bias" problem. Selection bias results from excluding observations on the dependent variable that are systematically different in some respect from the included observations.

In an attempt to address the implications of selection for our study, we analyzed responses to a question in the 1992 study that queried Perot voters about prior intentions to vote for Clinton or Bush (specifically, the question read: "Was there ever a time when you thought you were going to vote for Clinton or Bush?" Forty-five percent said they thought of voting for Clinton; 47 percent said they thought of voting for Bush; and 8 percent replied they had thought about voting for both). Using these responses, we created a surrogate, "second choice" variable, then estimated the 1992 models reported in this chapter with Perot voters included (we also estimated similar models for the Perot voters alone). This is an admittedly indirect attempt to get a handle on the selection bias problem, but it nonetheless raised our confidence in the purchase of our results, for we found that the differences between these estimates and those we report were trivial.

For a detailed analysis of the Perot vote, see chapter 6 by Herb Asher.

5. In a probit model, the probability that the dichotomous dependent variable is equal to one of its values is expressed as a nonlinear function of its right-hand-side variables. The model assumes normally distributed errors. See Aldrich and Nelson (1984) for a complete treatment of probit with binary variables and McKelvey and Zavoina (1975) for an extension to multi-category variables.

6. No attempt is made to distinguish between direct and indirect effects. (An indirect effect using the variables in this model might be that the voters' party affect would lead them to have a favorable perception of a candidate's personality, which in turn might lead them to favor that candidate's economic policy, which would finally lead them to vote choice.) Rather than make any assumption about a particular chain of attitudes that would lead ultimately to vote choice, each attitude category is given equal standing in terms of causal proximity; and the vote is estimated from all of them.

7. The coefficients associated with the three independent variables in table 4.1 and fourteen of the independent variables in table 4.2 are at least twice their estimated standard errors. All thus pass two-tailed hypothesis tests with 95 percent confidence intervals; most are significant, even, at less than .001.

8. A +.05 partisan valence corresponds to a 5 percent advantage for the Democrats because, if the neutral point were at its "real world" value of 50 percent, the Democratic vote resulting from this attitude would be 55 percent. Since we moved the neutral point to 0 from .50 for the calculation of the partisan valence scores, the partisan valence is +.05 (rather than +.55). Another consequence of setting the neutral point at 0 is the maximum advantage the Democrats can have is +.50; the maximum advantage the Republicans can have is −.50. To continue with our example, this means that while +.05 indicates a 5 percent advantage for the Democrats in votes cast, the same +.05 represents 10 percent of the maximum possible advantage for the Democrats.

9. The most often used strategy involves holding each independent variable at some "ordinary" value (usually its mean), generating a prediction of the probability of, say, a Democratic vote, then generating a series of second predictions by shifting one variable one unit while holding the others constant at their ordinary (mean) values. The difference between these two predictions is then interpreted straightforwardly as the change in the probability of a Democratic vote that results from shifting the (said) variable one unit with the others held constant at their means.

10. In the presidential elections since 1952, the 1976 contest was the only one in which attitudes about candidates appeared to be more important than attitudes about issues. Attitudes about parties have always been substantially less prominent voting determinants than attitudes about either issues or candidates (Kessel 1992, 265).

11. Because the probit coefficient for *agriculture* is statistically indistinguishable from zero, we do not report predicted probability changes for this variable, and the same is true for *people in the party*.

12. This represents an increased concern. From 1952 through 1980, voters were less concerned with intelligence than any other candidate attribute. In 1984, this attitude began to creep up to the middle ranks.

13. For the years in which systematic data have been available, the only time when party attitudes appeared to rank second (behind issues) in terms of the potential of these attitudes to sway vote choices was 1952. They have not been close to issues or candidates since.

14. Just for the record, Dan Quayle was the leading focus of negative comments about the Republicans in this category, and Al Gore was the leading focus of positive comments about the Democrats.

15. Trivia buffs may want to remember that George Bush was the second Yale infielder who failed to gain reelection as president. The first was William Howard Taft (who presumably weighed less in his playing days than when he got to the White House).

16. Kessel (1992, 286–87) describes this trend for the three elections in the 1980s as compared to those from the 1950s, and we have since conducted statistical tests of the differences between the probit results from 1992 and those from both 1980 and 1976. The results—derived from pooling the three data sets and estimating a single equation with slope dummies—provide rather dramatic evidence in favor of the thesis that issue attitudes have become a more important part of the average voter's calculus over time. The evidence is most striking when comparing 1992 to 1976, where statistically sig-

nificant increases in the probit coefficients associated with issue attitudes are apparent in the general category, international involvement, and civil liberties. And between 1980 and 1992, social benefits show an increase in importance as well. Thus, economic management remained as the most potent attitude, and all the other major issue attitudes (that is, all except natural resources and agriculture) gained in potency.

CHAPTER 5

The Candidates' Wives

ANTHONY MUGHAN AND BARRY C. BURDEN

Recent years have seen women become an influential force in the shaping of American electoral politics. After long commanding little attention as a force in its own right, gender has emerged to take on its own dynamic, its own role in shaping both the content of political debate and the outcome of electoral contests. Not the least reason for this structural change is that the political role of gender has become multifaceted. At one level, whether Americans are male or female is now important for their electoral behavior. Since 1980, women have tended to register and vote Democratic in consistently greater proportion than men. At another level, the number of female candidates running for elected office has grown steadily. And at yet another level, what might be called "women's issues" have become a prominent part of the political agenda. Moving on from such relatively specific themes as equal rights and sexual discrimination, these now also include diffuse areas long of special concern to women, such as abortion, family values, health care, children, and education.

Despite a contest between presidential and vice-presidential aspirants who were all male, gender assumed an unprecedented prominence in the 1992 presidential battle. The social, economic, and political forces that had brought it to the fore in previous contests were aggravated by two factors unique to this election. The first was anger stemming from the perception of the unfair treatment of Anita Hill, particularly by Republicans, during the all-male Senate Judiciary Committee's 1991 review of her allegations of sexual harassment against President Bush's Supreme Court nominee, Clarence Thomas. With their political consciousness raised to new heights, women mobilized as never before for the 1992 contest. An estimated 10 million more women were registered than men. In addition, the number of female candidates for state and national office increased, their fund-raising activities multiplied, and women's issues loomed large on the campaign agenda. The year 1992 would indeed appear to have been "The Year of the Woman" (Boles 1993; Carpini and Fuchs 1993; Cook et al. 1994; chap. 8 of this book).

The second reason for gender's unusual prominence in 1992 involves Barbara Bush and Hillary Rodham Clinton, the wives of the Republican and Democratic presidential candidates. Not only did they attract tremendous media coverage for "first wives" during the campaign, but they also embodied very different conceptions of the proper role of women in American society precisely when this issue was the subject of emotional debate in the country at large.[1] The highly popular Barbara Bush's image was that of a traditional wife, mother, and grandmother who had early given up her career ambitions to devote her life to her husband, family, and charitable causes. Hillary Rodham Clinton, by contrast, had refused to subordinate her own identity to her husband's throughout his political career. As well as being a wife and mother, she was a highly successful lawyer in her own right, her husband's long-time political confidante, and a woman who made no secret of having her own political agenda. Moreover, she appeared to imply contempt for homemakers like Barbara Bush when, early in the campaign and in response to Jerry Brown's charge that her Little Rock law firm had benefited unfairly from her marriage to the Arkansas governor, she retorted: "I suppose I could have stayed home, baked cookies and had teas."[2]

Sensing an advantage for their candidate, Republican strategists turned the question of the image and character appropriate to the nation's "first lady" into a campaign issue. Implicitly contrasting Hillary Clinton with the more traditional Barbara Bush, the chairman of the Republican National Committee used the platform of his party's nominating convention in Houston to distort the argument Hillary had made in an article written as a law student in 1973 by characterizing her as a lawsuit-mongering feminist who likened marriage to slavery and encouraged children to sue their parents. The contrast could not have been drawn more sharply.[3]

Of course, first ladies have not always been anonymous figures, especially in the twentieth century. With their husbands ensconced in office, for example, Edith Wilson was charged with exercising "petticoat government," Florence Harding with "running" her husband's career, and Eleanor Roosevelt with "putting words into the president's mouth." More recently, Rosalynn Carter was criticized for being present at cabinet meetings and Nancy Reagan for "getting people fired"

(Caroli 1987, xxi). The key difference in 1992 was that the candidates' wives were an issue in the campaign itself.[4]

Media commentators differed in their reaction to this new feature of presidential election campaigns. Some regretted it in principle. An editorial in the *Chicago Tribune* (16 August 1992), for example, was critical of the Republican National Committee chairman's attack on Hillary Clinton and insisted: "[She] is not running for president; her husband is. Why are her views relevant in the campaign.... Do Hillary's and Barbara's views on issues matter? Sure, but not near as much as Bill's and George's." Others were more sanguine, holding to the traditional view that the candidates' wives are of no consequence for the election outcome. In the words of a *Boston Globe* (1 September 1992) editorial: "One thing is certain: At the polls, voters will not be signifying their preference in first ladies, regardless of how much a helpmeet they are to their husband candidates." Still others took the view that the wives did indeed matter. A senior Clinton strategist, for example, enthused: "This campaign owes a debt of gratitude to the Republican convention for casting her [Hillary] in the role of heroine to a lot of people." While hardly welcoming it, many Republicans came reluctantly to share the Democratic view. Indeed, George Bush's press secretary sought to neutralize the backlash for the Republican candidate by insisting that "Hillary Clinton, good or bad, is not the issue in this campaign" (*New York Times*, 24 September 1992).

This divergence of opinion reflects the high visibility of both women in the campaign as well as the controversy surrounding Hillary Clinton, a new type of presidential wife perhaps more in keeping with the times. It also suggests the hypothesis that the two women were consequential for their husbands' fortunes in the election. Moreover, if they did indeed matter, the question whether their importance was unique to the 1992 election or represents a development with long-term implications for presidential election outcomes immediately raises its head.

The primary purpose of this chapter is to investigate the role of the two women in the 1992 election. Its secondary purpose is to draw some tentative conclusions about the implications of their 1992 role for future presidential contests. The chapter is divided into three sections. First, since for a candidate's wife to matter she must minimally have her own identity, Barbara Bush and Hillary Clinton are shown not simply to be extensions of their husbands in the eyes of Americans. Second, having established their independent identities for voters, we turn to the question of whether their separate identities had implications for the way people voted. It transpires that they did, and the final section addresses the question of what it is that shapes the distinctiveness of the wives vis-à-vis their husbands. Of particular interest is whether it is a function of forces unique to the 1992 election, what might be called the "Anita Hill factor," or whether it can be attributed to longer-term "pro-women" attitudes whose influence can be expected to persist in future elections.

Husbands and Wives in the Public Eye

The conventional wisdom about the presidential wife is that she helps her husband most by subordinating her personality and presence to his. She is his loyal, devoted, and adoring partner and to be seen to stand apart from him risks an adverse reaction from traditionalists still wary of women's assertion of their identity and its implications for core societal institutions such as marriage and the family. As *Newsweek* (8 June 1992) put it early in the campaign: "In a year when scores of women are running for office on their own, maybe voters need reassurance that there is one area of political life where the old rules still apply: First Ladies must remember they are extensions of their husbands." The fundamental difference between Barbara Bush and Hillary Clinton was that the former had always followed these "old rules," whereas the latter had refused to play by them from her earliest days as the governor's wife in Arkansas. Nor would Mrs. Clinton allow her husband's bid for the presidency to change things. From the outset of his campaign, she let it be known that she had no intention of changing her ways should she come to occupy the White House.

Table 5.1 presents the mean and distribution of responses to the NES thermometer questions, scored from 0 to 1, for the four individual

TABLE 5.1
HUSBAND AND WIFE THERMOMETER SCORES

	George	Barbara	Hillary	Bill
Mean score	0.52	0.67	0.54	0.56
Distribution of scores (%)				
Cold (0 to 0.49)	35.2	11.4	23.5	29.7
Indifferent (0.50)	14.1	16.2	28.4	14.6
Warm (0.51 to 1.0)	50.8	72.5	48.1	55.7
N	2,463	2,432	2,299	2,429

SOURCE: 1992 National Election Study.

spouses.[5] It is intended as a first look at the public's reaction to the wives relative to their husbands. Overall, the pattern in the scores provides little reason to conclude that the American public views either woman as a pale reflection of her husband. This is most immediately obvious in the case of Barbara Bush. Not only are Americans no more likely to be indifferent to her than they are to her president husband, but also the substance of their reaction is far more positive on the whole. The Clintons would seem to have similarly separate identities in the public eye, although, unlike the Bushes, their separateness is not obvious in mean scores that are about the same on average. Instead, it is the distribution of reactions to Bill and Hillary Clinton that is distinctive. For a start, more people are indifferent to Hillary than to her candidate husband. Indeed, Bill Clinton is more like the Bushes than his wife in respect to the number of people who have some reaction, positive or negative, to him. In addition, as with the Bushes, more people react coldly to husband than to wife. Finally, and in contrast to the Bushes, the Democratic candidate is regarded warmly by more people than is his wife. Indeed, fewer people react warmly to Hillary Clinton than to any other individual in the table, including an unpopular, soon-to-be-defeated incumbent president.

Both wives, then, have identities in the public eye that are substantially independent of their husbands'. The overwhelmingly positive reaction to Barbara Bush evident in table 5.1 would suggest that this is more true for her than it is for Hillary Clinton. This difference between the two wives is confirmed in table 5.2, which presents the zero-order correlations between their thermometer scores and those of their husbands. The correlation for the Bushes is 0.58, but is substantially higher for the Clintons at 0.70. Even here, though, husband and wife are still clearly differentiated by the public so that it is unwise to take the electoral role of either wife for granted, to dismiss her at the outset as a

TABLE 5.2
ZERO-ORDER CORRELATIONS BETWEEN INDIVIDUAL
THERMOMETER SCORES

	George	Barbara	Hillary
Barbara	.58		
Hillary	−.30	−.12	
Bill	−.39	−.26	.70

SOURCE: 1992 National Election Study.

clone of her candidate husband and therefore of no potential added electoral value to him.

That the wives are not simply extensions of their husbands is one good reason not to discount them as potential influences on the vote in their own right. Another is their identity vis-à-vis each other. Just as each of them has an identity that is separate from her husband's, so her identity is also separate from that of the other wife. This is evident in the correlation between their thermometer scores being a meager −0.12 on average, compared to a mean 0.64 when each's score is correlated with her husband's. Voters' reactions to Barbara Bush and Hillary Clinton, in other words, cannot be assumed to be opposite sides of a coin defined by a preference for a traditional role for women in society on one side and a more modern role on the other. Instead, voters' reactions to them seem to be more individualized, more sensitive to the two women as distinct personalities. Again, the conclusion is inescapable that their role in the 1992 presidential election is complex and must be investigated rather than taken for granted. Thus, our next task is to determine whether Barbara Bush and Hillary Clinton actually moved beyond the traditional anonymity of candidates' wives to make a difference to the distribution of the presidential vote as personalities in their own right.

The Candidates' Wives: A Closer Look

As independent electoral stimuli, Barbara Bush and Hillary Clinton may or may not have influenced the way people voted. Table 5.3 represents an initial look at whether they did. In it, the presidential vote is regressed on the individual husbands' and wives' thermometer scores, while controlling for party identification and a number of sociodemographic variables that can reasonably be expected to condition voters' attitudinal and behavioral reactions to the presidential candidates and their wives. The vote is coded 0 for Clinton, .5 for Perot, and 1 for Bush, and missing data are deleted pairwise. The coding of the independent variables is straightforward. Party identification is the usual seven-point scale ranging from weak Democrat (scored 0) to strong Republican (coded 1). Males, blacks, and union members are scored 0; females, nonblacks, and nonunion members 1. Two sets of coefficients are presented, unstandardized in the first column and standardized in the second. Holding the other variables in the equation constant, the former estimate how much more likely it is that a person will vote for Bush given a unit change in her score on the independent variable. Thus, a

TABLE 5.3

THE EFFECT OF SOCIODEMOGRAPHIC VARIABLES AND
HUSBAND AND WIFE THERMOMETER SCORES
ON THE PRESIDENTIAL VOTE

	b	B
Party identification	.38***	.28***
Age (in years)	.03	.02
Gender	−.02	−.02
Education (in years)	−.01	−.01
Race	.11***	.08***
Union membership	−.00	−.00
George: thermometer	.52***	.31***
Barbara: thermometer	.07*	.03*
Bill: thermometer	−.55***	−.30***
Hillary: thermometer	−.14***	−.07***
$R^2 = .67$		

SOURCE: 1992 National Election Study.

*$p < .05$.   **$p < .01$.   ***$p < .001$ (one-tailed test).

nonblack person is, in net terms, 11 percent more likely to vote for Bush than a black person. The standardized coefficients, or beta weights, estimate the explanatory power of individual variables relative to others in the same equation. Thus, Hillary Clinton's effect, at −.07, is a little more than twice as strong as Barbara Bush's, at .03.

In a nutshell, table 5.3 indicates that, of the various sociodemographic groupings, only nonblacks voted disproportionately for George Bush. This is also true of those giving George and Barbara Bush a high thermometer score and Bill and Hillary Clinton a low one. More to the point, though, the table also indicates that affect for both wives had an independent influence on the vote for their husbands, an influence that is noteworthy in two respects. First, it is relatively moderate; they may be players in the game, but they should not be taken for anything else but minor players. A comparison of the beta weights indicates quite clearly that party identification and affect for Bill Clinton and George Bush are far more powerful influences on the vote. Second, their effect was not of equal magnitude. Just crossing the 5 percent threshold of significance, it was only marginal for Barbara Bush, whereas it was appreciably stronger for Hillary Clinton. Bill Clinton's share of the presidential vote, in other words, benefited more from his wife than did George Bush's from his.

The question that follows naturally from these observations concerns what the wives brought to the election that their husbands did not have. What does each wife stand for that sets her apart from her husband and adds to his vote, and why was Hillary Clinton a greater benefit in this regard than Barbara Bush?

In view of the low correlation between the thermometer scores for Barbara Bush and Hillary Clinton (see table 5.2), these questions do not hold out the promise of an easy and neat answer. What works to distinguish Hillary from Bill Clinton will not necessarily also distinguish Barbara from George Bush. The identification of Hillary Clinton with women's issues, for example, could well bring her husband votes that he, not being as unambiguously "pro-woman," would not otherwise have picked up. Barbara Bush might be less successful in delivering the traditionalist vote on these issues because she did not take this side in the debate as clearly as Hillary Clinton took the progressive side. Such different degrees of identification notwithstanding, a perusal of the wives' role in the campaign suggests that, in general terms, it was in the area of women's issues that they were most distinctive from each other and in the area of children and family values that they were most distinctive from their husbands. It stands to reason, therefore, that these are the areas in which their special appeal will be found, the areas in which the public's response to them will be distinctive from its response to their husbands.

Table 5.4 is an effort to identify the common and the distinctive in the appeal of the Democratic and Republican presidential candidates and their wives. The dependent variables are their individual thermometer scores and the independent variables those already included in table 5.3 plus a battery of variables tapping women's issues and family values. The women's issues variables are two. One is long term and measures attitude to women's equality.[6] The second is a thermometer-scale-based measure of affect for Anita Hill and represents a measure of discontent in the short term with the plight of one woman. Gender, in other words, is likely to continue to be a political issue as long as there is a perception of structured sexual inequality in American society, whereas memories of Anita Hill's treatment by Clarence Thomas and the Senate Judiciary Committee is less likely to mobilize women beyond the 1992 election. Support for family values is measured by three variables: abortion, government spending on child care, and health care.[7] Since husband is to be compared with wife, only unstandardized coefficients are presented in the table, because they allow the calculation of a *t*-statistic indicating whether individual variables have a significantly different impact on each spouse's thermometer score (Jencks et al.

TABLE 5.4
SOURCES OF AFFECT: HUSBANDS AND WIVES COMPARED

	George	Barbara	t	Bill	Hillary	t
Party identification	.24	.03	8.74	−.20	−.03	7.37
Age (in years)	−.06	.11	8.22	.03	.00	1.47
Gender	.00	.04	3.54	.00	−.02	1.52
Education	−.07	.07	8.18	−.01	−.01	0.26
Race	−.01	.06	3.31	−.02	−.01	0.26
Union membership	.02	−.01	1.93	−.01	.01	1.58
George: thermometer	—	.46	—	−.01	−.03	0.73
Barbara: thermometer	.53	—	—	−.08	.11	6.55
Bill: thermometer	−.01	−.10	2.32	—	.54	—
Hillary: thermometer	−.05	.15	4.97	.58	—	—
Abortion	.05	.01	2.79	.00	−.03	1.92
Child-care spending	.00	.02	0.55	−.04	−.01	1.55
Health care	.05	.02	1.23	−.02	.00	1.64
Women's equality	.05	−.05	4.50	.02	−.03	2.95
Anita Hill	−.08	.03	4.06	.04	.15	4.80
R^2	.51	.41		.59	.53	

SOURCE: 1992 National Election Study.

1979, 39). It must have a value of 1.65 or greater for the difference to be statistically significant at the 5 percent level or better.

Table 5.4 provides several valuable insights into the role the candidates' wives played in shaping the outcome of the 1992 presidential election. Some of these insights appear to be general and, as such, may continue to have relevance beyond the 1992 contest, whereas others seem to be specific to it. We start with the general and work toward the particular.

First, insofar as affect for them is far more independent of party identification than is affect for their husbands, wives would seem to be relatively independent campaign stimuli with a very real potential to influence presidential election outcomes. This potential can take two forms. On the one hand, a candidate's wife may shore up her husband's support by having more appeal than he has to potential defectors (e.g., independents and weak partisans). On the other hand, she may add to his vote by appealing across party lines. Capitalizing on this potential is easier said than done. The right appeal has to be found and made successfully. A candidate's wife can be an asset or a liability but is not automatically either.

In this regard, the second important insight from table 5.4 is that high or low levels of affect are not sufficient to guarantee a meaningful electoral impact. Take Barbara Bush as an example. She can be seen to be far more popular than her husband among older, female, and better-educated Americans in particular, yet table 5.3 shows these groups to be no more likely to vote for President Bush than their younger, male, and less-well-educated counterparts. Moreover, carefully crafted appeals can backfire. The Republicans clearly hoped to pick up the traditional vote by painting Barbara Bush as the archetypal 1950s American wife and mother and Hillary Clinton as the equally archetypal modern woman who, rejecting this traditional female role, puts her own career before her husband and family. But table 5.4 shows that those unenthusiastic for women's equality in fact react negatively to both Barbara Bush and Hillary Clinton. Traditionalists, it would seem, react negatively to any form of political involvement on the part of politicians' wives regardless of the values these women purport to represent.

This brings us to the third insight in table 5.4, and it concerns the role of family values and women's issues in differentiating the public's reaction to husband and wife in the specific context of the 1992 election. Two conclusions stand out. First, among the family values of abortion, child-care spending, and health care, only abortion sets husband and wife apart in voter affect. This is particularly true of the Bushes, with those with antiabortion views feeling much more positively toward George Bush. This could be due to his unambiguous stand against abortion as incumbent president. Barbara Bush's rejection late in the campaign of her husband's blanket antiabortion stance might also have played a role. Second, the women's issues of gender equality and Anita Hill differentiate both husbands and wives very effectively, but their influence is more complicated than campaign rhetoric would lead us to expect. Put simply, Barbara Bush did not appeal simply to traditionalists and Republicans and Hillary Clinton to nontraditionalists and Democrats. The tendency for traditionalists to react negatively to both wives has already been mentioned. Equally surprising perhaps is that affect for each wife is positively associated with affect for the other wife and with affect for Anita Hill. The public would seem to tar all prominent female actors in the campaign with the same brush and to react to them all positively or negatively; it tends not to differentiate women into "good" and "bad" camps.[8]

This undifferentiated reaction stands to have profound, and counterintuitive, implications for the way women's issues affected the vote through their structuring of the public response to the candidates' wives. This complex relationship is explored next.

Women's Issues, Candidates' Wives, and the Vote

Republican strategists clearly anticipated that George Bush's vote could at the least not suffer from casting his wife in a very traditional feminine role. Equally, they could only have anticipated that the Anita Hill episode would reverberate roundly to the disadvantage of their candidate if it were to become an election issue. The analysis in the preceding section of this chapter suggests that an irony of the 1992 campaign may well be that the party's strategists were wrong on both counts. That is, to the extent that Barbara Bush was greeted coldly by traditionalists, she may well have cost her husband votes. Equally, to the extent she was greeted warmly by Anita Hill supporters, she may have brought him votes that would otherwise have been denied to him. Hillary Clinton, in contrast, appears to have been uncomplicated in the independent effect she had on the presidential vote. As expected, she was popular among proponents of women's equality and among Anita Hill supporters.

Such speculation should not be pushed too far, since it has already been demonstrated that variables predicting affect are not always equally successful in predicting the vote. Table 5.5 therefore focuses attention explicitly on the presidential vote. It manipulates the women's issues variables to specify how, if at all, they affect the vote indirectly through their structuring of the public response to the candidates' wives. With its five independent regression equations, the table is in effect a simulation exercise designed to clarify how these issues mediate the wives' impact on the vote. Its basic purpose is twofold. On the one hand, it seeks to determine whether it was the salience of women's issues in the campaign that accounts for the wives adding to their husbands' votes. If this is the case, then affect for the wives should disappear when voters' positions on these same issues are entered into the regression equation. On the other hand, by distinguishing between short- and long-term women's issues, it serves as the basis for some speculative conclusions about the role candidates' wives can play in future presidential elections.

Equation I in the table sets the baseline against which the others are to be compared in that it specifies the effect of Barbara Bush and Hillary Clinton when women's issues are discounted. It contains the same variables as table 5.3 plus the three family values variables. The major point it makes is that when women's issues are not taken into account, Barbara Bush represents a marginal electoral bonus for her husband and Hillary Clinton a more substantial one for hers. Equation II's inclusion of the long-term issue of women's equality in American society makes it the first step in determining whether the candidates' wives are effectively proxies for women's issues in the campaign. The answer is negative. Attitudes about women's equality may structure affect for the candidates' wives and distinguish them from their husbands (see table 5.4), but their impact on the vote is both insignificant and independent of how voters feel about Barbara Bush and Hillary Clinton. If their impact were mediated by the wives, then their influence on the presidential vote would decline. As it is, their effects remain unchanged in both cases.

TABLE 5.5
WOMEN'S ISSUES, CANDIDATES' WIVES, AND
THE PRESIDENTIAL VOTE

	I	II	III	IV	V
Party identification	.36***	.35***	.35***	.35***	.35***
Age (in years)	.01	.01	.01	.01	.01
Gender	−.01	−.00	−.00	−.00	−.01
Education	.01	.02	.01	.02	.01
Race	.11***	.12***	.12***	.12***	.12***
Union membership	−.00	−.01	−.01	−.01	−.00
George: thermometer	.48***	.47***	.47***	.47***	.48***
Barbara: thermometer	.06*	.07*	.07*	.07*	.07*
Bill: thermometer	−.54***	−.54***	−.53***	−.54***	−.54***
Hillary: thermometer	−.11**	−.11**	−.07*	−.07*	−.11**
Abortion	.10***	.09***	.10***	.09***	.09***
Child-care spending	.04*	.03	.03	.03	.04*
Health care	.07***	.07**	.07***	.07**	.07***
Women's equality	—	.04	—	.04	.04*
Anita thermometer	—	—	−.11***	−.11***	—
Anger over women	—	—	—	—	−.00
Sexual harassment	—	—	—	—	−.00
R^2	.68	.68	.68	.68	.68

SOURCE: 1992 National Election Study.

$*p < .05.$ $**p < .01.$ $***p < .001.$

This is not to conclude that women's issues are insignificant in shaping the electoral impact of candidates' wives. Equations III and IV indicate that Hillary Clinton's substantial addition to her husband's vote is partly explainable at least by the short-term goodwill accruing to her, a modern, independent woman, as a result of affect for Anita

Hill. Once Anita Hill's popularity is controlled, Hillary Clinton's impact on the presidential vote drops appreciably. This is not true of Barbara Bush. Whether one looks at short- or long-term women's issues, her marginal contribution to her husband's share of the presidential vote remains unaltered. It is hard to know whether the persistence of her effect is a function of the considerable warmth felt for her by the electorate as a whole or of some issue or set of issues not hinted at by campaign events and rhetoric. Hillary Clinton, in contrast, is clearly unlikely to have been the electoral force she was had it not been for the residue of the 1991 Anita Hill episode. It would appear premature, therefore, to conclude that her bolstering of her husband's vote signals a new electoral role for assertive, independent candidates' wives in the new age of the "liberated woman."

Those skeptical of this conclusion might counter that scores on the Anita Hill thermometer reflect not feelings toward the woman herself, but more deeply rooted and durable resentment over the way women are treated in contemporary American society. That is, Anita Hill was important for the election outcome, not because of herself and/or the transient events that surrounded her, but as the symbol of a long-term malaise over American men's attitudes about, and behavior toward, women. Equation V tests this alternative, more long-term explanation of the "Hillary effect" by substituting for the Anita Hill thermometer two questions tapping attitudes towards sexual harassment and anger over the way women are treated.[9] The results only confirm the short-term interpretation of the role of women's issues in the campaign. Taking the Anita Hill thermometer out of the equation serves only to restore Hillary Clinton to her status as a substantial force in her own right, while neither of the anger or harassment variables even approaches statistical significance.[10] The conclusion is clear: Hillary Clinton's rise to a position of influence in the 1992 election is largely a function of the bad taste left in many mouths by the Anita Hill episode in 1991 and not of Hillary Clinton's distinctive appeal to voters discontented over the longer term with the subordinate position of women in American society.

Conclusion

This chapter starts from the observation that a novel feature of the 1992 presidential contest was the highly prominent campaign role of the wives of the Democratic and Republican candidates. In addition, these women represented very different conceptions of the proper role of women in contemporary American society. Barbara Bush was a traditional, selfless wife and mother, whereas Hillary Clinton represented the new type of independent American woman concerned with her own career as well as her roles as wife and mother. The issue crystallized around the question whether Hillary Clinton, and the values she stood for, were preferable to the country's mainstream, traditional, and highly popular first lady, Barbara Bush. The stage was set for the wives to become an issue in the campaign, an issue that could influence how their husbands fared in the popular vote.

The fact that Bill Clinton won the presidency has persuaded many people that the "battle of the wives" represents the victory of the "new" over the "old" type of American woman. Hillary Clinton helped her husband to victory because of her appeal to the growing percentage of the population that accepts equality of the sexes and is uneasy about persistent vestiges of female disadvantage (e.g., sexual harassment). She could not, the argument goes, have played the role she did if attitudes toward and about women had not changed. In the words of one historian comparing her to Eleanor Roosevelt: "We have seen in the past two decades a sharper change in the ideal and practice of equality for women than occurred in the preceding two millennia—it is the most basic social change of our time. In this context, the prominence of Hillary Rodham Clinton is less a matter of personal rebellion (as it was, however genteelly, with Mrs. Roosevelt) than of a normal reflection of a larger social reality" (Wills 1993, 24).

Nobody could deny this change, but the clear lesson of the 1992 election is not to overstate its political importance. Attitudinal transformation has undoubtedly paved the way for acceptance of the new type of first lady that Hillary Clinton is. It does not, however, guarantee that future aspirants to the position, even if they model themselves after Hillary Clinton, will be players of the same magnitude in the presidential election game. She was an electoral asset to her husband less because she commanded the affection of liberated progressives and more because she was the pole around which there collected affect for a particular individual of passing importance in American politics, Anita Hill. Had it not been for the Clarence Thomas confirmation hearings and the controversy they generated, Hillary Clinton would likely not have been the electoral force she was in the 1992 contest. We accept, of course, that indignation over Anita Hill would not have become an issue in the election if the substantial advances made by the women's movement had not legitimated it. Our point is that these advances create the potential for an independent electoral role for a wife whose identity is no longer seen as being properly merged with her candidate husband's. This potential is now part of the routine background of elections in the United States, and it must be sparked to be consequential. The legacy of the Anita Hill episode would appear to have been the spark in 1992.

Notes

1. By contrast, Margot Perot, the wife of the third significant presidential candidate, Ross Perot, barely figured in the campaign. Her lack of a reasonably well-defined public image is the reason she is ignored in this analysis.

2. While this much-quoted remark did much to create Hillary Clinton's initial image in the public mind, it does not reflect the more balanced nature of her response to Jerry Brown. She went on to say: "The work that I have done as a professional, a public advocate, has been aimed ... to ensure that women can make their choices ... whether it's full-time career, full-time motherhood or some combination" (*Time,* 14 September 1992).

3. The contrast between the two wives did erode over the course of the campaign. Democratic strategists, fearful that voters were not yet ready for so independent a first lady, persuaded Hillary Clinton to moderate her image. She softened her hairstyle, clothes, and makeup and consciously steered clear of controversial issues. She also took pains to be seen to travel with her husband more often and to defer to him in public, and both were seen more often with their daughter, Chelsea. Barbara Bush, in turn, moved toward Hillary Clinton's initial image and asserted her independence from her husband. She took a position on the abortion issue decidedly to the left of his. She also chided an interviewer for being "very sexist" in asking about her husband's rumored love affair while not asking her whether she had one. Finally, she chastised the Republican National Committee chairman for "knocking" the Democratic candidate's wife and not the office seeker himself.

4. One simple indicator of the novelty of this development is that in 1992 the National Election Study (NES) contains a question on the Democratic and Republican candidates' wives for the first time since its inception. This question is the conventional one asking respondents to place each woman on a thermometer scale ranging from 0 to 100 degrees. Scores between 0 and 50 degrees reflect an unfavorable feeling toward the person, a score of 50 degrees represent neither a particularly warm nor a particularly cold feeling, and a score between 50 and 100 degrees signals a warm and favorable response. Thermometer questions were also asked about a number of other prominent actors in the 1992 contest, including, of course, the presidential candidates.

The fact that only one closed-ended question is asked on each of the two women sets clear limits on the kind of exploration of their electoral role that can be undertaken in this chapter. Nonetheless, we feel it better to undertake this exploration, no matter how partial, than to risk missing a "first ladies" personality contest that may well have been consequential for the outcome of the presidential election.

5. As note 4 mentions, responses to the thermometer scores actually range from 0 to 100. We have simply divided individuals' responses by 100 to make the metric of the thermometer scores comparable with that of the other independent variables, which are scored between 0 and 1, used in the analysis to come.

6. The NES question tapping women's equality is worded as follows: "Recently there has been a lot of talk about women's rights. Some people feel that women should have an equal role with men in running business, industry, and government. Others feel that women's place is in the home. Where would you place yourself on this scale, or haven't you thought about it much?" A seven-point scale follows with responses ranging from "Women and men should have an equal role" to "Women's place is in the home." These responses are coded from 0 to 1.

7. Again, these three variables have codes ranging between 0 and 1, with the low score representing the "Democratic" response and the high score the "Republican" one. The questions are worded in the following way:

Abortion: "There has been some discussion of abortion during recent years. Which one of the opinions on this page best agrees with your view? 1. By law, abortion should never be permitted. 2. The law should permit abortion only in case of rape, incest, or when the woman's life is in danger. 3. The law should permit abortion for reasons *other than* rape, incest, or danger to the woman's life, but only after the need for the abortion has been clearly established. 4. By law, a woman should always be able to obtain an abortion as a matter of personal choice."

Child-care spending: "If you had a say in making up the federal budget this year, for which of the following programs would you like to see spending increased and for which would you like to see spending decreased?" There then follows a list of programs, including child care.

Health care: "There is much concern about the rapid rise in medical and hospital costs. Some people feel there should be a government insurance plan which would cover all medical and hospital expenses for everyone. Others feel that all medical expenses should be paid by individuals, and through private insurance plans like Blue Cross or other company paid plans. Where would you place yourself on this scale, or haven't you thought about it much?" The seven-point scale ranges from "government insurance plan" to "private insurance plan."

8. What makes this especially interesting is that the same uniform reaction is not evident with the men. Affect for one presidential candidate does not predict to affect for the other, and albeit that it is insignificant in both cases, the relationship between them is negative. Equally, affect for Anita Hill predicts differentially to affect for the two presidential candidates, expectedly negative for Bush and positive for Clinton.

9. The wording of these questions is as follows:

Harassment: "Recently there has been a lot of discussion about sexual harassment. How serious a problem do you think sexual harassment is?" The possible responses are "very serious," "somewhat serious," or "not too serious."

Anger over women's treatment: "How often do you find yourself angry about the way women are treated in society?" The responses are "very often," "some of the time," "occasionally," or "almost never."

In both cases the responses are coded from 0 to 1.

10. The same nonresults emerge when we replace the anger and harassment variables with a question asking respondents whether they are feminists. The relative unimportance of long-term attitudinal predispositions to Hillary Clinton's effect on the vote is thereby given further support.

CHAPTER 6

The Perot Campaign

HERB ASHER

Ross Perot's campaign of 1992 was truly one of the most impressive and bizarre electoral events of recent decades. The impressive feature was Perot's winning 19 percent of the popular vote, a performance that far outdistanced those of recent third-party and independent candidacies, such as John Anderson in 1980 and George Wallace in 1968. What made Perot's performance even more noteworthy is that he did not have any inherent regional base of support, as did the Dixiecrats and Strom Thurmond in 1948, nor any particular ethnic or racial advantage. Instead, Perot's candidacy was a national one. He received at least 20 percent of the vote in twenty-eight states and exceeded 30 percent in Maine, where he narrowly edged out George Bush for second place. Perot also finished second in Utah with 27.3 percent of the vote, besting Clinton by almost three percentage points. Only in Mississippi and the District of Columbia did his support fall below 10 percent.

Perot's performance is even more remarkable considering the bizarre paths his candidacy took. He announced his willingness to run for president in February 1992, on the *Larry King Live* show, contingent on the ability of his supporters to place his name on the ballot in all fifty states, a task readily accomplished. To the consternation of his supporters, he dropped out of the race during the Democratic convention. He then orchestrated his reentry into the race in October, teasing the media for a few weeks. He more than held his own in the three presidential debates in October, but selected as a running mate a person for whom the debate format was cruel and who brought very little to the ticket. Throughout the campaign and particularly toward the end, many of the accusations that Perot made and the explanations that he offered for his actions became increasingly strange. Nevertheless, by the end of the campaign, Perot's support had increased, unlike recent third-party and independent candidacies whose support declined dramatically as election day approached.

Ross Perot demonstrated in 1992 that a well-funded independent candidate who is skillful in using the media can tap into voter dismay with politics and become a credible presidential challenger. Not only did Perot circumvent the two political parties, he also got around the traditional political media such as the national reporters and evening news shows through such means as lengthy infomercials, frequent appearances on television talk shows, and satellite feeds. Indeed, unlike Bush and Clinton, Perot did very little traditional campaigning.

The successful Perot campaign raises a number of questions that are addressed in this chapter. First, I examine the dynamics of the campaign, focusing on Perot's standing at different points in the campaign and trying to explain why it did not decline at the end of the campaign. Second is a descriptive analysis of who the Perot voters were. Here I examine a number of demographic, political, and issue variables to ascertain how Perot voters differed from Clinton and Bush supporters. Next I construct a multivariate model of support for Perot, trying to assess which factors help account for citizens' overall evaluations of him. The fourth part of the chapter assesses the impact of Perot's candidacy on the electoral fortunes of Clinton and Bush. The chapter concludes with a discussion of Perot's potential future political role and his likely impact on the political system.

The Dynamics of the Perot Campaign

The rise and fall and then the fall and rise of Perot's electoral fortunes are outlined in table 6.1, which presents the results of CBS News/*New York Times* polls conducted over the course of the campaign. The results are for registered voters only and are not adjusted for the likely electorate. Moreover, the results include only respondents who offered a preference in response to the vote-intention question and do not include those who expressed a leaning after initially saying they were undecided. Note that Perot was included as a vote option in three polls conducted after he dropped out of the race, a prescient decision on the part of the pollsters.

Table 6.1 shows the rapid rise in Perot's support from March to June. From a distant third-place showing in March, Perot quickly became competitive with Clinton, and by June he was essentially tied with George Bush for first place. A few surveys conducted by other polling

TABLE 6.1
THE STANDING OF THE CANDIDATES
DURING THE 1992 CAMPAIGN

Date of poll	Bush	Clinton	Perot	Don't know, Would not vote
26–27 Mar	44	31	16	9
20–23 Apr	38	28	23	11
6–8 May	36	30	25	9
27–30 May	35	27	26	12
17–20 Jun	32	24	30	14
8–11 Jul	33	30	25	12
Perot drops out.				
Aug	32	45	12	11
Sept	34	42	14	10
Perot reenters.				
2–4 Oct	37	45	7	11
First debate.				
12–13 Oct	34	47	10	9
Second debate.				
Third debate.				
20–23 Oct	35	39	15	11
27–28 Oct	33	44	14	9
27–30 Oct	34	43	15	8
29 Oct–1 Nov	34	43	15	8

SOURCE: CBS News/*New York Times* polls. The August and September surveys asked respondents to assume that Perot was in the race. The percentages in the table are based on registered voters unadjusted for the likely electorate. Undecideds are treated as such regardless of whether they "lean" toward a candidate.

outfits had Perot in the lead. The reader should recall that the early surveys were conducted at a time when the Democratic and Republican nominations (especially the former) were not yet locked up for Clinton and Bush and when their intraparty challengers were sharply criticizing the eventual nominees. Nevertheless, Perot's rapid ascendance in the polls to be competitive with the incumbent president was an impressive development. His March performance in the polls was particularly surprising because, as noted by Zaller with Hunt (1993), Perot received very little media attention between the time of his February *Larry King* interview and the middle of March.

Even as the Perot candidacy was soaring, the seeds for his early withdrawal from the race were being sown. The initial post-March media coverage of the Perot campaign focused on its novelty and on attractive features of the candidate such as his business success, his decisiveness, and his position as a nonpolitical outsider. But soon the media focus became more critical, with examinations of his business practices, his personality characteristics, and his dealings with others. Campaign difficulties and gaffes received major media attention, as illustrated by the departure of Ed Rollins from the Perot campaign and the insensitive words uttered by Perot at the NAACP convention. Thus, as more Americans became aware of Perot, the ratio of favorable to unfavorable impressions of him declined. For example, in the March CBS News/*New York Times* poll, Perot was rated favorably by 16 percent of the respondents and unfavorably by 8 percent; by June, the corresponding numbers were 26 versus 20 percent, and by July, 19 versus 27 percent.

Perot withdrew from the presidential campaign during the Democratic National Convention, in which the Democratic Party presented itself to the American public as united, capable of governing, and in the mainstream of American politics. Perot's timing gave Democratic nominee Bill Clinton the first opportunity to appeal to Perot's supporters, portraying himself as the Washington outsider and the candidate of change. Indeed, Clinton left the convention with the largest postconvention "bounce" in support ever measured in the polls and a lead over George Bush of 55 to 31 percent (Apple 1992). In addition, former Perot backers preferred Clinton over Bush by a margin of 45 to 26 percent, according to a CBS News/*New York Times* poll conducted at the time.

Although he ended his candidacy, Perot never removed his name from any of the fifty state ballots. And as the deadline for getting off the ballot passed in a number of states without any effort by Perot to remove his name, speculation arose as to whether Perot would reenter the race. Throughout much of September, Perot skillfully manipulated the Clinton and Bush campaigns as well as the media by carrying out an extensive political tease that culminated in his reentering the contest on 1 October, just one month before the election.

Starting at about 7 percent in the polls in early October, Perot quickly doubled his support by mid-October. His full participation in the three presidential debates and his strong performance therein strengthened his appeal. For example, a CBS News/*New York Times* poll conducted after the first debate showed that because of the debate, 57 percent of the viewers thought better of Perot and only 7 percent poorer, compared to 31 and 14 percent respectively for Clinton and 14 and 18 percent respectively for Bush. Perot performed well in all three debates; the only downside for him was the painful performance of his running mate, Admiral James Stockdale, in the vice-presidential debate.

Most of the national polls conducted close to election day showed

Perot with 14 to 15 percent of the vote. And many political observers, including political scientists, expected that his actual vote share would fall short of the opinion poll estimates. One reason for this expectation was the pattern of the Wallace and Anderson campaigns in 1968 and 1980. In both cases, the candidate's election day performance fell short of projections, in part because many Democrats and Republicans who had flirted with the idea of voting for the third-party candidate returned home to their own parties' nominees. A similar trend was expected in 1992. Moreover, third-party and independent candidacies are vulnerable to the "wasted vote" argument, which states that since the third candidate has no chance of winning, voters should not waste their votes but should instead turn to one of the two major-party nominees. Since the later polls showed that Perot was running a very distant third with no chance of winning, most observers believed that many of his supporters would move to Clinton or Bush on election day. And toward the end of the campaign, Perot himself became more flaky, as evidenced by his claim that he had initially dropped out of the race to protect his daughter's wedding from GOP sabotage.

Instead of fading, Perot received a higher percentage of the vote —19 percent—than any public opinion survey had projected. In hindsight, many explanations can be given for the accomplishment. First was Perot's extensive media presence in the final two weeks of the campaign. Unlike Wallace and Anderson, Perot had the financial resources to bring his message directly to the American people over the airwaves. Second, as mentioned earlier, Perot had more than held his own in the three debates with Clinton and Bush. Third was the unpresidential conduct of George Bush in the last days of the campaign, with his references to his Democratic opponents as "bozos" and his characterization of Al Gore as "ozone man." Observers speculated whether any late surge to Bush was hindered by these bizarre statements as well as by a last-minute revelation that the president had not been fully forthcoming about his involvement in the Iran-*contra* affair. Finally, there is the possibility that the polls consistently underestimated Perot's support.

There are two reasons to suspect that the polls could underestimate Perot's strength. One was the traditional challenge that polls face in determining which citizens will actually vote. Turnout increased sharply in 1992. If the polls failed to project this turnout and if the turnout increase were generated by an influx of Perot supporters into the electorate, then the polls would have underestimated Perot's support. The other potential problem with the polls would occur if Perot gained support in the last days of the campaign and the polls failed to capture these late voter movements. This seems unlikely because polling con-

tinued right to the very end of the 1992 campaign. Nevertheless, Perot
ran strongest among late deciders, an unsurprising result since he became a candidate again only one month before the election. According
to the 1992 American National Election Study (NES), of those respondents who made their vote choices in the last few days of the campaign,
38 percent supported Perot, 33 percent preferred Clinton, and 29 percent opted for Bush; these late deciders constituted almost 19 percent of
the sample. Likewise, of those who decided in the last month, 34 percent favored Perot, 43 percent Clinton, and 23 percent Bush; this group
constituted 19 percent of the sample. Perot of course ran poorly among
those citizens whose final decisions about candidate choice were made
early, since he was not a candidate at the time.

The success of Perot's candidacy was facilitated by a number of
changes in American politics. Access to the ballot has become easier for
third-party and independent candidacies in the past two decades because of a series of court decisions and actions of state governments;
certainly Perot faced a more hospitable legal environment than did Anderson in 1980 and, especially, Wallace in 1968. Moreover, there are
many more opportunities today for earned (free) media beyond the national nightly news shows and the traditional political talk shows such
as *Meet the Press* and *Face the Nation*. Candidates can now circumvent
the national political reporters by appearing on talk shows, local news
via satellite hookups, morning news shows, and other outlets. And if a
candidate has a personal fortune, the paid media become a path to the
voters. Perot's infomercials certainly elevated the level and content of
political advertising, especially his scholarly presentations about the
budget deficit and the national debt, replete with charts and graphs. At
the end of this chapter we speculate about Perot's future. But certainly
Perot's success may encourage others to emulate his efforts.

Characteristics of Perot Voters

One of the interesting features of Perot voters is that they were not distinctive with respect to many of the standard demographic and attitudinal variables traditionally used to analyze voting behavior. For example, according to the Voter Research and Surveys (VRS) exit poll of
the 1992 election, gender, marital status, education, income, union
membership, religion, employment status, and region had little relationship to the likelihood of voting for Perot. Women, Jews, and southerners were less likely than men, non-Jews, and nonsoutherners to vote for
Perot, but overall the differences were not large. Only with respect to

race were the differences dramatic; 7 percent of blacks supported Perot, compared to 20 percent of whites.

Likewise, there were scant differences in Perot support across categories of ideological self-identification. According to the VRS exit poll, 18 percent of liberals, 21 percent of moderates, and 17 percent of conservatives supported Perot. Only when we examine citizens' political party loyalties do sharp differences in Perot support emerge. According to the VRS data, 17 percent of Republicans and 13 percent of Democrats supported Perot, compared to 30 percent of independents. The NES data enable a more detailed examination of the relationship between citizens' party loyalties and their votes. The NES survey asked Americans whether they considered themselves to be Democrats, Republicans, or independents. If respondents replied Democrat or Republican, they were next asked if they thought of themselves as strong or not very strong (weak) Democrats or Republicans. If respondents first answered independent, they were then asked whether they leaned toward one party or the other. The responses to these items generated the seven-category classification of party identification shown in table 6.2, ranging from strong Democrat at one end to strong Republican at the other.

Each cell in table 6.2 contains two entries—the row percentage on top and the column percentage beneath it. Table 6.2 enables us to ex-

TABLE 6.2
THE RELATIONSHIP BETWEEN VOTE CHOICE
AND PARTY IDENTIFICATION

	Party identification						
Vote	Strong Dem	Weak Dem	Ind Dem	Ind	Ind Rep	Weak Rep	Strong Rep
Bush	1.8	6.9	2.5	5.7	22.5	27.0	33.6
	3.1	13.4	6.1	22.2	61.9	60.1	86.9
Clinton	38.7	25.3	20.3	7.4	2.8	4.8	.6
	92.8	68.5	70.6	40.8	10.8	14.9	2.3
Perot	4.3	16.7	16.8	16.9	17.8	20.1	7.5
	4.1	18.1	23.3	37.0	27.3	25.0	10.8

SOURCE: 1992 National Election Study.

NOTE: For each pair of entries in the table, the top entry is a row percentage and the bottom entry a column percentage. That is, the top entries in each row sum to 100 percent. Likewise, the bottom entries in each column sum to 100 percent. Thus, the 1.8 in the upper left cell indicates that of the total Bush vote, 1.8 percent came from strong Democrats. Likewise, the 3.1 in the upper left cell indicates that of the strong Democrats in the survey, 3.1 percent voted for Bush.

amine two questions: how people with different partisan preferences voted (based on the column percentages); and the partisan sources of support for Bush, Clinton, and Perot (based on the row percentages). Note that Perot ran strongest among independents, from whom he received 37 percent of the vote compared to 40.8 percent for Clinton and only 22.2 percent for Bush. In contrast, Perot ran weakest among strong Democrats and strong Republicans, where he received only 4.1 percent and 10.8 percent of the vote respectively. Table 6.2 clearly shows that citizens with strong political party ties were less susceptible to the appeal of the Perot candidacy. One interesting sidelight of 1992 was that Democrats were more loyal to the Clinton candidacy than Republicans were to the Bush candidacy, a pattern opposite the one witnessed in most presidential elections, wherein Republicans tend to be more "loyal" party voters than are Democrats. For example, table 6.2 indicates that fully 92.8 percent of the strong Democrats voted for Clinton, compared to the 86.9 percent support that Bush received from strong Republicans.

An examination of the row percentages in table 6.2 shows that Perot's vote coalition was much more heavily independent in its composition than the coalitions that supported Bush and Clinton. Of Perot's total vote, 16.9 percent came from pure independents, compared to only 5.7 percent and 7.4 percent for Bush and Clinton respectively. And when one combines the independent leaners with the pure independents, more than half of Perot's support (16.8 + 16.9 + 17.8) came from respondents who initially called themselves independents. This contrasts with the Bush and Clinton support coalitions, where about 30 percent of total support came from respondents in one of the three independent categories. Thus, the Perot support coalition consisted heavily of voters with weaker ties to the two major political parties, voters who were younger and more likely to be independents. Indeed, age and partisan strength are strongly related in that younger voters are much more likely to be independents than their older compatriots. Thus Perot ran strongest among young voters. According to the NES data, Perot received 27.7 percent of the vote from those between the ages of eighteen and thirty, but only 10.9 percent from voters sixty-five and older.

When we turn to domestic and international issues, we find little relationship between issue position and support for Perot. The VRS data show that, with respect to family financial situation, Perot did better (winning 25 percent of the vote) among respondents who felt worse off than among those who felt better off (where he got 14 percent of the vote). But even here, economic situation differentiated support for Bush versus Clinton much more. For example, those who felt worse off economically supported Clinton over Bush by a margin of 61 percent to 14 percent, while the much smaller number who felt better off supported Bush over Clinton by a margin of 62 percent to 24 percent. Those voters who felt that their economic future had not changed voted 41 percent for Clinton, 41 percent for Bush, and 18 percent for Perot.

The NES data permit us to examine in greater breadth and depth how economic issues and other policy matters affected the Perot vote. By and large, the message is the same: Perot supporters were not characterized by distinctive positions on many issues. Indeed, on many issues, respondents who took one side of the issue were as likely to support Perot as those who took a very different stance on that issue. The Democrats tried to make the 1992 election a referendum on the state of the economy, while the Republicans emphasized issues such as the role of government and Clinton's liberal ideology as well as the importance of traditional lifestyle and social values. Positions on all these issues differentiated Bush and Clinton voters, but they had little impact on support for Perot.

The NES survey included many measures of voters' perceptions of the performance of the economy and, in general, the more satisfied the respondents were, the more likely they were to vote for Bush, and the more dissatisfied, the more likely they were to support Clinton. But assessments of economic performance had little impact on support for Perot. For example, those whose own economic situation had gotten worse were almost equally likely to support Perot as those whose situation had improved—21 versus 20 percent. But for Clinton and Bush, there were sharp differences; those who thought their economic situation had gotten worse cast 57 percent of their votes for Clinton and 21 percent for Bush, while those whose finances had improved voted for Bush over Clinton by a margin of 43 percent to 37 percent.

With respect to the national economy, 19 percent of respondents who believed it had gotten worse supported Perot compared to 13 percent support for Perot among those who thought the economy had gotten better, a relatively small difference. But for Bush and Clinton, the differences were striking. Seventy-five percent of those who thought the economy had gotten better supported Bush, compared to only 26 percent support among those who thought it had gotten worse. Likewise, only 12 percent of those who believed the economy had improved backed Clinton, compared to 55 percent support among those who felt the economy had weakened. This pattern is repeated over and over again with other indicators of economic performance, including unemployment and inflation. Overall, voters' perceptions about the health of the economy were very much related to their support for Clinton versus Bush but had little impact on their support for Perot.

As discussed earlier in this chapter, respondents' ideological self-identification had little systematic impact on their likelihood of voting for Perot. The NES data enable us to develop this point in greater detail. Voters were asked how they viewed the presidential candidates ideologically; the responses showed much greater agreement as to where Bush and Clinton stood than Perot. Seventy-three percent saw Bush as conservative and only 13 percent as liberal. Likewise, 67 percent of respondents saw Clinton as liberal and only 12 percent as conservative. But for Perot, perceptions were less consistent; 47 percent saw Perot as a conservative, 28 percent as a liberal, and 25 percent as a moderate. Specific items about the role of the government in the economy differentiated among Bush and Clinton voters, but not among Perot voters. For example, 23 percent of respondents who said less government was better supported Perot, compared to 16 percent support among those who wanted government to do more, a difference of only 7 percent. In contrast, Bush received 52 percent of the vote from those who believed less government was better, compared to only 22 percent from those who wanted government to do more; for Clinton, the comparable figures were 25 percent and 62 percent. A similar pattern holds for a related item dealing with the government's role in the economy; there were scant differences in support for Perot whether voters advocated a strong role for government versus a free market economy, while there were huge differences in support for Clinton and Bush.

Finally, the NES data not only measured the direction of respondents' ideology, but also its strength. If we compare the voting behavior of extreme liberals and extreme conservatives, we find no difference in their support for Perot; both groups gave Perot about 18 percent of their vote. But we do find sharp differences with respect to support for Clinton and Bush; 82 percent of extreme liberals supported Clinton, while only 23 percent of extreme conservatives did so. Likewise, 58 percent of extreme conservatives supported Bush, while none of the extreme liberals did so. What all these numbers say is that Perot's support was not closely linked to voters' ideological positions and their views about the role of government. Part of the reason for this was lack of clarity and agreement as to just where Perot stood along traditional ideological cleavages defined by the proper role of the government in the economy. More respondents saw Perot as a conservative than a liberal, yet it was Perot who was calling for a substantial tax increase, a position more often linked politically with liberals than with conservatives. At the same time, Perot's major emphasis was on cutting the deficit, a stance more often seen as conservative. The point is that traditional ideological labels do not help in accounting for support or nonsupport of Perot.[1]

Certainly another focal point of the 1992 campaign was the emphasis on traditional values and their decline. Once again, we find that opinions on these matters differentiate Bush and Clinton voters, but have little impact on Perot support. For example, the NES survey presented voters with a number of statements to which they could agree or disagree. Three such items follow:

1. "We should be more tolerant of people who choose to live according to their own moral standards even if they are very different from our own."
2. "This country would have many fewer problems if there were more emphasis on traditional family ties."
3. "The newer lifestyles are contributing to the breakdown of our society."

On these three items (and others), a respondent's agreement or disagreement with the statement had little relationship to support for Perot. For example, 18 percent of those who agreed with the third item supported Perot, compared to 17 percent support from those who disagreed with the statement. But for Bush and Clinton there were sharp differences. Forty-two percent of those who agreed with the third item voted for Bush, compared to only 14 percent who disagreed; the comparable percentages for Clinton were 40 and 69.

The NES survey also included a set of questions on gay-related issues:

1. "Do you favor or oppose laws to protect homosexuals against job discrimination?"
2. "Do you think homosexuals should be allowed to serve in the United States Armed Forces or don't you think so?"
3. "Do you think gay or lesbian couples, in other words, homosexual couples, should be legally permitted to adopt children?"

One can construct an index based on these three items and identify respondents who are most and least supportive of gay rights. Once again, there is no relationship to support for Perot; 17 percent of those most sympathetic toward gay issues supported Perot and 17 percent of those most negative also supported Perot. But for Clinton and Bush, there were substantial differences in support. Seventy-one percent of the most supportive respondents voted for Clinton and only 26 percent of the least supportive did so, while for Bush the comparable figures were 13 and 57 percent.

Similar patterns hold for other issues. For example, comparing the polar extreme options on the issue of abortion—never permit abortion versus always allow the woman's choice—shows that abortion opinion is more closely tied to support for Bush and Clinton than to support for Perot. Thirteen percent of those who favored no abortions supported Perot, compared to 21 percent support from respondents who said abortion is the woman's choice, a difference of 8 percent. In contrast, Bush received 49 percent of the vote of those opposed to all abortions and only 21 percent from respondents who favored the woman's choice in all situations, while Clinton won 39 percent of the vote from the former group and 57 percent from the latter. Comparing the polar extreme positions on the issue of urban unrest—use all available force to curb urban unrest versus cure the underlying social ills—once again shows stronger linkages to the Clinton and Bush votes than to the Perot vote.

Thus far, we have shown that most demographic and many issue variables do not explain why citizens chose to vote or not vote for Perot. The only variable strongly related to the likelihood of supporting Perot is party identification; independents are much more supportive of Perot than are voters who have strong attachments to the Democratic or Republican parties. There are other political dispositions that are somewhat linked to the Perot vote, although the patterns are not dramatic. Overall, Perot ran stronger among those who were more cynical and distrustful of government, who were less convinced of the responsiveness of government, and who were less integrated into the political party system (younger and less partisan voters). For example, Perot ran stronger among those who believed the government wasted a lot of tax money and who never trusted the government to do the right thing. Perot also ran stronger among those who were very dissatisfied with the candidate choices available to them and who cared about the outcome of the election. Thus, one gets a sense of Perot voters being driven by frustration with the political system and the candidates and parties who dominate that system. In summary, Perot's vote can be seen as grounded more in a generalized disdain for politics and a distrust for politicians than in any specific public policy issue or set of issues. But while there may have been a protest component to the Perot vote, the key question becomes whether we can really explain support for Perot in any thorough and systematic way. This is the task of the next section.

A Multivariate Model of Support for Perot

In the previous section we examined sequentially how a number of variables affected the Perot vote. In this section we want to examine the impact of many factors simultaneously by moving to a multivariate analysis. Thus we construct and test a multivariate model of support for Perot where support is measured by thermometer evaluations that respondents gave to Perot rather than simple vote choice. The thermometer ratings rely on the analogy to a thermometer used to measure a person's temperature. A rating scale ranging from 0 to 100 is used where 100 represents the warmest (most positive) evaluation and 0 represents the coldest (most negative) assessment. Thus the thermometer evaluations provide for more refined assessments of Perot than does simple vote choice. I apply the same model to evaluations of Clinton and Bush to see whether citizens employ the same factors to rate all three candidates. If it turns out that our models can explain Bush and Clinton assessments fairly well but not Perot assessments, this will be important evidence attesting to the uniqueness of the Perot phenomenon and his basis of support and will have implications for Perot's future prospects.

I do not claim that the models to be tested are fully specified and include all relevant variables and exclude all irrelevant ones. But the models do include a range of demographic, issue, and attitudinal variables that one can plausibly link to vote choice in the 1992 election. The first model tested can be considered the "kitchen sink" model because it includes all our variables, including partisanship measures, ideological distance (proximity) measures, issue variables, demographic attributes, and items about the characteristics of Bush and Clinton (comparable items were not available for Perot). One could argue that this initial model is unfair to Perot because it includes partisan measures and Perot is not a member of a political party; hence we would expect the model to do a better job accounting for evaluations of the two political party candidates, Bush and Clinton. This "bias" in the model is further exacerbated by the inclusion of measures that tap attitudes toward Bush and Clinton; surely these measures will result in a better explanation of Bush and Clinton thermometer ratings than of those for Perot. Hence, the strategy of our analysis is to sequentially remove variables that "advantage" Bush and Clinton, ending up with a model that is not likely to be biased from the outset to do a better job of accounting for Bush and Clinton assessments. If, at the end of this process, we still find that we do a poorer job explaining why people liked or disliked Perot, this will strongly suggest that the bases for opinions about Perot lie beyond many of our standard explanations of voting behavior.

The explanatory power of the various models is summarized by the adjusted R^2 statistic, often referred to as the fraction of explained variance. The larger the R^2, the better we have accounted for the evaluations of the candidates. Note in table 6.3 that we do a much better job explaining assessments of Bush and Clinton than of Perot across all our models. In the first model, this is in part a methodological artifact (as discussed above) because the model includes partisan measures as well as indicators assessing the major-party candidates. Yet the model also includes many other measures (a total of thirty-nine) tapping demographic attributes, political dispositions, and issue stances, but it only accounts for 14.7 percent of the variance in Perot ratings, compared to 67.4 and 59.1 percent for Bush and Clinton.

In the second model we remove variables that directly measure views about Bush and Clinton—a Bush performance approval measure and an index of candidate characteristics for Bush and for Clinton. As expected, the removal of these items (which on their face seem very closely linked to a thermometer rating) lowers the explained variance for Bush and Clinton, but scarcely affects the R^2 for Perot. The third model removes three more variables—measures of the perceived ideological proximity between citizens and each of the three presidential

TABLE 6.3
THE EXPLAINED VARIANCE IN THERMOMETER RATINGS
OF BUSH, CLINTON, AND PEROT
BASED ON FOUR MODELS

	Bush	Clinton	Perot	Number of predictors
Model 1 (Complete model)	67.4	59.1	14.7	39
Model 2 (Model 1 minus Bush approval and a Bush and a Clinton trait assessment)	49.7	49.0	14.5	36
Model 3 (Model 2 minus three ideological proximity measures)	44.9	43.8	4.7	33
Model 4 (Model 3 minus party identification and strength of partisanship)	36.2	32.4	3.9	31

NOTE: Table entries are the percentage of explained variance—the adjusted R^2—for each of the explanatory models for each of the candidates.

candidates—and, as expected, the fraction of explained variance for all three candidates goes down. Finally, in the last model, party identification and strength of partisanship are also removed. Since Bush and Clinton are major-party candidates whose evaluations are likely to be colored by voters' own party preferences, the elimination of party identification should lower the explained variance in Clinton and Bush ratings, and that is indeed what happens. Likewise, since Perot was more popular among citizens without a partisan allegiance, the elimination of strength of partisanship should and does result in lessening our ability to explain assessments of Perot.

What remains in the fourth model is an explanatory structure that largely focuses on issues and demographic variables. The respondent's own ideological position is still included in the model, but measures of partisanship and specific candidate characteristics are no longer included. Hence this model becomes interesting because it is less biased in favor of the major-party candidates. Indeed, in some ways it is biased in favor of Perot because it includes two measures of respondents' perceptions of whether the major parties differ on issues as well as a general candidate satisfaction measure. One might intuitively expect that voters who cannot see differences between the parties and who are dissatisfied with the candidate choices would be more positive toward Perot, while it is not clear that those who can see differences between the parties should be more positive to Clinton or to Bush.

Whether or not this last model is stacked in favor of Perot, the key point is that this model, with thirty-one issue and demographic variables, can account for only 3.9 percent of the variance in Perot evaluations, compared to more than 36 and 32 percent for Bush and Clinton. A fuller understanding of this model is provided by examining the variables that achieve statistical significance (at the .05 level) for each candidate evaluation. These are listed in rank order in table 6.4.

First note that twelve variables reached significance in the Bush explanation, fourteen for Clinton, and only five for Perot. For Bush and Clinton, a respondent's own ideological stance was the top predictor; it did not even achieve significance in the Perot evaluation. More important, items dealing with the direction in which the country was moving, national economic conditions, and personal financial situation were all important in accounting for Bush and Clinton evaluations, although more so for the former. This strongly suggests that central to the 1992 election was a retrospective judgment on the economic performance of the Bush administration, a judgment that was largely negative. Voters who were unhappy about their own and the country's condition were more hostile to Bush. These same voters were more favorable toward

TABLE 6.4
THE STATISTICALLY SIGNIFICANT VARIABLES
IN EVALUATIONS OF BUSH, CLINTON,
AND PEROT IN MODEL 4

	Bush	Clinton	Perot
1.	ideology	ideology	age
2.	direction of country	candidate satisfaction	political knowledge
3.	national economic conditions	gay issues index	political interest
4.	gay issues index	party differences	gender
5.	race	direction of country	party differences
6.	personal economic situation	gov't. too powerful	—
7.	black issues index	age	—
8.	religiosity	income	—
9.	candidate satisfaction	black issues index	—
10.	cynicism	education	—
11.	efficacy	race	—
12.	party differences	national economic conditions	—
13.	—	personal economic conditions	—
14.	—	women's issues index	—

NOTE: The table lists the variables that achieved statistical significance in the equations for Bush, Clinton, and Perot evaluations respectively. The variables are listed in rank order, determined by the magnitude of the standardized regression coefficient in each equation.

Clinton, in part because they believed he could better deliver a brighter economic future. But none of the measures of economic conditions were important in explaining attitudes toward Perot.

In a similar pattern, race and attitudes about gay issues and black issues all achieved significance in predicting to Bush and Clinton evaluations, but not so for Perot. White respondents and those less supportive of gay and black issues were more favorable toward Bush than were blacks and those more supportive of gay and black issues. Likewise, black respondents and those more sympathetic toward gay and black (as well as women's) issues were more favorable toward Clinton. Income and education were statistically significant predictors of Clinton evaluations; respondents of lower income and education were more positive toward Clinton. Religiosity, cynicism, and efficacy all were significant predictors of assessments of Bush; more religious, more efficacious, and less cynical respondents were more supportive of Bush.

Thus, little of direct issue relevance affected evaluations of Perot. The most important predictor was age, but only because it is confounded with political independence as younger voters are less partisan and more favorable toward Perot. Next in importance were political knowledge and interest. More knowledgeable citizens were less favorable to Perot; more interested citizens were more favorable. Men liked Perot more than women did. And those who were less likely to see differences between the two major parties on a set of issues were more positive toward Perot. But overall we have been unable to uncover any systematic foundation underpinning evaluations of Perot. Age as a surrogate for weak political party ties and the belief that there are no major differences between the parties once again suggest that Perot's support was in large part a function of how integrated voters were into the political system and the party system. Although political cynicism did not turn out to be significant in explaining evaluations of Perot, one gets the sense from the various analyses conducted thus far that Perot's support came from citizens who were angry and frustrated with the performance of the political system, particularly with its processes and perhaps with its outcomes. The fact that we could find little issue basis to support for Perot may indicate that appeals to "clean up the mess in Washington" may have moved Perot supporters more than any specific policy proposals. Certainly, Perot himself seemed to understand this. With the exception of the deficit and some specific proposals dealing with taxes and spending cuts, Perot often fell back on assertions about process—getting the best minds together, sitting down and knocking some heads together, getting the lobbyists out of the room, using common sense, ending the gridlock and stalemate, and so on. Indeed, should a future Perot candidacy get very specific on issues, it may run the risk of driving away supporters.[2]

Perot's Effect on the Clinton and Bush Candidacies

An obvious question that emerges from a three-candidate presidential contest is how the third candidate affected the fortunes of the two major-party nominees. That is, did Perot hurt Clinton's or Bush's prospects more? This seems like a very straightforward question, yet a definitive answer is impossible. We can look at voters' preferences among the three candidates as well as their statements about who they would have voted for had Perot not been in the race. But one source of indeterminacy is that we can never rerun the presidential contest without Perot as a presidential candidate. His very presence in the contest may have changed its dynamics in fundamental ways. For example, in April through June of 1992, Perot's successes knocked the Clinton candidacy out of the media spotlight. In hindsight, this may have benefited the Clinton campaign because it gave Clinton the opportunity to reemerge at the Democratic convention in terms that he could largely define and control. Another difficulty arises because the presidential contest is essentially a fifty-state Electoral College contest. Even if we could assess Perot's effect on the popular vote, we would encounter problems in determining whether Perot's presence altered the outcome in any of the fifty states. For example, in all states except Arkansas, Maryland, Mississippi, and New York (and the District of Columbia), Perot's share of the popular vote far exceeded the margin of difference between Clinton and Bush.

Nevertheless, there are a number of ways to get a handle on Perot's support and its effect on the fortunes of Clinton and Bush. A very simple approach is simply to compare the aggregate popular vote in 1988 and 1992. In 1988, Bush received about 54 percent of the two-party vote and Dukakis 46 percent. In 1992, Bush received 37.7 percent of the three-candidate vote, Clinton 43.3 percent, and Perot 19 percent. Thus the victorious Clinton got a smaller share of the vote than did the loser Dukakis four years earlier. But the major decline was the share of the vote won by Bush, which plummeted by more than 16 percent. These numbers seem to suggest that Perot profited heavily at Bush's expense, but aggregate totals mask some important patterns.

A more direct examination of voter movements between 1988 and 1992 would be provided by panel data that are not available. Instead, using the NES data, one can compare respondents' reports of their 1992 presidential votes with their recall of their 1988 votes, recognizing that recall information may have problems of faulty memory and distortion. Table 6.5 shows that Perot received a higher share of the vote from 1988 Bush voters than he did from 1988 Dukakis voters; almost 22 percent of Bush voters in 1988 voted for Perot in 1992, compared to about 12 percent of Dukakis voters who went for Perot.

While table 6.5 shows that Perot attracted greater support from former Bush voters than from Dukakis supporters, it does not tell us how these Perot supporters would have voted had Perot not been in the race in 1992. In order to gain some insight into what Perot voters would have done had Perot not been in the race, we need to ascertain the preference orderings for the three candidates among Perot support-

TABLE 6.5
CITIZENS' 1988 AND 1992 PRESIDENTIAL VOTES

	1988 vote	
1992 vote	Dukakis	Bush
Bush	5.5	53.9
Clinton	82.7	24.3
Perot	11.8	21.8
Total %	100	100
N	(480)	(759)

SOURCE: 1992 National Election Study.

NOTE: Respondents were asked how they voted in 1992 and asked to recall how they voted in 1988.

ers. That is, we need to know who were the second- and third-choice presidential candidates for Perot voters. Two sets of items in the NES survey help us do this. The first asks respondents whether they ever considered a vote choice other than their final election day selection. The other items are thermometer ratings of Clinton, Bush, and Perot. With these thermometer ratings, one can establish a preference ordering among the three candidates for the entire sample as well as for subsets of the sample determined by vote choice.

For Bush and Clinton supporters, 59 and 56 percent respectively said they never considered voting for another candidate. But for Perot backers, 79 percent said that they had considered voting for another candidate. Of this group of Perot voters, 45 percent said they had once considered a Clinton vote, while 46 percent cited a Bush preference. Hence it appears that the Perot voters had been equally predisposed to Clinton and Bush at some time during the campaign. This result corresponds closely with the finding of the 1992 exit poll that approximately 38 percent of Perot supporters said they would have voted for Clinton and 38 percent said they would have voted for Bush had Ross Perot not been in the race. Thus, with respect to the national popular vote, it appears that Perot did not harm one candidate more than the other, although this still leaves open the possibility that his impact was more differential within particular states.

The thermometer ratings respondents gave to the three presidential candidates provide one last test of the impact of the Perot candidacy. The thermometer rankings allow us to examine the second and third choices of all respondents as well as the preference orderings of supporters of particular candidates. Moreover, the thermometer evaluations enable us to investigate how many voters felt warmest toward Perot, but failed to vote for him, perhaps because they feared wasting their votes. An examination of candidate assessments given by Perot voters reveals some interesting patterns. First, almost 12 percent of Perot voters evaluated Bush most warmly, while another 7 percent of Perot voters gave their highest evaluations to Clinton. Among the Perot voters who rated Perot most highly on the thermometer measures, 34 percent rated Bush over Clinton, 47 percent evaluated Clinton over Bush, and 19 percent gave identical ratings to Clinton and Bush. Thus it does not seem that Perot's voters would have gone heavily for a particular candidate had Perot not been in the race.

The thermometer assessments do indicate that Perot was not as successful as Clinton and Bush in actually winning votes from citizens who gave the warmest evaluations to a particular candidate. Table 6.6 shows the relationship between respondents' thermometer evaluations and their vote choices. Almost 93 percent of those who rated Bush most highly actually voted for him; likewise, 95 percent of those who evaluated Clinton most positively voted for him. But for Perot, only 76 percent of respondents who assessed him most favorably actually voted for him, with the rest of his supporters (as measured by the thermometer ratings) splitting fairly evenly between Bush and Clinton. This may be evidence, albeit indirect, that some citizens who liked Perot the most could not bring themselves to vote for him, perhaps because they feared wasting their votes.

In summary, it is difficult to show that Perot affected the vote outcome in any way that strongly helped Clinton or Bush. Perot's presence

TABLE 6.6
THE RELATIONSHIP BETWEEN PREFERRED CANDIDATES
AS MEASURED BY THERMOMETER RATING
AND ACTUAL VOTE CHOICE

	Thermometer-based first choice		
Actual vote	Bush	Clinton	Perot
Bush	92.8	2.3	10.1
Clinton	1.4	95.0	13.6
Perot	5.8	2.6	76.4
Total %	100	99.9	100
N	(485)	(685)	(258)

SOURCE: 1992 National Election Study.

in the race certainly changed the dynamics of the campaign, but it did not seem to affect the distribution of voter preferences. But, as mentioned earlier, one will never be able to ascertain how the Clinton-Bush contest would have differed had Perot not been in the race. Although early speculation focused on Perot splitting the anti-Bush, "change vote" with Clinton, thereby helping the president in his reelection bid, the available evidence suggests that Perot did not disproportionately take votes away from Clinton.

Conclusion

Perot has not faded into oblivion since the 1992 election. Instead he has maintained a high profile, being very vocal and active on such issues as NAFTA (the North American Free Trade Agreement) and the federal deficit. There is widespread speculation about his potential presidential aspirations in 1996. Because of strong GOP support for NAFTA, Perot became the focal point of opposition to the president and the pact, often appearing with Democratic members of Congress who were opposing President Clinton on this issue. Perot also was active in the health-care-reform debate of 1994. And he is moving to establish a United We Stand America organization in all fifty states. Toward the end of the 1994 campaigns, he issued a blanket endorsement of Republican candidates for Congress even as he supported Democrat Ann Richards in her unsuccessful bid for reelection as governor of Texas. There is already rampant speculation about Perot's role in 1996. Will he run again as an independent, or will he create a formal third party that will contest not only the presidency but also congressional seats? Or will he try to capture the GOP nomination?

Although Perot will certainly be able to command media coverage in the future, some of the results of this chapter suggest that his efforts to move from a surprisingly strong third-place finisher in 1992 to a major presidential candidate in 1996 may encounter some roadblocks. Some of these roadblocks are suggested by the results presented earlier. The fact that Perot's support base is so amorphous is both an advantage and a disadvantage to him. As long as Perot can focus on generalized discontent and attacks on the political process, he may be able to win support from very disparate individuals and groups. But as soon as he has to become more specific about a whole set of issues and policy concerns, some of his supporters may drift away as they recognize that they do not share his views on issues important to them. Perot's prospects for creating a successful new political party are diminished by the fact that, as our results show, in 1992 he did not enjoy any natural regional or demographic base as previous nontraditional candidacies had, nor did he have a particular issue or cluster of issues to mobilize his disparate followers.

Moreover, by late 1994, Perot himself seemed to have lost some of his luster, although one should not put too much weight on any particular slice of public opinion. Certainly NAFTA and, particularly, the debate with Vice-President Gore did little to enhance Perot's political and personal standing. But even here, should the economy be bad in 1996 and finger pointing the order of the day, Perot will be best positioned to blame the economic distress on the folly of NAFTA and to cite his own leadership in opposing the pact. Nevertheless, a poll sponsored by *U.S. News & World Report* in late November–early December 1993 showed that Perot's support had declined sharply since the previous May (Borger and Buckley, 20 December 1993). For example, 31 percent of respondents viewed Perot as a strong leader in the later poll compared to 62 percent back in May. Fifty percent now said that he was all talk compared to 27 percent seven months earlier. Overall, 55 percent viewed Perot unfavorably, compared to only 26 percent who were negative toward him back in May.

As Borger and Buckley argue, however, it would be premature to write off Perot. Indeed, the Perot organization United We Stand America played an active role in special elections for the House of Representatives in 1994. One item in the poll combines issues with attitudes about Perot and finds that many Americans like the issues Perot addresses even if they do not like Perot. For example, 13 percent of survey respondents said they like the issues Perot addresses and believe he would make a good president, while 60 percent like the issues, but have doubts about whether he would make a good president. It is clear that Perot's future success will be a function of Clinton's success, the behavior of Congress, and the performance of the economy. A weak economy with a scandal-ridden Congress and a discredited president would provide a promising scenario for Perot's success. The Republican capture of Congress in 1994 may give Perot the opportunity in 1996 to argue that both parties have had their chance to clean up the mess in Washington and both have failed; therefore, it is time for a new, third alternative. Likewise, a strong economy, with a "reformed" Congress, a reformed campaign financing system, and a popular president may undercut any opportunities that Perot might have. But as long as Perot has media access and personal wealth, as well as a political and economic system perceived as not working in the interests of the common person, his prospects or the prospects of the next Ross Perot should never be underestimated.

Acknowledgments

I would like to thank Mike Barr for his skillful assistance in data analysis.

Notes

1. In the multivariate analysis section later in this chapter, we construct measures of the ideological proximity between voters and the candidates. These measures are based on where voters stand ideologically and where they perceive the candidates to stand. Such measures enhance the likelihood that ideology will be important in explaining assessments of the candidates, especially for contestants such as Perot who are seen by different voters as ranging widely over the ideological spectrum. Indeed, our multivariate analysis shows that while voters' own ideological stances do not predict assessments of Perot, their perceived closeness to Perot does help account for their evaluations of him.

2. If one examines Model 1 in which the explained variance for Perot is 14.7 percent, one finds nine variables that achieved statistical significance, the five listed in table 6.4 as well as strength of partisanship, race, ideological proximity to Perot, and candidate satisfaction. Ideological proximity is the most important predictor, and its removal accounts for most of the decrease in explained variance between Models 1 and 3. The key point still holds, however: there are few issue variables that are related to evaluations of Perot.

PART II

Group Voting in 1992

CHAPTER 7

Structural Dependence or Group Loyalty? The Black Vote in 1992

KATHERINE TATE

> A correlation between the fact of being Negro and the casting of a Democratic ballot gives us interesting information, yet information pitched at a low level of abstraction.
> — Campbell, Converse, Miller, and Stokes, *The American Voter*

Since 1964, blacks have remained solidly Democratic in their voting preference, and 1992 proved to be no different. Taking a somewhat smaller share of the black vote than Michael Dukakis, who won 89 percent in 1988, Democratic challenger Bill Clinton still netted 83 percent of the black vote, according to the exit polls conducted by Voter Research and Surveys (VRS). Incumbent President George Bush received 10 percent of the black vote, just one percentage point short of what he earned in 1988. And while H. Ross Perot won 19 percent of the popular vote, he obtained only 7 percent of the black vote.[1] The black vote in 1992 confirms what has been shown for past three-way presidential races, namely that blacks represent the one voting bloc that has remained consistently loyal to one of the two major parties (Rosenstone, Behr, and Lazarus 1984, 179). In an era of increasing voter indifference to the major parties (Wattenberg 1986), blacks' continued loyalty to the Democratic Party remains all the more remarkable.

To conclude, however, that Clinton won the lion's share of the black vote because most blacks are Democrats is to tell only part of the story. Although partisans can be generally counted on to vote for their party's nominee in a given election, this is not always the case in American elections. Party defections and split-ticket voting are, in fact, what make American elections interesting. Unlike many other social and political groups, blacks generally do not cross party lines. In fact, in the past five presidential elections, blacks have voted more consistently Democratic than all other voters who claim to be Democrats (see table 7.1). What accounts for blacks' extraordinary allegiance to the Democratic Party?

In general, analysts of black voting behavior have presented two different accounts for the consistent pro-Democratic character of the black vote today. Several scholars of black politics claim that *structural dependence* on the Democratic Party explains blacks' strong record of party loyalty (Pinderhughes 1986; Walters 1988; Walton 1990). To un-

TABLE 7.1
PERCENTAGE OF DEMOCRATIC VOTE IN PRESIDENTIAL ELECTIONS, 1976–92, BY KEY SOCIAL AND POLITICAL GROUPS

	1976: Carter/ Mondale	1980: Carter/ Mondale	1984: Mondale/ Ferraro	1988: Dukakis/ Bentsen	1992: Clinton/ Gore
National	50	41	41	45	43
Black	83	83	91	89	83
Democratic	80	67	74	83	77
Republican	11	11	7	8	10
Independent	48	31	36	43	38
Liberal	74	60	71	82	68
Moderate	53	43	46	51	47
Conservative	30	23	18	19	18
Men	52	38	38	42	41
Women	52	46	42	49	45
White	48	36	34	40	39
Hispanic	82	56	66	70	61
Asian	n.a.	n.a.	n.a.	n.a.	31
Union	62	48	54	57	55

SOURCE: As reported in *The American Enterprise*, January/February 1993, 90–91. Exit polling conducted by CBS News/*New York Times* of 15,199 voters in 1976; CBS News/*New York Times* of 12,782 voters in 1980; CBS News/*New York Times* of 8,671 voters in 1984; CBS News/*New York Times* of 11,645 voters in 1988; and Voter Research and Surveys of 15,490 voters in 1992.

derstand their high level of support for the Democratic Party, one must recognize blacks' position as a cohesive political minority whose options are less than they would be in a multiparty system. Blacks' ideological liberalism greatly limits their political choices. Liberalism is often defined as support for government intervention in the economy to promote individual and group welfare, which most blacks favor, and most whites do not. For example, whereas one-quarter of all white Americans expressed support for the idea that government should guarantee all Americans jobs and a minimum standard of living in a 1988 national survey, nearly 60 percent of African Americans favored the idea.[2] In a two-party system in which blacks are ideologically to the left of both parties, blacks would gain politically little by strategically relocating to the right (Pinderhughes 1986). Thus political independence, or moving to the center of the two major parties, is not an option for a group as politically liberal as blacks.

A second option of third-party formation, while possible, is also of limited utility for blacks because the American party system works against the emergence of third parties. Moreover, third-party candidates rarely possess the financial resources to compete effectively against major-party candidates (Rosenstone, Behr, and Lazarus 1984). Given their liberalism and the structure of the American two-party system, blacks therefore are "structurally dependent" on the Democratic Party. Other than voting Democratic, blacks can still withhold their votes. Rational-voter theories, in fact, assert that when no candidate is favored, the optimal strategy is not to cast a vote (Downs 1957). Moreover, the collective nonparticipation of a politically cohesive group can serve to remind the party of the power of the group's voting strength as a bloc. In this scenario, blacks deny their vote to the party's nominee by staying home on election day (Walters 1988).

The "structural dependence" theory of black voting behavior goes far in explaining black voting behavior in presidential politics during the 1980s. It explains why a third-party candidacy of black civil rights leader Jesse Jackson was viewed as an attractive strategy by many blacks. Jackson had twice run as a candidate for the Democratic Party's presidential nomination, in 1984 and in 1988. Although not the first African American to run for president, he was able to mobilize a much higher percentage of the black community in support of his candidacy than had past black presidential contenders, including former New York Congresswoman Shirley Chisholm, who ran in 1972. As an African American championing minority causes, Jackson was never seen as able to attain the party's nomination. Still, millions of blacks supported his bid. Winning 3.3 million votes in his 1984 bid, he doubled his primary vote in 1988 to 6.7 million, winning 29 percent of the total votes cast in the nominating contest. Most of Jackson's votes came from black Democrats, who form nearly one-quarter of the party's membership. Although he did not appear on the general ballot in either election, more than half of those interviewed in national telephone surveys of black Americans in 1984 and 1988 said that they would have voted for Jackson over the Democrat in both presidential elections (Tate 1993). And although the Democratic Party's nominee, Michael Dukakis, won nearly 90 percent of the black vote in 1988, turnout among blacks fell to a record low, especially among those who had supported Jackson during the presidential primary contest (Tate 1993). Presumably, Jackson's supporters sat out the election because they disapproved of the party's choice for president.

In contrast to the structural account of black partisanship, there is the more mainstream, social-psychological view that blacks are more intensely partisan than other social groups in American politics and the strength of their partisanship explains their consistent record of support for the Democratic Party. Implicit in this view is the theory that blacks' strong group orientation toward politics promotes their strong partisanship (Campbell et al. 1980 [1960]). Further analysis bears this out: In 1984, racial-group identification among blacks was strongly related to the direction and strength of their party identification. Strong racial identifiers were more likely to be self-identified strong Democrats (Tate 1993). Race-conscious blacks may identify more closely with the Democratic Party than weak racial identifiers because they believe that the Democrats represent blacks' collective interests best. In a national telephone survey of blacks conducted in 1984, 73 percent felt that the Democratic Party works hard on issues "black people care about," while only a quarter of the black respondents felt that the Republican Party works hard on such issues (Tate 1993, 57).

The *group loyalty* account of black partisanship can help explain blacks' electoral behavior during the 1980s as well; despite nearly a decade of growing black criticism that the party took their votes for granted, blacks nevertheless stuck by the party. While black participation fell in 1988, black identification with the Democratic Party did not. In fact, in a four-year panel study of voting-age African Americans, what little partisan movement there was among the original 1984 black respondents reinterviewed in 1988 occurred among weak and independent Democrats who now considered themselves to be strong Democrats (Tate 1993). Disappointed with the party's nominee in 1988, blacks' strong attachment to the Democratic party nevertheless did not weaken for a number of reasons. First, the general unpopularity of

Ronald Reagan in the black community strengthened blacks' ties to the Democratic Party. Reagan's assault on blacks' civil rights agenda and on social welfare programs accentuated the policy differences between the major parties, increasing, as it were, the substantive significance of being a Democrat for blacks. In this way, as Ronald Walters put it, the Reagan presidency greatly "devalued" what little remained of the Republican option for black Americans (1988, 188). Second, blacks' perceptions that national conditions and blacks' economic situations had worsened during the Reagan years increased their motivation to vote Democratic and remain aligned with the Democrats (Tate 1993). Lastly, in spite of Jackson's flirtation with the idea of a third-party challenge in 1984 and 1988, he remained loyal to the party, endorsing and campaigning for the party's nominees. Jackson's decision to stick by the party undercut any movement among the most alienated black Democrats to break away from the party altogether.

While both perspectives can easily account for the stability of the pro-Democratic voting patterns of blacks, they depict two radically different kinds of black voters. In contrast to the group loyalty account, the structural dependence version of black voting behavior implies that blacks are less a loyal constituency group within the Democratic Party than a politically restive group (Lewis and Schneider 1983), one that would bolt en masse from the party if other alternatives existed. In contrast to the structural dependence account, the group loyalty perspective implies that blacks' psychological attachment to the party remains strong and that blacks are perhaps the most loyal members of the Democratic Party. Of the two, black voting behavior in 1992 appears to lend more support to the group loyalty account. The 1992 presidential election presented more options for blacks than they had in 1988, insofar as there was a third-party candidate on the ballot. Yet the bulk of black voters chose to cast ballots for the Democratic candidate. A majority of blacks supported Bill Clinton in spite of the fact that he did not aggressively pursue their support. Campaigning as a "New Democrat," Clinton stressed that he was against the "old style liberalism" of the traditional Democratic Party, which is a major basis of blacks' support.

In an attempt to determine whether black Democratic voting was structurally or attitudinally defined, I first examine black political participation rates. Did turnout among blacks rebound, suggesting that their support for Clinton was stronger than it had been for the 1988 Democratic nominee? Second, utilizing data from the 1992 National Election Study, I examine blacks' and whites' perceptions of policy differences between the two parties. Are blacks more likely than whites to attribute major policy differences between the two parties, and could such perceptions define their partisanship and account for the continuity of the black vote?

Black Participation in the 1992 Election

Campbell, Converse, Miller, and Stokes, in *The American Voter*, were the first to present an analytical framework linking identification with the parties to the vote and to show, among other things, that strong partisans are more likely to vote than weak partisans (1980 [1960], 101). They argued that strongly attached partisans are more inclined to vote given their higher levels of campaign interest, greater concern over the election outcome, and stronger sense of political efficacy or civic duty (1980 [1960], 103). Given the uniformity and degree of blacks' partisan attachment to the Democratic Party, their rates of participation should be higher than for other groups. Black participation in primaries and presidential elections has fluctuated greatly over the past two decades, however, and among registered voters, it remains markedly lower than that of white registered voters (see table 7.2).

In 1992, although Bill Clinton received about two-thirds of the black primary vote (this despite the fact that his rival, Edmund "Jerry" Brown, Jr., had pledged to select Jesse Jackson as his running mate, if nominated), black enthusiasm for Clinton, expressed, at least, in blacks' rates of participation, was decidedly muted. Black participation in most state presidential primaries fell substantially lower in 1992 than it had

TABLE 7.2
VOTING AND REGISTRATION BY RACE IN PRESIDENTIAL ELECTIONS, 1964–92

	1964	1968	1972	1976	1980	1984	1988	1992
Percentage reported voting								
Black	58.5 [a]	57.6	52.1	48.7	50.5	55.8	51.5	54.0
White	70.7	69.1	64.5	60.9	60.9	61.4	59.1	63.6
Gap	−12.2	−11.5	−12.4	−12.2	−10.4	−5.6	−7.6	−9.6
Percentage reported registered								
Black	n.a.	66.2	65.5	58.5	60.0	66.3	64.5	63.9
White	n.a.	75.4	73.4	68.3	68.4	69.6	67.9	70.1
Gap		−9.2	−7.9	−9.8	−8.4	−3.3	−3.4	−6.2

SOURCE: *Current Population Reports*, P20-466 (November 1992), tables A and B.

a. Includes blacks and other races in 1964.

been in the 1988 and 1984 primaries, when Jackson was on the ballot. Moreover, although overall voter turnout peaked in the 1992 presidential election (see chapter 2 by Nichols and Beck), reversing a thirty-year trend of decline, voter participation among blacks did not return to its 1984 level. The 1984 presidential election remains the highwater mark of black voter turnout (see table 7.2). Thus, even while the peak turnout rate for the 1992 election might be taken as a sign that voter confidence and trust are rebounding, this is not necessarily the case for black Americans. Notably, in spite of the dramatic rate of increase in voting in 1992 from 1988, racial differences in turnout in the 1992 election increased the racial gap by two percentage points. Also, the racial gap in voter registration nearly doubled in size from −3.4 percent in 1988 to −6.2 percent in 1992. Thus, although many whites apparently returned to the voting booths in 1992, many blacks did not.

The general increase in voter participation in the 1992 election was primarily the result of increases in turnout among registrants rather than increases in voter registration. Yet black voting rebounded less dramatically than white voting both because of the decrease in black voter registration and because of the lower rates of turnout among black registrants. Since 1968, nonvoting among registrants has been substantially higher among blacks than among whites (see table 7.3). In fact, among blacks who claimed to be registered voters, 15.4 percent reported not having voted in the 1992 election. In contrast, only 9.3 percent of white registrants reported not having voted in this election. Nonvoting among black registrants was especially pronounced during the 1972 and 1988 presidential elections, as was nonvoting among white registrants during these elections. The 1972 and 1988 elections were similar in that the Democrats were organizationally weak and divided in their effort to unseat incumbent Republican presidents. But indifference among black voters to presidential politics ran particularly high in the 1988 presidential election. As shown elsewhere (Tate 1993), many blacks who failed to vote in 1988 had solidly backed Jesse Jackson in the 1988 Democratic presidential primaries and caucuses. The nonvoting among black registrants in this election, in fact, exceeded 20 percent. Nevertheless, the rate of nonvoting among black registrants in the 1992 race was consistent with past presidential elections—around 15 percent.

Although the reemerging racial gap in voter participation may signal black dissatisfaction with current developments in national politics, the high rates of nonvoting among black registrants, in particular, lend strong support to the structural dependence account of black voting behavior. There appear to be substantial minorities of blacks who are

TABLE 7.3
PERCENTAGE OF REGISTERED VOTERS WHO DID NOT
VOTE, BY RACE AND HISPANIC ORIGIN, 1968–92

	Blacks	Whites	Hispanics
1968	13.0 [a]	8.4 [a]	n.a.
1972	20.4	12.2	15.7
1976	16.7	10.8	16.7
1980	15.9	10.9	17.8
1984	15.8	11.8	18.5
1988	20.1	13.0	18.9
1992	15.4	9.3	17.5

SOURCE: Calculated from tables 1 and 2 in *Current Population Reports,* P-20, no. 192, 253, 322, 370, 405, 440, 466.

a. Number of registered voters was estimated by adding to the total number who voted those registrants who did not vote in the 1968 presidential election.

indifferent to their choices and to presidential election outcomes, and who elect not to vote on election day. Who are these "nonvoting" black voters? Although black women are more likely than black men to be registered voters (Williams 1987), as registered voters they are not more likely to turn out to vote. As shown in table 7.4, among registered voters, the black gender gap in turnout among registrants is fairly negligible (under two percentage points). Generational differences in participation rates, in fact, are more striking than gender differences. Younger blacks are less likely to vote than older blacks, and even among those registered to vote, blacks under thirty-five years of age are less likely to turn out.

Gender-generational interactions also relate strongly to the propensity to vote among black registrants. Young black male registrants, in particular, are unlikely to vote. Over 30 percent of black men 18–24 years of age reported not having voted in the 1992 presidential election, in contrast to 21 percent of black women in the same age category (see table 7.4). Black registrants over the age of thirty-four, of both genders, are more inclined to vote. Less than 13 percent of the black male and female registrants over this age failed to vote in the 1992 presidential election. Young black males are less supportive of the Democratic Party than are women and older blacks (Tate 1993). Their lower levels of attachment to the Democratic Party are expressed through their higher rates of nonparticipation.

TABLE 7.4
REGISTERED BLACK VOTERS WHO REPORTED THAT
THEY DID NOT VOTE IN THE 1992
PRESIDENTIAL ELECTION

	Males		Females	
	%	N	%	N
Total, 18 and older	16.4	5,727	14.6	7,715
18–24 years old	31.3	775	21.4	966
25–34 years old	21.4	1,283	17.3	1,824
35–54 years old	12.3	2,133	11.9	2,884
55 and older	10.6	1,533	12.9	2,041

SOURCE: *Current Population Reports,* P20-466 (November 1992), calculated from table 2.

NOTE: Total numbers of registered voters in thousands.

Black Partisanship Reexamined

The high rates of nonvoting, particularly among black registrants, suggest that a minority of blacks are indifferent to their electoral choices. Many in this group do not bother to vote because they do not care which party wins. Attitudinal data, however, paint an altogether different picture of black voters. In the 1992 National Election Study, respondents were asked which party they thought would do a better job of handling the nation's economy and foreign affairs, solving the problem of poverty, and making health care more affordable. They were also asked which party was more likely to cut social security and raise taxes. Among those respondents who named a party, near-unanimous percentages of blacks felt that the Democrats would, in general, perform better on this set of policy matters. As shown in table 7.5, 94 percent felt that the Democrats would handle the nation's economy better than the Republicans and be more likely to solve the poverty problem, and 96 percent felt that the Democrats would make health care more affordable. Blacks were somewhat less uniform in the consensus that Democrats are superior to Republicans in handling foreign relations and in not raising taxes. Twelve percent of the black respondents felt that the Democrats were more likely than the Republicans to cut social security, and nearly 40 percent felt that the Republicans would perform better than the Democrats in foreign affairs.

The majority of white respondents (about 80 percent) felt that the Democrats would perform better than the Republicans on social wel-

188 KATHERINE TATE

TABLE 7.5
PERCENTAGE OF THOSE WHO NAMED THE DEMOCRATS
AS OPPOSED TO THE REPUBLICANS ON
POLICY MATTERS, BY RACE

	Blacks		Whites	
	%	(N)	%	(N)
Which party do you think would do a better job of:				
Handling the nation's economy?	94	(203)	60	(1,149)
Handling foreign affairs?	61.5	(200)	28	(1,377)
Solving the problem of poverty?	94	(226)	80	(1,253)
Making health care more	96	(237)	80	(1,330)
affordable?	96	(237)	80	(1,330)
Which party is more likely to:				
Cut social security?	12	(192)	23	(1,011)
Raise taxes?	27	(164)	69.5	(1,124)

SOURCE: 1992 National Election Study.

NOTE: Total number of respondents appears in parentheses.

fare matters: poverty, health care, and social security. But, unlike blacks, whites were divided in their assessments of whether the Democrats or Republicans were better equipped to handle the economy and which party was more likely to raise taxes. In the area of foreign affairs, in fact, a majority of the white respondents felt that Republicans, by and large, would do a better job than the Democrats.

While an overwhelming majority of blacks were of the opinion that the Democrats perform better than the Republicans across a number of policy domains, a substantial minority nevertheless failed to see any difference between the Republicans and the Democrats on such matters. Table 7.6 shows the percentages of respondents who voluntarily stated that neither party would do a better job or who expressed no opinion on this matter by race. As the table shows, while fewer blacks than whites thought that neither party would perform better, 25 to 37 percent expressed such views. Similarly, 40 percent thought that both parties were likely to cut social security, and nearly half felt that both parties were equally likely to raise taxes. Thus, although blacks uniformly reject the Republican Party on policy matters in favor of the Democratic Party, a sizable minority felt, as did whites, that on these

TABLE 7.6
PERCENTAGE WHO SAID "NEITHER PARTY" OR HAD
NO OPINION ON POLICY MATTERS,
BY RACE

	Blacks		Whites	
	%	(N)	%	(N)
Which party do you think would do a better job of:				
Handling the nation's economy?	36	(317)	44	(2,067)
Handling foreign affairs?	37	(317)	33	(2,068)
Solving the problem of poverty?	29	(317)	39	(2,066)
Making health care more affordable?	25	(317)	36	(2,064)
Which party is more likely to:				
Cut social security?	40	(318)	51	(2,068)
Raise taxes?	48	(318)	46	(2,070)

SOURCE: 1992 National Election Study.

NOTE: Total number of respondents appears in parentheses.

five policies, differences between the two major parties were trivial. Blacks, in other words, while overwhelmingly pro-Democratic in their party preference, may still be no more partisan in their political orientation than whites. To assess more formally the issue of the degree of black partisanship, I regressed the perceptions of major-party difference items on a set of social demographic and attitudinal variables, including racial group membership. Those identifying with a party are defined as partisans and are expected to see large differences between the parties, as well as those who have experienced politics longer (older Americans) and those likely to be better informed about politics (better-educated Americans). Income might or might not have an independent impact on such perceptions. Finally, gender was included in the model because since 1980 significant gender differences in party preferences have emerged. Because the measure of party difference is a dummy variable, logit analysis was performed. The results are reported in table 7.7.

While partisanship was consistently related to the perception of party difference, as expected, racial group membership had an independent effect on four of the six items and mostly on the social welfare items: poverty, health care, and social security.[3] Blacks were also more

SOURCE: 1992 National Election Study.

TABLE 7.7
LOGIT ANALYSIS OF PERCEPTION OF PARTY DIFFERENCE ON POLICY MATTERS
(REPUBLICANS OR DEMOCRATS VS. NEITHER PARTY OR NO OPINION)

	Nation's economy	Foreign affairs	Solve poverty	Health care	Social Security	Raise taxes
Intercept	-.61* (.25)	.12 (.26)	-.13 (.25)	-.09 (.26)	.46 (.24)	.41 (.24)
Gender (male)	-.22* (.09)	-.23* (.10)	-.11 (.09)	-.22* (.10)	.02 (.09)	-.45** (.09)
Race (black)	.29* (.14)	-.10 (.14)	.47** (.15)	.54** (.15)	.42** (.14)	-.05 (.13)
Partisan (yes)	1.09** (.09)	.72** (.10)	.85** (.09)	.75** (.10)	.27** (.09)	.43** (.09)
Age	.00 (.00)	.00 (.00)	.00 (.00)	.00 (.00)	-.01** (.003)	.00 (.00)
Education	.15** (.03)	.10** (.03)	.14** (.03)	.10** (.03)	-.03 (.03)	.11** (.03)
Income	-.01 (.01)	.01 (.01)	-.01 (.01)	-.01 (.01)	-.00 (.01)	.00 (.01)
Total cases	2,130	2,132	2,129	2,127	2,131	2,134
Log likelihood	-1363.8	-1310.8	-1340.7	-1305.4	-1457.7	-1432.8
% correct	64.5	68.2	65	67.2	53.7	58.5

$*p < .05.$ $**p < .01.$

likely to recognize differences between the parties in how they managed the health of the economy. Interestingly enough, gender mattered for four of the six items as well. Women were more likely than men to recognize differences between the two major parties in handling the nation's economy, on foreign affairs, on health care, and in raising taxes. No consistent patterns were found for age and income, while better-educated respondents were more likely to discern party differences on the six policy items than less-educated respondents.

The results of this analysis imply that blacks are evaluating the parties solely on two policy dimensions—the economy and social welfare—since race differences emerged only on the items corresponding to these dimensions. These findings throw new light on what may have accounted for the surge in black Democratic identification during the late 1960s and early 1970s and what sustains it today. Although some historians have argued that blacks had begun voting Democratic during the 1930s out of economic necessity, large-scale identification with the party did not take off until the 1964 election. By 1964, a full 80 percent of blacks identified with the Democratic Party, while between 1952 and 1962, only some 56 to 66 percent identified themselves as Democrats. While I have stressed the Democratic Party's championship of landmark civil rights legislation as key to the new surge in black identification with the Democratic Party, President Johnson's War on Poverty legislation, the set of federal programs aimed at creating new social service structures, also strengthened blacks' Democratic identification.

Because no direct question on the performance of the parties on civil rights was included in the 1992 National Election Study, it is not possible to determine whether blacks continue to see substantial differences between the parties on racial issues and thereby link race policies to black Democratic identification. Given the racial conservatism of the Republican Party that emerged in 1964 with Barry Goldwater's nomination and persisted up to, possibly, George Bush's signing the 1991 Civil Rights Act, both racial issues and social welfare policies likely explain the preponderance and strength of blacks' pro-Democratic preferences. But it is possible that in the weighting of these two factors, the party's performance on economic issues and social welfare policy matters more to black Democrats today than does the party's performance on race.

Conclusion: Whither Black Partisanship?

Although Clinton's victory had been interpreted by some as evidence that the Democratic Party had finally repaired its fractured New Deal coalition of blacks, labor, Catholics, Jews, and southerners, tensions between the warring factions within the Democratic Party persisted. Those in the center of the party have expressed their disappointment and dismay at the liberal cast of Clinton's political appointees, while black liberals were outraged over the president's abandonment of Lani Guinier, a liberal black law professor, whom he had nominated in his first year of office to head the civil rights division of the Justice Department. As the president struggles to maintain his coalition, such tensions will likely persist. While there is a "new Democrat" in the White House, a "new," more stable Democratic electoral coalition has yet to evolve.

Analysis of the Census Bureau's turnout data and the 1992 NES attitudinal data lends support to both the social-psychological and structural accounts of black partisanship. First, despite the ongoing feuding between blacks and conservative white Democrats, there remains the perception that enough substantive differences between the two parties exist to nurture and sustain the strong Democratic identity of blacks. Those analysts positing a structural version of black partisanship have failed to appreciate the widening political gulf between the parties that emerged during the Reagan-Bush years, creating conditions that reaffirmed and hardened black voters' preference for the Democrats. Bush's standing among blacks, which had been higher than Ronald Reagan's in 1984, fell from 46 to 38 percent from 1988 to 1992. Bush's low standing among blacks, coupled with their negative view of the nation's economy, prompted more blacks to go to the polls and vote Democratic in 1992.

At the same time, analysts working with traditional survey and exit poll data have failed to grasp blacks' position as a political minority in a two-party system. Jackson's 1984 and 1988 candidacies heightened and were fueled by mounting black dissatisfaction with the Democratic Party's nominees and policies, and in particular, its inadequate response to Reagan's assault on the social welfare state and blacks' civil rights agenda. Since 1988 the racial gap in voter participation has been increasing, rather than decreasing, as had been the trend since the 1968 election. Moreover, even among registered voters, turnout among blacks is considerably lower than turnout among whites. Two political scientists have found that a significant part of the overall decline in black voter participation between 1968 and 1988 can be explained by the reduction in the efforts made by the Democrats to mobilize and get out the black vote (Rosenstone and Hansen 1993, 222–24).

If the returning racial gap in voter participation is to be reduced, state and national Democratic Party organizations need to increase their efforts at registering and mobilizing black voters. Eliminating the racial gap in participation is electorally vital for the Democrats, given that when blacks vote, they usually vote Democratic. Although a high black turnout cannot guarantee a Democratic victory, low turnouts can have disastrous consequences for the Democrats, as was illustrated in the 1993 governor's race in New Jersey. Jim Florio, the incumbent Democratic governor, was narrowly defeated by his Republican challenger, Christine Todd Whitman, thanks in part to the poor showing of blacks at the polls and the markedly higher rate of participation by white suburbanites, who mostly voted Republican. Even without concentrated efforts by the Democratic Party to boost black participation, if the record of the Clinton administration evinces a sharp departure from past Republican policies, particularly on health care and in combating crime, black Democrats are more likely to return to the polls in 1996. Demonstrating that the Democrats perform better than the Republicans on policies blacks care about will motivate more blacks to vote.

Notes

1. A scant 2.5 percent of blacks interviewed in the 1992 National Election Study claimed to have voted for Perot.

2. These figures are from the American National Election Studies, 1952–88 Cumulative Data File; see also Tate (1993, 36–38). If one excludes the issue of capital punishment, however, blacks today are no more or no less liberal than whites on many social issues.

3. To determine if the six policy evaluations of party differences are interrelated, the items were factor analyzed using LISREL 7. Because these items were recoded as dichotomies, a generalized weighted least squares (WLS) technique was used. (In this procedure, it is assumed that there is a latent continuous variable that is normally distributed for each dichotomous variable; see Bollen 1989.)

Estimating several different factor models, the best-fitting model was obtained when four factors were specified. Only the social welfare latent variable consists of more than one item: solving poverty, health care, and social security. While the best fit was obtained when the social welfare dimension was estimated with all three items, the social security item was only modestly associated with the latent variable. This could reflect the different wording of the item relative to the others. In this model, three of the latent factors were estimated by single items (items were fixed to one and their corresponding error terms then fixed to zero). In addition, the best-fitting model was obtained when the error terms of the "social security" and "raise taxes" items were allowed to correlate. This improvement in fit probably resulted from the similarity in the question working of the two items, especially since the ϕ coefficient for the two latent constructs (ksi 3 and ksi 4) is moderately weak (.27), suggesting that they are not strongly linked constructs. Of the four latent constructs defined, the perceptions of major-party differences on economic performance and social welfare policy between the two parties were the most strongly linked ($\phi = .70$). Because the χ-square statistic obtained is statistically significant at the 0.04 probability level, the results reported here are more suggestive than conclusive. Nevertheless, it appears that most Americans evaluate parties on at least four separate policy dimensions: economic performance, foreign affairs, social welfare, and taxation policies (see table 7.8).

TABLE 7.8
WLS CONFIRMATORY FACTOR ANALYSIS OF PERCEPTION OF PARTY DIFFERENCE ON POLICY MATTERS: FOUR-FACTOR MODEL
(STANDARDIZED SOLUTION)

	Economic performance KSI 1	Foreign policy KSI 2	Social welfare KSI 3	Taxation KSI 4
Lambda X				
Nation's economy	1.00	.00	.00	.00
Foreign affairs	.00	1.00	.00	.00
Solve poverty	.00	.00	.93	.00
Health care	.00	.00	.91	.00
Social security	.00	.00	.45	.00
Raise taxes	.00	.00	.00	1.00
Phi				
KSI 1	1.00			
KSI 2	.53	1.00		
KSI 3	.70	.51	1.00	
KSI 4	.37	.41	.27	1.00

Number of observations = 2,487
Chi-square = 11.58; 5 d.f.
Probability = .041
Goodness of Fit index = .999
Adjusted Goodness of Fit index = .997
Root mean square = .022

CHAPTER 8

Women Voters in the "Year of the Woman"

ELIZABETH ADELL COOK AND CLYDE WILCOX

On the second night of the 1992 Democratic National Convention, many of the ten women who had won their party's nominations for seats in the U.S. Senate took to the stage in a series of speeches. At one point all of them stood on stage together, with incumbent Senator Barbara Mikulski (D-Md.) in the center. They were joined by most of the women who had won their party's nomination for seats in the U.S. House. These photo opportunities were irresistible to many journalists, who began to write seriously that the 1992 elections might finally result in the long-awaited "Year of the Woman." With many Democratic and Republican women seeking election to the U.S. Congress, women were poised to make significant gains.

A number of events during George Bush's presidency had increased the salience of gender-related policy issues to the presidential election as well: the Supreme Court's *Webster* decision, which allowed states new authority to regulate abortion and had reenergized the pro-choice forces (Cook, Jelen, and Wilcox 1992); the televised hearings on Anita Hill's charge that Clarence Thomas had sexually harassed her; and Bush's veto of family leave had all brought renewed attention to gender-related issues. Moreover, the Republican National Convention, with its anti-feminist rhetoric and attacks on Hillary Clinton, suggested that gender would be especially salient in the presidential election (Conover and Sapiro 1993b).

Journalists had written about possible "Years of the Woman" in previous election years (Duerst-Lahti 1993). In 1990, for example, the Republicans had nominated a record number of women to run for Senate seats, but only incumbent Nancy Kassebaum (R-Kans.) won. Yet the 1992 election proved different. Four women won new Senate seats and one woman incumbent won an easy reelection, tripling the number of women in that body; and twenty-four new women were elected to the House, raising the number of women in the lower chamber from twenty-nine to forty-seven (Wilcox 1994). These unprecedented gains were made almost entirely by Democratic women. All four of the newly elected women in the Senate are Democrats, as are twenty-one of the twenty-four newly elected women in the House (Chaney and Sinclair 1994).[1]

Most of the media attention to the "Year of the Woman" focused on the victories of women candidates in the Senate and House, but most feminists also viewed the election of Bill Clinton as a major victory. Clinton issued executive orders liberalizing abortion policy and signed the Family and Medical Leave Act early in his presidency. He appointed women to highly visible positions, including attorney general, secretary of health and human services, ambassador to the United Nations, and associate justice of the Supreme Court (Bendyna and Lake 1994). Hillary Clinton became a visible symbol of politically powerful women, presiding over the administration's deliberations in drafting a new plan for national health care.

Thus 1992 was declared by many analysts to be the "Year of the Woman" (see Cook, Thomas, and Wilcox 1994 for an extended discussion). The successes of women congressional candidates and the salience of gender issues and symbolism in the presidential election suggest that men and women may have voted differently from one another in 1992. In this chapter we focus on gender differences in voting for Senate and presidential candidates.

The phrase "gender gap" achieved popularity after the 1980 election and has received increasing attention ever since. The term usually refers to the differences in the vote decisions of men and women, but it has also been used to indicate that men and women may base their votes on different factors. We therefore also examine the sources of vote decisions for men and women, to see if men and women based their votes on different factors.

Most of the research on the gender gap has focused on the attitudes and behaviors of women, but it is important to understand that the gender gap results equally from the decisions of women and men. To say that women were more likely to support Michael Dukakis in the 1988 presidential election is exactly the same as saying that men were more likely to support George Bush. In this chapter we most often discuss how women's votes differed from men's, but in each instance we could instead word our analysis to show how men's differed from women's.[2]

We examine the impact of gender on vote decisions in 1992 in this chapter. First, we offer an explanation for women's gains in Congress in 1992. Second, we focus on gender differences in vote choice in Senate elections, especially those in which a woman was running. Third, we examine the gender gap in the 1992 presidential vote and its sources. We use data from the 1992 National Election Study (NES), from the 1992 VRS (Voter Research and Surveys) primary and general election exit polls, and from tracking polls conducted during the campaign by the polling firm Greenberg and Lake.[3]

The "Year of the Woman" in the House and Senate: Explaining the Gains

Throughout the 1980s, increasing numbers of women sought their party's nominations for House or Senate seats. Many were experienced, savvy politicians who had served in state legislatures and other political offices. Nearly all of them lost. The number of women in the U.S. House of Representatives increased very slowly throughout the decade, and the number of women in the Senate held steady at two. The 1992 election brought a substantial change in the number of elected women. Why did women candidates succeed in 1992 when in earlier elections they had failed?

Our explanation centers on three factors: the decisions by potential candidates, activities by political elites, and decisions by voters. In part, women won in 1992 because they ran in record numbers. Barbara Burrell (1993) reports that 218 women sought their party's nomination to the House in 1992, a large increase over the 1986 record of 134.

The women who ran in 1992 were generally well-qualified, experienced politicians. Candidates with previous electoral experience are much more likely to win election to the House than those without such experience, and state legislators are often considered a pool of eligible candidates for the House. Throughout the 1970s and 1980s the number of women in state legislatures increased steadily (Thomas 1994), and women elected more recently were politically ambitious (Dolan and Ford 1993). Thus there existed a pool of qualified, ambitious women serving in state legislatures and other state and local offices, ready to seize an opportunity to run for higher office.

Ambitious politicians generally seek to time their bids for higher office to maximize their chances for election. Strategic female politicians saw 1992 as a good year to launch their bids. Redistricting and a large number of retirements created ninety-one open seats in the House, providing the opportunity for women to run for office without the necessity of running against an incumbent. It was qualified women running for open seats who won election in 1992. Nearly all the newly elected women won in open seats (Chaney and Sinclair 1994), and among the Democratic women who won Senate seats, none defeated an elected incumbent in a general election contest.[4] In 1992, as in previous elections, most women who ran against incumbents lost, as did most of their male counterparts.

Although 1992 was a good year for nonincumbents in general to run for the House or Senate, it was an especially inviting year for Democratic candidates. Democratic women (and men) were inspired to run by the stagnant economy and President Bush's low job-approval ratings —two factors that typically inspire experienced candidates from the opposition party to seek election (Jacobson and Kernell 1983).

Some women candidates were additionally motivated by a specific event in 1991. The televised Senate hearings on the confirmation of Clarence Thomas to the U.S. Supreme Court left a lasting image in the minds of many women: a room full of men grilling Anita Hill on her accusations that Thomas had sexually harassed her. A number of Democratic women who ran for the Senate and a few who sought House seats listed the Thomas-Hill hearings as a prime motivation for their candidacies.

Women were running in record numbers in 1992, but their victories were not assured. The second factor that explains women's gains in 1992 was the behavior of political elites, especially female political contributors. Although women have traditionally contributed less often and in smaller amounts than men (Wilcox, Brown, and Powell 1993), the Thomas-Hill hearings and the *Webster* and *Casey* decisions energized potential women contributors. Contributions to political action committees (PACs) that sought primarily to elect more women to Congress increased dramatically, as did gifts to PACs that promoted abortion rights (Nelson 1994; Thomas 1994). The receipts of EMILY's List, a PAC that supports pro-choice Democratic women, increased fourfold, and WISH List formed to help pro-choice Republican women (Rimmerman 1994).[5] PACs such as EMILY's List recruited candidates, offered campaign advice and training, made direct cash contributions, and frequently encouraged members to give directly to women's campaigns (Roberts 1993; Nelson 1994). Members of women's PACs formed the core of the House list for direct-mail solicitations for many women candidates (Babcock 1992).

The third factor that helped elect more women in 1992 was the willingness of voters to support women candidates. To some extent this was part of a generalized yet amorphous desire for change: electing women clearly represents a deviation from the status quo. In addition, the issue mix of the 1992 elections was auspicious for women candidates. Women are generally perceived as better at handling "compassion" issues such as unemployment, health care, and education, while voters generally believe that men are better able to deal with "force" issues such as war and crime (Sapiro 1981–82; Alexander and Andersen 1993; Huddy and Terkildsen 1993). The electorate in 1992 cared about unemployment, education, and health care, not about defense spending or foreign policy. Women candidates responded to this favorable issue environment by playing up their advantages on compassion issues (Williams 1994; see also Kahn 1993).[6]

All of this translated into an electorate that was quite willing to support women candidates. Indeed, although most polls showed that Americans were generally indifferent in the abstract to the sex of candidates, among those who did voice a preference there was a substantial advantage for women candidates. This was especially true in Democratic primary elections: in California, for example, prospective voters told pollsters that they preferred a generic woman to a generic man by a ratio of 5–1 (DiCammillo 1993).

These three factors combine to explain the election of women candidates to the House and Senate in 1992. A ready pool of skilled, ambitious officeholders took advantage of the unique opportunities of 1992. Many realized that 1992 would be their best shot at higher office for many years; others were motivated by specific policy concerns; and still others were recruited by party elites or women's PACs. They were well funded by an energized core of women contributors. Finally, they faced an electorate anxious for change, concerned with education, health care, and the economy, and uninterested in foreign and defense policy.

Although much of the explanation for women's successes in 1992 lies in the decisions of candidates and contributors, especially on the unique opportunities from the record number of open seats in the House, in this chapter we focus on the decisions of individual voters. In 1992, women candidates won more votes from women than from men, as did the Democratic presidential ticket. In the next section we discuss gender differences in partisanship and ideology that are a major factor in these vote decisions.

The Voter Context: Gender Differences
in Partisanship and Policy Positions

Vote decisions are influenced by long-term attitudes such as partisanship and certain enduring political issues (Asher 1992). Men and women differ in their partisanship and in their positions on issues that have long been on the national agenda. These differences lead us to expect differences in the vote decisions between men and women. The gender gap in vote choice is due in no small part to gender gaps in party identification and in issue positions.

The gender gap in partisanship was first observed in the original National Election Studies conducted in the 1950s, but in these early elections, it was women who were more likely than men to identify as Republicans (Bendyna and Lake 1994). This pattern was also evident in Europe, where women were more likely to support conservative, especially Christian Democratic, parties. Women in most Western democracies, including the United States, were more likely than men to call themselves conservatives and to take conservative positions on many political issues.

During the 1960s, the gender gap in partisanship disappeared, and by the 1972 election women were significantly more likely than men to identify as Democrats. In 1976 the gender gap in partisanship temporarily narrowed, only to widen again in the 1980s. Figure 8.1 shows the percentage of men and women who identified as or leaned toward each party in NES surveys since 1952. The data show a widening partisan gap in recent elections.

Most scholars have explained the emerging gender gap in partisanship as a function of the movement of white men toward the Republican Party, especially in the South (Bolce 1985; Miller 1991). In figure 8.1, there is some evidence for this view. In 1988 women were less likely to consider themselves Democrats than in 1952 and were more likely to call themselves Republicans. The gender gap in partisanship existed because men had made a much larger shift toward the Republicans than had women.[7] In the 1992 data there is evidence that women moved away from the Republican Party.[8]

Why are women more likely than men to identify as Democrats? Part of the answer lies in social location: women earn less than men and are more likely to be poor. Democratic officeholders are more likely to support social programs that benefit the disadvantaged and therefore benefit women.[9] Yet in 1992 NES data, controls for social location reduce gender differences in partisanship by only 30 percent, suggesting that economic inequality is only part of the explanation.

Women and men also differ in their political attitudes and ideolo-

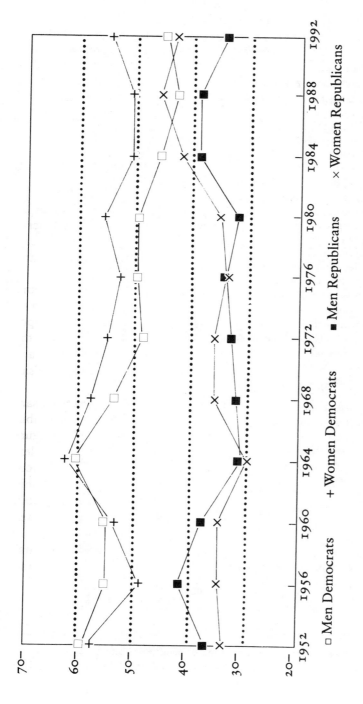

FIGURE 8.1. GENDER DIFFERENCES IN PARTISANSHIP, 1952–92.

□ Men Democrats   + Women Democrats   ■ Men Republicans   × Women Republicans

SOURCE: National Election Studies, 1952–92.

TABLE 8.1
PARTIAL CORRELATIONS BETWEEN SEX AND ISSUE
POSITION WITH PARTISANSHIP CONTROLLED

Foreign policy	
Bush's handling of Gulf War	.04*
Anything good from Gulf War	.11**
Isolationism	.07**
Did right thing in Gulf War	.10**
Defense spending	.05*
Social issues	
Equal role for women	.03
Sexual harassment is serious	.16**
Ban discrimination against gays	.11**
Abortion policy	.02
Death penalty	.13**
School prayer	.00
Racial issues	
Colleges reserve spaces for blacks	.07**
Preferences in hiring	.03
Economic policy issues	
Guaranteed jobs	.09**
Government services and spending	.12**
Government health insurance	.05*
Spending on:	
Social security	.14**
Child care	.11**
Unemployed	.08**
Poor people	.11**
Food stamps	.07**
Welfare	.09**
Homeless	.08**
Former USSR	−.06**
Schools	.06**
Science and technology	−.12**
Environment	.01
Crime	.04*
AIDS	.03
Blacks	.03
Short-term economic evaluations	
Evaluation of national economy	.10**
Personal situation vs. past	.07**
Personal situation in future	.10**

SOURCE: 1992 National Election Study.

NOTE: All items coded so that high scores are more liberal or indicate more spending.

*$p < .05.$ **$p < .01.$

gies. These differences have been modest but enduring. In table 8.1 we show the gender gap on policy issues, holding constant the partisan gap described earlier. There are large differences in support for the use of military force, with men far more likely than women to support using U.S. troops in foreign countries (Shapiro and Majahan 1986; Fite, Genest, and Wilcox 1990) and in support for the Gulf War (Conover and Sapiro 1993a; Wilcox, Ferrara, and Allsop 1993).

On social issues, studies generally find no gender differences on policy matters commonly called "women's issues," such as abortion (Cook, Jelen, and Wilcox 1993), the Equal Rights Amendment, or family leave. In 1992, however, there were significant gender gaps on two such issues: whether a married woman should be required to notify her husband before obtaining an abortion, and whether enough was being done about sexual harassment. In addition, women were less willing to allow discrimination against homosexuals and less supportive of the death penalty. Women were also more likely than men to support social spending on programs to help the poor and the unemployed and on education and other social services, and these differences appear to be enduring as well (Conover 1988; Cook and Wilcox 1991).

These differences in positions on concrete issues are mirrored in ideological self-identification. Women are more likely than men to call themselves liberals and are less likely to call themselves conservatives. Yet gender differences in policy preferences do not always fit neatly on a simple liberal-conservative dimension. In a variety of other areas (e.g., limitations on immigration and censorship of certain sexual and even political speech), studies have occasionally reported that women are more conservative than men (Jelen, Thomas, and Wilcox 1994).

Finally, women differed from men in their short-term reactions to the recession. Women were more likely to evaluate the performance of the national economy over the past four years negatively and to believe that their personal financial situation had deteriorated and would continue to worsen in the next year.

Gender differences in policy positions help explain the gender gap in partisanship. Our analysis suggests that in 1992, the gender gap in support for spending for social programs accounted for the largest share of the policy component of partisan differences, with foreign policy attitudes also playing a significant role.[10]

Voting for Women for the U.S. Senate

These gender differences in partisanship and ideology suggest that women should be expected to be more supportive of liberal Democratic candidates than men. Yet when the sex of the candidate is factored into the equation, the results may be less predictable. It is possible that women will also be more likely to support women candidates, regardless of their party and ideology. When liberal Democratic women run against conservative Republican men, all factors point toward women disproportionately supporting the Democratic woman candidate. Yet when a liberal Democratic man runs against a conservative Republican woman, there may be some cross pressures that would lead to a smaller gender gap than in other elections.

How might the sex of the candidate matter to voters? There are at least four possibilities. First, the sex of the candidate may be irrelevant to voters. If this is true, women voters will be more likely to support Democratic candidates than male voters, regardless of the candidate's sex. Female Republican candidates will receive relatively fewer votes from women than from men, while their Democratic male opponents will win more votes from women. Second, it is possible that women will be more likely than men to support women candidates, and that partisanship will be relatively unimportant in races when a woman runs against a man. Third, it is possible that women will consider both party and the sex of the candidate independently, so there will be large gender gaps when women run as Democrats and smaller ones when women run as Republicans. Finally, women may especially respond to Democratic women candidates, but may be unaffected by women running as Republicans.[11]

In 1992, eleven women sought election to the U.S. Senate, and five won. Data from the VRS exit polls provide an opportunity to examine the sources of women's votes in 1992 Senate races.[12] In 1992, only one woman ran as a Republican in a Senate general election. To help sort out the relationship between gender and party, therefore, it is helpful to consider earlier elections as well. In 1990, Republican women won Senate nominations in several states, including three women who were currently serving in the U.S. House of Representatives. We examine both 1990 and 1992 so that we can include a number of Senate races in which highly qualified, experienced women won nomination as Democrats and Republicans. By considering both elections, we can examine the interaction of voter and candidate partisanship, and of voter and candidate gender.

Table 8.2 shows the percentage of men and women who voted for the Democratic candidate in Senate elections in 1990 and 1992 in a number of states. Most of the elections in this table involve a male candidate from each party, and the average gender gap in these elections is

3.8 percent. We can use this figure as a baseline to examine the effects of women candidates on the gender gap in Senate elections.

In 1990 Republican incumbent Nancy Kassebaum (R-Kans.) won many more votes among women than among men.[13] In most of the other states, women were more likely than men to vote for the Democratic male candidate. Among all Senate elections that featured Republican women candidates in 1990, the average gender gap was 1 percent, with women more likely than men to vote for the Democratic male candidate. With the incumbent Kassebaum excluded, the average was 3.6 percent. In New Jersey, women's votes were responsible for the victory of Democrat Bill Bradley over Christine Whitman, his Republican challenger. In Illinois, women were more likely than men to vote for incumbent Paul Simon over his Republican challenger, Lynn Martin. In Hawaii and Rhode Island, there were no gender gaps. When highly qualified women ran as Republicans in 1990, the average gender gap was somewhat smaller than in states where the male candidate was a Republican.

In the two states in which Democratic women ran against Republican men in 1990, the gender gap varied widely. In Colorado, Democrat Josie Heath opposed the Gulf War and supported sharp cuts in defense spending. She narrowly lost among women and lost by 14 percent among men. In Wyoming, in contrast, women were slightly more likely than men to vote for the Republican male incumbent instead of the Democratic woman challenger.

In 1992 the average gender gap in states in which two male candidates won their parties' nominations was 4.4 percent. When Democratic women ran against Republican men, the average gap was 9.1 percent. The gender gap was substantial in all states with Democratic women candidates. In Kansas, where Republican Kassebaum had a 10 percent advantage among women voters in 1990, Democrat Gloria O'Dell had a 6 percent advantage over Bob Dole in 1992. In California, fully 60 percent of women who reported voting for both Senate seats cast ballots for Democrats Dianne Feinstein and Barbara Boxer.[14] Boxer's victory came because of her margin among women voters, but she lost narrowly among men.

In South Dakota women were more likely than men to vote for Republican antifeminist Charlene Haar, suggesting that women may have been voting for women candidates in 1992 regardless of party and ideology. It is also possible that women in South Dakota are simply more Republican than men, for in 1990 the Republican male Senate candidate in South Dakota also won more votes among women than among men.

TABLE 8.2
VOTING FOR DEMOCRATIC CANDIDATE IN SENATE
ELECTIONS, 1990 AND 1992

	1990			1992		
	Women	Men	Gap	Women	Men	Gap
Alabama	61	54	7	69	63	6
Alaska				36	35	1
Arizona				33	31	2*
Arkansas				62	55	7
California (full)				57	43	14*
California (short)				64	50	14*
Colorado	46	38	8*	58	53	5
Connecticut				63	60	3
Delaware	66	58	8**			
Florida				67	65	2
Georgia				52	46	6
Hawaii	54	54	0**	60	60	0
Idaho	38	37	1	45	41	4
Illinois	67	63	4**	58	51	7*
Indiana	46	46	0	41	41	0
Iowa	56	52	4	34	22	12*
Kansas	21	31	−10**†	35	29	6*
Kentucky	49	46	3	64	64	0
Maine	39	35	4			
Maryland				76	66	10*†
Minnesota	50	48	2			
Missouri				49	40	9*
Nevada				54	50	4
New Hampshire	34	29	5	49	45	4
New Jersey	54	47	7**			

Overall, then, it appears that voters consider the party *and* the sex of Senate candidates. When both candidates are men, women are consistently more likely to vote for the Democratic candidate. In states with qualified, moderate women running as Republicans, women are still more likely than men to support the Democratic man, but the gender gap in those states is smaller than in states with two men running. In states with qualified, liberal women running as Democrats, the gender gap is larger than in states with two men running.

To see if both partisanship and candidate gender mattered in vote choice in 1992, we controlled for partisanship in each Senate election. In 1992 twelve Senate contests had statistically significant gender gaps in bivariate analysis, but after controls for partisanship, this number

TABLE 8.2 —*continued*
VOTING FOR DEMOCRATIC CANDIDATE IN SENATE
ELECTIONS, 1990 AND 1992

	1990			1992		
	Women	Men	Gap	Women	Men	Gap
New Mexico	23	24	−1			
New York				53	44	9
North Carolina	53	42	11	51	44	7
North Dakota				63	54	9
Ohio				57	53	4
Oklahoma	86	82	4	41	37	4
Oregon	48	44	4	56	40	16
Pennsylvania				54	44	10*
Rhode Island	61	62	−1**			
South Carolina	34	33	1	52	51	1
South Dakota	44	47	−3	64	70	−6**
Tennessee	74	64	10			
Texas	39	34	5			
Utah				40	43	−3
Vermont				61	51	10
Washington				58	51	7*
West Virginia	74	61	13			
Wisconsin				54	52	2
Wyoming	35	36	1*			

SOURCE: Voter Research and Surveys exit polls. This table includes all states with a
Senate election in either year that was included in the VRS exit polls.

* Dem candidate is female. ** Rep candidate is female. † Woman is incumbent.

was reduced to six. These six states all featured Democratic women
candidates who ran credible races. In both California seats, in Illinois,
Maryland, Missouri, and in Pennsylvania, women were more likely to
vote for the Democratic candidate than men, even after gender differences in partisanship had been controlled. Only in Washington did a
strong Democratic woman candidate not draw votes disproportionately
from women, after controlling for partisanship.[15]

In 1992 women voters were an important part of the electoral coalitions of Democratic women senatorial candidates. This support appears partially to reflect a belief in the value of greater numbers of
women in Congress. In states with nonincumbent women who were
strong candidates, the exit polls asked voters how important it was to
elect more women to the U.S. Senate. In all five states, women voters

were significantly more likely than men to believe that it was very important to elect more women to the Senate. In California and Washington, more than half the women surveyed indicated that it was very important to send more women to the Senate; in Illinois and Pennsylvania, the figure was only slightly less than half. In contrast, in no state did as many as a third of men believe that it was very important to send more women to the Senate.

The preference for women candidates was also evident in Democratic primary election voting. The VRS primary election exit polls show that there were gender gaps of between 8 and 12 points in the California long seat, in Illinois, and in Pennsylvania, where half the women but only slightly more than a third of the men voted for Lynn Yeakel. Dianne Feinstein also benefited from a smaller gender gap of 4 points. Both Carol Moseley-Braun and Yeakel won their primary victories because of women's votes; both candidates lost among male voters.

This suggests that when partisanship is not a factor, women voters are attracted to women candidates, at least when those candidates are liberals. When all things are equal, a large number of women (and many men) would like to see more women in elected office. In elections in which partisanship is a factor, however, women are more likely than men to prefer liberal Democratic men to moderate Republican women, although the presence of the woman candidate reduces the magnitude of the gender gap. When liberal Democratic women run against Republican men, the gender gap is fairly substantial, with women more likely than men to vote for the Democratic woman candidate.

Gender and Presidential Voting

The 1992 presidential election campaign was laden with gender-related symbolism. The Republicans tried for a time to make an issue of Hillary Clinton, and strove throughout the campaign to focus media attention on Bill Clinton's rumored philandering. Ross Perot's language was clearly aimed at men: he frequently used metaphors of automobile repair to describe his economic plans. Moreover, Perot's generalized insensitivity to various social groups was evident in his attempts to court women voters as well. He told one rally that he understood the concerns of women because he was married to one and had daughters.

On election day, women were more likely than men to vote for Clinton, while men were more likely than women to vote for Perot. Clinton won among both men and women, but his victory margin came almost entirely among women. It is frequently argued that presidents who win easily have a mandate to accomplish their programs. Although the notion of a mandate is controversial (Dahl 1992), it is clear that Bill Clinton owes any mandate he might claim to women voters.

Table 8.3 shows the percentage of men and women who voted for each presidential candidate according to the VRS exit polls and the NES surveys. The columns labeled "All" show the percentage of all voters who reported supporting each candidate. The VRS data, based on a very large sample, is closer to the actual election outcome. The NES data overestimate the Clinton vote, primarily among women voters. In both surveys, however, Clinton did far better among women than among men. Women in the exit polls preferred Clinton to Bush by 9 points, and in the NES the margin was an astonishing 20 percent.

The VRS data show a gender gap of 5 points for Clinton on election day. This gap was slightly smaller than the average gender gap in tracking polls taken before the election. Polls by Greenberg-Lake showed an average gender gap of 7 points in Clinton support in the month of October, and an average of 9 points in the five polls after the final debate but before the final preelection poll. Moreover, the Greenberg-Lake data show that the gender gap in candidate preference increased to 11 points after the election. In the final days before the election, men's support for Clinton increased, narrowing the gender gap in actual vote.

The gender gap varied across various social and political groups. The data in table 8.3 show the gender gap among subgroups of voters in both the NES and VRS data. These data show that the gender gap in support for Clinton was largest among younger voters and among professionals and those in two-income families. Bendyna and Lake (1994) reported that young professional women were among the earliest Clinton supporters and the most loyal throughout the campaign. Professional men and men in two-income families supported Bush by a small margin, while women in these households gave strong support to Clinton.

The exit polls show a larger gender gap among black than among white voters.[16] Indeed, the VRS data suggest that white women split their votes evenly between Bush and Clinton. The exit polls also show that there was no significant gender gap among white Born-Again Christians, with women slightly more likely than men to support Bush over Clinton.

These data make another important point: the differences among women are far larger than the differences between women and men. In the VRS data, 5 percent more of women than men voted for Clinton. In contrast, 46 percent more of black women than of white women voted

TABLE 8.3
GENDER DIFFERENCES IN PRESIDENTIAL VOTE
(IN PERCENTAGES)

NES data	Bush		Clinton		Perot	
	Men	Women	Men	Women	Men	Women
All	35	33	42	53	24	14
Professional	41	28	37	55	23	16
Other	32	34	45	52	21	14
Homemakers		39		46		14
Other		32		54		14
Feminists	15	12	60	71	25	17
18–30 years old	27	28	38	54	35	19
31–40	40	36	40	46	20	18
41–50	34	28	44	60	22	12
51–60	37	32	41	56	22	11
61+	35	37	51	52	14	11
Black	7	4	89	95	4	1
White	37	36	36	47	26	16
White Evangelicals	58	52	27	35	16	14
White Catholics	28	30	40	54	31	16

VRS Exit Polls	Bush		Clinton		Perot	
	Men	Women	Men	Women	Men	Women
All	38	37	41	46	21	17
Democrats	9	10	76	78	15	12
Independents	32	31	35	40	33	29
Republicans	71	75	11	10	19	16
Household with 2 wage earners	40	37	36	46	24	18
Homemakers		36		45		19
18–29 years old	37	33	38	48	25	20
30–44	38	38	39	43	23	19
45–64	39	39	41	44	20	17
65+	37	42	50	50	13	8
Black	14	8	78	87	9	5
White	40	41	37	41	23	19
White Born-Again Christian	60	62	24	22	16	14
White, attends church weekly	54	53	28	33	18	15

for Clinton. The NES data show that white evangelical women preferred Bush to Clinton by 52 percent to 35 percent, while professional
women preferred Clinton to Bush 55 percent to 28 percent. Women,
like men, do not speak with a single voice; they are deeply divided on
most political issues, including abortion, family leave, and other policy
concerns commonly called "women's issues."

TABLE 8.4

ISSUE SALIENCE IN VOTE DECISIONS,
VRS EXIT POLLS

	Men				Women			
	All	*Bush*	*Clinton*	*Perot*	*All*	*Bush*	*Clinton*	*Perot*
Economy (general)	12	34	60	59	17	30	56	60
Deficit	29	21	24	54	21	16	17	41
Taxes	18	28	10	13	16	23	9	16
Health care	21	10	34	15	24	14	34	18
Education	12	8	18	9	17	11	22	14
Environment	6	2	11	5	6	3	10	4
Abortion	9	16	6	4	18	24	16	8
Family values	14	25	7	8	20	35	9	12
Foreign	12	25	2	2	8	18	1	3

NOTE: Percentage of voters for each candidate mentioning each issue as influencing their
vote. Question allowed for multiple responses.

The "woman's vote" is composed of many different groups of
women whose votes are influenced by many different factors. Yet men's
votes also vary along similar lines, and in the aggregate, women were
more likely to support Clinton than men, while men were more likely
than women to vote for Perot. Despite the diversity of women's political
preferences, then, it is useful to examine why men and women differ in
the vote decisions. We examine three sources of vote choice: partisanship, issue positions, and candidate evaluations.

PARTISANSHIP

As we saw in figure 8.1, women are predisposed to support Democratic
candidates by their partisanship. The partisan differences between men
and women are sufficient to explain entirely the gender gap in vote
choice between Clinton and Bush: there is no gender gap in vote for the
two major candidates after controls for party identification. In the

1972, 1980, and 1984 elections, partisanship did not fully account for the gender gap in vote choice, but it did in both 1988 and 1992.

This means that the gender gap in vote choice was at one time larger than the gender gap in partisanship, but that eventually the gender gap in partisanship caught up. During the 1980s, men continued steadily to march into the ranks of the Republicans, and there is some evidence that suburban pro-choice Republican women have become Democrats over the past several years.[17] Although partisanship may account for the gender gap in vote choice, the partisan gap itself may be the result of a series of vote decisions made during the 1970s and 1980s (see Jackson 1975 for an account of issue-driven partisan change).

Yet partisanship (or strength of partisanship) does not explain gender differences in reactions to Ross Perot. Even after controls for the direction and strength of partisanship, women were still significantly less likely to support Perot's candidacy. We need to look elsewhere to explain the partisan gap in support for Perot.

ISSUE POSITIONS

A second attitude generally used to explain vote decisions is one's attitude toward policy issues. We saw in table 8.1 that women differ in modest but enduring ways in their positions on policy matters. Clinton's campaign spoke directly to the economic insecurities of women evident in the data in table 8.1, and to their attitudes about the "social deficit" that Clinton promised to remedy. In contrast, Bush's emphasis on foreign policy experience was not an attractive issue to women. Although women rallied to support the Gulf War after the outbreak of hostilities, the data in table 8.1 show that their doubts reemerged afterward. Thus Clinton's platform had a stronger appeal to women voters than did the issue program of the Bush campaign.

In addition to differences in policy positions, women differed in the *salience* of the issues to their votes in 1992. The VRS exit polls show that regardless of partisanship or candidate preference, women were more likely than men to mention health care and education as important issues in deciding their votes. The data are presented in table 8.4. Women were also more likely than men to mention abortion and family values, regardless of the candidate they finally supported. Men were far more likely than women to indicate that foreign policy was an important issue and to indicate that Clinton's efforts to avoid the draft was a factor in their vote decision.

To determine the effects of partisanship and issue positions on evaluations of Bush and Clinton, we estimated separate regression equations for each candidate for men and women.[18] We include as predictor variables partisanship, general ideology, evaluations of the national economy and of the respondent's personal finances, scales measuring opposition to domestic spending, support for an assertive foreign policy, feminist consciousness and sympathy, and opposition to liberal abortion policies. We also include single items on societal policy on sexual harassment, family leave, and child care. Finally, we include dummy variables to identify blacks and evangelical Christians.

The results are shown in table 8.5. The relationships are complex, for different factors predict evaluations of each candidate, and by each gender. Partisanship is a stronger influence on women's evaluations of the candidates than men's, while general ideology is more important for men's evaluations of Clinton and women's evaluations of Bush. Men are more generally concerned with their personal finances, while women are more responsive to national economic evaluations.

Men and women alike responded to the candidates based in part on their positions on domestic spending, and men were especially likely to evaluate Bush based on foreign policy. Women were more likely to evaluate Clinton based on their feminist sentiments and abortion stands than men. Race mattered more among women, evangelical religious attachments were more important among men.[19]

It is important to remember that the gender gap is a function of both the importance of an issue in influencing candidate evaluations and of the differences between men and women in their positions on the issue. Thus partisanship contributes to the gender gap because it influences the votes of both men and women, and men and women differ significantly in their party identification. Abortion attitudes also contribute somewhat to the gender gap, for although men and women do not differ in their support for legal abortion, abortion is more important in influencing the candidate evaluations of women than of men. Finally, issues such as foreign policy are a source of the gender gap because men and women differ in their opinions, and the issue matters more to men than to women. Overall, partisanship and issue positions were important sources of the gender gap in 1992.

ATTITUDES TOWARD CANDIDATES

The final attitude commonly used to explain vote decisions is one's attitude toward the candidates. The VRS exit polls asked voters a series of questions about each candidate and gave voters a chance to mention specific characteristics that they found most attractive about each one. The NES asked respondents to evaluate each candidate on a series of characteristics such as intelligence, leadership, and honesty and asked about certain emotional reactions to candidates.

TABLE 8.5
SOURCES OF CANDIDATE EVALUATIONS FOR MEN AND WOMEN, 1992 NES

| | Bush | | | | Clinton | | | |
| | Men | | Women | | Men | | Women | |
	b	β	b	β	b	β	b	β
Partisanship	3.75	.32**	4.48	.35**	-2.96	-.26**	-4.60	-.37**
General ideology	1.46	.09*	2.87	.15**	-2.91	-.18**	-.10	-.01
National economy	2.48	.09**	4.43	.14**	-.54	-.02	-2.05	-.07*
Personal finances	1.70	.08*	1.07	.05	-1.44	-.07*	-.78	-.03
Domestic spending	6.16	.12**	5.02	.08*	-7.30	-.14**	-6.52	-.09*
Foreign policy	4.67	.18**	2.72	.10*	-1.20	-.05	-2.43	-.09*
Feminist conscious-ness/sympathy	-1.73	-.05	-1.79	-.05	1.83	.06	3.36	.09*
Abortion	.34	.02	.51	.03	-1.56	-.08*	-3.16	-.16**
Sexual harassment	.23	.01	2.64	.06*	-.84	-.02	-1.47	-.04
Family leave	5.44	.10**	1.44	.03	-1.39	-.03	-2.38	-.05
Child care	.44	.03	.51	.04	-.23	-.02	-.25	-.02
Black	-10.52	-.12**	-15.32	-.18**	2.58	.03	2.14	.03
Evangelical	1.59	.03	.02	.00	-5.21	-.09**	-2.63	-.05
Constant	-8.86		5.75		22.36**		-6.71	
R^2	.45		.44		.37		.33	

SOURCE: 1992 National Election Study.

*$p < .05$.   **$p < .01$.

It was once thought that women might cast their votes more on the basis of emotional reactions to candidates than did men, although research has discounted this suggestion (Shabad and Andersen 1979). It might be, nonetheless, that men and women reacted differently to the various "character" issues of the campaign, including Clinton's rumored affairs with women and his avoidance of the draft.

The data suggest, however, that men and women reacted in very similar ways to the candidates. After partisan differences are controlled, women were slightly more likely than men to believe in Bush's morality, honesty, and compassion and Clinton's honesty and compassion. They were more likely than men to indicate that Bush made them afraid, less likely to indicate that Bush made them proud, more likely to indicate that Clinton made them both proud and angry. These candidate traits and emotional reactions were strongly associated with vote choice among both men and women, with no obvious differences in the patterns.

This suggests that evaluations of the candidates did not differ much by gender, after partisan differences are controlled. Indeed, when partisan and policy differences are simultaneously held constant, women were actually warmer than men toward Bush, and cooler toward Clinton. We estimated the equations in table 8.5 with men and women in the same analysis and measured the impact of gender on candidate evaluation. Women were significantly warmer toward Bush, and cooler toward Clinton, than were men. If anything, then, women were more likely than men to prefer Bush to Clinton on personal qualities, but were drawn to Clinton by partisanship and policy issues.

THE PEROT PUZZLE

The preceding analyses have focused primarily on the Clinton-Bush match-up. We have not discussed evaluations of Perot for one important reason: few variables in the NES or VRS data help explain gender differences in Perot's support. The NES and the VRS did not include many questions on Perot, which makes analysis more tenuous. The gender gap in vote choice is echoed in other data as well. Men who voted for either Bush or Clinton were more likely to have considered a Perot vote than were women, and men who voted for Perot were more likely to indicate that they had never considered another candidate than were women Perot voters.

The gender gap in support for Perot was more sizable throughout the campaign and narrowed on election day. The NES data show that fully one in five of the women who voted for Perot decided to do so on election day, more than twice the number of men. Moreover, most of the women who made last-minute decisions for Perot preferred Clinton to Bush.

Why were women more negative toward Perot? Although the data do not allow us to offer definitive answers, we can offer some possible explanations. First, it appears that women were more frightened of Perot than were men. Perot's authoritarian style may have been especially unattractive to women: he frequently told voters to "just do it," and implied at times that a suspension of constitutional guarantees might be needed to solve certain problems. Perot's economic focus was on reducing the budget deficit, which was a far lower priority among women than men, and he was skeptical of additional spending on the "social deficit," which women supported more often than men. Finally, Perot's campaign used language designed to appeal to men. He frequently used metaphors that compared economic policy to tinkering under the hood of a car, and his references to women were occasionally patronizing. For these reasons, Perot was less attractive to women than to men.

Conclusions

The 1992 election constituted a major victory for liberal feminists. The number of Democratic women in the U.S. House and Senate increased sharply, and the newly elected Democratic president reversed many of the antifeminist policies of the Reagan-Bush years. These victories were hailed by male and female feminists and were denounced by women and men who oppose feminist policies.

Many of the Senate campaigns of women candidates emphasized gender-related symbolism: Washington's Democratic nominee for the Senate, Patty Murray, referred to herself as a "Mom in Tennis Shoes."[20] Sue Tolleson Rinehart (1994) has argued that the nominations to the U.S. Senate of Democrats Dianne Feinstein and Barbara Boxer in California immediately transformed the nature of the campaigns and invoked complicated considerations of gender.

The gender gap in most Senate elections was modest but statistically significant, with women more likely than men to support the liberal Democratic candidate, regardless of which, if any, candidate was a woman. It appears, however, that women were also somewhat more likely than men to vote for women candidates, regardless of party. All this suggests that women (and men) vote more on the basis of partisanship and policy than on the sex of the candidate but that women are more likely than men to prefer to elect more women after partisanship and policy are controlled. Both men and women indicated that they wanted to elect more women in 1992, but this sentiment was more widespread among women, and more intensely held.

The gender symbolism of the presidential campaign was a continuation of the "family values" debates of the 1980s. The Republicans continued to stake out a pro-life, antifeminist position on many issues, and the Democrats continued their support for abortion choice and gender equality. For a time the symbolism was personified in the Republican attacks on Hillary Clinton, and the Democrats' frequent references to Clarence Thomas.

In the presidential election, there was a modest but significant gender gap, with women contributing the lion's share of Clinton's victory margin. Women were more likely to support Clinton than men, not because they liked him or disliked Bush personally, but because of partisanship and their positions on various policy issues. The greater willingness of men to back Perot is less explainable with available data, but we think it likely that Perot's issue package, his authoritarian style, and his style of communication may have limited his support among women.

Nonetheless, men and women had the same ordering of candidates; among both sexes, Clinton received a plurality of the vote, Bush came in second, and Perot came in third. It is important to remember that there were greater differences among members of each sex than between women and men. Race was a far greater factor in presidential and Senate voting than gender, and white evangelical women preferred Bush to Clinton by a wide margin, while young, white professional women were strong elements of Clinton's coalition. Yet women and men do hold somewhat different policy positions and care about different issues. Women now vote more frequently than men, and the gap in campaign contributions may be narrowing as well. It seems likely that women's policy concerns will be a major focus of elections for many years to come.

Notes

1. In 1993, Republican Kay Bailey Hutchison became the second Republican woman in the Senate. She won easily in an open seat created by the retirement of Lloyd Bentsen, who joined the Clinton cabinet. Hutchison was returned to the Senate in 1994, as was Dianne Feinstein (D-Calif.), while Olympia Snowe of Maine became the third Republican woman in the Senate.

2. We do not intend to imply that men are the baseline from which to evaluate women's electoral behavior. Instead, we are merely following the

most common conventions in focusing on women's behaviors and attitudes. In fact, much of the gender gap in partisanship has resulted from rapid changes in the partisanship of white men, which were not mirrored by those of white women (Miller 1991).

3. VRS conducts exit polls on election day for media subscribers. For the general election, precincts in all fifty states and the District of Columbia were sampled, with the probability of sampling proportionate to the total vote cast in a recent past election. "Within precincts, respondents were selected on a systematic random basis. The interviewer had no control over respondent selection" (Voter Research and Surveys 1993). The surveys were self-administered. The primary election exit polls were similarly conducted, but not all states were sampled. These data were made available by the Inter-University Consortium for Political and Social Research (ICPSR).

Greenberg-Lake, The Analysis Group, conducted polls for the 1992 Clinton campaign. These were national surveys conducted by telephone. These data were made available to us by Celinda Lake.

4. Democrat Dianne Feinstein of California defeated an appointed incumbent from a divided party, and Democrat Carol Moseley-Braun of Illinois beat an incumbent in a three-candidate primary in which the two other candidates concentrated their negative advertisements on each other.

5. EMILY's List stands for "Early Money Is Like Yeast," a phrase that emphasizes that this PAC focuses on providing seed money early in the campaigns of women candidates. WISH List stands for "Women in the Senate and House," and it also provides early money and training for women candidates.

6. In contrast, in 1990, Colorado Democrat Josie Heath's campaign foundered when her calls for deep defense cuts were unpopular during the Gulf buildup (Barone and Ujifusa 1992).

7. Miller (1991) reported that white women in the South had made a small shift back toward the Democrats after 1972, while men had moved in large numbers toward the Republicans. He found that the gender gap was confined to whites in the South, with whites outside the South and African Americans showing no gender gap. Jelen and Wilcox (1994), however, find evidence of a significant gender gap in partisanship in most states.

8. The 1992 NES overestimates the Clinton vote among women and may also overestimate Democratic identification.

9. Women also live longer than men, and are therefore more dependent on social security and Medicare. Voters generally perceive that the Democrats are more likely than Republicans to favor generous social security benefits.

10. Our analysis strategy is similar to that of Gilens (1988). The relative effects suggest that attitudes on domestic spending were twice as important in explaining the gender gap in partisanship as foreign policy attitudes. This reverses the ordering that Gilens reported. Although Gilens's study was also conducted during a recession, it was a period in which foreign policy was more salient than in 1992.

11. Of course, this can occur in a variety of ways. Women may be more likely to vote for female candidates than they are to vote for male candidates while sex of the candidate may not make a difference to male voters. It is also possible that men will be less likely to vote for female candidates than male

candidates while sex of the candidate may be irrelevant to women. Finally, both men and women may respond to the sex of the candidate.

12. The VRS data are representative within states, providing large samples for states with and without women candidates. They do not permit analysis of individual House races.

13. Interestingly, this gender gap was confined to older voters, and among the youngest members of the Kansas electorate women were more likely than men to support her Democratic male challenger.

14. California presented an unusual situation in 1992 in that there were elections for two Senate seats. One of California's senators, Republican Pete Wilson, had left his Senate seat in 1991 after he was elected governor of the state. As governor, Wilson appointed fellow Republican John Seymour to fill this seat temporarily until after an election could be held in 1992. This is referred to as the "short" seat because the term for this Senate seat was to expire in 1994. The other California Senate seat was also up for election in 1992. It is referred to as the "long" seat because it has a normal six-year term.

15. In 1990 neither state with Republican women candidates had a significant gender gap after controls for partisanship and income. In Kansas, Republican Nancy Kassebaum won more women's votes than men after controls for party and income, and in New Jersey, Democrat Bill Bradley had a statistically significant advantage among women voters after party and income were controlled.

16. Usually the number of blacks in national surveys makes such a comparison tenuous. The national exit polls had sufficient numbers of black voters to make the difference in gender gaps among white and black voters statistically significant, however.

17. Personal communication from Celinda Lake, a Democratic pollster who specializes in gender issues.

18. Our dependent variable is an adjusted feeling thermometer toward each candidate. For each candidate, we began with the feeling thermometer toward that candidate and subtracted the higher of the feeling thermometers toward the other two.

19. We selected these two demographic variables because they were the only two with statistically significant relationships with candidate evaluations in our various model specifications.

20. When Patty Murray was first elected to Washington's state senate, she was dismissed by a fellow lawmaker as "just a mom in tennis shoes" who would never have any influence in politics. As Schroedel and Snyder (1994) discuss, she adopted this term to her own advantage early in her 1992 Senate campaign to cast herself as an underdog and evoke images of "family, the middle class, and womanhood."

CHAPTER 9

The Demise of the New Deal Coalition: Partisanship and Group Support, 1952–92

HAROLD W. STANLEY AND RICHARD G. NIEMI

The makeup of the party support coalitions—who favors the Democrats, who favors the Republicans—is of long-standing interest. Of particular concern to political scientists is the pattern of support over medium to long periods. White southerners, for example, were very heavily Democratic in the 1950s and earlier. How much less Democratic, how much more Republican, has this group become since the 1950s? Young people in the 1980s were slightly more Republican than their elders. Did they remain more Republican in the early 1990s?

Of special interest is what happened to the New Deal coalition. Beginning in the 1930s, and for a long time after, a number of demographic groups voted more Democratic than Republican, often by a wide margin. These groups included southern whites, African Americans, Catholics, Jews, labor union members and their households, and poorer individuals in general, such as those who regarded themselves as working class. In the 1960s and later, it began to be observed that support from some of these groups was weakening (e.g., Nie, Verba, and Petrocik 1976, chap. 13). Yet in election after election, the remnants of voting patterns established in the Great Depression could be detected. Southern whites, for example, still tended to be more Democratic than Republican.

The nomination of a southerner for president—and the fact that

Bill Clinton had the strongest Democratic showing in the two-party presidential vote since 1964—would seem to make the persistence of the New Deal coalition likely. Yet by 1992 more than a half-century had elapsed since the 1930s. Even after this amount of time, were the Democrats able to marshall support from their long-time allies? Or did the stronger-than-expected support for Ross Perot suggest an even further weakening of the old coalition? Were the Republicans—even in a losing battle—able to attract support from any of the traditionally Democratic groups? In short, were the party coalitions unchanged? Was the New Deal coalition alive or dead?

Using survey data from 1952 to 1992, we can answer such questions.[1] The answers turn out to be both more interesting and more difficult to come by than one might suppose. First, exactly what does it mean to support a party? If it simply means "how do people vote?" we could just show which candidates various groups have supported over the years. Understandably, however, voting is affected by which contest one considers (presidential, congressional, etc.). In addition, the qualities of the candidates affect voting in a given contest; some groups of voters could be moderately Republican in some respects but vote heavily Democratic (as in the 1964 presidential contest) or moderately Democratic and yet vote heavily Republican (as in 1972). Can we assess party support in some more enduring or "underlying" sense? Often, political scientists attempt to do so by observing party identification, which is what we do in this chapter: we look at party coalitions over the years in terms of which party people say they "generally" support.[2]

A second consideration is how, statistically, we should assess the support of each group for a party. We could simply show the partisanship of each group—that is, how many native southern whites, urban residents, blacks, white Protestant fundamentalists, and so on, say they generally support Democrats versus Republicans. For some purposes this approach is exactly what one wants. A problem is that such simple accounts are misleading because the groups are overlapping. For example, blacks tend to reside in urban areas. Thus, if one finds that blacks and urban residents tend to support Democrats, one is talking largely about the same people. Do both characteristics tend to make people Democratic? Trying to answer such questions raises several problems, but one is certainly aided by the use of multivariate statistical procedures (i.e., procedures that incorporate multiple variables "all at once" rather than one at a time). In this chapter we use multivariate logit analysis. While this technique is complicated, a careful reading of our tables and of the explanations we provide for them should make the results understandable.

The Models

We begin by describing the multivariate models that form the basis of our analysis. In this presentation, we draw on National Election Studies data from nineteen presidential and congressional elections since 1952. Because our interest is in the nature of party support over time, we might ideally have a single equation, one that assesses the contribution of a variety of groups over the entire period under study. In fact, we need several models. This is primarily because the groups considered relevant change over time. Hispanics, for example, were simply not a large enough group to be considered politically significant before the 1980s. Religious fundamentalists were a large enough group, but they were not considered a coherent political force until the mid-1970s. And, obviously, certain groups defined by birth dates—such as those born after 1958—could not be relevant until recently.[3]

With these constraints in mind, we defined three models of party support that collectively cover the 1952–92 period. For comparisons over the entire period, it is important to consider all three models, and we have previously done so. For the present analysis, we emphasize the latest model, which can be estimated without change since 1980. That model incorporates the New Deal elements, gender, church attendance, income, white Protestant fundamentalists, Hispanic origin, 1943–58 birth cohort, and 1959–74 birth cohort. The primary dependent variables are Democratic identification and Republican identification.[4]

We use separate models for Democratic and Republican identification. To the extent that the New Deal coalition has broken up, we want to be able to see the breakup in process—how quickly the coalition dissolved and the timing and consistency with which various groups left the party. We also want to see whether formerly Democratic groups subsequently support the Republican Party. For new groups, we want to see whether hypothesized connections to the Republicans have taken hold. Since we have analyzed these changes previously (Stanley, Bianco, and Niemi 1986; Stanley and Niemi 1991), our focus here is on the continuing nature of the changes as reflected in 1990–92 period.[5]

Results

We begin by considering the estimates of recent group effects for the core groups of the New Deal coalition. The top half of table 9.1 presents the mean predicted probability that a group member claims Democratic identification in each election year since 1952. (See also appendix, p. 238.) Essentially, these numbers are the proportions of

Democrats in each group before imposing any controls for other group memberships.[6] The latest figures show a small resurgence among certain of the New Deal coalition groups in 1990 and 1992. Overall, however, the mixed pattern of gains and declines raises strong doubts that the old Democratic coalition still exists.[7]

Most noteworthy is the continued decline of support among native southern whites. The proportion of Democratic identifiers among native southern whites reached a new low in 1990. In 1992, despite having a moderate Democratic presidential nominee from the South, another new low was reached.[8] These lows of around one-third Democratic were a marked decline from nearly three-quarters Democratic in the 1950s. In direct contrast, Jewish support for the Democrats rebounded sharply, reaching levels about as high as any time since 1960. The proportion of Democrats among Catholics also rebounded from 1988, but their level of support has not recovered the highs of the period before 1980. Members of union households and the working class—though overlapping in membership—went divergent ways. Those in union homes increased Democratic identification to levels that had been typical in the 1970s and 1980s. In contrast, support among the working class held steady in 1990 and then dropped to an all-time low in 1992. Support among blacks—despite unhappiness by some prominent blacks such as Jesse Jackson with their role in the Clinton campaign—continued at approximately the same levels.

The most recent figures show quite clearly what has happened to the New Deal coalition. The coalition, which persisted for years after its heyday, did not break apart precipitously. Nor, except for native southern whites, have the Democratic loyalties of the coalition groups declined steadily since the 1950s. Even now, some groups, on occasion, can rally to Democratic loyalty levels reminiscent of decades ago. But these exceptions should not distract from the larger point: Support from the various groups rises and falls without a clear pattern; the components often *tend* toward Democratic support, but the components cannot be counted upon to register the formerly high support levels. In brief, the former Democratic coalition, as such, no longer exists.

The incremental impact of membership in a particular group is isolated in the bottom half of table 9.1. These numbers show how much more likely an individual is to be a Democratic identifier because of membership in a specific group; that is, they consider all of the other group ties of each individual and how likely those other ties are to make the person Democratic. Their movements sometimes diverge considerably from the overall support levels in the top half of the table. For 1990 and 1992, however, the details differ but the incremental proba-

Table 9.1

Mean and Incremental Probabilities of Democratic Identification for Members of Each Group

	1952	1956	1958	1960	1964	1966	1968	1970	1972	1974	1976	1978	1980	1982	1984	1986	1988	1990	1992
Mean probabilities [a]																			
Black	.54	.51	.51	.44	.74	.63	.85	.80	.67	.71	.74	.66	.74	.82	.63	.71	.65	.66	.64
Catholic	.56	.51	.58	.66	.60	.54	.52	.53	.50	.51	.50	.50	.43	.54	.43	.45	.37	.46	.41
Jewish	.76	.63	.71	.52	.56	.67	.51	.55	.52	.52	.59	.55	.83	.62	.60	.36	.36	.61	.60
Female	.47	.43	.51	.49	.54	.47	.48	.46	.43	.43	.42	.42	.45	.49	.41	.42	.40	.43	.39
Native southern white	.76	.70	.75	.72	.72	.60	.53	.45	.52	.51	.51	.43	.50	.55	.41	.43	.40	.38	.32
Union household	.54	.51	.59	.57	.64	.56	.51	.57	.46	.47	.47	.49	.47	.52	.47	.45	.43	.51	.48
Working class	.54	.49	.55	.51	.61	.52	.52	.48	.45	.43	.47	.45	.47	.51	.42	.45	.44	.44	.41
Regular churchgoer	.50	.47	.47	.49	.54	.48	.47	.47	.44	.40	.43	.43	.40	.47	.37	.43	.39	.43	.35
Income: top third	.43	.40	.46	.44	.43	.42	.39	.39	.34	.31	.31	.33	.35	.36	.32	.33	.28	.35	.30
White Protestant fundamentalist	—	—	—	—	—	—	—	—	.45	.44	.42	.42	.54	.48	.41	.38	.37	.33	.30
Hispanic, non-Cuban	—	—	—	—	—	—	—	—	—	—	—	—	.54	.60	.49	.58	.54	.54	.44
Born 1959–70	—	—	—	—	—	—	—	—	—	—	—	—	.32	.35	.31	.35	.27	.30	.28
Born 1943–58	—	—	—	—	—	—	—	—	—	—	—	—	.40	.43	.35	.35	.34	.43	.37
Incremental probabilities [b]																			
Black	.16	.17	.12	.08	.28	.23	.48	.43	.36	.41	.42	.35	.45	.47	.35	.41	.37	.32	.36
Catholic	.20	.19	.21	.31	.18	.16	.18	.15	.20	.21	.21	.20	.14	.20	.14	.15	.09	.12	.14
Jewish	.43	.34	.33	.19	.20	.37	.22	.22	.28	.25	.38	.33	.58	.36	.35	.08	.18	.31	.37
Female	-.01	-.05	.04	.05	.02	.03	.04	.02	.05	.04	.03	.04	.09	.06	.05	.05	.09	.02	.05
Native southern white	.44	.41	.40	.41	.32	.26	.19	.11	.18	.22	.21	.11	.15	.20	.08	.12	.10	.05	.05
Union household	.10	.10	.12	.13	.16	.14	.06	.16	.08	.09	.11	.14	.10	.12	.12	.10	.10	.15	.15

Working class	.12	.08	.08	.09	.09	.09	.01	.05	-.02	.07	.06	.06	.04	.03	.04	.11	.02	.07
Regular churchgoer	.00	-.00	-.09	-.03	-.01	.02	.00	.03	.03	-.03	.03	-.04	.02	-.04	.01	.02	.01	-.03
Income: top third	-.04	-.02	-.02	-.04	-.11	-.03	-.04	-.07	-.06	-.12	-.09	-.05	-.11	-.06	-.06	-.04	-.08	-.07
White Protestant fundamentalist	—	—	—	—	—	—	—	.08	.05	.04	.09	.22	.07	.10	.04	.06	-.01	.01
Hispanic, non-Cuban	—	—	—	—	—	—	—	—	—	—	—	.16	.10	.08	.14	.15	.14	.08
Born 1959–70	—	—	—	—	—	—	—	—	—	—	—	-.17	-.17	-.16	-.16	-.20	-.19	-.17
Born 1943–58	—	—	—	—	—	—	—	—	—	—	—	-.08	-.06	-.11	-.12	-.10	-.05	-.07

SOURCE: 1952–92 National Election Studies.

NOTE: The three models containing the different variables were evaluated through 1992. However, presentation is greatly simplified by showing only the following: 1952–70 values are based on the model with nine variables; 1972–78 values are based on the model with ten variables; 1980–92 entries are based on the model with thirteen variables. Values that can be estimated with more than one model seldom differ by more than .01 from one model to another.

a. Cells are the mean of the predicted probabilities of Democratic identification for all group members in each year.
b. Cells are the average of the difference, for each group member, between the individual's predicted probability of Democratic identification and what the individual's probability would have been without the effect of the group membership.

bilities support the interpretation above. Being a native southern white now propels one hardly at all in the direction of Democratic support; other characteristics are variable in their effects.

As we turn to the newer groups, some of whom are said to be attracted to the Republicans, we draw on table 9.1 and on a parallel table for the Republicans (table 9.2). Beginning with observed support for President Reagan in 1980, a great deal was written about the so-called gender gap—the tendency of women to be noticeably more Democratic than men. Indeed, the incremental push toward Democratic identification was greater in 1980 than in any previous year and rose to that same level again in 1988. In the past two election years, however, it dropped down to earlier levels and then rose again. Despite the brief decline in 1990, it clearly could not be said that women were moving in the direction of the Republican Party; table 9.2 shows the largest ever incremental probabilities away from the Republican Party. To the extent that women have moved away from the Democratic Party, Republicans have yet to attract them as a group.

The relationship between religion and partisanship was allegedly reinvigorated during the Reagan years as the president supported traditional moral values consistent with fundamentalist Christianity. The Bush administration continued to support those values, sometimes less vigorously (as was alleged with respect to abortion policy) and sometimes very vocally (as with the family values debate sparked by Vice-President Dan Quayle's highly publicized critical remarks about television's fictionalized Murphy Brown bearing a baby out of wedlock). During the 1992 primary campaign, these values were emphasized by the candidacy of Pat Buchanan (Baker 1993, 46). Both of our measures of religiosity seem to reflect these developments, but they leave unclear what the long-term impact will be for partisanship.

Church attendance at first appears to have had only a minor effect on partisanship over the period under study. Those who attend church often are more frequently Democratic (compare the top portions of tables 9.1 and 9.2). But this partly stems from the fact that Catholics and blacks attend church more regularly; the incremental probabilities in table 9.1 show little push in a Democratic direction associated with regular attendance. On the other hand, a modest push toward Republican identification appears in 1980, 1984, and 1992 (table 9.2, bottom half). That this weak push was not sustained in 1988 or in the off-years perhaps suggests that it arises only when religious values are actively debated or supported by political leaders.

When we measure religiosity among whites in terms of affiliation with a fundamentalist religion, the results reveal a considerable change

TABLE 9.2

MEAN AND INCREMENTAL PROBABILITIES OF REPUBLICAN IDENTIFICATION FOR MEMBERS OF EACH GROUP

	1952	1956	1958	1960	1964	1966	1968	1970	1972	1974	1976	1978	1980	1982	1984	1986	1988	1990	1992
Mean probabilities [a]																			
Black	.14	.19	.16	.17	.07	.09	.02	.05	.08	.03	.06	.06	.04	.02	.03	.05	.06	.05	.04
Catholic	.18	.20	.17	.14	.16	.17	.15	.17	.14	.15	.16	.14	.18	.17	.20	.22	.27	.23	.20
Jewish	.00	.12	.12	.08	.06	.05	.05	.05	.09	.12	.09	.05	.00	.19	.10	.21	.12	.11	.05
Female	.29	.31	.28	.31	.24	.25	.23	.25	.24	.23	.27	.23	.23	.23	.28	.26	.29	.23	.23
Native southern white	.09	.12	.11	.11	.09	.11	.09	.15	.15	.11	.16	.17	.16	.18	.22	.22	.21	.20	.25
Union household	.22	.21	.17	.17	.14	.18	.19	.15	.16	.13	.14	.14	.14	.18	.20	.21	.21	.20	.15
Working class	.21	.23	.23	.24	.16	.20	.20	.20	.21	.19	.19	.16	.18	.17	.22	.20	.19	.21	.20
Regular churchgoer	.28	.29	.31	.30	.26	.25	.24	.25	.26	.25	.28	.24	.28	.26	.32	.27	.32	.28	.30
Income: top third	.31	.34	.33	.31	.31	.26	.27	.30	.30	.28	.30	.25	.30	.33	.35	.30	.35	.33	.32
White Protestant fundamentalist	—	—	—	—	—	—	—	—	.20	.16	.21	.18	.17	.20	.22	.26	.27	.29	.30
Hispanic, non-Cuban	—	—	—	—	—	—	—	—	—	—	.18	.14	.14	.05	.09	.13	.05	.12	.17
Born 1959–70	—	—	—	—	—	—	—	—	—	—	—	.14	.28	.25	.27	.25	.29	.27	.24
Born 1943–58	—	—	—	—	—	—	—	—	—	—	—	—	.20	.20	.28	.25	.27	.24	.25
Incremental probabilities [b]																			
Black	− .24	− .18	− .23	− .23	− .23	− .22	− .33	− .28	− .24	− .28	− .25	− .22	− .26	− .28	− .35	− .29	− .29	− .27	− .29
Catholic	− .22	− .19	− .25	− .27	− .20	− .18	− .22	− .18	− .19	− .17	− .17	− .18	− .13	− .16	− .17	− .12	− .07	− .11	− .17
Jewish	− .42	− .32	− .27	− .34	− .35	− .35	− .34	− .35	− .28	− .21	− .29	− .31	− .34	− .24	− .35	− .16	− .34	− .27	− .35
Female	.03	.07	− .01	.02	− .00	− .01	− .02	.01	.01	.00	.06	.02	− .02	− .03	− .00	− .01	− .02	− .04	− .04
Native southern white	− .33	− .30	− .33	− .36	− .29	− .27	− .29	− .22	− .16	− .19	− .16	− .11	− .12	− .14	− .07	− .11	− .13	− .13	− .10
Union household	− .06	− .10	− .13	− .14	− .12	− .09	− .07	− .13	− .11	− .12	− .14	− .10	− .13	− .10	− .10	− .07	− .11	− .10	− .13

Working class	−.13	−.09	−.04	−.11	−.11	−.09	−.05	−.06	−.01	−.01	−.03	−.08	−.04	−.07	−.06	−.07	−.13	−.04	−.07
Regular churchgoer	.05	.04	.10	.06	.04	.02	.03	−.00	.05	.06	.04	.08	.03	.09	.08	.04	.05	.05	.09
Income: top third	.01	.04	.03	−.02	.05	−.03	.01	.04	.08	.05	.07	.04	.07	.09	.07	.03	.02	.09	.06
White Protestant fundamentalist	—	—	—	—	—	—	—	—	−.06	−.05	−.08	−.10	−.07	−.14	−.04	−.04	.00	−.02	
Hispanic, non-Cuban	—	—	—	—	—	—	—	—	—	−.03	−.13	−.11	−.10	−.17	−.11	−.05			
Born 1959–70	—	—	—	—	—	—	—	—	—	—	−.06	.04	.02	.04	.03	.05	.00		
Born 1943–58	—	—	—	—	—	—	—	—	—	—	.03	−.01	−.01	−.02	−.02	.00			

SOURCE: 1952–92 National Election Studies.

a. Cells are the mean of the predicted probabilities of Republican identification for all group members in each year.

b. Cells are the average of the difference, for each group member, between the individual's predicted probability of Republican identification and what the individual's probability would have been without the effect of the group membership.

since the 1970s, when church membership was first recorded so that we could identify "neofundamentalists." The initial effects are contrary to popular rhetoric: in every election between 1972 and 1988, membership in a Protestant fundamentalist denomination pushed whites away from a Republican identification and inclined them toward the Democrats (incremental probabilities, tables 9.1 and 9.2). In the last two election years, however, there was almost no incremental impact. What remains to be seen is whether the changes in 1990 and 1992 are only the beginning of a new trend, with fundamentalism—presumably because of links to issues such as abortion and school prayers—in the future making people not marginally more Democratic but more Republican.

Moreover, we get a very different picture of the relationship between religion and politics if we examine the overall probabilities of Democratic and Republican identification (tables 9.1 and 9.2, top half). Since 1980, the likelihood of fundamentalists identifying with the Republican Party has increased steadily. The corresponding figure for the Democrats has dropped just as steadily and even more sharply, reaching parity in 1992. Thus, in an overall sense, the relationship between fundamentalism and Republican identification has increased dramatically. Indeed, the greater overall connection between fundamentalism and partisanship could "snowball," making religious fervor a more powerful partisan force for the Republicans.[9]

Another group thought to be part of the Republican rejuvenation is the well-to-do (Petrocik and Steeper 1987). In earlier analyses we noted that a small but clear increase in the incremental probabilities of Republican identification appeared in the 1970s and 1980s, though the change did not seem to be sustained in the late 1980s (Stanley and Niemi 1991, 199). With the most recent observations, however, we can see that the well-off population continued to receive a push in the Republican direction nearly equal to that of the Reagan era.

Young voters—those born after 1958, who were first able to vote for president in the 1980 Reagan election—were thought to have been part of the Republican upsurge of the 1980s (Norpoth 1987; Norpoth and Kagay 1989). We found, however, that the incremental push of being young was better described as an anti-Democratic force (note the relatively large, negative coefficients for the youngest cohort in table 9.1). That tendency continued into the 1990s. Baby boomers—those born between 1943 and 1958, who first cast presidential ballots in the changing political context of the mid-1960s—also continued their anti-Democratic tendencies, though to a lesser degree than the young. For the Republicans, conflicting recent results among the young (table 9.2) give them no reason to be complacent about their success in attracting new voters, and baby boomers are essentially neutral toward the Republicans. Both these groups have consistently high increments in favor of independence (not shown), a reflection of the dealigning forces that have characterized American politics since the mid-1960s.[10]

The final group to gain significance in the past decade or so is Hispanics. Apart from a presumably pro-Republican segment (those of Cuban origin, of whom there are too few for analysis), group attachments clearly push Hispanics toward the Democratic Party and away from the Republican Party (e.g., Southwest Voter Institute 1988). The figures for 1990 and 1992 give encouragement to the Republicans, however. The incremental pushes are smaller, especially for 1992, though these results would have to be sustained for additional elections before one could confirm a more neutral partisan stance among Hispanic voters.

We observed previously, in summarizing the effects of group attachments through the 1988 election, that the extra push from membership in new groups was generally weaker than that from traditional ones, and that what we were observing was not so much a realignment of group support as a general weakening between group attachments and party ties. That observation holds true for the 1990s. Despite Democratic gains in the 1990 midterms and the capture of the White House in 1992, the incremental push toward Democrats weakened after 1988 in more than two-thirds of the groups. "Gains" were more frequent among the Republicans, but the only substantial change meant a larger *negative* increment, as Catholics returned to a more traditional level of eschewing Republican identification.[11]

As far as the new groups are concerned, perhaps the most significant trend uncovered by the addition of data from the 1990s was the movement of Protestant fundamentalists toward the Republican Party, to parity in their overall identification. Ironically, this change, even if it continues unabated or picks up speed in the years to come, is not sufficient to give Republicans majority status in the electorate as a whole. There are simply not enough fundamentalists. Moreover, close association with fundamentalists could drive other groups further away from the party. The Republicans still need to find a comfortable *set* of group attachments if they expect to regain the majority-party status they enjoyed before the New Deal.

Group Support and the Party Coalitions

So far we have focused on the probability that individuals with a given characteristic identify with one party or the other. Now our attention turns to the party coalitions. In the first two sections of tables 9.3 and 9.4 we show the mean predicted probability of Democratic or Republican identification in the United States and, below that, the percentage of each coalition with a given group characteristic. This breakdown of the coalitions is in terms of overlapping groups. The percentages describing the party coalitions thus add to more than 100, as, for example, a black female churchgoer is counted in each of three categories.

Several changes are notable, even if we concentrate only on the past few years. The most striking change is the decline in the proportion of females in the Republican coalition.[12] In the 1980s, the term gender gap was used to describe the greater support of women, compared with men, for the Democrats. That meant, coincidentally, that a greater proportion of the Democratic coalition was female—from three to six percentage points more than in the Republican coalition (tables 9.3 and 9.4).[13] Beginning in 1988 the gap widened, first because of a jump in the proportion of women among Democrats and then because of a substantial drop in the proportion of women among Republicans. In 1992, for the first time since at least 1952, men outnumbered women in one of the party coalitions.

Another noteworthy change also affected both parties in the same way. The proportion of Hispanics rose between 1988 and 1992 in both coalitions. The proportion is still no more than 10 percent, even among Democrats, but it is bound to rise, and as it does, so too will Hispanic influence on party policy. Hispanics now constitute about the same share of the Democratic Party as blacks did before 1964.

In 1990 and 1992, fundamentalists in the Republican coalition continued to strengthen their position. Southerners also increased their proportion slightly, as part of a long-term trend. This, combined with movement away from the Democrats, meant that in 1992, for the first time since the 1950s (and presumably since the 1850s), native southern whites were a larger fraction—though just barely—of Republican than of Democratic identifiers.

On the Democratic side, the proportion of identifiers in union households continued a downward slide from about a third of the coalition in 1966 and earlier to just over a fifth in 1992.[14] The proportion of identifiers who are black dropped slightly from its peak in the late 1980s, but this small change was made up for by recent increases in the proportions that were Jewish and Hispanic, leaving unchanged our assessment of 1992 that the Democratic Party may increasingly be viewed as the party of racial and ethnic minorities and liberal whites.

What would happen to the coalitions if they were to lose the partisan tendency due to each group characteristic? Here we show results

TABLE 9.3
SIZE AND COMPOSITION OF THE DEMOCRATIC COALITION

	1952	1956	1958	1960	1964	1966	1968	1970	1972	1974	1976	1978	1980	1982	1984	1986	1988	1990	1992
Predicted probability of Democratic identification in the U.S. [a]	48	44	50	47	53	46	45	45	41	41	40	40	41	46	38	40	36	41	36
Percentage of Democratic coalition with a given group characteristic [b]																			
Black	11	10	9	8	14	14	18	17	16	16	18	16	19	20	18	25	25	23	24
Catholic	27	25	26	30	26	27	26	25	31	30	33	33	27	29	32	29	26	32	31
Jewish	5	4	4	4	3	5	3	4	3	3	4	4	7	3	4	1	2	3	4
Female	54	53	55	58	57	57	60	58	60	62	60	58	62	59	60	60	65	58	59
Native southern white	25	28	26	28	21	19	20	19	21	25	21	16	21	23	20	21	23	18	17
Union household	32	31	31	34	30	34	28	30	30	31	29	32	29	25	27	24	24	23	22
Working class	70	68	66	73	66	65	61	56	60	58	61	58	56	58	55	56	62	57	56
Regular churchgoer	41	46	43	51	45	43	41	42	42	43	44	42	38	44	38	44	42	45	42
Income: top third	38	28	32	39	29	35	27	34	27	23	29	29	25	29	27	25	26	29	27
White Protestant fundamentalist	—	—	—	—	—	—	—	—	17	19	15	15	19	18	16	16	20	16	16
Hispanic, non-Cuban	—	—	—	—	—	—	—	—	—	—	—	—	4	2	7	6	7	7	10
Born 1959–70	—	—	—	—	—	—	—	—	—	—	—	—	5	7	13	16	16	16	22
Born 1943–58	—	—	—	—	—	—	—	—	—	—	—	—	35	35	34	34	34	36	35

a. These estimates, derived from the model, are virtually identical to the actual percentage of Democratic identifiers.

b. Figures derived from taking the mean predicted probability of Democratic identification for a group in a particular year (table 9.1) multiplied by that group's number of respondents, and dividing this product by the number of Democratic identifiers.

Percentage of Democratic identifiers in group continuing to claim Democratic identification after removing Democratic tendency of defining group characteristic [c]

Group																			
Black	71	66	76	81	63	64	43	46	46	42	42	47	39	43	45	42	43	52	43
Catholic	65	64	64	52	70	70	67	72	61	58	58	59	68	63	68	67	76	74	66
Jewish	43	45	53	63	65	44	57	60	45	52	36	41	30	42	41	77	51	48	38
Female	103	111	93	90	97	93	91	97	89	91	93	91	80	89	86	88	77	95	88
Native southern white	43	42	47	43	55	57	64	76	64	58	59	74	71	63	81	73	74	86	83
Union household	81	80	79	77	76	74	88	71	84	80	77	71	79	78	74	79	76	70	70
Working class	78	83	85	84	85	82	84	98	88	105	86	86	87	92	92	91	75	95	84
Regular churchgoer	100	101	119	106	101	96	100	94	92	106	93	94	110	97	110	98	94	97	110
Income: top third	110	104	104	109	126	107	110	117	117	139	129	128	114	130	118	120	114	124	122
White Protestant fundamentalist	—	—	—	—	—	—	—	—	83	89	91	78	59	86	75	89	84	104	96
Hispanic, non-Cuban	—	—	—	—	—	—	—	—	—	—	—	—	70	83	85	76	73	74	83
Born 1959–70	—	—	—	—	—	—	—	—	—	—	—	—	153	150	152	145	172	161	158
Born 1943–58	—	—	—	—	—	—	—	—	—	—	—	—	121	114	131	133	129	112	119

c. Figures derived by recalculating the probabilities of Democratic identification without the effect of, say, working-class identification, then taking the mean of these probabilities for all respondents who claimed working-class status. The ratio of this revised mean probability to the mean probability that includes the effect of working class gives the ratio of the hypothetical size to the actual one.

Continued ...

TABLE 9.3 — Continued

SIZE AND COMPOSITION OF THE DEMOCRATIC COALITION

Relative size (percentage) of Democratic coalition after removing group characteristic

	1952	1956	1958	1960	1964	1966	1968	1970	1972	1974	1976	1978	1980	1982	1984	1986	1988	1990	1992
Black	97	97	98	99	95	95	90	91	92	90	90	92	88	89	90	86	86	89	86
Catholic	91	91	91	85	92	92	91	93	88	88	86	86	91	89	90	91	94	92	90
Jewish	97	98	98	99	99	97	99	98	98	99	98	97	95	98	98	100	99	99	98
Female	101	106	96	94	98	96	94	98	93	94	96	95	87	93	92	93	85	97	93
Native southern white	86	84	86	84	91	92	93	95	92	90	91	96	94	92	96	94	94	98	97
Union household	94	94	94	92	93	91	97	91	95	94	93	91	94	95	93	95	94	93	93
Working class	85	88	90	89	90	88	90	99	93	94	92	92	93	95	96	95	85	97	91
Regular churchgoer	100	100	108	103	100	98	100	97	97	103	97	98	104	99	104	99	97	99	104
Income: top third	104	101	101	103	108	103	103	106	105	109	108	108	104	109	105	105	104	107	106
White Protestant fundamentalist	—	—	—	—	—	—	—	—	97	98	99	97	92	97	96	98	97	101	99
Hispanic, non-Cuban	—	—	—	—	—	—	—	—	—	—	—	—	—	99	100	99	99	98	98
Born 1959–70	—	—	—	—	—	—	—	—	—	—	—	—	102	103	107	107	111	113	113
Born 1943–58	—	—	—	—	—	—	—	—	—	—	—	—	107	105	111	110	104	104	106

SOURCE: 1952–92 National Election Studies.

TABLE 9.4

SIZE AND COMPOSITION OF THE REPUBLICAN COALITION

Predicted probability of Republican identification

	1952	1956	1958	1960	1964	1966	1968	1970	1972	1974	1976	1978	1980	1982	1984	1986	1988	1990	1992
in the U.S. [a]	28	29	28	29	24	25	24	25	24	22	25	21	23	25	28	26	29	25	26

Percentage of Republican coalition with a given group characteristic [b]

	1952	1956	1958	1960	1964	1966	1968	1970	1972	1974	1976	1978	1980	1982	1984	1986	1988	1990	1992
Black	5	6	5	4	3	4	1	2	3	1	2	3	2	1	1	3	3	3	2
Catholic	15	15	14	10	16	15	14	14	15	16	17	17	21	17	21	22	24	26	21
Jewish	0	1	1	1	1	1	1	1	1	1	1	1	0	1	1	1	1	1	0
Female	58	60	55	56	56	57	54	59	57	60	66	60	57	53	57	57	57	51	48
Native southern white	5	7	7	6	5	6	6	12	10	10	10	12	12	14	15	17	15	15	18
Union household	23	20	16	15	15	21	20	14	17	16	14	17	15	15	16	17	15	14	10
Working class	46	50	52	51	38	45	44	42	48	48	41	39	39	37	40	38	33	44	37
Regular churchgoer	40	43	53	47	47	41	39	41	43	50	48	43	48	45	45	44	44	47	50
Income: top third	47	37	43	41	46	40	37	47	40	38	46	41	40	49	40	37	39	44	40
White Protestant fundamentalist	—	—	—	—	—	—	—	—	13	13	12	13	11	14	12	17	17	23	22
Hispanic, non-Cuban	—	—	—	—	—	—	—	—	—	—	—	—	2	0	2	2	1	2	5
Born 1959–70	—	—	—	—	—	—	—	—	—	—	—	—	4	10	14	19	20	31	26
Born 1943–58	—	—	—	—	—	—	—	—	—	—	—	—	31	31	38	37	34	30	32

SOURCE: 1952–92 National Election Studies.

a. These estimates, derived from the model, are virtually identical to the actual percentage of Republican identifiers.

b. Figures derived from taking the mean predicted probability of Republican identification for a group in a particular year (table 9.2) multiplied by that group's number of respondents, and dividing this product by the number of Republican identifiers.

for only the Democratic coalition.[15] These results show, again, the shattered nature of the New Deal coalition. Compared to 1988, Catholics, Jews, and members of union households would be more likely to drop their Democratic identification were they to lose the party's appeal to them as members of these groups. But native southern whites and working-class members would be less likely to alter their identifications. Also significant are the numbers near 100 for churchgoers and fundamentalists, suggesting that the Democratic Party would retain the loyalty of almost all its supporters from these groups even if its group-based appeals to these individuals were to vanish. The latest figures suggest that without the Democratic tendency of the group membership, less than half of blacks and Jews and only about two-thirds of Catholics and union household members would remain Democratic. Females, native southern whites, working-class individuals, and Hispanics would have about 85 percent retention of Democratic identification.

The final panel in table 9.3 shows the effect on the size of the Democratic coalition of removing the group characteristic. As of 1992, the party benefits from a combination of overlapping characteristics and the small size of some groups that would most likely desert it. Only blacks dip below 90 percent, suggesting that the party would remain close to its current size even if it lost its specific appeal to any one group. This may be partly a result of President Clinton's studied effort to appeal to a broad range of groups and to avoid being "captured" by any one. Ironically, a broad-based appeal may have made the Democrats simultaneously more appealing to members of each specific group.

Conclusion

One might view the changes in the party coalitions over the past few years as merely a continuation of processes that have been under way for decades. After all, movements away from the Democratic Party by native southern whites began in the 1960s and by members of union households in the 1970s. Hispanics were too few to be a politically potent group before the 1980s, but the Democratic ties of another prominent minority group—blacks—became very strong in the 1960s.

While not denying these links to the past, we think it would be a mistake to view recent changes in the party coalitions as merely more of the same. With respect to the remnants of the New Deal coalition, two very important points can be made about 1990 or 1992. First, native southern whites were estimated to be a greater fraction of Republican than of Democratic identifiers. Second, members of union households continued to fall toward one-fifth of Democratic identifiers. In both cases, the trends and differences were small, but the symbolism is clear. At the same time, Hispanics were becoming a larger support group for both parties, but especially for the Democrats.

A significant threshold was also passed when, in 1986 and again in 1990 and 1992, white Protestant fundamentalists became a larger fraction of Republican than of Democratic identifiers. Despite overt Republican appeals since the early 1980s, the incremental push from being a fundamentalist was toward the Democrats until the last two elections. Now Republicans have pulled even in their appeal, and more of their identifiers claim to be a part of this group.

Considering these changes, it is time to declare the New Deal coalition dead. The groups that were part of the coalition will obviously continue to be of interest, as they include some of the largest and most visible groups in the country; political scientists and pundits can therefore be expected to analyze the movements of these groups well into the future. But the party support coalitions definitely differ from what they were in the 1950s. If this was not obvious even as recently as 1988, the latest probabilities make it clear. Democrats can no longer rely on native southern whites; conversely, Republicans can potentially attract them in large numbers. Union households and working-class individuals, now fewer in number, are unlikely to return to their former partisanship. Both parties have to appeal to the middle class. The number of Hispanics has increased to the point that they can no longer be ignored; non-Cuban Hispanics lean toward the Democrats, but not to the extent of the pro-Democratic groups of the 1950s. The gender gap is something both parties must address. Arguments may continue over whether these changes make up a "realignment" of support. But one thing is clear: we can at long last declare one very prominent coalition dead.

Appendix

Dependent Variables[a]

Democratic	1 if strong or weak Democratic identifier, 0 if independent, Republican, apolitical, or other
Republican	1 if strong or weak Republican identifier, 0 if independent, Democratic, apolitical, or other

Independent Variables[b,c]

Black	1 if black, 0 otherwise
Catholic	1 if Catholic, 0 otherwise
Jewish	1 if Jewish, 0 otherwise
Female	1 if female, 0 otherwise
Native southern white	1 if white native of South (grew up in Alabama, Arkansas, Florida, Georgia, Louisiana, Mississippi, North Carolina, South Carolina, Tennessee, Texas, or Virginia), 0 otherwise
Union household	1 if union member in household, 0 otherwise
Working class	1 if self-reported working class, 0 otherwise
Regular church-goer	1 if attends church regularly or as often as "almost every week," 0 otherwise
Income	1 if family income in upper third, 0 otherwise
Fundamentalist	1 if "neo-fundamentalist" white Protestant, 0 otherwise
Hispanic	1 if of non-Cuban Hispanic origin, 0 otherwise
Born 1959–70	1 if born in 1959 or later, 0 otherwise
Born 1943–58	1 if born between 1943 and 1958 inclusive, 0 otherwise

a. With one exception, the results are very similar if one defines partisans to include those leaning toward the parties.

b. Whites migrating into the South, education, metropolitan residence, Sun-belt residence, rural residence, blue-collar workers, white-collar workers, farmers, Protestant, Irish or Polish descent, and foreign-born parents were incorporated at earlier stages of the analysis but failed to exhibit a consistently significant relationship with partisanship.

c. "Otherwise" includes only other valid data codes. Missing data (primarily "not ascertained" cases) were excluded from the analysis.

Notes

1. For a complementary analysis of ideology and the groups making up the Democratic coalition, see Carmines and Stanley (1992).

2. Party identification, or partisanship, has been measured regularly (since 1952) by both commercial pollsters and academic researchers. The Gallup poll, for example, regularly reports proportions of Democrats, independents, and Republicans in *The Gallup Report,* available in most university libraries. In political science, there is a long history of research on the meaning and measurement of partisanship, both in the United States and abroad. See, for example, Niemi and Weisberg (1993a, b). For the distribution of partisanship over time, see Stanley and Niemi (1994).

3. A second, related reason for multiple models is that the survey questions needed to identify the appropriate groups have not been asked over the entire period. There was no reason to think about measuring religious fundamentalism in the 1950s and 1960s. In addition, how to measure this concept has been debated widely (see, for example, Rothenberg and Newport 1984); given this debate, it is not surprising that the relevant survey items have changed over the years, resulting in a further complication.

4. The survey question used by the National Election Studies to measure partisanship is: "Generally speaking, do you usually think of yourself as a Republican, a Democrat, an independent, or what?" Democrats and Republicans are asked if they are "strong" or "weak," and independents are asked if they lean toward the Democratic or the Republican Party. This results in seven categories: strong Democrats, weak Democrats, independents leaning Democratic, "pure" independents, independents leaning Republican, and weak and strong Republicans (plus a small group of respondents who are "apolitical"). For our analysis, the first two categories are considered Democrats and the last two Republicans. (Regarding the handling of the "leaners," see Niemi and Weisberg 1993b, 278–79.)

5. Reliance on the NES cumulative data file through 1990, refined coding of certain variables and percentages, and use of a logistic procedure with different convergence criteria make the results reported here differ slightly from those in our earlier articles.

6. These mean predicted probabilities of identification from the logit analysis closely match the percentages of identifiers from a simple frequency count. Since the incremental boosts to identification and subsequent presentations are taken from the logit analysis, we present these probabilities rather than the simple percentages. Data are unavailable for 1954 and 1962.

7. For a somewhat different reading on 1992, see Pomper (1993, 135–40). Note, however, that Pomper analyzed voting in 1992, whereas we use the more durable indicator of party identification. Also note that our interpretations are not wholly inconsistent. For example, we note that Hispanics are a new force in the Democratic coalition; Pomper considers them a traditional element in that they, like some other Democratic support groups, are "among America's disadvantaged" (p. 135).

8. Differences of just a few points may have no basis in reality—that is, they may not be statistically significant. Thus, changes such as the decline from .40 to .38 among native southern whites between 1988 and 1990 should

be interpreted cautiously. One of the ways of being cautious, which is of obvious relevance here, is to observe patterns across time. Often, small changes will not be interpretable, but a long, clear trend is meaningful even if each step along the way is a small one.

9. See also Green and Guth (1988). The fact that mean and incremental probabilities are divergent might seem oddly inconsistent. They can be explained, at least in part, by a change observed earlier—that among native southern whites. One of the major groups of white fundamentalists is Southern Baptists. As native southern whites moved away from the Democrats and toward the Republicans, this coincidentally moved Southern Baptists from the Democratic to the Republican side. But that change may not have had religious motivation, since until 1990, fundamentalism itself carried with it a small incremental nudge in favor of the Democrats.

10. "Dealignment" refers to the fact that more Americans began calling themselves independent in the mid-1960s, a change that has continued up to the present. See the distributions of party identification in Stanley and Niemi (1994, 158–60).

11. Although we analyze partisanship rather than the vote, if we had instead analyzed the presidential vote, many of the conclusions about the political significance of group membership would have been the same. Most vividly, change among native southern whites has left them voting less Democratic than the nation as a whole. The lack of a strong group basis for the Republican vote is also apparent. In these and other respects, a comparable analysis focusing on presidential voting would establish complementary findings.

12. Another striking change in the party coalitions, the greater proportion of the young, is politically significant but demographically inevitable as the older generations are replaced by the younger.

13. Historically, a greater proportion of men than women have been independent (Miller, Miller, and Schneider 1980, 88), so females constituted a majority of both parties.

14. This is a function, in part, of declining membership in unions. We noted earlier that the tendency for union members in 1990 and 1992 was for greater support of Democrats.

15. Comparable results for Republicans would be convenient, but those results have a distorting mirror-image aspect. Given the general Democratic tendencies of the group ties, removing the group ties means that the group's share of Republican identifiers, perhaps tiny to begin with, often swells to greater than 100 percent of its former size.

CHAPTER 10

Social-Group Polarization in 1992

HERBERT F. WEISBERG, AUDREY A. HAYNES, AND JON A. KROSNICK

Politics always involves clashes of social groups. The interests of some groups come into conflict with the interests of others, and government must decide how to manage such conflicts. Whether it is unions versus businesses debating labor policies, fundamentalist religious groups versus feminists debating abortion laws, or gun owners versus law enforcement officials debating gun-control laws, group conflicts are at the heart of the American political process. Thus it is interesting to study and compare the roles of Catholics, Protestants, and Jews (see chapter 9), blacks (see chapter 7), and other such groups in the American political process.

Elections provide an opportunity for such group conflicts to become apparent, and 1992 was no exception. Bill Clinton's campaign clearly endorsed the interests of groups such as environmentalists, abortion rights activists, and homosexuals, and these groups publicly supported Clinton's candidacy. Similarly, George Bush's campaign stands were consistent with the preferences of fundamentalist religious groups, the U.S. military establishment, and law enforcement advocates. And presumably in response, these groups supported Bush's candidacy. Campaign rhetoric also focused at times on other social groups, including immigrants, especially illegal immigrants, Asian Americans, and Hispanics.

Over the course of the campaign, one set of social groups came together in a coalition supporting Clinton and the Democrats, and another set of groups banded together in support of Bush and the Republicans.[1] Even though the basic values and concerns of the various groups supporting a candidate did not always have much in common with one another, they came together in opposition to a common enemy. Because of the choice that Americans faced in the 1992 election, the two coalitions of groups came into conflict with one another.

These group coalitions are usually ideological as well as partisan. The world of politics that confronts American citizens through the daily newspaper and the television news is powerfully organized along ideological lines. That structure is evident at the elite level where votes in Congress often divide liberals from conservatives and where the two major political parties are distinguished principally by the Democrats' more liberal and Republicans' more conservative positions. For example, in the social welfare arena, liberals are more likely to desire governmental solutions to societal problems, whereas conservatives are more likely to favor nongovernmental solutions. Thus, in the early 1990s, liberals proposed a bill requiring businesses to grant new parents unpaid leave to take care of their children, while conservatives felt that businesses should decide such matters for themselves. Liberals thought government could help solve a problem in the private sphere, whereas conservatives viewed government itself as a problem. Group coalitions are likewise usually ideological, so elections often become conflicts between Democratic-liberal coalitions and Republican-conservative coalitions.

One purpose of this chapter is to explore the extent to which Americans' feelings toward social groups in 1992 reflected these coalitions. That is, did people who liked some groups associated with the liberal coalition tend to like all the groups in that coalition? And did people who liked some conservative groups like all of them? Or did people have loyalties to specific groups without liking other members of their coalitions?

Our second question is whether people's liking of these groups reflected opposition between them. In other words, did people who liked conservative groups also dislike liberal ones? And did liberal group supporters dislike the conservative groups? Or did most individual American voters like some liberal groups *and* some conservative groups, thus transcending the competition between them and failing to take sides? Stanley and Niemi report in chapter 9 that the New Deal coalition has died. This demise would be even more poignant if the polarization between liberal and conservative groupings were no more.

We find that Americans' loyalties toward social groups in 1992 did indeed reflect the clumping of the liberal and conservative coalitions. Some groups dominated these two coalitions in voters' minds, reflecting the 1992 campaign itself. Perhaps most important, Americans saw these as opposing coalitions only to a limited extent, much more weakly than they had during most of the prior twenty-five years. Thus the 1992 election represents a weakening in the ideological cleavage of group conflict in American politics.

Social Groups in the 1992 Election

Social-group involvement in the 1992 election paralleled recent elections, but with some differences. For one thing, the Republican Party aligned itself with social conservatives more than in 1988, partly because of the emphasis on family values in the Republican campaign and at the Republican National Convention. At the same time, the Democratic standard-bearers were less tied to the liberal side than in 1988 when Bush attacked Democrat Michael Dukakis as a card-carrying member of the liberal American Civil Liberties Union.

Some social groups that have been traditionally aligned with the parties were out of the limelight during the 1992 campaign. In particular, candidate Clinton campaigned as a moderate rather than fully embracing traditional Democratic liberal groups. He distanced himself from black activists, as when he criticized African-American rap singer Sister Souljah. Clinton came out in favor of welfare reform, so he was also not closely tied to those on welfare. He had union support, but that support was not a prominent part of the campaign. Clinton even received some support from retired military leaders, though Bush was more likely to be seen as favoring a strong defense establishment. The Republicans pushed for tort reform, so the Democratic campaign was seen as more favorable to trial lawyers.

The liberal social groups that were most prominent in the election included the women's movement (after the Anita Hill hearings by the Senate Judiciary Committee raised the issue of sexual harassment to political prominence), homosexuals (given Clinton's promise to allow gays to serve in the military), and environmentalists (due to Al Gore's strong pro-environmental position). The conservative social groups that were prominent in the 1992 campaign included right-to-life groups and Christian fundamentalists.

The extent to which these campaign appeals were mirrored in public opinion can be checked by looking at public opinion data from the 1992 campaign. To do so, we analyzed data from the National Election

Studies, which have measured attitudes held by representative national samples of American adults toward a wide array of social groups in presidential election surveys since 1964. In these surveys, attitudes were measured on a 101-point feeling thermometer scale, which ranges from 0 (indicating very cold feelings toward the group) to 100 (for very warm feelings).

The social groups asked about in the 1992 NES survey are listed in table 10.1. They include most of the groups that played a prominent role in the 1992 campaign (except the right-to-life movement) as well as several groups that are traditionally prominent in politics (such as those discussed by Stanley and Niemi in chapter 9).

The average popularity of each group in 1992 is shown by the column of means in table 10.1. Some groups were clearly popular with the American public, whereas others were not. The groups liked most were whites, the poor, the military, and the police. Republicans, people on welfare, liberals, Congress, lawyers, and the federal government were rated close to neutral. The only groups that were definitely disliked in 1992 were homosexuals and illegal immigrants.

Some of these groups were also more controversial than others. The standard deviations in table 10.1 measure the amount of disagreement among respondents in terms of the scores given to a group: large standard deviations indicate that the group was controversial, with many high and many low ratings, whereas small standard deviations indicate that the scores different people gave a group were fairly similar. We would expect that the groups most linked to the 1992 campaign would be the most controversial, whereas groups that include the majority of the public (such as whites) would not be controversial.

In fact, the groups on which there was most disagreement were homosexuals and fundamentalists—two groups fairly new on the political scene—plus unions, Republicans, and Democrats—three groups that have long been prominent in politics. The groups on which there was least disagreement were the poor, Asian Americans, conservatives, Jews, whites, and Hispanics. These groups were not very visible in the 1992 campaign, and they turned out not to be controversial.

Are attitudes toward all social groups polarized along ideological lines? We would expect that the groups most relevant to the 1992 campaign would have received the most polarized responses. We can test this by comparing the thermometer ratings of social groups by respondents who called themselves liberals, moderates, and conservatives. (This test uses a survey question that asked respondents to locate themselves on an ideological scale ranging from strong liberal to strong conservative.)

TABLE 10.1
SOCIAL-GROUP POPULARITY IN 1992

	Mean	Standard deviation
Whites	71.1	19.0
Poor	70.6	18.0
Military	70.0	20.0
Police	69.4	20.3
Environmentalists	67.7	20.2
Southerners	66.1	19.5
Blacks	65.3	20.0
Catholics	65.0	19.6
Jews	64.6	18.8
Women's movement	62.0	22.3
Hispanics	61.0	19.1
Asian Americans	59.4	18.2
Democrats	58.9	22.8
Legal immigrants	57.7	19.9
Conservatives	55.8	18.4
Big business	54.9	20.0
Fundamentalists	54.8	23.5
Unions	53.8	23.4
Feminists	53.5	22.2
Republicans	51.6	23.4
People on welfare	51.0	19.8
Liberals	51.0	20.3
Congress	51.0	19.7
Lawyers	49.8	22.6
Federal government	48.0	21.7
Homosexuals	37.7	26.9
Illegal immigrants	36.1	22.8

SOURCE: 1992 National Election Study.

NOTE: Values shown are the mean thermometer rating of each group along with the standard deviation of the ratings given to that group.

The columns of table 10.2 divide the sample into these three ideological positions. Here we see that liberals liked one set of groups more than conservatives did, whereas conservatives liked a different set of groups more than liberals did. The largest differences, not surprisingly, are in ratings of liberals and conservatives. Liberal respondents also rated homosexuals, the women's movement, Democrats, and feminists much more favorably than conservatives did. Environmentalists, unions, and people on welfare were seen somewhat more positively by

TABLE 10.2
SOCIAL-GROUP POPULARITY BY IDEOLOGY IN 1992

	Liberals	Moderates	Conserva-tives	Difference be-tween Lib-erals and Con-servatives
Liberals	70	51	33	37
Homosexuals	56	40	25	31
Women's movement	74	62	49	25
Democrats	69	58	44	25
Feminists	64	54	39	25
Environmentalists	75	68	59	16
Unions	57	52	44	13
People on welfare	57	50	46	11
Illegal immigrants	41	35	33	8
Congress	52	49	46	6
Blacks	70	63	65	5
Poor people	73	68	69	4
Hispanics	66	60	62	4
Legal immigrants	63	58	60	3
Lawyers*	50	47	47	3
Federal government*	47	46	44	3
Jews	68	64	67	1
Asian Americans	63	59	62	1
Catholics*	64	65	66	-2
Whites	69	69	72	-3
Southerners	63	65	69	-6
Big business	48	54	61	-13
Police	63	68	77	-14
Military	59	69	75	-16
Fundamentalists	42	52	66	-24
Republicans	35	52	64	-29
Conservatives	41	55	71	-30

SOURCE: 1992 National Election Study.

NOTE: Values shown are the mean thermometer scores given to each social group by the ideological categories. The last column is the difference between the mean score given to the group by liberals and by conservatives.

*Unless noted with an asterisk, the differences in the groups' ratings are statistically significant ($p < .05$).

liberals than conservatives. By contrast, Republicans and fundamentalists were rated much more favorably by conservatives than by liberals. Conservative respondents also gave somewhat higher ratings on average to the military, the police, and big business as compared to ratings of those same groups by liberals.

It is also interesting to see how minimal the ideological differences were in ratings of nearly half the social groups. Liberals and conservatives gave about the same ratings of Jews and of Asians, and differences in ratings of lawyers, Catholics, and the federal government were not statistically significant. While statistically significant, differences by ideology in ratings of whites, Hispanics, the poor, blacks, southerners, Congress, and immigrants were still very small. The 1992 campaign did not sharply polarize the public ideologically along religious lines, while positive reactions to poor people and negative reactions to illegal immigrants were shared across the ideological spectrum.

Next, we employed a procedure (explained in the appendix to this chapter) to see how much attitudes toward each social group were associated with either a liberal coalition or a conservative coalition in voters' minds.[2] Table 10.3 shows the results of this mapping of the social groups for 1992. The two columns indicate how strongly each group was associated with what are called liberal and conservative "factors."[3]

Feminists, the women's movement, the Democratic Party, and homosexuals were particularly strongly associated with the liberal side in 1992, as were labor unions, environmentalists, and the federal government. By contrast, the Republican Party, fundamentalist Christians, and the military were strongly associated with the conservative side, along with big business and the police. These results confirm our initial analysis, shown in table 10.2.

The strong presence of feminists and the women's movement on the liberal side may not have been new to 1992, but may have been heightened by the major role Hillary Rodham Clinton played in her husband's presidential campaign (see chapter 5). The relatively strong presence of homosexuals and the strong presence of environmentalists probably reflects the positioning of Clinton and Gore on issues relevant to those groups.

It is interesting to note that people on welfare and blacks had only relatively weak presences on the liberal factor. These groups are traditionally aligned with the Democratic Party and are often advantaged by legislation initiated by self-identified liberal politicians. Welfare policy and racial issues were relatively peripheral in the 1992 campaign, however, which may have decoupled them somewhat from the liberal end of the spectrum. The weak presence of blacks on the liberal factor is mir-

TABLE 10.3
LOADINGS OF ATTITUDES TOWARD SOCIAL GROUPS
ON LATENT FACTORS

Social group	Conservative factor	Liberal factor
Republican Party	1.21	
Conservatives	1.00	
Fundamentalists	.78	
Military	.71	
Big business	.61	
Police	.58	
Southerners	.28	
Whites	.23	
Catholics	.18	
Jews		
Asian Americans		
Legal immigrants		
Feminists		1.13
Women's movement		1.00
Liberals		1.00
Democratic Party		.89
Homosexuals		.82
Labor unions		.65
Environmentalists		.52
Federal government		.47
Congress		.46
People on welfare		.44
Illegal immigrants		.42
Lawyers		.36
Blacks		.14
Hispanics		.07
Poor people		

$N = 2,205$

SOURCE: 1992 National Election Study.
NOTE: All groups shown have a loading of 1.0 on the method factor.

rored by the weak presence of whites on the conservative factor. In times of more overt racial hostility in the course of political debate, we would expect both blacks and whites to have a stronger presence on these factors. President Bush did not play the racial card as much in 1992 as in the 1988 campaign, while Bill Clinton tried to distance himself from some black leaders, which fits in well with these weak loadings for the races on the 1992 factors. The federal government, Congress, and lawyers appeared on the liberal factor in 1992.

On the conservative side, the strongest groups were fundamentalist Christians, the military, big business, and the police. During the 1992 campaign, George Bush had the vocal support of most conservative religious leaders, and he received endorsements from many (though not all) police organizations. Of course, the alignments of the military and big business with the Republican Party have been long-standing. All these groups saw their interests championed by Bush during his presidency, which helps account for their strong appearances on the conservative factor. That southerners had only a weak presence on the conservative factor may reflect the fact that the most nationally visible southerners (Bill Clinton and Al Gore) were the Democratic Party's candidates.

Also of interest in table 10.3 is the lack of association of some groups with either a liberal or conservative outlook in 1992. In particular, Jews, Asian Americans, legal immigrants, and poor people were not found to be particularly related to either the liberal or conservative factor. Table 10.2 shows that these groups were given relatively similar ratings by liberals and conservatives. Lawyers, the federal government, and whites were also given fairly similar ratings by liberals and conservatives, but lawyers and the federal government appear on the liberal side of table 10.3, while whites were clearly on the conservative factor.

A crucial question that remains is how polarized were attitudes toward liberal and conservative groups? Were they seen as opposites, or were ideological positions less polarized in 1992? This question is answered by estimating the correlation between the liberal and conservative factors. In principle, this correlation can range in value from −1.0 to +1.0. A value of −1.0 would indicate the strongest possible ideological organization: people who like liberal groups a great deal would also dislike conservative groups a great deal, and people who like conservative groups a great deal would also dislike liberal groups a great deal. A value of zero would indicate complete independence of the liberal and conservative factors: knowing how much a respondent likes liberal groups reveals nothing about how much he or she likes conservative groups. A value of +1.0 would indicate that the more a respondent likes liberal groups, the more he or she likes conservative groups.

The estimated correlation between the liberal and conservative factor is −.40. This negative and statistically significant correlation indicates that there was ideological organization underlying these attitudes, but it was relatively weak. Thus, it seems, Americans' attitudes toward social groups in 1992 did reflect ideological organization to some extent, but this was not at all the only organizing principle at work.

This relatively weak correlation appears consistent with the content of the 1992 campaign, in that ideology was not discussed frequently. Although Bush did occasionally ridicule Clinton for endorsing liberal policies or pursuing liberal agendas, the words liberal and conservative were not as prominent in the candidates' speeches as had been the case just four years earlier when Bush frequently used "the L word" to describe Michael Dukakis (meaning that he was a tax-and-spend liberal who was not to be trusted). The campaign did not focus on ideology, so the electorate did not view social groups in very ideologically polarized terms.

Putting 1992 in Historical Context

Politics is dynamic in nature, so it is important to examine how attitudes toward social groups and the ideological underpinnings of those attitudes change over time. Is 1992's mapping of social groups divergent from previous years? Are there any general trends or similarities in the way the general public feels toward particular social groups? And were there changes in the degree of ideological polarization? Are people becoming more likely or less likely to see ideological clashes?

To answer these questions, we compared the social-group thermometers of 1992 with those of previous years. The list of social groups asked about in the National Election Study surveys has changed over the years, as different groups have become more and less prominent in political debates. For example, environmentalists, homosexuals, and religious fundamentalists are but three of the relevant social groups of the 1990s that were not asked about in the surveys of the 1960s. Similarly, some groups asked about in the late 1960s and early 1970s, such as radical students, protesting ministers, and marijuana users, would be seen as anachronistic by the 1990s and were therefore not asked about in 1992.

At the same time, the political meaning of other social groups can change over time. A group might have been seen as liberal in an earlier time but conservative today. Such change is inevitable over a lengthy time period and tells us a good deal about how politics has shifted in the intervening years.

The most important over-time comparison is in seeing whether there has been change in the degree of ideological polarization. By comparing the correlation between the liberal and conservative factors over time, we can see the extent to which there was change in polarization between them. We have repeated the analysis of table 10.3 for all the

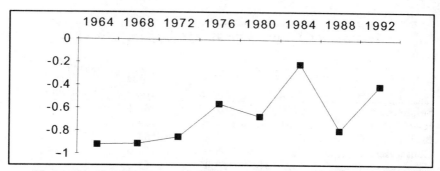

FIGURE 10.1. CORRELATION OF LIBERAL AND CONSERVATIVE
FACTORS, 1964–92.

presidential election years since the group thermometer question was
first asked in 1964. Figure 10.1 portrays the trends in the correlation
between the liberal and conservative factors.

Interestingly, ideological structuring of social-group attitudes was
extremely strong during the 1960s and early 1970s. Liberal and conservative positions were polar opposites during that period of American
politics. By contrast, the late 1970s and early 1980s witnessed less ideological conflict. There was a slight surge at the time of Ronald Reagan's
election in 1980, an election that returned ideological themes to the
fore. Ideological structuring fell during Reagan's 1984 reelection (with
its nonideological "Morning in America" theme), surged again in 1988
when Bush attacked Dukakis for his liberal ideology, and then fell again
in the 1992 campaign when the focus was more on the economy and
trust than on ideology per se.

To understand these changes over time better, we can compare the
1992 results with the group ratings for two earlier years: 1964, the
height of ideological polarization, and 1976, an early instance of diminished polarization. These years also happen to be the last two elections
before 1992 in which a Democrat won the White House; 1964 was the
year of Johnson's landslide defeat of Goldwater, while 1976 was the
year of Carter's very narrow win over Ford.

How much did attitudes toward these social groups change over
the time period? Has the popularity of these groups stayed fairly constant, or have some groups become much more popular or unpopular?
Table 10.4 displays net trends in thermometer scores by comparing the
average ratings for each group in 1964, 1976, and 1992. The table
shows only groups asked about in all three years.

TABLE 10.4
TRENDS IN GROUP RATINGS, 1964, 1972, AND 1992

	1964 Mean	1976 Mean	1992 Mean	Difference between 1964 and 1992
Southerners	63.4	62.1	66.1	2.7
Jews	62.0	57.2	64.6	2.6
Blacks	63.0	60.6	65.3	2.3
Conservatives	56.7	59.0	56.0	−.7
Catholics	65.9	63.0	65.0	−.9
Liberals	53.2	52.2	51.0	−2.2
Labor unions	57.7	46.7	54.0	−3.7
Military	74.7	73.4	70.0	−4.7
Big business	60.2	48.4	55.0	−5.2
Republicans	59.5	57.6	51.6	−7.9
Whites	83.0	73.4	71.1	−11.9
Democrats	71.1	62.7	59.0	−11.1

SOURCE: 1964, 1976, and 1992 National Election Studies.

NOTE: Values shown are the mean thermometer rating of each group.

The average ratings of the groups were remarkably stable over the twenty-eight years, with most changes being under 10 points. The largest difference is the substantial drop in ratings of the Democrats, though this probably reflects the Democrats' atypical popularity when Johnson won election by landslide proportions in 1964. Ratings of the Republicans also fell during this period, though somewhat less sharply.

The other large change involves ratings of whites, which also fell sharply; ratings of blacks did not change, but the difference between ratings of the two races fell from a 20-point difference in 1964 to a 13-point difference in 1976 and a 5-point difference in 1992. There was also a substantial drop in ratings of big business and labor unions between 1964 and 1976, but their ratings went back up by 1992 to intermediate values. Note that average ratings of liberals and conservatives barely changed throughout the period, in contrast to claims of some observers that the country moved to the right in this era.

There also seems to have been a slight general decline in the ratings of nearly all these groups. This may reflect increased polarization, with opposing groups becoming more critical of their opposites. Or it might reflect an increase in public cynicism more generally.

Another useful over-time comparison is in how polarized ratings of the groups are by ideology. To what extent did liberals, moderates, and conservatives agree or disagree in their ratings of the groups? And are the patterns different from that found for 1992? Table 10.5 shows the average ratings of the social groups in 1976 by self-identified liberals, moderates, and conservatives. (The 1964 survey did not ask respondents to locate themselves in liberal-conservative terms, so this analysis cannot be done for that year.)

Liberals, on average, gave much higher ratings to liberals, marijuana users, radical students, black militants, and civil rights leaders than did conservatives, plus somewhat higher ratings to the women's movement, Democrats, unions, and blacks. By contrast, conservatives, on average, gave much higher ratings to conservatives and Republicans than liberals did, plus somewhat higher ratings to big business, military, and the police.

The biggest change to observe here between 1976 and 1992 is at the liberal end: the groups whose ratings differed the most in 1976 were new countercultural groups—marijuana users, radical students, and black militants—which were no longer relevant social groups by 1992. Another important change involves racial groups: ratings of both blacks and whites were more polarized ideologically in 1976 than in 1992. The difference between how these groups were rated by liberals and by conservatives fell by half over these sixteen years. Liberals actually rated blacks and whites about equally both years. Conservatives in 1976 on average rated whites 17 degrees more favorably than blacks; that difference had fallen to 7 degrees in 1992. The relevance of race to ideological polarization clearly declined during this period.

Finally, we can trace how the loadings of some groups on the ideological factors changed. In particular, were the parties consistently tied to liberal-conservative conflict over the years, or has the relation between ideology and political parties changed? To test this, figure 10.2 compares the loadings of ideological and partisan groups on the liberal and conservative factors over the period in which these group thermometer ratings are available. Not surprisingly, the liberal thermometer always loaded high on the liberal factor and the conservative thermometer always loaded high on the conservative factor. More change is evident for the party thermometers. The Democrats loaded high on the liberal factor in 1964, but that loading fell sharply in the 1968–80 period until it returned to its prior strength in 1984. A comparable result is evident for Republicans: loading high on the conservative factor in 1964, with a much smaller loading for 1968–80, and large loadings since 1984.

The patterns found here are both complex and important for understanding changes in American politics during this era. First, there

TABLE 10.5
SOCIAL GROUP POPULARITY BY IDEOLOGY IN 1976

	Liberals	Moderates	Conserva- tives	Difference be- tween Liber- als and Con- servatives
Liberals	70	53	38	32
Marijuana users	51	36	25	26
Radical students	45	31	21	24
Black militants	39	24	15	24
Civil rights leaders	66	50	43	23
Women's movement	64	53	45	19
Democrats	69	61	56	13
Unions	50	46	39	11
Blacks	69	59	59	10
People on welfare	58	49	49	9
Chicanos	62	55	55	7
Poor people	77	68	71	6
Young people	78	74	74	4
Jews*	61	58	59	2
Women	80	77	81	−1
Working men	75	75	78	−3
Protestants	66	64	70	−4
Older people	80	81	84	−4
Catholics	61	62	66	−5
Southerners	60	60	65	−5
Men	69	72	75	−6
Middle class	70	73	77	−7
Whites	68	71	76	−8
Police	62	70	77	−15
Military	55	65	73	−18
Big business	37	48	56	−19
Republicans	46	58	66	−20
Conservatives	47	58	71	−24

SOURCE: 1976 National Election Study.

NOTE: Values shown are the mean thermometer scores given to each social group by the ideological categories. The last column is the difference between the mean score given to the group by liberals and by conservatives.

*Unless noted with an asterisk, the differences in the groups' ratings are statistically significant ($p < .05$).

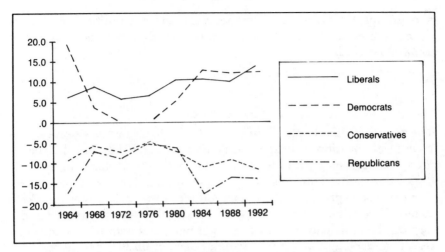

FIGURE 10.2. LOADINGS OF PARTY AND IDEOLOGY GROUPS, 1964–92.

was a shift in the ideological mapping of American politics after 1964. The 1964 results fit well with our understanding of ideological competition in party politics since the New Deal realignment, with liberal groups associated with the Democratic Party and conservatives with the Republican Party. The Vietnam war fractured these usual linkages. Politics shifted from an economic basis to concerns with the war, civil rights, and social issues. That shift is evident in the weaker associations of the parties with the liberal and conservative factors in the 1968–80 period (seen in figure 10.2), in the milder correlations between the liberal and conservative factors starting in 1976 (figure 10.1), and in the large differences in table 10.5 between how liberals and conservatives rated marijuana users, radical students, and black militants in 1976. The meaning of ideology changed in the mid-1970s. The old economic basis to liberalism was less salient to the public than were its new social linkages.

A second change is evident since the late 1970s. The degree of polarization between attitudes toward liberal and conservative social groups remains low, but the linkage of parties to the main ideological blocs has returned. Radical students and black militants seemed important in the 1970s, but by the 1990s new social groups were salient to the public: homosexuals, religious fundamentalists, the women's movement, and anti-abortionists. The public is polarized in its view of these new groups, but what is more important is that the political parties are at the core of ideological conflict in ways that they were not during the 1968–80 period.

Conclusion

The results of this chapter fit in well with the focus on the demise of the New Deal coalition in chapter 9. Politics has changed, and the social-group relationships with ideologies and parties have changed. Yet it is difficult to move from this analysis into speculation about the future. The new social groups that seem important in the early 1990s are likely to fade in relevance as quickly as did the social groups prominent in the 1970s. The basic pattern evident is tight party ties with liberal and conservative ideology but without strong polarization between liberal and conservative groupings. The linkage of parties with ideology is the same as in 1964, but the lack of polarization between liberals and conservatives is very different from then. The public still sees groupings between ideologically similar social groups and again puts the political parties into those ideological groupings, but there is not a deep ideological divide between once opposite ideological camps. Ideology exists, without intrinsic ideological cleavage.

We would suspect that the current pattern is best seen as transitional, though it would be premature to guess what the next pattern will be. The current pattern fits with party dealignment, and it shows how Ross Perot could run as a nonparty candidate and could gain 19 percent of the vote. In a more ideologically polarized situation, it would have been difficult for a nonparty candidate to attract support. But when ideological cleavages are reduced, a nonparty candidate can assemble support outside of usual social groups or ideological lines.

More generally, our results show how interesting lessons can be learned about American politics by studying citizens' attitudes toward social groups. Group conflict will probably never disappear, so it will be interesting to repeat our analysis in a decade to see how the lines of polarization shift in the coming years.

Appendix

In this chapter we employ a new method to examine the ideological structure of attitudes toward social groups. (Krosnick and Weisberg 1988 provide a full report on this method.) Briefly, we performed a confirmatory factor analysis (using the LISREL computer program of Jöreskog and Sorbom 1978) of the group thermometers, with 3 factors specified: a factor on which only liberal groups loaded, a factor on which only conservative groups loaded, and a method factor on which all groups loaded equally.[4]

The method factor controls for "perspective differences" in how different respondents rate the social groups (see Ostrom and Upshaw 1968). Typically, some respondents view 100 on the 0–100 thermometer scale as an extremely positive score and rate all groups in the middle of the scale (say, 40–70). Other respondents view 100 as a more moderately positive score, so their ratings are in the top region of the scale (say, 70–100). Because of the perspective differences, the latter set of respondents rate all the groups higher than the other set of respondents, even if their actual feelings are identical. The statistical result of this perspective difference is to make the correlations between ratings of different groups more positive than they would otherwise be, since people who like one group more also like the other groups more (see Green and Citrin 1994). The method factor removes this artifactual correlation, so the remaining correlations may be viewed as free from perspective effects (Alwin 1974).

Other studies have also examined the degree of polarization between liberal and conservative groups. Conover and Feldman (1981) found essentially zero correlations between attitudes toward liberal and conservative political objects, but this correlation might be much more negative if perspective effects had been removed. Indeed, Green (1988) controlled for "charitability" differences between respondents and found that adjusted correlations between attitudes toward liberals and conservatives were much more negative. Similarly, Knight (1990) subtracted each respondent's mean rating on all the thermometers from his or her ratings of liberals and conservatives and found that this correction made the correlation very negative. But these studies focused only on liberals and conservatives and parties, instead of obtaining a more general ideological mapping of the social groups.

It is also important to contrast this method with two alternative approaches. One is an exploratory factor analysis of the group thermometers, as was done by Miller, Wlezien, and Hildreth (1991). Exploratory factor analysis can determine the number of factors needed to account for the social group ratings. It does not control for perspective differences, however, and by finding several smaller factors, it gives less emphasis to tracing changes on the dominant liberal and conservative factors over time. Another approach is to correct just the correlation between the liberal and conservative thermometers for perspective differences, as by subtracting the mean score each person gives to all the groups from the liberal and conservative thermometers before correlating them (Wilcox, Sigelman, and Cook 1989). Random measurement error can have substantial effects on ratings of one or two groups, however, and our use of multiple measures better removes such random measurement effects.

Notes

1. One distinctive aspect of the Perot candidacy is that it was not based on a coalition of social groups, which may be one reason that there were few strong correlates of voting for Perot (see chapters 3 and 6).

2. Miller, Wlezien, and Hildreth (1991) provide an important alternative analysis of the structure of the social-group thermometers, with an emphasis on partisan coalitions rather than the emphasis here on ideological polarization.

3. To be more specific, table 10.3 shows the extent to which each group loads on either a liberal or conservative factor, with the perspective factor explained in the appendix being controlled. Groups on the same factor share a lot of covariation, meaning that people who tend to like one group more tend to like the other groups on the same factor more, and people who tend to dislike one group more tend to dislike the other groups on the same factor more.

4. For this analysis, we estimated the parameters of the structural equation model described by the following equation:

$$X_i = \alpha_1 \xi + \alpha_2 \eta + \alpha_3 \zeta + u$$

This equation specifies that any given attitude, X_i, is a function of an underlying attitude toward liberals (ξ), an underlying attitude toward conservatives (η), a perspective anchor point defined by the respondent's definitions of the positivity and negativity of the end points of the attitude scale (ζ), and a disturbance term (u). The terms α_1, α_2, and α_3 are regression coefficients estimating the impact of each of the latent factors on the individual attitudes. The disturbance term, u, includes variance due to random measurement error and item-specific true variance not shared with the other variables. The specification of a liberal and a conservative factor in this way is in line with Kerlinger's (1967, 1972; Kerlinger, Middendorp, and Amon 1976) assertion that attitudes toward liberal and conservative objects represent separate underlying factors.

In order to identify this model, we must assume that the liberal and conservative factors are uncorrelated with the method factor. It is also necessary to fix some of the loadings of items on the liberal and conservative factors to be zero. We based our initial decisions about which loadings to constrain to zero on a preliminary analysis in which two factors were specified—a single substantive factor plus a method factor on which each group again loads equally. Groups were assigned to the liberal or conservative factor (or to neither) on the basis of whether their loadings on the substantive factor in the preliminary analysis were positive or negative (or not significant). The loadings for groups were fixed at zero on both factors if they had negative loadings on their assigned factor in an initial three-factor model, which indicates that they do not belong on that factor.

Respondents failed to answer some questions, and we replaced these missing data points with the number 50, the conceptual midpoint of the thermometer scale, so as to retain the largest possible sample of respondents for the analysis.

PART III

The Elections for Congress

Congress Bashing and the 1992 Congressional Election

SAMUEL C. PATTERSON AND MICHAEL K. BARR

The 1992 congressional election unfolded under extraordinary circumstances. Most notably, the election followed a staccato of congressional scandals, a plummeting of public approval of congressional job performance, and a rash of highly negative commentary in the media about the efficacy of Congress as a political institution (see Ceaser and Busch 1993; Nelson 1993; Pomper 1993). Six out of ten House members were implicated in a scandal involving overdrafts in their accounts with the House bank, following on the heels of negative publicity about a congressional salary increase, and the savings-and-loan crisis involving some members of Congress. Congress's public image reached unprecedented depths as, by mid-April, only 17 percent of Americans said they approved of its job performance, and for the first time fewer than half of all poll respondents expressed approval in the way their own representative was "handling his or her job." The airwaves and print media carried tales of congressional infidelity and inaction, decried the "gridlock" between Republican president and Democratic Congress that seemed to prevent resolution of the nation's problems, and wallowed in stories of members' ethical peccadillos and even criminal behavior. Congress bashing was in full swing.

Amid the anti-Congress, anti-incumbent malaise, two sideshows promised at least partial remedies to congressional maladies: redistricting and term limitation. In accord with the 1990 federal census, congressional district boundary lines were redrawn to realign populations, particularly to compensate for large population shifts from the rust belt states of the northeast to the sunbelt states of the South and Southwest, and to construct districts that could elect representatives from ethnic and racial minorities. These circumstances combined to indicate a potential for substantial change in congressional representation, perhaps even an upheaval of unprecedented proportions, with Republicans seemingly the main beneficiaries. In the event, the election itself produced both stability and change. Term-limit propositions were on the ballot in fourteen states, providing a focus for public debate about the quality of representation they enjoyed and the turpitude of their Congress.

In this chapter we rehearse the results of the 1992 congressional election and characterize the role of Congress bashing, congressional scandal, and efforts to reform and restrain Congress in the environment of that election. We adumbrate the role of Congress bashing as an important part of the climate of politics for the 1992 congressional contests. More extensively, we make use of the 1992 National Election Study (NES), using this public opinion survey to investigate voters' attitudes and behavior in order to explore congressional election voting. We demonstrate that Congress bashing and congressional scandal exerted a significant influence on the preferences voters expressed for incumbent or challenger candidates for election to the House of Representatives. Other things being equal, voters clearly preferred House candidates who were not tainted by the House bank scandal, and attentive voters' candidate preferences were affected by their appraisals of Congress as an institution. Moreover, while contemporary reporting about election events amplified their Congress-bashing features, the results of our analysis underscore the powerful effects of political party affinities and constituency linkages even when important anticongressional sentiments and emotions are at play.

The Congressional Election Outcome

As the congressional election campaign unfolded, the rising impact of these unusual circumstances was felt. Before the campaign got under way, a large number of incumbents simply withdrew altogether, either retiring from politics or opting to run for other offices. By the time the primary season had ended, sixty-five House incumbents and seven senators had announced decisions not to run for reelection, the largest proportion of retirees in more than half a century.

CONGRESSIONAL CANDIDACIES

In the instance of House incumbents, this meant that somewhat more than 15 percent of Democrats and just over 14 percent of Republicans opted out of renomination events. As figure 11.1 indicates, the 1992 retirement rate substantially exceeded retirement in previous years, especially among Democrats. Moreover, nineteen House incumbents and one sitting senator (Alan Dixon, D-Ill.) were defeated in primary battles.

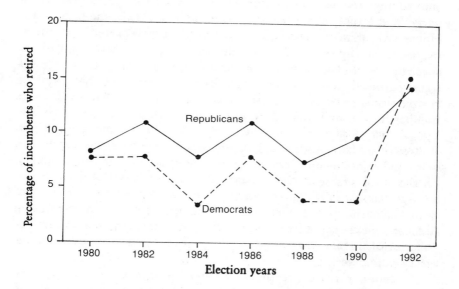

FIGURE 11.1. RETIREMENTS FROM THE HOUSE, 1980–92.

SOURCE: Norman J. Ornstein, Thomas E. Mann, and Michael J. Malbin, *Vital Statistics on Congress, 1993–94* (Washington, D.C.: CQ Press, 1994), 42, 50.

NOTE: Includes representatives who did not run for reelection, or who ran for other offices; members who died or resigned before the end of the Congress are excluded.

Some of the incumbents who retired, deciding not to run for renomination, did so because redistricting had radically changed the composition of their districts, in a few cases throwing them into potential contention with other incumbents. Some House incumbents withdrew because of the devastating publicity given to their check overdrafts in the so-called House bank, and a sizable majority of incumbent House members suffering primary defeat were on the check-overdraft roster. Some incumbents retired because of their dissatisfactions with public office in an atmosphere of scandal, declining comity within Congress, hostility toward Congress and its members, and more general negativism and cynicism about politics. For some, public service was not fun anymore, and it was more difficult than ever to serve constructively in public life.

At the same time, candidate participation in the general election campaign reached an all-time high. About 1,300 candidates ran for House seats, most of them Democrats and Republicans.[1] Minor parties entered many House races; the Libertarian Party, the largest minor party in the race, contested 120 seats. In more than one-fifth of the House races (ninety-one districts) no incumbent was present, the largest incidence of "open" seats in a half century. At the other end of the spectrum, fewer House seats were uncontested by one of the major political parties than had been the case for many years. In only thirty-four congressional districts was there no contest, fewer than half the average number of uncontested races over the previous decade (Jacobson 1993a, 168). Only one senator seeking reelection ran unopposed (John B. Breaux, D-La.). Additionally, there is some evidence that candidates who challenged incumbents in 1992 were of somewhat better quality, on the whole, than in recent congressional elections (Jacobson 1992, 167–70; 1993a, 168). This appears to have been true largely because of the unusual number of open seats, which attracted a larger than usual number of experienced candidates. Finally, among the contenders for congressional seats was an extraordinary proportion of women and minority candidates.

The opportunities presented by the congressional races in 1992 encouraged Republicans, who thought they might enjoy substantial House and even Senate seat gains. Redistricting had altered the composition of a number of congressional districts, requiring incumbents to cultivate new constituents. In general, candidacies were stimulated by better-quality challengers, by women, and by African Americans and Hispanics. More competitive campaigning by a larger-than-usual number of candidates produced a surge in congressional campaign spending, mostly on the part of House incumbents, who averaged spending almost $595,000, or 41 percent more than in the previous congressional election (Ornstein, Mann, and Malbin 1994, 69). Competitiveness stimulated voter turnout; more than 96 million people voted for congressional candidates. The national turnout rate was 50.8 percent for House contests (compared to 55.2 percent for the presidential race), the highest voter turnout in two decades.

THE NEW CONGRESS

Considering the exceptional atmosphere and unusual conditions under which the congressional election took place, it produced only limited changes. In partisan terms, the 103d Congress changed little; the gains Republicans had hoped for did not materialize (Cook 1993). The new House of Representatives would have 258 Democrats (59.3 percent), 176 Republicans (40.5 percent), and 1 independent—a nine-seat Republican gain. The Senate would be Democratic by a 57–43 margin, one more Democrat than in the previous Congress.

Although the House acquired 110 new members, most were elected in open-seat contests. Fully 93 percent of House incumbents who were renominated won their reelection bids, and the overall incumbent return rate (taking both primary and general elections into account) was 88.3 percent. This incumbent success was ten percentage points below the incumbent reelection rate in 1988, and was the lowest mark of incumbent success since 1974. Senate results ran parallel, with 82.1 percent of incumbent senators returned as a proportion of those seeking reelection. Moreover, not only did a somewhat smaller percentage of incumbents succeed in 1992 than in previous years but also incumbents suffered shrinkages in their margins of victory.

The new Congress—the 103d—included 110 freshmen representatives and 13 freshmen senators. The House's 25 percent freshmen membership made it the largest new class in the post–World War II era. Notable in this membership is the significant increase it reflects in the numbers of women, blacks, and Hispanics in Congress. The House membership included thirty-nine African Americans, a historic record; and one black senator was elected to the 103d Congress, Senator Carol Moseley-Braun (D-Ill.). Black representatives were elected in some southern states for the first time since the Reconstruction following the Civil War. Hispanic representation increased in the House to seventeen members, an increase from ten in 1983 and five in 1973 (Hershey 1993, 179).

These increases in minority representation were made possible by congressional redistricting, which carved out minority districts in accord with amendments to the Voting Rights Act of 1965. An unusually large number of well-qualified women ran for Congress in 1992, and a record number were successful. Women's gains in 1992 began in the primaries, where their success rates in open-seat districts exceeded men's, especially on the Democratic side (Jacobson 1993a, 171). The 103d Congress included forty-eight women representatives (thirty-six Democrats and twelve Republicans) and six women senators (five Democrats and one Republican).

Nevertheless, the partisan environment of the congressional houses was not much changed by the 1992 election. Although House Republicans chalked up the largest net gain in seats since 1984, the House retained a substantial Democratic majority. With only a third of its seats up for election, only four Senate seats changed party hands in 1992, with no net partisan change. In the early days of the 103d Congress there were a few signs that the unusually large freshmen class might affect the partisan climate of the House, particularly by taking bipartisan actions to change House rules. As time passed, the new members became better integrated into the House's institutional life, and the patterns of partisan cleavage developing in the previous decade came to be evident, so the viscosity of partisanship notable in the previous Congress was soon reached.

The Rise of Congress Bashing

It would be an overstatement to say that the political atmosphere was poisonous by the time of the 1992 congressional elections, but the climate certainly was negative. And it would be ahistorical to say that a negative climate for congressional politics was unique to the election of 1992; low esteem for Congress has been a persistent feature of American political life (see Patterson and Caldeira 1990). Nevertheless, a new wave of "Congress bashing," and a fairly virulent form of it, washed over the 1992 congressional elections and took a toll on their outcomes (Polsby 1990).

The volume and amplitude of Congress bashing increased markedly in the mid-1980s, as the Reagan administration jousted repeatedly with the determined Democratic congressional leadership. The new wave of negativism was initiated in an article in the *Atlantic Monthly* entitled "What's Wrong with Congress?" (Easterbrook 1984), whose author recounted the litany of congressional failures:

> The end of the seniority system; the arabesque budget "process" and other time-consuming new additions like the War Powers Act; the transformation from party loyalty to political-action-committee (PAC) loyalty; the increased emphasis on media campaigning; the vogue of running against Washington and yet being a member of the Washington establishment; the development of ideological anti-campaigns; a dramatic increase in congressional-subcommittee power and staff size, and a parallel increase in the scope and intensity of lobbying—all are creations of the past fifteen years. (p. 58)

Newsweek's staff writers ripped "The World of Congress," claiming that Congress had become removed from the real world of American life. "CongressWorld," they wrote, "is a fortress of unreality, its draw-bridges only barely connected to life beyond the moat." More viciously, they asserted that "it used to be that calling a member of Congress a 'press whore' ... was considered an insult ... [but] today's Congress is a brothel" (Alter, Fineman, and Clift 1989, 28, 29).

The Washington staff of *Business Week* excoriated Congress in a widely quoted article entitled "Congress: It Doesn't Work. Let's Fix It" (Dwyer and Harbrecht 1990), replete with proposals for congressional reform. Its authors asserted that "Congress produces very little of tangible value" (p. 55).[2] These highly visible samples of Congress bashing in widely circulated magazines were harbingers of a spate of books denouncing Congress, with such titles as *Kick the Bums Out, The Cardinals of Capitol Hill, The Best Congress Money Can Buy,* and *Congress: America's Privileged Class.*[3] In these publications Congress was portrayed as ineffective, inefficient, unrepresentative, illegitimate, and corrupt. The drumbeat of attacks on Congress reverberated to television and radio commentary, newspaper editorializing, and the rhetoric of congressional campaigning.

"Congress bashing," wrote political scientist Nelson W. Polsby, "is back in style." A leading congressional commentator, Norman Ornstein, proclaimed that "Congress bashing has become America's favorite indoor sport." Columnist Richard E. Cohen's preelection speculation was that "in their worst nightmares, few Members could have dreamed that public cynicism about Congress would become as intense as it did in 1991."[4] The crescendo of public cynicism fed diminishing public confidence in Congress and its work, and provided fuel for surging, organized efforts to limit congressmen's terms of office. What was the overall shape of public feelings about Congress?

The Mood of the 1992 Voters

Historically, Americans' feelings about Congress have waxed and waned, sometimes quite favorable (as in 1965, when it won high public ratings following the outpouring of Great Society legislation), and sometimes highly negative (in the 1970s congressional popularity fell very low, principally due to public disillusionment with the Vietnam war). How favorably or unfavorably citizens evaluate Congress's job performance depends very strongly on the popularity of the president, the negativity of media coverage of the institution, and the extent of reporting about ethical conduct rather than about other aspects of congressional life (Patterson and Caldeira 1990).

During much of the 1980s and early 1990s, Congress was assailed by Presidents Reagan and Bush as intractable, unwilling to adopt presidential programs, and responsible for "gridlock." Congress bashing became the leitmotif of media coverage of Congress. And reports of congressional scandal abounded—the S&L bailout, the disgrace of Speaker Jim Wright, the events of the Senate confirmation of Justice Clarence Thomas, the House bank scandal, and the ethical misconduct of a number of individual members (see Ceaser and Busch 1993, 127–58).

THE HOUSE BANK SCANDAL

The most damaging scandal, which arose first in late 1991 and continued throughout 1992 until election day, concerned the archaic operations of the so-called House bank. The scandal entailed revelations by the General Accounting Office that well over half the members of the House had, at one time or another, overdrawn their accounts (the final list included 355 current and former members). The House bank, abolished in 1991, had existed since 1830. Not really a bank in any modern sense, this House agency provided check overdraft protection for those who used its services.

Some members opted to have their paychecks deposited in non-interest-bearing accounts maintained by the bank on which they could write personal checks. Forty-seven members had accumulated 100 overdrafts or more, and the worst offenders showed several hundred overdrafts. Although no public funds were risked or lost, the revelation of bank overdrafts created a media sensation. Members were assailed as "check-kiters" or "bad check" writers or writers of "bounced checks." Some Republicans sought to make political hay from the check overdraft issue: House Ethics Committee Republican Fred Grandy (R-Iowa) touted that "as of today, ... your talk show hosts have a topic, your opponent has an issue, and your constituents have a reason to support term limits" (quoted in Hershey 1993, 163). But partisan advantage was hard to come by because many of the overdrafters were Republicans. The savings-and-loan (S&L) bailout involved far more money than the check overdraft problem, but its impact remained generalized and distant for most voters. The bank overdraft scandal provided voters with a gauge of the ethical culpability of their individual representatives, in terms of the number of overdrafts and the amounts.

CITIZENS' SUPPORT FOR CONGRESS

Interestingly, candidates themselves frequently campaign for Congress by running against Congress, criticizing the institution and demanding reform. Moreover, it is well known that incumbent members of Congress are often insulated from public negativism about the institution, "if they have taken steps to ensure they are seen as part of the solution and not as part of the problem" (Patterson and Magleby 1992, 541). Generally, incumbents win high popularity ratings from the public and are almost always reelected if they seek to be returned to Congress (Jacobson 1992, esp. 25–60; Abramowitz and Segal 1992, esp. 93–121).

Americans are regularly asked to evaluate congressional job performance. Pollsters ask their respondents whether they think Congress is doing an "excellent, pretty good, only fair, or poor" job, how much confidence they have in Congress or the people running it, how they rate Congress on a "feeling thermometer" ranging from 0 to 100 degrees, or whether they "approve or disapprove of the way Congress has been handling its job." On the eve of the 1992 congressional elections, Americans' ratings of Congress's performance dropped very low.

In figure 11.2 we portray this precipitous decline in congressional support for seven election years, drawing data from the National Election Studies (NES). For the sake of comparison, we include in figure 11.2 ratings of the performance of incumbent representatives. Typically, citizens appraise their own representatives much more favorably than they rate Congress as an institution. Figure 11.2 depicts the difference between the percentage of respondents who said they "approve" and those who said they "disapprove" of Congress or their own representative. Accordingly, in the 1992 NES survey only 28 percent approved of Congress's work and 63 percent disapproved, a difference of 35 percent. By the same token, in 1992 63 percent approved of the performance of their own representative, while only 12 percent disapproved, a difference of 50 percent. Such differences are plotted in figure 11.2 for 1980 to 1992.

The story in figure 11.2 is one of a dramatic plunge in citizens' approval of Congress. In 1990 the gap between approval and disapproval had nose-dived to −18; by 1992 the difference between them was −35. On the eve of the 1992 congressional election, the NES survey showed that nearly two-thirds of Americans disapproved of congressional performance. Although incumbents enjoyed a fairly steady approval level across the election years considered in figure 11.2, incumbent approval was trending downward. The ABC/*Washington Post* and CBS/*New York Times* polls (Patterson and Magleby 1992, 550) showed incumbent approval diminishing from 64 percent (October 1991) to 55 percent (February 1992) to 49 percent (March 1992) to 47 percent (October 1992). Polls conducted in March 1992 showed 76 percent agreeing that "it's time to turn most of the rascals out of office," and 72 percent

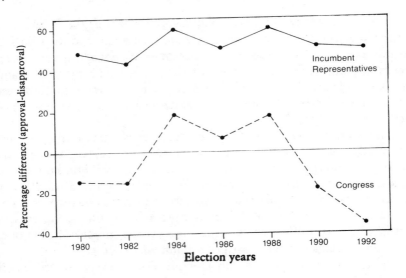

FIGURE 11.2. CONGRESSIONAL FEVER CHART, 1980–92.

SOURCE: National Election Studies, 1980–92.

NOTE: The questions were: "In general, do you approve or disapprove of the way the U.S. Congress has been handling its job?" and "In general, do you approve or disapprove of the way Representative _____ has been handling his/her job?"

agreeing that most members of Congress were not doing "a good enough job to deserve reelection."

The House bank scandal peaked in April 1992 with the full release of the names of incumbent members showing check overdrafts. The bank scandal soured public attitudes toward Congress and congressmen even more, if that were possible. At mid-March 1992, 72 percent of those questioned in the ABC/*Washington Post* poll said the bank scandal represented "business as usual in Congress" and not "an isolated exception." Nearly two-thirds indicated that they thought "representatives who bounced checks did something illegal," and 79 percent indicated that they would be "less likely" to vote for their representative if he or she was "one of the members who repeatedly wrote bad checks." The bank scandal gave voters a direct and immediate gauge of their own representative's performance, and it proved to be a significant threat to incumbents. As we noted earlier, many retired; some were defeated in the primary; a few lost in the general election; incumbents' margins of general election victory declined (see Banducci and Karp 1994; Jacobson and Dimock 1994).

THE TERM-LIMITATION MOVEMENT

At the same time, organized efforts to punish Congress and its members were well under way in the form of the term-limitation movement. In 1990, term limits had been approved by voters in California, Colorado, and Oklahoma for state legislative offices, and for congressional terms in Colorado. Washington state voters defeated a congressional term-limitation proposal in 1991. In 1992, congressional term-limit propositions were on the ballot in fourteen states, and these won pervasive public support (see figure 11.3). An April 1992 Gallup poll gave a typical result: 67 percent favored a twelve-year limit on the number of years a representative or senator could serve, and this level of support was about the same for both Democratic and Republican respondents.

Polls in the states in which a congressional term-limit proposal was on the ballot showed pervasive support for it, although some striking party differences appeared. Indeed, in five states—Arkansas, Michigan, Montana, North Dakota, and Washington—fewer than half of the state's Democrats expressed support for term limits, and the term-limit propositions succeeded by smaller margins in these states than in states where term-limit proposals were favored by majorities of Democrats and Republicans alike. In fact, Democrats in all fourteen states were substantially less supportive than Republicans. Congressional term limits (and limits on state legislators' terms in all states except North Dakota) were adopted in every one of the fourteen states by impressive margins, ranging from 52 percent in Washington to 77 percent in Florida and Wyoming.

The Impact of Congress Bashing

What were the effects of the public's negative attitudes and perceptions of Congress and its members on the 1992 election outcomes? Did Congress bashing make a difference? We have already noted that by the eve of the general election, most of the highly vulnerable incumbents had been taken out of the contest through their own retirement or primary defeat. The general atmosphere of Congress bashing and the more selective check-overdraft revelations took their toll well before voters went to the polls for the final reckoning in November. When the electoral verdict was rendered, only a few incumbents actually lost their congressional seats.

CONGRESSIONAL ELECTION MARGINS

Nevertheless, the verdict in the aggregate gives evidence of the pervasive

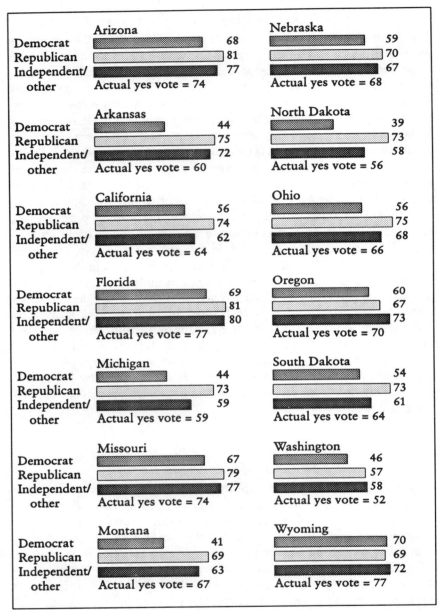

FIGURE 11.3. SUPPORT FOR TERM LIMITS IN FOURTEEN STATES,
1992 (IN PERCENTAGE).

SOURCE: *American Enterprise*, January/February 1993, 97.

effects of anti-incumbent sentiment in 1992 (see Jacobson 1993b, 390–91). That evidence is not to be found in the ubiquity of electoral defeat but in the diminution of voters' support for incumbents. Figure 11.4 shows the trace lines in congressional election margins for the elections of the 1980s and 1990s. These are depicted in two forms: as the proportion of House incumbents who won large majorities—60 percent of the vote or more; and as the differential election margins of northern Democrats, southern Democrats, and Republicans.

The aggregate election margins of congressional incumbents embrace marked stability over time. But the bottom part of figure 11.4 portrays a decline in the election margins of House Democrats, both northern and southern, between the 1990 and 1992 elections. Of course, what is also revealed in figure 11.4 is that within the period of the 1980s through the early 1990s, Democrats showed an erosion of election margins from a high in 1986. Republican margins in 1992 were, in fact, slightly higher than in 1990, recording their small net competitive success in financing quality challengers and perhaps the in-

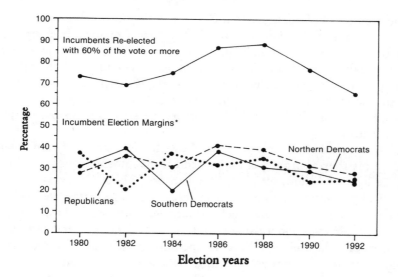

FIGURE 11.4. HOUSE ELECTION MARGINS, 1980–92.

SOURCE: National Election Studies, 1980–92; Norman J. Ornstein, Thomas E. Mann, and Michael J. Malbin, *Vital Statistics on Congress, 1993–94* (Washington, D.C.: CQ Press, 1994), 61.

NOTE: *Data points plotted represent the average percentage differences between incumbent vote shares and challenger vote shares in contested races; the election in Louisiana is excluded.

cidental Republican gains on account of redistricting. But Republican margins in the first two congressional elections of the 1990s fell substantially short of their showing during the Reagan era.

At the top part of figure 11.4 we display the trend in one-sided congressional races since 1980—given as the proportion of incumbents who were returned by margins of 60 percent of the vote or more. Over the 1980s, the percentage of incumbents elected in lopsided contests grew steadily, only to plummet in the 1990s. In 1992, 65.6 percent of House incumbents who ran for reelection won by at least 60 percent of the two-party vote, down from 76.4 percent in 1990 (the average for the 1980s was 78.3 percent). By the same token, Senate incumbents running for reelection in 1992 experienced declines in aggregate election margins. Half the twenty-six incumbents running in 1992 captured at least 60 percent of the vote, compared to a 57.5 percent average for Senate contests in 1986–90 (Ornstein, Mann, and Malbin 1994, 62).

VOTING BEHAVIOR IN THE CONGRESSIONAL ELECTION

These patterns of congressional election voting in the aggregate are revealing; they underscore the possibility that Congress bashing influenced the extent of voters' support for incumbents. Existing research has revealed the extent to which charges of corruption can influence voting in congressional elections (Peters and Welch 1980). The pre- and postelection surveys of the 1992 National Election Study provide rich resources for analyzing individual voters' perspectives on the congressional races.

For instance, in table 11.1 we show the percentage of respondents indicating they approved of and voted for incumbent House candidates in the light of various attitudes they harbored about Congress, scandal, political party, and the government in general. The "approve" column of the table indicates how much respondents approved of the performance of their own congressman, and the "vote" column indicates what proportion said they voted for the incumbent. We have divided the respondents up into two groups: those whose own political party affinities are the same as the party affiliation of their representative, and those whose party differs from that of their member. Notice that party affinity looms very large in support for House incumbents: where survey respondent and incumbent representative belong to the same party, percentages of approval and voting are substantially higher than is true in the condition where citizens' and incumbents' party is incongruent.

Americans often tend to think and talk about congressional elections as if partisan differences played little part. These elections, schol-

TABLE 11.1
EVALUATING AND VOTING FOR HOUSE INCUMBENTS:
1992 CONGRESSIONAL ELECTION

Attitudes	Respondent's political party identification			
	Same as incumbent's		Different from incumbent's	
	% Approve	% Vote	% Approve	% Vote
Approve of House incumbent's job performance	–	97	–	71
Disapprove of job performance	–	25	–	7
Approve Congress's job performance	94	94	87	65
Disapprove Congress's job performance	89	89	67	46
Favor term limits	91	91	73	52
Oppose term limits	91	92	75	59
Respondent knows incumbent wrote bad checks	84	88	66	52
Respondent knows incumbent did not write bad checks	97	96	80	58
Bad checks don't disqualify the member from serving	92	95	85	57
Check bouncers should be voted out	88	87	60	44
Check bouncers broke the law	89	93	72	54
Check bouncers didn't break the law	94	89	80	52
Incumbent bounced no checks	95	93	79	56
1–99 checks bounced	90	89	74	50
100–920 checks bounced	77	89	55	39
Congress to blame for S&L crisis	90	88	64	33
Congress not at fault for S&L crisis	95	91	75	53
Quite a few people running the government are crooked	89	90	69	45
Hardly any are crooked	89	88	82	60

SOURCE: 1992 National Election Study.

ars say, are "candidate-centered" affairs in which the qualities, traits, behavior, or characteristics of the individuals running for Congress are by far the dominant considerations in citizens' conjectures about their voting choice. In fact, congressional elections are surprisingly partisan contests in terms of the propensity of citizens to vote for the congressional candidate sharing their own partisan predispositions. But the powerful pull of party congruence or affinity, while very evident in the comparisons shown in table 11.1, is modulated somewhat by attitudes voters have about Congress and by their reactions to incumbents' peccadillos or involvements in scandal. Citizens who approve of the job performance of their incumbent representative are substantially more prone to vote for that incumbent than are voters who disapprove. Moreover, citizens who feel that Congress as an institution is doing a good job are more supportive of incumbents, and more inclined to vote for them, than is true for those who disapprove of the work of Congress. Whether citizens favored or opposed provisions placing limits on the maximum number of years a person could serve in Congress did not appear to have an impact on their inclination to support or vote for their own representative.

The comparisons shown in table 11.1 provide interesting indications of the ways in which certain attitudes about the behavior of members of Congress may impinge on citizens' willingness to vote in the congressional contest or their propensity to support incumbent or challenger. If citizens lose confidence in a democratic political institution and scorn their elected representatives, they may withdraw their participation and support. Citizens' supportiveness of their representative assembly and its members is, as table 11.1 suggests, powerfully refracted through individuals' partisan attachments. At the same time, voters supported their incumbent representative more firmly if they knew he or she had not written check overdrafts at the House bank, if they felt such overdrafts did not disqualify their member from serving, if they thought the check overdrafts were not a violation of law, or, relatedly, if they felt that Congress was not to blame for the savings-and-loan crisis. And when we actually counted incumbents' House check overdrafts, we could see (as table 11.1 indicates) that the raw number of overdrafts affected citizens' support for incumbents—those who "bounced" checks more than a hundred times were the least supported, irrespective of party congruence.

The Influence of Partisan Attachments

We can underscore the impact of partisanship in the congressional election by comparing degrees of partisan strength for "partisan congruents" and "partisan incongruents" who express approval of incumbent representatives, report voting for the incumbent, and rate the incumbent highly (above 70 degrees) on the feeling thermometer. We display these interesting comparisons in table 11.2. Strong partisans whose congressman shares the same party identification are much more

TABLE 11.2

STRENGTH OF PARTISAN CONGRUENCE AND EVALUATIONS OF HOUSE INCUMBENTS IN 1992

	Respondent's political party identification												
	Same as incumbent's						Independent		Different from incumbent's					
	Strong		Weak		Lean				Lean		Weak		Strong	
Incumbent evaluations	%	N	%	N	%	N	%	N	%	N	%	N	%	N
Percentage who approve of the incumbent	92	(261)	93	(228)	86	(165)	79	(136)	74	(115)	74	(140)	68	(107)
Percentage voting for the incumbent	95	(229)	90	(206)	85	(155)	74	(105)	57	(102)	49	(134)	33	(120)
Percentage rating the incumbent above 70 degrees on the thermometer scale	41	(263)	26	(250)	24	(174)	17	(167)	17	(132)	15	(163)	12	(120)

SOURCE: 1992 National Election Study.

NOTE: The numbers in parentheses are numbers of cases. The mean feeling thermometer rating given to incumbents was 61, and the standard deviation was 21. The cutoff of 70 degrees was chosen because it is about half a standard deviation above the mean rating.

supportive than those who only "lean" toward the incumbent's party. By the same token, strong party identifiers whose incumbent representative adheres to a different party are least likely to approve of the way in which the incumbent had done his or her job, substantially less likely to vote for the incumbent, and far less likely to rate the incumbent highly on the feeling thermometer.

The results in table 11.2 simply punctuate the profound effects of partisan attachments and affinities on citizens' support for, and inclination to vote for, the incumbent. In our subsequent analyses, we find that other variables influence incumbent support and congressional voting, but it is profoundly true, in every case, that congressional support and voting are unequivocally rooted in partisan orientations and linkages. The tantalizing comparisons shown in tables 11.1 and 11.2 give some urgency to a multivariate analysis that can bring order out of interrelated effects and allow the underlying pattern of relationships to emerge.

ANALYZING SUPPORT FOR INCUMBENTS

In order to unravel the influences of a variety of factors that help account for variations among citizens in the extent of their support for (or opposition to) incumbent representatives, we have chosen to estimate a multivariate analytical model using the 1992 NES survey data. In everyday terms, this means that we offer estimates of the weights of several explanatory factors (independent variables) on voters' support (the dependent variable) for candidates for the House of Representatives, where our estimates for each factor or variable hold the influences of other factors constant. We aim to explain voters' net preferences for or comparative evaluations of the major party House candidates.

In the 1992 NES interviews, respondents were asked to rate congressional candidates on a scale ranging from 0 to 100, as if rendering a judgment of their feelings of "warmth" or "coldness" toward incumbent members of Congress. Interviewers told respondents: "Ratings between 50 degrees and 100 degrees mean that you feel favorable and warm toward that person. Ratings between 0 degrees and 50 degrees mean that you don't feel favorable toward the person and that you don't care too much for that person." The phenomenon we are trying to account for—the dependent variable—is the relative level of support for the incumbent candidate, obtained by subtracting the challenger's thermometer score from the rating given to the incumbent.

This "difference between thermometer scores for Democratic and Republican candidates ... represents the net gain (or loss) in utility which the citizen would expect to receive as a result of the election of the Republican rather than the Democratic candidate" (Page and Jones 1979, 1072). These thermometer rating differences allow us to assay a wide range of voter evaluations of candidates, a range potentially sensitive to influences beyond the weight of party attachments or candidate familiarity. As such, this measure of voter preferences is more suitable than merely the dichotomous report of the voters' choice between one or the other of the major-party candidates. And our thermometer-based measure of candidate preference is a good stand-in for explicit vote choice. Indeed, 89 percent of those who rated the challenger relatively warmer than the incumbent actually voted for the challenger. And 94 percent of those voters who gave their incumbent representative higher thermometer ratings voted for the incumbent. It is a testimony to the power of incumbency in congressional politics that 65 percent of the survey respondents who gave incumbent and challenger the same thermometer ratings actually voted for the incumbent.

We model citizens' support for House incumbents with seven sets of independent variables: (1) socioeconomic status and economic evaluations, (2) party affiliation, (3) relations with the incumbent representative, (4) contact with and awareness of the challenger, (5) political attentiveness and trust in the government, (6) reactions to the House check-overdraft scandal, and (7) evaluations of Congress's job performance.[5] These measures have become quite conventional in research on congressional election behavior (e.g., see Patterson, Ripley, and Quinlan 1992), although few election studies include the scandal variables (but see Jacobson and Dimock 1994 or Peters and Welch 1980). We have analyzed the effects of these sets of variables for all respondents in the 1992 election survey who resided in districts where an incumbent was in the fray.

Our model of relative incumbent support contains a variety of interaction terms intended to disentangle the effects of variables that may influence one another. A good example of such an interaction is between partisan congruence and the effects of check overdrafts, such as we evidenced in table 11.2—writing bad checks appears to have much less impact on incumbents' ratings when the respondent identifies with the incumbent's political party. Rather than test only the hypothesis that check overdrafts lower voters' support for incumbents, we show the effects of check bouncing under conditions where the voter and the incumbent have different party identifications.

VOTER SUPPORT FOR HOUSE INCUMBENTS

The results of our analysis of citizens' support for their incumbent representative vis-à-vis the challenger are shown in table 11.3. The first

TABLE 11.3
SUPPORT FOR HOUSE CANDIDATES IN THE 1992 CONGRESSIONAL ELECTION

Variable	Unstandardized regression coefficient	t-ratio	Range
Constant	− 31.59***	− 7.77	
Socioeconomic status, economic evaluations			
Education	.18	.55	0–17
Age	.01	.23	17–91
Federal policies hurt the economy	1.79*	1.90	1–5
Federal policies hurt family finances	− .19	− .17	1–5
Partisanship of respondent and incumbent			
Same party identification	11.62***	7.26	0, 1
Party ID: seven-point scale	− .32	− .74	− 3 − +3
Awareness, contact, evaluations: incumbent			
Awareness through media	2.33**	2.19	0–3
Awareness × different party ID	− 3.60**	− 2.61	
Sum of contacts with incumbent	4.68***	5.18	0–4
Satisfaction with assistance	6.98***	3.43	0, 1
Incumbent stays in touch	8.96***	9.04	1–4
Critical of public officials, members of Congress	− 5.70*	− 1.88	0, 1
Awareness, contact: challenger			
Awareness through media	− 2.45**	− 2.46	0–3
Sum of contacts with challenger	− 8.79***	− 5.90	0–4

*p < .10;   **p < .05;   ***p < .01 (all tests are two-tailed).

Continued . . .

column of numbers gives estimates of the effect on the differences in thermometer ratings that each variable has when the other variables are held constant at their mean values. It is apparent from these estimates that neither education nor age nor perceptions of the government's effects on family finances had any significant influence on levels of support for incumbents. The positive coefficient associated with attitudes about the impact of federal policies on national economic conditions indicates that incumbents were rated more warmly than challengers when voters thought that government policies hurt the economy. This is a rather surprising result that runs counter to our expectation; we anticipated that incumbents would fare worse when the government is blamed

TABLE 11.3 — *Continued*
SUPPORT FOR HOUSE CANDIDATES IN THE 1992
CONGRESSIONAL ELECTION

Variable	Unstandardized regression coefficient	t-ratio	Range
Political attentiveness and efficacy			
Follows government and public affairs	− 2.68**	− 2.65	1–4
Government responsiveness	.04	.27	1–20
Trust in the government	.04	.11	3–20
House banking scandal			
Punishment for bad checks	− 2.89***	− 3.72	0–3
Number of bounced checks	.001	.78	0–920
Checks bounced × different party ID	.002	.10	
Checks bounced × incumbent media contact	− .02**	− 2.04	
Checks bounced × punishment	− .01*	− 1.69	
Congressional Evaluations			
Favor term limits	1.48	.79	0, 1
Approve of Congress	− .59	− .33	1–4
Congress approval × following politics	1.80*	1.86	

Adj R^2 = .38;   standard error = 21.22;   N = 907.

SOURCE: 1992 National Election Study.

NOTE: The dependent variable is the arithmetic difference between the scores given to House candidates (incumbent scores minus challenger scores) on the 0–100-point feeling thermometers. The parameter estimates are unstandardized two-stage least squares regression coefficients. The values for approval of Congress are the predicted levels of approval obtained from the first-stage regressions.

*$p < .10$;   **$p < .05$;   ***$p < .01$ (all tests are two-tailed).

for declines in economic conditions. But because there were more Democratic than Republican incumbents, it may be that Democrats were simply advantaged by voters' inclinations to blame the Republican president, George Bush, for the recession.

Looking at the second set of variables, we can see that partisan congruence between citizens and incumbents leads to a considerable pro-incumbent rating differential. The coefficient of 11.62 means that the incumbent is rated almost 12 degrees warmer than the challenger when respondent and incumbent come from the same party rather than from different parties.[6] Party identification, coded as a seven-point scale ranging from strong Democrat to strong Republican, is not related to differences in feeling thermometer ratings, indicating that Republican and Democratic voters do not differ as such, and the strength of their partisan attachments are not at issue here. What counts in partisan terms is party congruence—the nexus between voter and representative.

The effects of party identification are also apparent in the way partisan differences interact with awareness of the incumbent through the media. When respondents and House members have different party identifications, then higher levels of media attention are related to lower feeling thermometer differentials ($b = -3.60$). At the same time, the interaction between partisan congruence and the number of checks incumbents bounced was not a significant predictor of incumbent support.

Other variables that significantly affect incumbent-challenger differences in thermometer scores are the extent to which the incumbent is perceived to stay in touch with constituents ($b = 8.96$), satisfaction with the incumbent's assistance with a problem ($b = 6.98$), and receiving mail from the incumbent ($b = 4.68$).[7] Similarly, awareness of the incumbent through the media—learning something about him or her on the radio, on television, or through the print media—leads to moderately greater incumbent support ($b = 2.33$). The positive influences of these variables reveals something important about the sources of incumbents' electoral security. Each of them is associated with a behavior anticipated or controlled, to some extent, by the incumbent.

In contrast to the effects of awareness of the incumbent, paying attention to political and governmental affairs more generally actually reduces the advantage incumbents enjoy over their challengers ($b = -2.68$). In the glare of the anti-incumbent and anti-Congress milieu of the 1992 election campaign, it should not be surprising that people "tuned in" to politics are also more critical of government officials such as congressmen. Interestingly, the attention-to-politics variable is positively correlated with disapproval of Congress—to be an aware and attentive citizen is, unsurprisingly, to deplore Congress's performance. Finally, as we anticipated, the more contact respondents had with and the more attention they paid to a challenger through the media, the greater was their support for the challenger. But more general appraisals of government responsiveness and trust in government showed no independent effects on citizens' preferences among congressional candidates.

Another group of variables shows that the House banking scandal and perceptions of dishonesty among public officials substantially influenced thermometer rating differentials. Respondents holding to the view that incumbents should be punished for writing bad checks were prone to support their opponents, by a moderate amount ($b = -2.89$). Again, although the sheer number of checks bounced by incumbents had no independent impact on voter suppportiveness, writing bad checks did interact with respondents' media contacts with incumbents and their endorsements of more severe punishment for check overdrafts to produce relatively lower net preferences for incumbents.

Finally, the estimates in table 11.3 indicate that the extent of citizens' approval or disapproval of Congress does not, by itself, impinge on their candidate preferences. Thermometer rating differentials do not differ as between those who think Congress does a good job and those who castigate Congress. The key to assaying the influence of pro- or anti-Congress sentiments lies in attentiveness to political affairs. When attention to politics and evaluations of Congress are working together (as shown in the interaction term), support for congressional candidates is significantly affected ($b = 1.80$). Put differently, at higher levels of political awareness the effect of evaluation of Congress on candidate support increases, so politically attentive people are more likely to link their evaluations of Congress to their evaluations of the incumbent and challenger.[8] It is the alert citizenry that invokes evaluations of institutional performance to make voting choices in electing members for that institution, as surely would be predicted by democratic political theory.

Interestingly, when the analysis was performed using incumbent thermometer ratings (rather than the differences between incumbent and challenger ratings), we found that evaluations of Congress were positively related to evaluations of members of Congress. That is, citizens who approve of Congress tend to give their incumbent member warm thermometer ratings, and citizens who think Congress has done a poor job are inclined to rate their own congressmen relatively low on the scale. At the same time, the analysis shown in table 11.3 indicates that the comparative thermometer evaluations of incumbents and challengers are sensitive to appraisals of Congress only for the politically aware.[9]

SCANDAL, CONGRESS BASHING, AND VOTER TURNOUT

In addition to analyzing support for incumbents, we expected scandal, anti-incumbent sentiments, and anti-Congress attitudes to affect voter turnout in 1992. In keeping with this expectation, we estimated a model in which the dependent variable is whether or not the respondent claimed to have voted in the congressional election. Here the dichotomous nature of turnout at the individual level dictates using logit re-

TABLE 11.4
PREDICTING VOTER TURNOUT IN THE 1992
CONGRESSIONAL ELECTION

Variable	Logit coefficient	t-ratio	Range
Constant	−8.62***	−7.28	
Socioeconomic status			
Education	.11**	2.40	0–17
Race (1 = White; 0 = nonwhite)	.87***	3.41	0, 1
Age	−.01*	1.22	17–91
Gender (1 = male; 0 = female)	−.31*	−1.70	0, 1
Family income	.02	1.42	1–77
Residential mobility	−.002	−.23	−40–0
Partisan orientations			
Party ID: 7-point scale	−.02	−.31	−3–+3
Strength of party ID	.1207	1.19	0–3
Political activity, interest, knowledge			
Index of campaign activities	.17	1.45	0–4
Cares about presidential election outcome	.37*	1.73	0, 1
Cares about congressional election outcome	.31***	2.47	0, 1
Presidential race will be close	.40*	1.77	0, 1
Interest in the campaign	.42***	2.80	1–3
Follows government and public affairs	.15	1.16	1–4
Index of political knowledge	.25***	2.70	0–4
Should vote even if not concerned	.12**	1.94	0, 1

Continued . . .

gression. For independent variables in the model we draw on previous research on participation, adding to the analysis measures of scandal, as well as evaluations of incumbents and appraisals of Congress. We expected to find that public hostility toward Congress and its incumbents might well exacerbate more general feelings of political cynicism or alienation, thereby dissuading citizens from participating in the congressional election.

The results of the analysis of voter turnout is presented in table 11.4. As expected, better-educated respondents and white respondents are more likely to cast votes in the congressional election, as, interestingly enough, are women.[10] In addition, variables in one way or another tapping electoral mobilization (caring about the outcome of the election, expecting a close presidential race, interest in the presidential campaign, political knowledge, and believing that citizens should vote

TABLE 11.4 — *Continued*
PREDICTING VOTER TURNOUT IN THE 1992
CONGRESSIONAL ELECTION

Variable	Logit coefficient	t-ratio	Range
Political efficacy, trust			
Internal efficacy	.00	.25	1–20
Government responsiveness	.01	.90	3–20
Trust the government	.08*	1.79	3–20
Incumbent-related attitudes			
Punishment for bad checks	.11	1.20	0–3
Number of bounced checks	.001	.77	0–920
Incumbent-feeling thermometer rating	.05***	5.59	0–100
Congress-related attitudes			
Support for term limits	.12	.52	0, 1
Approve Congress's job performance	−.44**	−2.00	0–100

$-2 \times$ LLR = 836.3 (df = 24; p = .000); N = 987. % who voted = 74; % voters correctly predicted = 93; % nonvoters correctly predicted = 47; % of all cases correctly predicted = 81.

*$p < .10$; ** $p < .05$; *** $p < .01$, two-tailed.

SOURCE: 1992 National Election Study.
NOTE: The dependent variable is voter turnout in House races. Respondents who reported voting were given a score of 1; those who said they did not vote were scored 0. The measure of congressional approval and incumbent feeling thermometer ratings are predicted values obtained from the first-stage regression.

even if they do not care about the election outcome) are quite powerfully associated with the probability of voting. We might say that the election campaign performed its purpose of arousing citizens and mobilizing them to go to the polls and, while there, to vote for their favorite congressional candidate (see Caldeira, Clausen, and Patterson 1990; Caldeira, Patterson, and Markko 1985).

The House bank overdraft scandal does not seem to have stimulated voter turnout or attenuated it. Voters do not appear to have gone to the polls because they wanted to punish incumbents who had accumulated bounced checks (although the positive coefficient indicates that endorsing a harsher punishment increased the chances of voting). The insignificant effect may occur because, as noted earlier in this chapter, the biggest abusers of the House bank did not run for reelection and were not available for "punishment" on election day. By the same to-

288 SAMUEL C. PATTERSON AND MICHAEL K. BARR

ken, citizens who favor congressional term limits did not, on that account, go to the polls (with a negative sign, there is the hint that term-limit supporters were, if anything, a bit "turned off").

Finally, both evaluations of incumbents and of Congress itself are related to the probability of voting, although the two variables have opposite effects. It seems that *disapproval* of Congress increases the odds of turning out to vote, while it is incumbent *approval* that promotes voting in the election.[11] The positive relationship between incumbent feeling thermometers and turnout is fairly easy to explain. Campaign activity, interest in the campaign, and contact with campaign organizations all stimulate voter turnout, but they also have the effect of generating support for particular candidates. Strong partisans and political activists tend to compose the core support for congressional candidates, and these people are also more likely to turn out to vote. Next, the turnout-depressing impact of approving Congress is reasonable when the determinants of congressional ratings and voter turnout are compared. Better-informed respondents are more likely to vote and are also more disapproving of Congress.

The Heritage of 1992

What are the main lessons to be drawn from the 1992 congressional election? The election was tumultuous in various respects, occurring in a climate of unusual hostility toward Congress and toward incumbent representatives. Certainly, the decibel count in Congress bashing was higher than normal in the few months before the election, and voters were influenced to the extent they were, themselves, Congress bashers. And the accumulated annoyance with Congress for failing, in highly publicized ways, to prevent bank (S&L) failures, reduce the deficit, clean up the malpractice involved in congressional services to members (the bounced-check scandal), and for other peccadillos significantly diminished voter support for incumbents.

Nevertheless, ultimately the congressional election process worked admirably well in 1992. Congressional politicians who committed misdeeds, who exhibited dishonesty, who took improper advantage of congressional services or amenities, or who egregiously neglected their responsibilities as public policymakers, were the losers in the electoral process. Many of those tainted by corruption or malpractice were motivated to withdraw, determining not to run for reelection. Support for incumbents who ran for reelection hinged very much on voters' attitudes toward the House bank scandal. Those incumbents who ran for reelection tended to be evaluated by voters in terms of the sheer number of their bounced checks when information about check overdrafts was disseminated through the communications media.

Our analysis of voters' candidate preferences in 1992 underscores the effects of Congress bashing and scandal. Even when voters' preferences are analyzed in the light of very powerful predictors—partisanship, awareness and attentiveness to politics, and contact with incumbents and challengers—citizens' attitudes toward perceived improper incumbent behavior and their evaluations of Congress itself strongly affect these preferences. More succinctly, our analysis gives direct evidence of Congress-bashing effects in demonstrating how check overdrafts affected voters' preferences when the media spread the word, and how affective orientations toward Congress influenced the choices of voters attentive to governmental and political realities, activities, and events. That indicators of Congress bashing and scandal independently affect voters' choices among congressional candidates is sober testimony to the part that evaluative and affective attitudes can play in congressional election politics. "Voters," V.O. Key, Jr., once said, "are not fools." Congressional politicians will enjoy the electoral benefits that flow from their partisanship, their politicking, and their constituency-side manner more fully as they attend properly to their ethical conduct and avoid appearances of impropriety, dishonesty, or disingenuousness.

In 1992, however prepared they may have been to punish incumbents, voters went to the polls principally on the basis of conventional influences—socioeconomic status, party identification, political mobilization factors—and not inordinately on the basis of resentment of politicians or alienation from politics. Voters' preferences among congressional candidates were, as usual, strongly colored by party congruence and by the strength of linkages between voter and incumbent. But, perhaps more than previous congressional elections of recent vintage, Congress bashing and congressional scandal contributed measurably to understanding the size and shape of voters' choices.

If the rumblings of voter discontent evident in 1992 did not play out in major retaliation against incumbent politicians, in hindsight they foreshadowed the political earthquake of the 1994 election. In the two years between congressional elections, public disaffection from Congress and its members, disappointment with the Clinton administration, and a skillful Republican campaign to capture a congressional majority fueled a dramatic change in electoral geography. Republicans gained 52 House seats and 9 Senate seats, defeating Democratic incumbents and winning in the unusually large number of open seats without losing an incumbent of their own running for reelection. For the first time in four decades, the Republicans would hold majorities in both the House of Representatives and Senate of the 104th Congress. Congress bashing had paid off.

Acknowledgment

This chapter was prepared while Patterson was a Fellow at the Center for Advanced Study in the Behavioral Sciences, Stanford, California. He is grateful for the financial support provided by a grant from the National Science Foundation, SES-9022192.

Notes

1. Specifically, 1,298 House candidates were either on ballots or were write-ins who earned at least .1 percent of the vote.

2. For a spirited defense of Congress against these attacks, read Representative David R. Obey's (D-Wisc.) 1991 speech in the House under special order—see *Congressional Record* 137 (5 November 1991): H9377–H9382. Recently Congress has also been defended vigorously by Nelson W. Polsby (see Polsby 1990a, 1990b).

3. The full citations are: Americans to Limit Congressional Terms, *Kick the Bums Out* (Washington, D.C.: National Press Books, 1992); Richard Munson, *The Cardinals of Capitol Hill* (New York: Grove Press, 1993); Philip M. Stern, *The Best Congress Money Can Buy* (New York: Pantheon, 1988); and H. Lon Henry, *Congress: America's Privileged Class* (Rocklin, Calif.: Prima Publishing, 1994).

4. See Nelson W. Polsby, "Congress-Bashing through the Ages," *Roll Call* 36 (10 September 1990): 27; Norman Ornstein, "Congress Confidential," *Washington Post*, 3 November 1991, C5; Richard E. Cohen, "Congress in Distress," *National Journal* 24 (18 January 1992): 118.

5. We are interested in the effects of citizens' evaluations of Congress on incumbent thermometer ratings, but as Born (1990) has demonstrated, attitudes about Congress are themselves influenced by evaluations of the incumbent. In order to single out the impact of congressional evaluations on incumbent approval, we analyzed the survey data using two-stage least squares regression. In the first stage, we employed the variables listed in table 11.3 (excluding the variables for approval of Congress and the interaction terms), plus additional variables not shown, to obtain a predicted score for congressional approval for every survey respondent. Then these predicted values "stand in" for the actual values of congressional approval in the second stage of the analysis, where we account for incumbent approval. This "second stage" analysis is what is reported in table 11.3. The independent variables used to construct the instrument for approval of Congress include the ones

used in the second stage plus these additional variables: feeling thermometer ratings of the federal government, the belief that the federal government is too powerful, blaming Congress for the size of the budget deficit, and blaming Congress for the savings-and-loan scandal. The adjusted R^2 for the instrumental equation was .32.

6. Specifically, partisan congruence obtains when the incumbent is from the same party that the respondent leans toward, weakly identifies with, or strongly identifies with. By construction, then, there never is partisan congruence between an incumbent and a respondent who claims to be a political independent or who identifies with a minor political party.

7. Respondents could have had as many as four types of contact with the incumbent and the challenger: (1) receiving mail, (2) contact with someone from his or her staff, (3) attending a meeting or rally where the candidate was present, or (4) personal contact.

8. The model was replicated using a set of dummy variables representing approval of Congress and high attention, disapproval of Congress and high attention, and neither approval nor disapproval with little attention. The coefficients are as anticipated, and the signs of the dummy variables are in the expected direction. Compared to the baseline category of low attention, the high attention–approve variable was positively signed, while the high attention–disapprove variable wore a negative coefficient.

9. In a similar line of analysis, college education was used as a surrogate for political sophistication and citizenship norms (Born 1990). The results generally contradicted the hypothesis that better-educated people would show a closer linkage between congressional and incumbent evaluations. That study employed a dependent variable different from ours: it predicted to incumbent feeling thermometers alone, and the rest of the model was specified differently from ours.

10. The positive relationship between being a woman and the probability of voting contrasts with the commonplace finding. Far from being an artifact of the model or method, we observed the same relationship between gender and turnout simply by controlling for political knowledge or attention to politics. At every level of political knowledge, women were more likely to vote than men in the 1992 congressional election.

11. These two variables are included in Nichols's and Beck's turnout analysis, presented in chapter 2, with the same signs, although the statistical significance of congressional approval decreases to the .10 level (two-tailed).

CHAPTER 12

The Long Campaign: Senate Elections in 1992

JANET M. BOX-STEFFENSMEIER AND
CHARLES H. FRANKLIN

All members of Congress serve a fixed term of office, after which they must stand for reelection, retire, or run for another office. The vast majority seek reelection.[1] In going before the voters, incumbents often say they "run on the record." They point to things they have done in Congress as reasons for voters to reelect them. Challengers often point to other things they have done (or not done) as reasons not to reelect them. In either event, it is clear that the time of governing, the period between elections, is crucial to the reelection bid. We call this time the *long campaign*. Members of Congress are clearly aware of the consequences of their actions in office for their future reelection chances. They worry about how their votes will play back home (Kingdon 1989), they anticipate likely challengers and what might be done to avert or prepare for those challengers (Fenno 1992), they raise money for the next campaign (Box-Steffensmeier 1993), and they constantly seek to explain their actions to their constituents (Mayhew 1974; Fenno 1978). This is all part of the long campaign, which culminates in the short campaign between Labor Day and election day.

Studies of voters and elections have focused almost exclusively on the short fall campaign. If our primary interest is in the psychology of the vote choice, then this is a good period to study. During the fall campaign voters learn about the candidates, especially the challenger

(Alvarez and Franklin 1994b). The fall campaigns may also affect citizens' beliefs about the candidates, through speeches, news coverage, and advertising. Exactly how voters "boil down" their beliefs and perceptions of candidates to make a voting choice is the subject of a vast literature on elections that focuses on the short campaign.[2]

The long campaign has been much less studied. This is unfortunate, for it is the period of governing that sets the stage for the final fall contest. What is more, the consequential actions of elected representatives during their terms of office provide the substance of republican government. How these actions make themselves felt in reelection choices is the essence of the politics (as opposed to the psychology) of voting.

In this chapter we dip into the long campaign by considering how U.S. senators position themselves for reelection during their term of office. Our interest is in how a senator's standing during the time of governing influences the outcome of the reelection contest. We want to trace a senator's standing with the voters to his or her actions in office over the time from election to reelection (or defeat). We also want to examine the extent to which voters appear to respond myopically to only the short campaign or alternatively incorporate the senator's performance over an entire term.

To do this we look at three pieces of evidence. First, we demonstrate that how a senator stands with the voters throughout a term of office plays a significant role in the outcome of the reelection bid. Second, we look at how a senator's voting in Congress during the six-year term affects voters' evaluations of performance and voters' perceptions of the senator's positions. Finally, we turn to the ultimate vote choice, asking if the voters appear to incorporate past performance in their vote decisions, rather than attend only to the moment of the short fall campaign.

Data and Design

Studies of voting behavior in presidential and congressional elections have relied heavily on surveys of voters taken during the short campaign. The earliest major academic study of campaigns was conducted by Lazarsfeld, Berelson, and Gaudet in 1940. They studied how citizens made their vote choices from May to November during the 1940 presidential campaign. While their study was intended to show how voters were affected by the campaign, they actually found surprisingly little change. It seemed that most voters entered the election campaign with their minds pretty well made up.[3] Lazarsfeld and colleagues explained this as being the result of stable partisan predispositions, which largely determine political preferences.

Our interpretation is somewhat different. In 1940 Franklin D. Roosevelt sought his third term as president, having presided over the most devastating depression of the century and the beginnings of a gradual recovery. Roosevelt had truly reinvented government, giving it a role in social and economic affairs unimagined previously in American history. All of these changes were controversial, arousing passions among both supporters and opponents. If we view his eight years in office as the long campaign leading to the 1940 election, it is far less surprising that preferences were well set before the fall contest. It is difficult to imagine how even an inattentive voter could fail to have reached a judgment of Roosevelt as president after eight years in office.[4] If we wish to understand the 1940 election, therefore, we would be better rewarded by asking how, over eight years, judgments of Roosevelt were formed, rather than focus only on the events of the last few months before the election.[5]

In the half century since the Lazarsfeld study, academic surveys have, for the most part, focused on an even shorter campaign period, from about Labor Day through election day. The National Election Study (NES), which is the leading academic survey of voters, has kept to the same basic design since 1952.[6] In presidential election years, the NES conducts interviews through the roughly eight weeks leading up to election day. After the election, these same respondents are reinterviewed. This allows an analysis of any changes in preferences that may have taken place during the campaign between the preelection and the postelection interview. There are no interviews taken before the beginning of the fall campaign, however, and hence there is no possibility of studying the development of the long campaign between elections using NES data.[7] In nonpresidential election years, the NES interviews citizens only once, after the election is over. This design can capture the outcome of the election, but is obviously unable to illuminate the dynamics of the campaign, either long or short.

While the NES surveys have not been designed to study the long campaign, a recent NES effort is much better able to address the Senate case. The NES sponsored a project known as the Senate Election Study (SES), which focused on the Senate elections of 1988, 1990, and 1992. The SES interviewed voters in all fifty states after each of the three elections, focusing primarily on perceptions of the senators from each state, and the Senate election when there was one. A new sample of respondents was drawn each year, so we cannot follow the same individuals across the three elections, but we can track aggregate opinion in each state over time. This provides the opportunity to explore the long campaign that culminated in the Senate elections of 1992.

There were thirty-four incumbent senators eligible for reelection in 1992. Of these, twenty-six sought reelection and eight chose to retire.[8] We can use the SES to follow the perceptions of these senators in the years leading up to and including 1992. Our aim is to show how perceptions of these senators were formed during the long campaign, how these perceptions changed over time, and how they shaped the fall election campaign in 1992. We can do this because the SES allows us to estimate the aggregate perception of each senator in each year. In 1992 we can relate these past aggregate perceptions to individual perceptions and voting choices in the fall campaign. Thus we can combine the study of the short and long campaigns of 1992.

A Model of Public Opinion

Before moving to the analysis, it is important to be clear about what our assumptions are concerning the dynamics of public opinion. The model we adopt plays an important role in our interpretation of the results.

The key element of our model of public opinion is the concept of memory. At one extreme, the public could have no memory at all. In this case, perceptions of and opinions about senators would be formed anew every election. Under this model, voters in 1992 would not give any weight to what they thought of a senator in 1990 or 1988. Their opinions would be based entirely on perceptions formed in the 1992 campaign.[9] If this were the case, our concept of the long campaign would be entirely irrelevant because only events of the reelection year would have any effect on voters. Such a model would place great emphasis on the strategy and tactics of the candidates over the short campaign only.

At the opposite extreme, the public could have long memories indeed. Under this model, previous evaluation of a candidate would continue to affect preferences even after taking account of current evaluations. Rather than let bygones be bygones, these voters hold a grudge. The empirical evidence for this would be seen in the continued effect of 1988 or 1990 opinion on vote, for example, even after controlling for 1992 opinion.

A model of public opinion that falls between these extremes is the Bayesian learning model. Bayesian theory is a means of formally taking prior information into account. According to this model, current opinions are updated based on a combination of prior beliefs and new information.[10] Bartels (1993) points out that Bayesian analysis provides a systematic way to characterize both the relative weight of the old and new information in voters' current opinions (1993, 268). Once updated, current opinion should include all relevant past information. There is memory in this model because the past affects current opinion. Once incorporated in current opinion, however, the past no longer has any direct impact on current behavior.

Empirically, under this model we should see approval in 1990 affect approval in 1992. Once we control for 1992 approval, however, there should be no remaining direct influence of prior approval on vote in 1992.[11]

Our expectation is that the Bayesian model is a reasonable approximation of the dynamics of opinion over the long campaign. Thus we expect that there will be an influence of past opinions on current ones, but that the past will exert little direct influence on election choices once current opinion is included in the model. Such a result does not reduce the importance of the long campaign at all. Instead, it shows how the long campaign is incorporated into the short contest. If our expectation is wrong, then the data can tell us this by showing either that the past has no effect on current opinion or choice or, alternatively, that the past continues to exert an influence after accounting for current opinion. The important point is that the data can distinguish between these alternatives. Thus our expectations are testable hypotheses, rather than preconceptions that will determine our conclusions.

Analysis

In this section we look at three aspects of the long campaign: the development of fundamental perceptions of senators; how the long campaign sets the stage for the election year; and how the election year choice is affected by the past.

DEVELOPING PERCEPTIONS OF SENATORS

How a politician presents himself or herself to the voters is a fundamental piece of the long campaign. Indeed, Fenno (1978) argues that the presentation of self is virtually the defining activity of members of Congress when they make contact with constituents. Incumbents must tell voters who they are. Voters, by the same token, need to know who the incumbent is. Without an established image of the incumbent, the voter will be unable to evaluate his or her performance.

Political folk wisdom paints a picture of politicians as veritable chameleons, able to change their hue to suit the surroundings. For the most part, this is a misleading picture. While politicians may find equivocation a useful skill in some circumstances, in general the politician who tries to be all things to all people is soon out of office. Obvious inconsistency is rapidly discovered and punished. Rather than constantly changing positions, incumbents attempt to define an image that will serve their need to appeal to a majority of voters. In order to appeal to voters successfully, the incumbent must also succeed in making that position known. This presentation of self is fundamental to the long campaign. There are many possible avenues along which senators can travel in presenting themselves to the voters. This section focuses on one crucial aspect of this presentation: political ideology.

One of the key elements of a senator's presentation of self is position taking (Mayhew 1974; Fenno 1978). In some cases, position taking is a rhetorical device, mere words, cheap talk. But once in office, position taking includes the far more consequential action of voting on legislation. Incumbents inevitably create a record of positions taken on the policy choices of government through their roll-call voting. Because this record is public, it is necessarily subject to debate in the next election campaign. Thus senators must take positions that they are prepared to defend and, indeed, to use as electoral weapons. This record is built up almost entirely during the long campaign. How it is established, and how it is linked to voters, is our primary concern in this section.

For our measure of roll-call voting, we use scores computed by the American Conservative Union (ACU). The ACU selects a number of votes that it considers important for conservative interests and scores each senator for the percentage of the time the senator took the conservative position. A score of 100 represents support for the conservative position on all votes, while a score of 0 represents opposition to the conservative position on all votes.[12] Similar scores are constructed by liberal groups, such as Americans for Democratic Action (ADA). The ADA and ACU scores are very highly correlated with each other, so there is little reason to prefer one over the other. Our results are the same with either measure.

Past research has found that the voting behavior of members of Congress is highly consistent over their time in office (Clausen 1973; Asher and Weisberg 1978; Kingdon 1989; Jackson and Kingdon 1992). In figure 12.1 we find that this is confirmed for the senators eligible for reelection in 1992. The figure shows that there is a strong relationship between ACU score in 1988 and in 1991. The correlation is a very high .96. (A correlation of +1.0 indicates a perfect relationship, while 0 indi-

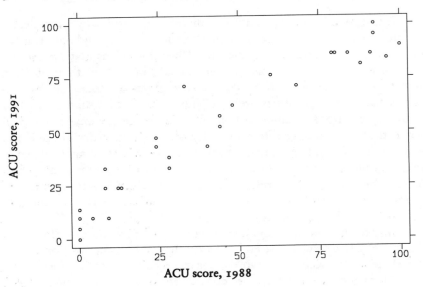

FIGURE 12.1. STABILITY OF ROLL-CALL RECORD.

cates no relationship at all and −1.0 indicates a perfect negative relationship.) Regardless of how they present themselves rhetorically, the
consequential behavior of these senators is remarkably consistent over
time.

Such consistent policy positions form a core of the presentation of
self. Over the course of the long campaign, senators transmit their policy positions to voters. Figure 12.2 shows the relationship between
ACU score in 1991 and mean liberal-conservative placement of the senator in 1992, as measured by the SES survey.[13] The correlation is a robust .83. This is all the more remarkable when we realize that virtually
no one knows what a senator's ACU score actually is. This relationship
demonstrates that through all the behaviors that communicate positions
to voters, the senator is successful in conveying an image that is congru-
ent with his or her behavior.

While citizens form perceptions of the incumbent that are strongly
related to roll-call voting behavior, it is important for us to examine
what learning takes place over the course of the long campaign. If citizens respond to the initial position taking of the incumbent (either during or immediately after the first election) but then ignore later developments, then our model of Bayesian learning is incorrect. Likewise, if
perceptions are developed anew each year, then there is no memory and
no learning. We address each of these possibilities.

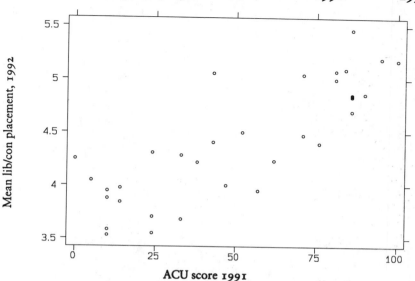

FIGURE 12.2. MEAN LIB/CON PLACEMENT BY
ROLL-CALL VOTING RECORD.

The images voters have of the incumbent are not static, though given the consistency of senators' behavior it is not surprising that the images among voters are quite stable. Figure 12.3 shows the relationship between mean liberal-conservative placement in 1990 and in 1992. The correlation is .83, indicating that average perceptions are highly stable over the two years. This stability, however, does not answer our primary question.[14]

It is critical to our argument that this stability is not stasis with a bit of noise. Instead, we want to show that perceptions are responsive to the behavior of the senator even as they incorporate past information. We show this by regressing mean liberal-conservative placement in 1992 on mean placement in 1990 and ACU score in 1991. In keeping with the Bayesian model of public opinion, 1992 perception should respond to both prior perception and the intervening roll-call behavior. It does, as table 12.1 shows.

The coefficients in the table show how much change in the average rating on a liberal-conservative scale we should expect given a change of one point on the independent variables, past perception and 1991 ACU score. Both are statistically significant, meaning we can reject the hypothesis that there is no effect of the independent variables on mean perception in 1992.[15] It is not surprising that the coefficient on 1990

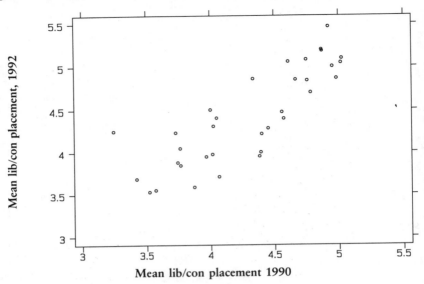

FIGURE 12.3. STABILITY OF MEAN LIB/CON PLACEMENT.

perception is larger than that for ACU score. In part, this is simply a reflection of the scales of each variable. The mean perception ranges from
about 3 to about 5, or just two points. The ACU scale, in contrast,
ranges over 100 points. A way of comparing these effects, then, is to
think what would happen to perceptions if the most liberal senator
were miraculously transformed into the most conservative. For past
perception, this means changing perception from a 3 to a 5. The predicted change in 1992 perception is .49 × (5 − 3) = .98, or about one
unit. For a similar reversal of ACU score, we would have .008 × (100 −
0) = .80. So it looks, from this, as if the effect of past perception is a
little stronger than that for ACU score, though not by a whole lot.

In fact, we should expect the effect of ACU score to be less than
that for past perceptions. According to our model, past perceptions incorporate all previous ACU scores plus everything else that affects the
perception of a senator's ideological position. The 1991 ACU score is
just one more observation of behavior. There should therefore be more
information represented by past perception than by the new ACU score.
According to the Bayesian model, more weight should be given to the
more reliable information, which in this case should be past perceptions
because they incorporate more information. By this light, the fact that
the ACU score is as powerful as it is suggests that the behavior which it
reflects is perceived by voters as quite reliable.

TABLE 12.1
DEVELOPMENT OF IDEOLOGICAL PERCEPTIONS
OF THE INCUMBENT, 1992

Variable	Coefficient	Standard error	Significance
Constant	1.91	.66	.007
Mean Lib/Con, 1990	.49	.18	.011
ACU Score, 1991	.008	.003	.015

$N = 34$
Adjusted $R^2 = .729$
Standard error = .288

SOURCE: Senate Election Study, 1988–92.

A second major element of the Bayesian model is the assumption that prior information is completely incorporated when updating is done. In this case, we would expect that 1988 mean liberal-conservative placement will add nothing to our prediction of 1992 mean placement, once 1990 placement and 1991 ACU score are taken into account. Figure 12.4 shows just this. The figure shows the scatter plot of residuals from the regression in table 12.1 against 1988 mean liberal-conservative placement.[16] The correlation is .0796, comfortably close to zero; if 1988 placement had a lingering effect on 1992 perceptions, there would be a positive correlation.

It is important to understand that this finding does not mean that perceptions in 1988 are irrelevant. Quite the contrary. What this shows is that 1988 perceptions are incorporated in 1990 perceptions, which in turn affect 1992 perceptions. It also shows that all the information from 1988 is absorbed in the 1990 perceptions, so there are no bits of information left over to have an independent effect on perceptions in 1992. Shifting slightly to negative campaigning, this also shows why old charges are unlikely to matter in a later campaign. If they were already incorporated in prior opinions, bringing them back up will have no effect on current opinion. In contrast, if a new scandal could be uncovered, there would likely be substantial impact.

The conclusions of this subsection are that senators behave consistently and that the public perceives their behavior rather accurately. Citizens behave consistently with the Bayesian model, and it appears that past information has no value once updated beliefs are incorporated. From the perspective of the long campaign, these results show just how

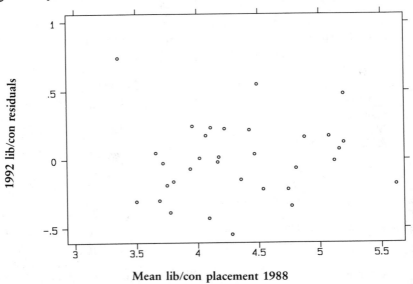

FIGURE 12.4. PRIOR PERCEPTION AND CURRENT RESIDUALS.

effective senators can be in communicating to voters, and how acute voters can be in receiving and processing those signals.

SETTING THE STAGE

The long campaign is not only a time for voters to learn about incumbents. It is also a time in which potential challengers make decisions about whether to run or not. Jacobson and Kernell (1983) have made a strong argument that conditions a year or more before an election play a powerful role in encouraging or discouraging strong challengers. Wilcox (1987) provides empirical evidence supporting Jacobson and Kernell's argument and finds that many serious challengers decide even earlier than spring of the election year. Ambitious politicians, those seeking to make politics their lifelong profession, must be especially selective in choosing the races they attempt.[17] A losing race can end a promising career. By the same token, an opportunity missed can forever foreclose advancement.

The events of the long campaign are summarized in the job approval of the incumbent at any point in time.[18] We can, in turn, use job approval as a measure of the incumbent's standing with voters. The abundance of public polls and the use of private polls by parties and those considering a race make it likely that the incumbent's standing with the public is known to potential challengers.

It is reasonable to assume that incumbents calculate the likely impact of their actions on voter approval. Fenno (1992) describes the considerable calculation behind an incumbent's actions. Studies of roll-call voting have often found that incumbents consider the impact of votes on their standing with the constituency (Kingdon 1989). It is reasonable, therefore, to think of the incumbent as choosing actions with some attention to the effects of these actions on voter approval. In some circumstances, an incumbent may choose actions that will lower his or her standing with voters in order to achieve some other goals, such as supporting the party's president or enhancing power within Congress. There is an obvious limit to such strategic behavior, however: low approval can lead to a strong challenge and the risk of electoral defeat. This means that few if any incumbents ignore the effects of their actions on their standing with voters. This calculus of action and approval then is an essential element of the long campaign.

We would expect high approval for the incumbent to deter the entry of strong challengers, while low approval would invite challengers into the race. Several measures of challenger quality have been proposed in the literature, including past officeholding and electoral experience. All such measures are aimed at the extent to which the challenger can run an effective campaign. We use total spending by the challenger as a measure of quality. The amount a candidate can raise is a good indication of whether potential contributors see the candidate as viable. Challengers almost always spend everything they are able to raise. Thus the total spending is a reasonable measure of how convincing the challenger is.[19]

Figure 12.5 shows the relationship between challenger spending in 1992 and mean incumbent job approval in 1990. The correlation is −.52. Thus an incumbent who can maintain popular support among voters through the middle years of his or her term can make substantial progress in assuring a relatively easy reelection bid.

Voters are not the only participants acting consistently with the Bayesian model. Candidates seem to also update their beliefs based on recent information. Table 12.2 shows the regression of challenger spending on incumbent job approval in 1990 and 1988. If potential challengers are Bayesians, we would expect the incumbent's standing in 1990 to matter, but not in 1988. That is what we find.

In addition to polishing their images with voters, incumbent senators spend an extraordinary amount of time planning for their next reelection bid by raising campaign funds. Table 12.3 shows the incumbents' activity in terms of the amount of money raised and the size of war chests between the 1986 and 1992 elections. Incumbents clearly do not wait

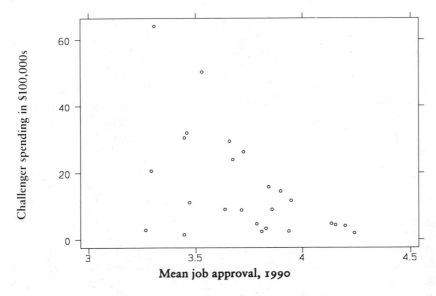

FIGURE 12.5. CHALLENGER SPENDING BY
INCUMBENT JOB APPROVAL.

until the fall of the election year to start raising money. Instead, it is an ongoing process and an integral part of the long campaign.

Incumbents who anticipated a tough race in 1992 began preparing for the challenge very early in the election cycle by raising large amounts of money. Safe incumbents helped ensure their success by building large war chests. Potential challengers are deterred from entering a race when the incumbent has a large war chest because potential challengers and contributors know that a challenger can never raise as much money as the incumbent and because contributors will be hesitant to contribute money to a strong incumbent's opponent. Without substantial financial backing, the challenger is doomed to fail because of the central role of money in successful modern campaigns. The distinction between unsafe incumbents who seek contributions because they are reacting to a threat and safe incumbents who build their war chests to deter quality challengers is important. Comparing the 1988 contributions and 1988 war chests exemplifies this point. The median unsafe incumbent, who received less than 55 percent of the 1992 vote, raised a whopping $544,646 but the war chest contained only $52,857. In contrast, the median safe incumbent, who received over 65 percent of the vote, raised less than one-third of the contributions that the unsafe incumbent raised and yet has a war chest that is six times larger.

TABLE 12.2
CHALLENGER STRENGTH IN 1992 AS A FUNCTION OF PAST INCUMBENT APPROVAL

Variable	Coefficient	Standard error	Significance
Constant	114.50	51.74	.038
Approval, 1990	−31.61	11.93	.015
Approval, 1988	4.96	14.46	.735

$N = 24$
Adjusted $R^2 = .210$
Standard error = 14.53

SOURCE: Senate Election Study, 1988–92.

Box-Steffensmeier (1993) separates incumbents' reaction and deterrence strategies and finds empirical evidence that incumbents who build large war chests effectively deter quality challengers.[20]

By their actions during the long campaign, incumbents both affect the decisions of their potential challengers and prepare themselves for the reelection bid. Their actions affect their job approval, which in turn has a significant impact on the strength of the eventual challenger. The large amount of time and effort devoted to fund raising has effects both on the strength of the challenger and on how well prepared the incumbent is to meet whatever challenge arises.

TABLE 12.3
MEDIAN INCUMBENT CONTRIBUTIONS AND WAR CHESTS OVER THE COURSE OF THE ELECTION CYCLE

	1988	1990	1992
Contributions			
Less than 55% of the vote	$544,646	$816,090	$4,322,671
55% to 65% of the vote	$85,375	$185,190	$2,317,149
More than 65% of the vote	$155,454	$515,242	$2,816,778
All incumbents	$155,454	$515,242	$2,889,357
War chests			
Less than 55% of the vote	$52,857	$751,373	$106,621
55% to 65% of the vote	$127,775	$286,901	$172,582
More than 65% of the vote	$349,721	$490,202	$354,763
All incumbents	$163,616	$423,862	$176,003

SOURCE: Federal Election Commission, 1990.

RUNNING THE RACE

By the time the short campaign begins on Labor Day, the stage has largely been set by the events of the long campaign. This does not mean that the short campaign is meaningless. There are clearly visible effects of the last eight weeks, as we shall see. In this section we trace the path incumbents travel to reelection (or defeat) and give an account of the relative contributions of the long and short campaigns to the final vote tally.

One way to approach the long campaign is to trace the paths of incumbents to these outcomes. We distinguish among four outcomes: retirement, winning less than 55 percent of the vote, winning between 55 and 65 percent, and winning over 65 percent in the 1992 election. These categories also happen to divide the set of incumbents into roughly equal numbers (eight or nine in each group). We want to know if these groups have distinctive histories over the long campaign. We summarize these histories by the mean job approval for the incumbent and the mean feeling thermometer score.[21]

Table 12.4 presents the histories of job approval and feeling thermometer for the four groups of incumbents. The results are striking in two ways. First, the paths diverge rather sharply, but only after initial similarity. Second, the retirees are unmistakably similar to the incumbents who run the closest races, suggesting that anticipation of the coming election plays a significant role in retirement decisions. In 1988 there is no reliable difference in the job approval of retirees and those

TABLE 12.4
INCUMBENT JOB APPROVAL AND THERMOMETER HISTORY
BY 1992 VOTE OUTCOME

Outcome	1988	1990	1992
Job approval			
Retiree	3.73	3.60	n.a.
Less than 55%	3.70	3.51	3.29
55% to 65%	3.71	3.78	3.76
More than 65%	3.99	3.95	4.03
Thermometer			
Retiree	56.7	56.0	51.7
Less than 55%	58.5	57.0	51.5
55% to 65%	60.2	61.0	61.0
More than 65%	65.1	65.2	65.6

SOURCE: Senate Election Study, 1988–92.

with less than 65 percent of the vote. Only the strongest vote getters appear distinctive in 1988. By 1990, however, a clear separation has begun to appear, with the eventual retirees and close-race incumbents showing a decline in job rating, while the other two groups hold steady or improve slightly. By the end of the reelection campaign in 1992, those in close races have fallen still further in the voters' eyes, while the two stronger finishers retain their levels of approval. The mean thermometer scores present the same picture, but confirm that by 1992 the retirees are as unpopular as those in the tightest races, even though retirees, by definition, had avoided the negative effects of a highly competitive short campaign. Had they chosen to seek reelection, it appears likely that the retirees would have been in for a tough fight.[22]

A second factor that distinguishes among the groups of outcomes is the relationship between incumbent and voter ideologies. We saw earlier that incumbents do a rather good job of transmitting their ideological positions to voters. This naturally raises the question of how the fit between incumbents and the voters plays into the eventual outcomes of races.

Table 12.5 shows the correlation between mean perceived incumbent liberal-conservative ideological placement and the mean voter's ideology in the state on the same scale, for each group of incumbents by the 1992 vote outcome. These measures are from 1990, so there are no effects of the short campaign. Once more, the groups are distinctive. The retirees show only a modest correlation with state opinion. Those in the closest races, by contrast, show a very strong negative relationship with state opinion. Senators earning at least 55 percent of the vote, in contrast, show a rather strong positive relationship to the average voter's ideological position. It seems that those who end up in electoral trouble are first out of step with their constituents. Those who match the voters do much better.[23]

TABLE 12.5
CORRELATIONS OF SENATORS' PERCEIVED IDEOLOGY
WITH MEAN VOTER IDEOLOGY IN 1990,
BY 1992 VOTE OUTCOME

Outcome	Correlation
Retiree	.159
Less than 55%	−.715
55% to 65%	.487
More than 65%	.535

SOURCE: Senate Election Study, 1988–92.

These results make it plain that the course of events over the long campaign is related to distinctive outcomes. But we are also interested in the short campaign. The model of public opinion we have adopted predicts that learning occurs throughout the election cycle, so while we expect the long campaign to set the stage, the short campaign should also play an important role in the final results. We now turn to this issue.

Comparing the Long and Short Campaigns

Our model of public opinion allows us conceptually to decompose public opinion into two components, prior opinion and new information. This corresponds rather closely to our ideas of the long and short campaign. If we were able to measure opinion before the short campaign begins, this would provide an observation of the end product of the long campaign. The short campaign would be captured by deviations from this initial position. Unfortunately, the design of the SES does not provide us with this. The SES measures for 1992 are all collected after the election is over and thus incorporate the events of the fall contest. Despite this difficulty, we can make some progress by adopting a simple statistical model of the campaign components.

As we argued earlier, it is possible to think of the incumbent job-approval measure as a summary of the net effects of the many elements that make up a campaign. In 1992 we have a measure of this approval taken after the completion of the fall campaign. This measure therefore incorporates both the long campaign effects and those of the short campaign. Given only the 1992 measure, we could not possibly separate these components. Thanks to the design of the SES, however, we have additional information in the form of the 1990 survey data, which includes job approval in 1990. Job approval in 1990 is clearly the result of the long campaign alone, since the short campaign does not begin for another two years. This gives us the leverage we need to examine the long and short campaigns.

The estimation of long and short campaign effects requires the decomposition of 1992 job approval into long and short components. This is a somewhat technical maneuver that is fully discussed in Box-Steffensmeier and Franklin (1994). Here we try to give a feel for the logic of what we are doing without resorting to the algebra necessary for the full proof.

Think about the 1992 approval measure. According to our Bayesian model of learning, this measure incorporates both the long and the short campaigns. If we had a way to separate these components, we could estimate the effects of each. The problem is how to do this. There are two ways, one that underestimates the effect of the long campaign and one that overestimates it. By doing both we can get a pretty good, but not perfect, estimate of the relative importance of the long and short campaigns.

The first way to decompose the campaign is to subtract the 1990 job approval from the 1992 approval. The 1990 measure, obviously, depends only on the long campaign. The 1992 measure depends on three parts: the long campaign up through 1990, the long campaign between 1991 and 1992, and the short campaign of 1992. After we subtract the 1990 approval, we are left with a combination of the 1991–92 long campaign and the 1992 short campaign. If we predict the vote using this difference as a measure of the short campaign, and 1990 approval as a measure of the long campaign, we will underestimate the long campaign effect (since some of it will be included in our short campaign measure) and overestimate the impact of the short campaign. This gives us our first estimate of the two effects.

The second way to decompose the effects is to subtract everything in the 1992 approval measure that is related to the 1990 long campaign measure.[24] This is clearly going too far, since we would expect that the 1992 short campaign is surely related to the long campaign (strong long campaigns are likely to be followed by strong short campaigns and likewise for weak campaigns). What this means is that we will overestimate the long campaign effect using this approach, since our measure will include some elements of the short campaign.

The virtue of these two approaches is that they set bounds on what the true effects are, since one is an overestimate and the other an underestimate. This means we can be confident that the actual effects of long and short campaigns are somewhere between our two estimates, though we cannot say exactly where. As it turns out, these bounds are close enough together to give us a reasonably good estimate of the two effects.

To estimate the effect of long and short campaigns on vote, we regress the incumbent's share of the two-party vote on our two alternative measures of the long and short campaign. We also include challenger spending to account for any short campaign effects not accounted for by our other measure. The results for both the over- and underestimates are presented in table 12.6.

Since both long and short campaign variables are measured on the same scale, job approval, we can compare their coefficients. The estimated coefficients for the long campaign effects are 20.6 and 17.1, a

TABLE 12.6
ESTIMATES OF LONG- AND SHORT-CAMPAIGN INFLUENCES
ON THE 1992 VOTE

Variable	Coefficient	Standard error	Significance
Overestimating long-campaign effects and under-estimating short-campaign effects			
Constant	−15.95	21.47	0.466
Long	20.64	5.68	0.002
Short	11.74	2.43	0.000
Challenger spending	−.07	.07	0.325
$N = 25$			
Adjusted $R^2 = .71$			
Standard error = 3.96.			
Underestimating long-campaign effects and over-estimating short-campaign effects			
Constant	−3.37	14.73	0.821
Long	17.13	3.78	0.000
Short	11.74	2.43	0.000
Challenger spending	−.07	.07	0.325
$N = 25$			
Adjusted $R^2 = .71$			
Standard error = 3.96.			

SOURCE: Senate Election Study, 1988–92.

relatively small range. The short campaign estimate is the same in both cases, 11.7. Both make a statistically significant contribution to the vote. In comparing the relative influence of long and short campaigns, we can conclude that the long campaign has from 46 to 76 percent greater impact on vote than does the short campaign. Nevertheless, this does not diminish the fact that the short campaign has a clear influence on the ultimate outcome as well. While the long campaign sets the stage, the short campaign clearly has a role to play.

We can get a visual picture of how the various senators fared by plotting the vote against long and short campaign effects. To this point, we have treated senators as a group. Here, however, we include the name of each senator, so we can see if our statistical evidence makes political sense in the light of the fortunes of each incumbent.

Figures 12.6 and 12.7 plot vote share against our estimated long and short campaign effects. Based on the long campaign, it appears that three incumbents should have been in precarious electoral circum-

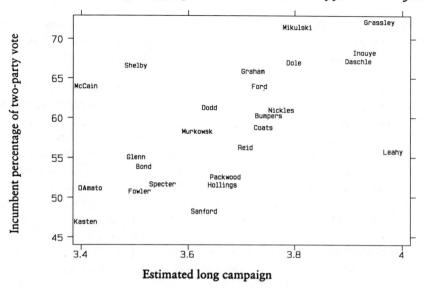

FIGURE 12.6. INCUMBENT VOTE BY LONG CAMPAIGN.

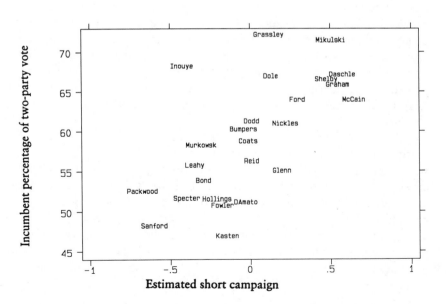

FIGURE 12.7. INCUMBENT VOTE BY SHORT CAMPAIGN.

stances: Kasten, D'Amato, and McCain. A second group of five should have expected close races: Fowler, Specter, Bond, Glenn, and Shelby. In fact, all but McCain and Shelby were held to under 55 percent of the vote.

The short campaign rescued some of them, while hurting others. Both McCain and Shelby had unusually strong short campaigns. In McCain's case, this represented a rebound from his entanglement in the savings-and-loan scandal. Glenn, like McCain, was implicated as a member of the "Keating five" and was thus the subject of an Ethics Committee investigation looking into involvement with a failed savings-and-loan institution controlled by Keating. Like McCain, Glenn bounced back with a strong short campaign, even against a quality challenger. Both McCain and Glenn may have benefited from the seemingly widespread perception that they were the least involved in the Keating affair and arguably should not have been made part of the Ethics Committee investigation (Barone and Ujifusa 1991, 953). Shelby benefited from drawing a rather weak opponent, a political consultant Shelby attacked for being basically unemployed: "He needs a job, but not in the U.S. Senate." (Barone and Ujifusa 1993, 7).

At the other end, Sanford, Packwood, Inouye, and Specter had the most negative short campaigns. In Sanford's case, heart surgery and a strong opponent snatched defeat from the jaws of what should have been victory, based on his long campaign. Packwood faced a bruising campaign against a strong opponent (Congressman Les AuCoin), though subsequent charges of sexual harassment did not emerge until after the election. Inouye faced charges of sexual misconduct, resulting in a negative short campaign performance, and a finish some 6 to 10 percent off his recent results. (Subsequent investigation by the Senate Ethics Committee ended when none of the alleged victims would come forward.)

Specter was the target of a challenge based on his role in the confirmation hearings for Supreme Court nominee Clarence Thomas and what some perceived as his hostile questioning of Anita Hill, who accused Thomas of sexual harassment. The Specter case is a good example of how a senator's actions in office, part of the long campaign, can affect the short campaign. His opponent, Lynn Yeakel, made the Thomas hearings a central issue in the campaign. Were it not for Specter's previously strong performance in the long campaign, the short campaign might well have cost him his seat in the Senate. In each of these cases, then, there is ample reason to expect the negative short campaign result which we observe.

Our results in this section have shown that there are distinctive paths to the reelection bid. While most incumbents are in similar circumstances four years before the election, clear differences emerge over the next two years. Those destined for a close race and those who eventually retire, are quite distinctive two years out. While not all retirees do so for electoral reasons, our results suggest that this is a common motivation, if not the only one.

We have also been able to partition the election campaign into long and short components. From this effort, we conclude that the effects of the long campaign are about one and a half times as large as the effects of the short. But the short campaign also has substantial effects on the outcome. Thus we would be unwise to ignore either of these elements of electoral competition.

Conclusions

We have seen that both the long and short campaigns are important elements of electoral politics. During the long campaign, a senator's actions play a substantial role in the development of citizens' perceptions. Perceptions of ideological position are closely tied to the senator's roll-call voting behavior. The evolution of these perceptions are consistent with the Bayesian model of public opinion that we use. The events of the long campaign also set the stage for the coming election. We found substantial differences in the ultimate outcome of reelection bids that were related to elements of the long campaign. In particular, we found that retirees seem very likely to have faced tough reelection battles. Finally, we were able to estimate the relative impacts of the long and short campaigns on the outcomes of the 1992 Senate races. The larger effect of the long campaign demonstrates the importance of what happens between elections. The significant effect of the short campaign shows that what happens after Labor Day can tip the balance in a close race. Incumbents cannot afford to neglect either campaign.

This chapter contains optimistic findings about the behavior of both incumbents and voters in a republican system. In contrast to numerous articles about the deplorable state of voter information in American politics, we find that constituents' aggregate perceptions are quite responsive to incumbent behavior in office. This finding is not necessarily inconsistent with studies that show that many individual voters are not well informed. As long as at least some citizens are informed, aggregate opinion will reflect incumbent behavior.[25] At the same time, our results imply that incumbents' presentation of self to voters is generally in line with their behavior in Congress. Instead of systematically misleading or confusing voters, senators adopt positions that they believe will attract majority support and convey these positions to voters.

The long campaign is the time in which these perceptions of performance are developed, though our results also show that the short campaign can be an important factor in the ultimate election outcome. As Franklin points out, however, if elections are to reflect the public's collective judgment of a representative's record, it is crucial that the record not be entirely a creation of the short campaign (1993, 228.) Our results show that the time of governing strongly affects public perceptions and evaluations, and so provides a key linkage between representatives and their constituents.

Acknowledgment

We would like to thank Laura Arnold and Christopher Zorn for research assistance on this chapter.

Notes

1. This was not always so. In the nineteenth century most members of Congress served only a term or two and then retired. See Polsby (1968), Fiorina, Rohde, and Wissel (1975), Price (1975), and Kernell (1977) for details on how this has changed.

2. For a glimpse at this literature, see Niemi and Weisberg (1993a, 1993b).

3. To be sure, some people did change their vote intention during the campaign, but Lazarsfeld and his colleagues found that most of this change reflected people returning to their partisan "home" after flirting with the opposition. To explain both the stability of most voters and this homing tendency, the authors developed the notion of a "partisan predisposition," defined by social class and other demographic factors. In their words: "A person thinks, politically, as he is, socially. Social characteristics determine political preference" (1944, 27). In the half century since they wrote, this verdict has been modified by a much greater emphasis on psychological factors, which are more malleable than are social characteristics, and by theories of rational choice, which assume voters make calculations of the expected benefits and costs of political alternatives and choose the option with the highest net benefit. Even modern theories, however, continue to acknowledge that social characteristics play a major role in the structuring of political preferences, though perhaps not as deterministic a role as Lazarsfeld and colleagues envisioned.

4. Niemi and Weisberg concur: "The problem with this model [the 1940 Columbia research team's model] is that the people knew how they would

vote even before the national conventions were held, particularly since President Franklin D. Roosevelt was running for a third term in office in 1940. People knew whether or not they were going to vote for him without listening attentively to the campaign" (1993a, 8).

5. This argument is somewhat at odds with another of the classic works on voting behavior, *The American Voter* (Campbell, Converse, Miller, and Stokes 1960). Campbell et al. argue for viewing elections as the results of "proximal forces," which are captured by the attitudes, perceptions, and preferences voters hold at the moment of the election. These proximal forces may themselves be the result of past political events, but the past is assumed to affect vote choice only through them and not directly. Our model is compatible with theirs on this point, but we differ in arguing that understanding how the proximal attitudes were formed, and relating them to the past political events of the long campaign, is more important for understanding the political origins of the vote choice.

6. The NES has also conducted several innovative studies that focus on a longer campaign period. In 1980 the NES conducted a study that repeatedly interviewed respondents in February, June, September–October, and November. This study is invaluable for studying the workings of the nomination process that leads to the fall campaign. The NES also conducted a continuous monitoring of public opinion throughout the 1984 election year, interviewing a new, small sample of the public each week throughout the year. (See Bartels 1988 for an excellent example of the use of these data.) These two studies provide many opportunities for analysis of public opinion through the eleven months leading to an election, but fall somewhat short of what is needed for studies of the longer campaign, which is our focus. Other scholars have also conducted studies over the course of the election year (e.g., Patterson 1981), but none have covered the interval from first election to first reelection that would be the key to a study of the long campaign.

7. Twice the NES has interviewed the same respondents over a period of four years. These panel studies of respondents between 1956 and 1960, and between 1972 and 1976, provide a glimpse of developments in the long campaign. But they are unfortunately placed insofar as they bracket the second terms of incumbent presidents as they sought reelection and after they became ineligible for another term. It would be far better to study the first terms of presidents as they initially establish their records with the public and to see the consequences this has for their reelection bids. The NES has begun a study that may provide this coverage for Bill Clinton's first term. Survey respondents interviewed in 1992 were reinterviewed in 1993. Current plans call for another reinterview in 1994. Whether this study will be continued into the 1996 election is as yet undecided.

8. Not all the retirements where voluntary: Alan Dixon of Illinois was defeated in a three-way primary race by Carol Moseley-Braun.

9. This model is also consistent with the scenario of uninformed constituents that have not formed past opinions.

10. The basic Bayesian model specifies how opinion at time t, Y_t, is related to prior opinion, Y_{t-1}, and new information, X_t. The formal model is $Y_t = aY_{t-1} + bX_t$, where a and b are weights that depend on the precision (or

reliability) of prior and new information respectively. You can see that if prior information were considered particularly dubious, the weight given it would be very little and in the model a would be close to zero. Then the Bayesian model would predict that current opinion, Y_t, would depend almost entirely on new information, X_t. Substantively, this would say that voters would pay attention to the short campaign and ignore the past. That would make sense if they thought that senators were apt to change their positions, so the past would be no guide to the future. Alternatively, suppose voters thought that "actions speak louder than words." In such a case, they might discount what senators say during a campaign and rely almost entirely on their past actions. In the formal Bayesian model, this corresponds to a near zero value for b, while the value of a is relatively large. You can see from this how the Bayesian model allows us to understand what voters are doing in terms of the weight they give to both prior and new information. In reality, we expect that most of the time voters give some weight to both prior and new information. The Bayesian model allows us to formalize this and estimate how much weight is actually given to each. For an exposition of the formal Bayesian model and an application to public opinion, see Franklin (1992) and Bartels (1993).

11. Consistency also plays a role in the Bayesian model. If an incumbent sends a consistent stream of messages to the constituency, then the Bayesian model predicts that perceptions of the incumbent will become more precise. The effect of this is that a challenger will find it more difficult to change voter perceptions of the incumbent in the next election. While we largely ignore this aspect of the model in this chapter, it is worth noting that we find a great deal of consistency in senators' roll-call voting. This suggests that it should usually be difficult to change voter perceptions of the ideology of their senators, a perception that is well established during the long campaign.

12. See Shaffer (1980) and Collie (1985) for a discussion of the use of interest-group ratings.

13. The SES asked respondents to place the senator on a seven-point scale, where 1 represents extremely liberal and 7 represents extremely conservative. When respondents are uncertain where a senator stands, they have a strong tendency to use a placement of 3, 4, or 5 (Alvarez and Franklin 1994a). This, plus the fact that some respondents place liberal senators on the conservative end of the scale and vice versa, means that the average scores are never as extreme as 1 or 7, but are instead drawn into the middle range of the scale. The important issue for us is whether these average perceptions vary with roll-call records.

14. One limitation of aggregate correlations over data spanning several years is that the aggregate correlations may mask individual level changes.

15. The significance indicates the confidence we have that the relationship we find is real and not just a random fluke. A significance value of .015 indicates that there is only a 1.5 in 100 chance that we would find a relationship this strong if there were actually no relationship. An easy way to think about this is to consider flipping a coin. If it is a fair coin, you know you ought to expect heads about half the time. But even a fair coin could come up heads more often than tails in, say, ten flips. The significance value is a way of specifying how likely you are to get, for example, eight heads in ten flips, if

the coin is really a fair one. (The answer, by the way, is .055, or a little over 5 percent of the time you would get eight or more heads in ten flips, even with a fair coin.) A low significance value says that the result is unlikely to come about by chance, so we should be more confident that the relationship is "real." By convention, a significance level of .05 or less is usually taken as convincing evidence of a real relationship.

16. The residuals are the observed mean perception minus the predicted perception based on the model in table 12.1.

17. See Canon (1993) for an interesting discussion of differences in ambition and how it affects entry into races.

18. There are far more elements of the long campaign than we could possibly specify or measure. These elements, however, are assumed to carry positive and negative implications for the incumbent and should all be incorporated into the incumbent's job approval as respondents update their evaluations of the senator, according to our model of public opinion.

19. Other factors certainly affect whether challengers receive contributions, such as whether the incumbent was involved in a scandal and whether the race is narrowing. These factors are also correlated with a stronger challenger emerging and with greater fund-raising success (Squire 1992). For example, if the incumbent was involved in a scandal, a stronger challenger is likely to enter the race than if there was no scandal. It is not that a weak challenger gets more money but that a strong challenger gets more money, unless the scandal becomes public knowledge in the short campaign after the challenger has already been determined in the primary. Our measure is not perfect, however. To the extent that contributions and spending reflect the events of the short campaign period, then our measure will not be confined to the preelection quality of the challenger alone. This means that our results may confound effects of candidate entry decisions with those due to the fall campaign.

20. Box-Steffensmeier (1993) uses an event history model with time varying covariates to establish this conclusion.

21. The feeling thermometer is a 0 to 100 scale where 100 means the respondent feels very warm or positive toward the incumbent and 0 means very cool or negative feelings. A score of 50 means neither warm nor cool feelings. The advantage of the thermometer is that it is available for retiring incumbents in 1992, where job approval is not available for the retirees. Job approval is a 1 to 5 scale where 5 means the respondent strongly approves of the incumbent's job performance.

22. Virtually no incumbents announce their retirement by admitting to poor standing with voters. Undoubtedly some retire for nonelectoral reasons. Our evidence, however, shows that as a group retirees could have expected a tight race. A question that deserves further attention is why, given similar standing with voters, some incumbents choose to retire while others are willing to wage a hard-fought reelection campaign.

23. Again, these results apply to the senators as a group, rather than to specific individuals, some of whom may be rather close to the state mean. Our aim is to focus here on the overall pattern.

24. Technically, we can do this by regressing 1992 approval on 1990 ap-

proval and saving predicted values and residuals (our second measures of long and short campaigns respectively).

25. In fact, Franklin (1991) shows that even individual voters' perceptions of senators' ideology is responsive to roll-call voting, though there is considerably more noise in the relationship than we find in the aggregate data here. Our interpretation of this is that individuals are imperfectly informed (some very imperfectly!) but that there is enough "signal" in the noise to produce perceptions that are, when aggregated, quite responsive to actual incumbent behavior.

Chronology of the 1992 Presidential Campaign

BARRY C. BURDEN

1991

March Bush's popularity reaches an all-time high of nearly 90 percent following U.S. success in the Persian Gulf. For the first time since at least 1972, no significant presidential aspirants have declared their candidacies at this point. Bush has scared away potential opponents in both parties.

30 April Former Senator Paul E. Tsongas (D-Mass.) declares his candidacy for the presidency. He begins campaigning with around 2 percent name recognition in New Hampshire.

17 July House Majority Leader Richard A. Gephardt (D-Mo.) publicly decides not to run in 1992.

7 August Senator John D. "Jay" Rockefeller (D-W.Va.) announces that he will not seek the presidency.

21 August Senator Al Gore (D-Tenn.) declares that he also will not run for president, largely due to a recent car accident involving one of his children. Gore was thought to be a front-runner given his success in the 1988 primaries.

13 September Governor L. Douglas Wilder (D-Va.) declares his candidacy. He is the first significant black contender for the office since Jesse Jackson.

15 September	Senator Tom Harkin (D-Iowa) announces his intention to run for president.
30 September	Senator Bob Kerrey (D-Neb.) declares his candidacy.
3 October	Governor Bill Clinton (D-Ark.) announces that he will run for president in 1992. He is an early leader in the contest.
21 October	Former Governor Edmund G. "Jerry" Brown (D-Calif.) declares his presidential candidacy. Brown is the first candidate to establish a toll-free number and states that he will take no donations larger than $100; both become trademarks of his campaign.
2 November	The Reverend Jesse Jackson (D-D.C.) declines to run for president. Because his candidacy gave nominee Dukakis trouble in 1988, this decision settles a number of questions in the minds of other potential candidates.
4 December	State Representative David Duke (R-La.) publicly announces that he will run. The Republican Party distances itself from Duke, a former Ku Klux Klan leader.
5 December	Bush announces the senior staff of his reelection campaign. His candidacy is not yet official.
10 December	Political columnist and former presidential adviser Pat Buchanan announces that he will challenge Bush for the Republican nomination.
20 December	After months of speculation, Governor Mario M. Cuomo (D-N.Y.) chooses not to run. Cuomo asserts that New York's budget difficulties require that he not run.

1992

8 January	Wilder becomes the first Democratic contender formally to withdraw his candidacy.
20 January	Clinton's widening lead in the Democratic pack is hurt as allegations of marital infidelity circulate. The tabloid *Star* hits newsstands on 21 January with the accusations, though the stories were widely rumored beforehand.
23 January	Former singer and television reporter Gennifer Flowers announces, via the *Star,* that she had a twelve-year affair with Clinton and has recorded conversations to prove it. The now-damaged Clinton calls

	the accusations lies. The incident recalls one in 1987 involving leading Democratic contender Gary Hart (D-Colo.).
28 January	President Bush delivers a State of the Union address that revolves around a slowly growing economy. His speech gets poor reviews as Buchanan challenges him in New Hampshire.
10 February	The Iowa caucuses pass with little drama. Harkin, the favorite son, receives over 76 percent of the vote. No other candidate gets even 5 percent in Iowa.
12 February	President Bush formally declares his candidacy for re-election.
18 February	In the New Hampshire primary, Tsongas leads the Democrats with 33 percent of the vote. Clinton bounces back from accusations to receive 25 percent. Other Democrats include Kerrey (11 percent), Harkin (10 percent), Brown (8 percent), and write-in Cuomo (4 percent). Clinton is labeled "The Comeback Kid" for his strong showing in the election despite rumors about Vietnam war draft evasion, affairs, and marijuana experimentation. Bush wins the Republican primary with 53 percent, though Buchanan strikes a blow to his candidacy with a "protest vote" of 37 percent.
20 February	Texas billionaire H. Ross Perot speculates on his presidential campaign. On *Larry King Live,* he agrees to run if his name is placed on all fifty state ballots by his supporters.
3 March	Three early primaries are held. Brown, Clinton, and Tsongas score about 25 percent each in Colorado. Clinton and Tsongas each receive about 35 percent of the Maryland vote. Clinton does well in Georgia, the first of the important southern primaries, receiving nearly 60 percent of the vote. The focus is now on the battle between Clinton and Tsongas. Buchanan makes a final stand against Bush with 36 percent of the vote in Georgia.
5 March	Kerrey drops out of the race.
9 March	Harkin ends his campaign for the presidency and endorses Clinton as he exits.
10 March	The 1992 version of Super Tuesday occurs as eight states hold primaries. Clinton sweeps all but two

	(Massachusetts and Rhode Island), which go to New England native Tsongas. One important victory for Clinton here is delegate-rich Texas.
17 March	Clinton takes two important midwestern states, Illinois and Michigan.
19 March	Though a winner in New Hampshire, Tsongas "suspends" his campaign following his poor showing in the 10 March primaries as well as those in Illinois and Michigan on 17 March.
7 April	Clinton gets 41 percent of the vote in the hard-fought New York primary. Brown and Tsongas each receive under 30 percent.
28 April	Clinton wins the important Pennsylvania primary with 56 percent of the vote. Brown continues to chase him with 26 percent.
29 April	Riots break out in Los Angeles as the Rodney King trial ends with a "not guilty" verdict for four white police officers accused of beating King. Over fifty people are dead. Hundreds of businesses are looted and destroyed.
2 June	Clinton officially gathers enough delegates to be the Democratic nominee for president. He wins six primaries, most important of which is Brown's home state of California, where the ex-governor is able to garner 40 percent, for a respectable second. Perot, however, takes the spotlight, announcing that Democrat Hamilton Jordan and Republican Edward J. Rollins will manage his still undeclared campaign. Bush ends the primary/caucus season with 73 percent of the Republican votes; Clinton enters the convention period with 52 percent of the Democratic votes.
3 June	Bill Clinton appears on *The Arsenio Hall Show* and plays "Heartbreak Hotel" on the saxophone, apparently to change his image and take attention from Perot.
9 July	Clinton selects Al Gore as his running mate. The Clinton-Gore team quickly becomes identified as a ticket of southerners, moderates, and baby boomers. Gore is known for environmental policy, his Vietnam veteran status, and his wife, Tipper, who crusaded against obscene music lyrics.

13 July	The Democratic National Convention begins in New York City. Attempting to portray a "New Democrat" image, the convention features Mario Cuomo, Bill Bradley, Ann Richards, and Jesse Jackson. Jerry Brown speaks but refuses to endorse Clinton as the others had. The convention ends with Clinton-Gore leading Bush-Quayle by a huge 24-point lead.
16 July	Undeclared independent candidate Ross Perot announces, the same day that Clinton accepts his party's nomination, that he will not seek the presidency. His candidacy is not needed, he claims, due to the revitalization of the Democratic Party. Perot maintains that he wanted to win the election outright, not with a plurality of votes; a strong Democratic showing causes his retreat.
13 August	Bush announces that Secretary of State James A. Baker III will leave his post to salvage the president's re-election effort. Clinton leads Bush at this point by nearly 20 points.
17 August	The Republican National Convention begins in Houston. The tone of the 1992 convention is more conservative than recent gatherings. The platform, for example, includes tough language about abortion, AIDS, and homosexuality. In addition to Ronald Reagan, Pat Buchanan and Pat Robertson speak. "Family values" seems to be the event's theme. The convention fails to provide the popularity "bounce" the Republicans expect.
1 October	Perot reenters the presidential race as an official independent candidate. He trails the other two candidates in the polls.
11 October	The first presidential debate is held in St. Louis. The three-man contest does little to alter the standings of either Bush or Clinton, though Perot gains substantially from the affair. Three journalists pose questions to the candidates, who stand at lecterns.
13 October	The only vice-presidential debate of the season is held in Atlanta. Gore, Quayle, and unknown Admiral James Stockdale respond to a moderator and other journalists. Quayle holds his own, Gore manages looking a bit stiff, and Stockdale is merely an observer here.

15 October	A second debate is held in Richmond, Va. The three candidates sit on stools while a moderator fields questions from an audience of undecided voters. Clinton is clearly at ease in this "talk show" format.
19 October	The final debate occurs in East Lansing, Mich. The first half has a single moderator, the second a panel of journalists.
3 November	Clinton-Gore wins the presidential election. Clinton receives 43 percent of the popular vote (370 electoral votes), Bush 38 percent (168 electoral votes), and Perot 19 percent (no electoral votes). Clinton becomes the first winning presidential candidate in decades to have lost the New Hampshire primary. Clinton takes California, Pennsylvania, Ohio, and Illinois, while Bush wins in Texas and Florida. Voter turnout rises significantly for the first time since 1960, with 55 percent of the electorate voting in the presidential election. Over 100 million Americans cast ballots, the highest number in U.S. history. Democrats lose ten seats in the House, though women win an unprecedented twenty-four new seats; the partisan balance in the Senate remains unchanged.

References

Abramowitz, Alan I., and Jeffrey A. Segal. 1992. *Senate Elections*. Ann Arbor: University of Michigan Press.

Abramson, Paul R., and John H. Aldrich. 1982. "The Decline of Electoral Participation in America." *American Political Science Review* 76:502–21.

Abramson, Paul R., and Charles W. Ostrom, Jr. 1991. "Macropartisanship: An Empirical Reassessment." *American Political Science Review* 85: 181–92.

Aldrich, John R., and Forrest D. Nelson. 1984. *Linear Probability, Logit, and Probit Models*. Sage University Paper Series on Quantitative Applications in the Social Sciences, 07-045. Beverly Hills and London: Sage.

Alexander, Deborah, and Kristi Andersen. 1993. "Gender Role Beliefs as Frameworks for Candidate Evaluation." *Political Research Quarterly* 46: 527–45.

Allsop, Dee, and Herbert F. Weisberg. 1988. "Measuring Change in Party Identification in an Election Campaign." *American Journal of Political Science* 32: 996–1017.

Alter, Jonathan, Howard Fineman, and Eleanor Clift. 1989. "The World of Congress." *Newsweek,* 24 April, 28–34.

Alvarez, R. Michael, and Charles H. Franklin. 1994a. "Uncertainty and Political Perceptions." *Journal of Politics* 56:671–88.

———. 1994b. "Voter Learning in Senate Campaigns." California Institute of Technology Working Paper.

Alvarez, R. Michael, and Jonathan Nagler. 1993. "Choice Models for Multi-Candidate Elections." Paper presented at the Political Methodology Summer Conference, Tallahassee, Fla.

Alwin, Duane F. 1974. "Approaches to the Interpretation of Relationships in the Multitrait-Multimethod Matrix." In *Sociological Methodology 1973–1974*, ed. H. L. Costner, 79–105. San Francisco: Jossey-Bass.

Apple, R. W., Jr. 1992. "Poll Gives Clinton a Post-Perot, Post-Convention Boost." *New York Times,* 18 July 1992, 1, 8.

Arnold, Laura W., and Herbert F. Weisberg. 1994. "Murphy Brown Meets Al Bundy: Parenthood, Family Values, and the 1992 Presidential Election."

Paper presented at the annual meeting of the Midwest Political Science Association, Chicago.

Asher, Herbert B. 1992. *Presidential Elections and American Politics.* 5th ed. Belmont, Calif.: Wadsworth.

Asher, Herbert B., and Herbert F. Weisberg. 1978. "Voting Change in Congress: Some Dynamic Perspectives on an Evolutionary Process." *American Journal of Political Science* 22:391–425.

Babcock, Charles. 1992. "Women Are Filling Coffers of Female Candidates: Nominees Build Financial Strength through Direct-Mail Fund-Raising." *Washington Post,* 22 October 1992.

Baker, Ross K. 1993. "Sorting Out and Suiting Up: The Presidential Nominations." In *The Election of 1992,* ed. Gerald M. Pomper, 39–73. Chatham, N.J.: Chatham House.

Banducci, Susan A., and Jeffrey A. Karp. 1994. "Electoral Consequences of Scandal and Reapportionment in the 1992 House Elections." *American Politics Quarterly* 22 (January): 3–26.

Barone, Michael, and Grant Ujifusa. 1992. *The Almanac of American Politics.* Washington, D.C.: National Journal.

Bartels, Larry M. 1988. *Presidential Primaries and the Dynamics of Public Choice.* Princeton: Princeton University Press.

———. 1993. "Messages Received: The Political Impact of Media Exposure." *American Political Science Review* 87(2):267–85.

Bendyna, Mary E., and Celinda C. Lake. 1994. "Gender and Voting in the 1992 Presidential Election." In *The Year of the Woman: Myths and Realities,* ed. E. Cook, S. Thomas, and C. Wilcox. Boulder, Colo.: Westview.

Berelson, Bernard R., Paul F. Lazarsfeld, and William N. McPhee. 1954. *Voting.* Chicago: University of Chicago Press.

Bibby, John F. 1992. *Politics, Parties, and Elections in America.* Chicago: Nelson-Hall.

Biersack, R., Paul Herrnson, and Clyde Wilcox, eds. 1994. *Risky Business? PAC Decisionmaking in Congressional Elections.* Armonk, N.Y.: M.E. Sharpe.

Bolce, Louis. 1985. "The Role of Gender in Recent Presidential Elections: Reagan and the Reverse Gender Gap." *Presidential Studies Quarterly* 15: 372–86.

Boles, Janet K. 1993. "The Year of the Woman." In *America's Choice: The Election of 1992,* ed. William Crotty. Guilford, Conn.: Dushkin.

Bollen, Kenneth A. 1989. *Structural Equations with Latent Variables.* New York: Wiley.

Borger, Gloria, and Jerry Buckley. 1993. "A Giant New Sucking Sound." *U.S. News and World Report,* 20 December 1993, 18–20.

Born, Richard. 1990. "The Shared Fortunes of Congress and Congressmen: Members May Run from Congress, but They Can't Hide." *Journal of Politics* 52:1223–41.

Box-Steffensmeier, Janet M. 1993. "Candidates, Contributors and Campaign Strategy: It's About Time." Ph.D. dissertation, University of Texas.

Box-Steffensmeier, Janet M., and Charles H. Franklin. 1994. "The Decomposition of the Long and Short Campaign." University of Wisconsin. Typescript.

Boyd, Richard. 1986. "Election Calendars and Voter Turnout." *American Politics Quarterly* 14:89–104.

Burnham, Walter Dean. 1965. "The Changing Shape of the American Political Universe." *American Political Science Review* 59:7–28.

Burrell, Barbara. 1993. "Just a 'Mom in Tennis Shoes': Exploring the Distinctiveness of Women's Campaigns for National Office in 1992." Paper presented at the annual meeting of the Midwest Political Science Association, Chicago.

Caldeira, Gregory A., Aage R. Clausen, and Samuel C. Patterson. 1990. "Partisan Mobilization and Electoral Participation." *Electoral Studies* 9:191–204.

Caldeira, Gregory A., Samuel C. Patterson, and Gregory A. Markko. 1985. "The Mobilization of Voters in Congressional Elections." *Journal of Politics* 47:490–509.

Campbell, Angus, Philip E. Converse, Warren E. Miller, and Donald E. Stokes. 1960. *The American Voter.* New York: Wiley; reprinted 1980 by University of Chicago Press.

Canon, David. 1993. "Sacrificial Lambs or Strategic Politicians? Political Amateurs in U.S. House Elections." *American Journal of Political Science* 37:1119–41.

Carmines, Edward G., and Harold W. Stanley. 1992. "The Transformation of the New Deal Party System: Social Groups, Political Ideology, and Changing Partisanship among Northern Whites, 1972–1988." *Political Behavior* 14:215–37.

Caroli, Betty Boyd. 1987. *First Ladies.* New York: Oxford University Press.

Cassel, Carol A., and Robert Luskin. 1988. "Simple Explanations of Turnout Decline." *American Political Science Review* 82:1321–30.

Ceaser, James, and Andrew Busch. 1993. *Upside Down and Inside Out: The 1992 Elections and American Politics.* Lanham, Md.: Rowman and Littlefield.

Chaney, Carole, and Barbara Sinclair. 1994. "Women in the 1992 House Elections." In *The Year of the Woman: Myths and Realities,* ed. E. Cook, S. Thomas, and C. Wilcox. Boulder, Colo.: Westview.

Clausen, Aage R. 1973. *How Congressmen Decide: A Policy Focus.* New York: St. Martin's.

Collie, Melissa P. 1985. "Voting Behavior in Legislatures." In *Handbook of Legislative Research,* ed. Gerhard Loewenberg, Samuel C. Patterson, and Malcolm E. Jewell. Cambridge: Harvard University Press.

Conover, Pamela J. 1988. "Feminists and the Gender Gap." *Journal of Politics* 50:985–1010.

Conover, Pamela J., and Stanley Feldman. 1981. "The Origins and Meaning of Liberal/Conservative Self-Identifications." *American Journal of Political Science* 25:617–45.

Conover, Pamela J., and Virginia Sapiro. 1993a. "Gender, Gender Consciousness, and War." *American Journal of Political Science* 37:1079–99.

———. 1993b. "Gender in the 1992 Electorate." Paper presented at the annual meeting of the American Political Science Association, Washington, D.C.

Converse, Philip E. 1964. "The Nature of Belief Systems in Mass Publics." In *Ideology and Discontent,* ed. David E. Apter. New York: Free Press.

———. 1972. "Change in the American Electorate." In *The Human Meaning of Social Change,* ed. Angus Campbell and Philip E. Converse. New York: Russell Sage Foundation.

————. 1976. *The Dynamics of Party Support*. Beverly Hills: Sage.

Converse, Philip E., Warren E. Miller, Jerrold G. Rusk, and Arthur C. Wolfe. 1969. "Continuity and Change in American Politics: Parties and Issues in the 1968 Election." *American Political Science Review* 63:1083–1105.

Cook, Elizabeth Adell, Ted G. Jelen, and Clyde Wilcox. 1992. *Between Two Absolutes: Public Opinion and the Politics of Abortion*. Boulder, Colo.: Westview.

Cook, Elizabeth Adell, Sue Thomas, and Clyde Wilcox, eds. 1994. *The Year of the Woman: Myths and Realities*. Boulder, Colo.: Westview.

Cook, Elizabeth Adell, and Clyde Wilcox. 1991. "Feminists and the Gender Gap: A Second Look." *Journal of Politics* 53:1111–22.

Cook, Rhodes. 1993. "House Republicans Scored a Quiet Victory in '92." *Congressional Quarterly Weekly Report* 51 (17 April): 965–68.

Dahl, Robert. 1992. "The Myth of the Presidential Mandate." In *The Quest for National Office*, ed. S. Wayne and C. Wilcox. New York: St. Martin's.

Delli Carpini, Michael X., and Ester R. Fuchs. 1993. "The Year of the Woman? Candidates, Voters, and the 1992 Elections." *Political Science Quarterly* 108:29–36.

DiCamillo, Mark. 1993. "How 1992 Truly Became 'The Year of the Woman' in California Politics." Paper presented at the annual meeting of the American Association for Public Opinion Research, St. Charles, Ill.

Dolan, Kathleen, and Lynne E. Ford. 1993. "Changing Times, Changing Styles: The Professionalization of Women Legislators." Paper presented at the annual meeting of the Midwest Political Science Association, Chicago.

Downs, Anthony. 1957. *An Economic Theory of Democracy*. New York: Harper & Row.

Duerst-Lahti, Georgia. 1993. "The Year of the Woman, the Decade of the Women: Wisconsin Legislative Elections." Paper presented at the annual meeting of the Midwest Political Science Association, Chicago.

Duncan, Phil, ed. 1993. *Politics in America 1994*. Washington, D.C.: CQ Press.

Dwyer, Paula, and Douglas Harbrecht. 1990. "Congress: It Doesn't Work. Let's Fix It." *Business Week*, 16 April, 54–63.

Easterbrook, Gregg. 1984. "What's Wrong with Congress?" *Atlantic Monthly*, December, 57–84.

Erikson, Robert S., Thomas D. Lancaster, and David W. Romero. 1989. "Group Components of the Presidential Vote, 1952–1984." *Journal of Politics* 51:337–46.

Feldman, Stanley, and Pamela J. Conover. 1984. "The Structure of Issue Positions: Beyond Liberal-Conservative Constraint." *Micropolitics* 3:281–308.

Fenno, Richard F., Jr. 1978. *Home Style: House Members in Their Districts*. Boston: Little, Brown.

————. 1992. *When Incumbency Fails*. Washington, D.C.: CQ Press.

Fiorina, Morris P. 1981. *Retrospective Voting in American National Elections*. New Haven: Yale University Press.

Fiorina, Morris P., David W. Rohde, and Peter Wissel. 1975. "Historical Change in House Turnover." In *Congress in Change*, ed. Norman Ornstein. Philadelphia: American Academy of Political and Social Science.

Fite, David, Marc Genest, and Clyde Wilcox. 1990. "Gender Differences in Foreign Policy Attitudes: A Longitudinal Analysis." *American Politics Quar-*

terly 18:492–512.

Fleishman, J.A. 1986. "Trends in Self-Identified Ideology from 1972 to 1982: No Support for the Salience Hypothesis." *American Journal of Political Science* 30:527–41.

Franklin, Charles H. 1991. "Eschewing Obfuscation? Campaigns and the Perception of Senate Incumbents." *American Political Science Review* 85: 1193–1214.

———. 1992. "Learning the Consequences of Actions: Public Opinion and the Gulf War." Paper presented at the Brookings Institution Conference on the Consequences of the Gulf War, Washington, D.C., 28 February.

———. 1993. "Senate Incumbent Visibility over the Election Cycle." *Legislative Studies Quarterly* 18(2):271–90.

Gilens, Martin. 1988. "Gender and Support for Reagan: A Comprehensive Model of Presidential Approval." *American Journal of Political Science* 32:19–49.

Green, Donald P. 1988. "On the Dimensionality of Public Sentiment toward Partisan and Ideological Groups." *American Journal of Political Science* 32:758–80.

Green, Donald P., and Jack Citrin. 1994. "Measurement Error and the Structure of Attitudes: Are Positive and Negative Judgments Opposites?" *American Journal of Political Science* 38:256–81.

Green, Donald P., and Bradley Palmquist. 1990. "Of Artifacts and Partisan Instability." *American Journal of Political Science* 34:872–902.

Green, John C., and James L. Guth. 1988. "The Christian Right in the Republican Party: The Case of Pat Robertson's Supporters." *Journal of Politics* 50:150–65.

Hershey, Marjorie Randon. 1993. "The Congressional Election." In *The Election of 1992*, ed. Gerald M. Pomper, 157–89. Chatham, N.J.: Chatham House.

Huddy, Leonie, and Nayda Terkildsen. 1993. "The Consequences of Gender Stereotypes for Women Candidates at Different Levels of Government." *Political Research Quarterly* 46:503–25.

Jackson, John E. 1975. "Issues, Party Choices, and Presidential Votes." *American Journal of Political Science* 19:161–85.

Jackson, John E., and John W. Kingdon. 1992. "Ideology, Interest Group Scores, and Legislative Votes." *American Journal of Political Science* 36:805–23.

Jacobson, Gary C. 1987. *The Politics of Congressional Elections*. Boston: Little, Brown.

———. 1992. *The Politics of Congressional Elections*. 3d ed. New York: HarperCollins.

———. 1993a. "Congress: Unusual Year, Unusual Election." In *The Elections of 1992*, ed. Michael Nelson, 153–82. Washington, D.C.: CQ Press.

———. 1993b. "Deficit-Cutting Politics and Congressional Elections." *Political Science Quarterly* 108:375–401.

Jacobson, Gary C., and Michael A. Dimock. 1994. "Checking Out: The Effects of Bank Overdrafts on the 1992 House Elections." *American Journal of Political Science* 38:601–24.

Jacobson, Gary C., and Samuel Kernell. 1983. *Strategy and Choice in Congressional Elections*. 2d ed. New Haven: Yale University Press.

Jelen, Ted G., Sue Thomas, and Clyde Wilcox. 1994. "The Gender Gap in Comparative Perspective." *European Journal of Political Research* 25:171–86.

Jelen, Ted G., and Clyde Wilcox. 1994. "The Geography of the Gender Gap in Partisanship." Paper presented at the biannual Citadel Symposium on Southern Politics, Charleston, S.C.

Jencks, Christopher, Susan Bartlett, Joseph Schwartz, Sherry Ward, and Jill Williams. 1979. *Who Gets Ahead? The Determinants of Economic Success in America.* New York: Basic Books.

Jöreskog, Karl G., and D. Sorbom. 1978. *LISREL: Analysis of Linear Structural Relationships by the Method of Maximum Likelihood.* Chicago: National Educational Resources.

Kahn, Kim Fridkin. 1993. "Gender Differences in Campaign Messages: The Political Advertisements of Men and Women Candidates for the U.S. Senate." *Political Research Quarterly* 46:481–502.

Keith, Bruce E., et al. 1992. *The Myth of the Independent Voter.* Berkeley: University of California Press.

Kellam, Susan, ed. 1993. *1992 Congressional Quarterly Almanac.* Washington, D.C.: CQ Press.

Kerlinger, Frederick N. 1967. "Social Attitudes and Their Criterial Referents: A Structural Theory." *Psychological Review* 74:110–22.

———. 1972. "The Structure and Content of Social Attitude Referents: A Preliminary Study." *Educational and Psychological Measurement* 32:613–30.

Kerlinger, Frederick N., C.P. Middendorp, and J. Amon. 1976. "The Structure of Social Attitudes in Three Countries: Tests of a Critical Referent Theory." *International Journal of Psychology* 11:265–79.

Kernell, Samuel. 1977. "Toward Understanding 19th Century Congressional Careers: Ambition, Competition, and Rotation." *American Journal of Political Science* 11:669–94.

Kessel, John H. 1974. "The Parameters of Presidential Politics." *Social Science Quarterly* 55 (June): 8–24.

———. 1980. *Presidential Campaign Politics.* Homewood, Ill.: Dorsey.

———. 1992. *Presidential Campaign Politics.* 4th ed. Pacific Grove, Calif.: Brooks/Cole.

Kingdon, John W. 1989. *Congressmen's Voting Decisions.* 3d ed. Ann Arbor: University of Michigan Press.

Kingston, Paul William, and Steven E. Finkel. 1987. "Is There a Marriage Gap in Politics?" *Journal of Marriage and the Family* 49:57–64.

Knight, Kathleen. 1990. "Ideology and Public Opinion." *Research in Micropolitics* 3:59–82.

Kramer, Gerald H. 1965. "Decision Theoretic Analysis of Canvassing and Other Precinct Level Activities in Political Campaigning." Ph.D. dissertation, Massachusetts Institute of Technology.

Krosnick, Jon A., and Herbert F. Weisberg. 1988. "Ideological Structuring of Public Attitudes toward Social Groups and Politicians." Paper presented at the annual meeting of the American Political Science Association, Washington, D.C.

Lazarsfeld, Paul, Bernard Berelson, and Helen Gaudet. 1944. *The People's Choice.* New York: Duell, Sloane, and Pearce.

Lewis, I.A., and William Schneider. 1983. "Black Voting, Bloc Voting, and the

Democrats." *Public Opinion* 6(5):12–15, 59.

Lipset, Seymour Martin. 1981. *Political Man*. Baltimore: Johns Hopkins University Press.

McKelvey, Richard D., and William Zavoina. 1975. "A Statistical Model for the Analysis of Ordinal Level Dependent Variables." *Journal of Mathematical Sociology* 4:103–120.

MacKuen, Michael B., Robert S. Erikson, and James A. Stimson. 1989. "Macropartisanship." *American Political Science Review* 83:1125–42.

Markus, Gregory B., and Philip E. Converse. 1979. "A Dynamic Simultaneous Equation Model of Electoral Choice." *American Political Science Review* 73:1055–70.

Mattei, Franco, and Herbert F. Weisberg. 1994. "Presidential Succession Effects in Voting." *British Journal of Political Science* 24:269–90.

Mayhew, David. 1974. *Congress and the Electoral Connection*. New Haven: Yale University Press.

Miller, Arthur H., Christopher Wlezien, and Anne Hildreth. 1991. "A Reference Group Theory of Partisan Coalitions." *Journal of Politics* 53:1134–49.

Miller, Warren E. 1990. "The Electorate's View of the Parties." In *The Parties Respond,* ed. Sandy Maisel. Boulder, Colo.: Westview.

———. 1991. "Party Identification, Realignment, and Party Voting: Back to Basics." *American Political Science Review* 85:557–70.

Miller, Warren E., Arthur H. Miller, and Edward J. Schneider. 1980. *American National Election Studies Data Sourcebook*. Cambridge: Harvard University Press.

Nelson, Candice. 1994. "Women's PACs in the Year of the Woman." In *The Year of the Woman: Myths and Realities,* ed. E. Cook, S. Thomas, and C. Wilcox. Boulder, Colo.: Westview.

Nelson, Michael, ed. 1993. *The Elections of 1992*. Washington, D.C.: CQ Press.

Nie, Norman H., Sidney Verba, and John R. Petrocik. 1976. *The Changing American Voter*. Cambridge: Harvard University Press.

Niemi, Richard G., and Herbert F. Weisberg. 1993a. *Classics in Voting Behavior*. Washington, D.C.: CQ Press.

———. 1993b. *Controversies in Voting Behavior*. 3d ed. Washington, D.C.: CQ Press.

Norpoth, Helmut. 1987. "Under Way and Here to Stay: Party Realignment in the 1980s?" *Public Opinion Quarterly* 51:376–91.

Norpoth, Helmut, and Michael R. Kagay. 1989. "Another Eight Years of Republican Rule and Still No Partisan Realignment?" Paper presented at the annual meeting of the American Political Science Association, Atlanta.

Ornstein, Norman J., Thomas E. Mann, and Michael J. Malbin. 1994. *Vital Statistics on Congress, 1993–1994*. Washington, D.C.: CQ Press.

Ostrom, Thomas M., and H.S. Upshaw. 1968. "Psychological Perspective and Attitude Change." In *Psychological Foundations of Attitudes,* ed. Anthony G. Greenwald, Timothy C. Brock, and Thomas M. Ostrom. New York: Academic Press.

Page, Benjamin I., and Calvin C. Jones. 1979. "Reciprocal Effects of Policy Preferences, Party Loyalties, and the Vote." *American Political Science Review* 73:1071–90.

Patterson, Kelly D., and David B. Magleby. 1992. "Public Support for Congress." *Public Opinion Quarterly* 56:539–51.

Patterson, Samuel C., and Gregory A. Caldeira. 1990. "Standing Up for Congress: Variations in Public Esteem Since the 1960s." *Legislative Studies Quarterly* 15:25–47.

Patterson, Samuel C., Randall B. Ripley, and Stephen V. Quinlan. 1992. "Citizens' Orientations toward Legislatures: Congress and the State Legislature." *Western Political Quarterly* 45:315–38.

Patterson, Thomas E. 1981. *The Mass Media Election: How Americans Choose Their President.* New York: Praeger.

Peters, John G., and Susan Welch. 1980. "The Effects of Charges of Corruption on Voting Behavior in Congressional Elections." *American Political Science Review* 74:697–708.

Petrocik, John R. 1974. "An Analysis of Intransitivities in the Index of Party Identification." *Political Methodology* 1:31–47.

Petrocik, John R., and Frederick T. Steeper. 1987. "The Political Landscape in 1988." *Public Opinion* 10(5):41–44.

Pinderhughes, Dianne. 1986. "Political Choices: A Realignment in Partisanship among Black Voters?" In *The State of Black America,* ed. Janet Dewart. New York: National Urban League.

Plutzer, Eric, and Michael McBurnett. 1991. "Family Life and American Politics: The 'Marriage Gap' Reconsidered." *Public Opinion Quarterly* 55:113–27.

Polsby, Nelson W. 1968. "The Institutionalization of the U.S. House of Representatives." *American Political Science Review* 62:144–68.

———. 1990a. "Congress-Bashing for Beginners." *Public Interest* 100:15–23.

———. 1990b. "Congress-Bashing through the Ages." *Roll Call* 36 (10 September): 27–32.

Pomper, Gerald M., ed. 1993a. *The Election of 1992.* Chatham, N.J.: Chatham House.

———. 1993b. "The Presidential Election." In *The Election of 1992,* ed. Gerald M. Pomper, 132–56. Chatham, N.J.: Chatham House.

Powell, G. Bingham, Jr. 1986. "American Voter Turnout in Comparative Perspective." *American Political Science Review* 80:17–44.

Price, H. Douglas. 1975. "Congress and the Evolution of Legislative 'Professionalism.'" In *Congress in Change,* ed. Norman Ornstein. Philadelphia: American Academy of Political and Social Science.

Rahn, Wendy M., John H. Aldrich, Eugene Borgida, and John L. Sullivan. 1990. "A Social-Cognitive Model of Candidate Appraisal." In *Information and Democratic Processes,* ed. John Ferejohn and James Kuklinski. Urbana: University of Illinois Press.

Riker, William H. 1982. "The Two-Party System and Duverger's Law." *American Political Science Review* 76:753–66.

Rimmerman, Craig. 1994. "New Kids on the Block: National Gay and Lesbian Caucus and WISH List in 1992." In *Risky Business? PAC Decisionmaking in Congressional Elections,* ed. R. Biersack, P. Herrnson, and C. Wilcox. Armonk, N.Y.: M.E. Sharpe.

Rinehart, Sue Tolleson. 1994. "The California Senate Races: A Case Study in the Gendered Paradoxes of Politics." In *The Year of the Woman: Myths and Realities,* ed. E. Cook, S. Thomas, and C. Wilcox. Boulder, Colo.: Westview.

Roberts, Susan. 1993. "Furthering Feminism and Female Representation? The

Role of Women's PACs in Recruitment." Paper presented at the annual meeting of the Midwest Political Science Association, Chicago.

Rosenstone, Steven J., L.R. Behr, and Edward H. Lazarus. 1984. *Third Parties in America*. Princeton: Princeton University Press.

Rosenstone, Steven J., and John Mark Hansen. 1993. *Mobilization, Participation, and Democracy in America*. New York: Macmillan.

Rosenstone, Steven J., and Raymond E. Wolfinger. 1978. "The Effects of Registration Laws on Voter Turnout." *American Political Science Review* 72:22–45.

Rothenberg, Stuart, and Frank Newport. 1984. *The Evangelical Voter*. Washington, D.C.: Free Congress Research & Education Foundation.

Rusk, Jerrold G. 1970. "The Effect of the Australian Ballot Reform on Split Ticket Voting." *American Political Science Review* 64:1220–38.

Sapiro, Virginia. 1981–82. "If U.S. Senator Baker Were a Woman: An Experimental Study of Candidate Images." *Political Psychology* 2:61–83.

Scammon, Richard M., and Alice V. McGillivray. 1993. *America Votes*. Washington, D.C.: Elections Research Center, Congressional Quarterly.

Schroedel, Jean and Bruce Snyder. 1994. "Patty Murray: The Mom in Tennis Shoes Goes to the Senate." In *The Year of the Woman: Myths and Realities*, ed. E. Cook, S. Thomas, and C. Wilcox. Boulder, Colo.: Westview.

Shabad, Goldie, and Kristi Andersen. 1979. "Candidate Evaluations by Men and Women." *Public Opinion Quarterly* 43:18–35.

Shaffer, William R. 1980. *Party and Ideology in the United States Congress*. Lanham, Md.: University Press of America.

Shanks, J. Merrill, and Warren E. Miller. 1991. "Partisanship, Policy and Performance: The Reagan Legacy in the 1988 Election." *British Journal of Political Science* 21:129–97.

Shapiro, Robert, and Harpreet Mahajan. 1986. "Gender Differences in Policy Preferences: A Summary of Trends from the 1960s to the 1980s." *Public Opinion Quarterly* 50:42–61.

Silver, Brian, Barbara Anderson, and Paul Abramson. 1986. "Who Overreports Voting?" *American Political Science Review* 80:613–24.

Southwest Voter Research Institute. 1988. *Research Notes*. California ed. 2(3).

Squire, Peverill. 1992. "Challenger Quality and Voting Behavior in U.S. Senate Elections." *Legislative Studies Quarterly* 17:247–64.

Stanley, Harold W., William T. Bianco, and Richard G. Niemi. 1986. "Partisanship and Group Support Over Time: A Multivariate Analysis." *American Political Science Review* 80:969–76.

Stanley, Harold W., and Richard G. Niemi. 1991. "Partisanship and Group Support, 1952–1988." *American Politics Quarterly* 19:189–210.

———. 1992. "Partisanship and Group Support Over Time." In *Controversies in Voting Behavior*, ed. Richard G. Niemi and Herbert F. Weisberg. 3d ed. Washington, D.C.: CQ Press.

———. 1994. *Vital Statistics on American Politics*. 4th ed. Washington, D.C.: CQ Press.

Tate, Katherine. 1993. *From Protest to Politics: The New Black Voters in American Elections*. Cambridge: Harvard University Press and the Russell Sage Foundation.

Teixeira, Ruy A. 1987. *Why Americans Don't Vote: Turnout Decline in the United States 1960–1984*. Westport, Conn.: Greenwood.

Thomas, Sue. 1994. "Women in State Legislatures: One Step at a Time." In *The Year of the Woman: Myths and Realities,* ed. E. Cook, S. Thomas, and C. Wilcox. Boulder, Colo.: Westview.

Verba, Sidney, and Norman H. Nie. 1972. *Participation in America.* New York: Harper & Row.

Verba, Sidney, Norman H. Nie, and Jae-on Kim. 1978. *Participation and Political Equality.* Cambridge, England: Cambridge University Press.

Voter Research and Surveys. 1992. Voters Research and Surveys Presidential Primary Exit Polls, 1992. Computer file. New York: Voter Research and Surveys (producer). Ann Arbor, Mich.: Inter-University Consortium for Political and Social Research (distributor).

————. 1993. Voters Research and Survey General Election Exit Polls, 1992. Computer file. New York: Voter Research and Surveys (producer). Ann Arbor, Mich.: Inter-University Consortium for Political and Social Research (distributor).

Walters, Ronald W. 1988. *Black Presidential Politics in America: A Strategic Approach.* Albany: SUNY Press.

Walton, Hanes, Jr. 1990. "Black Presidential Participation and the Critical Election Theory." In *Social and Political Implications of the 1984 Jesse Jackson Presidential Campaign,* ed. Lorenzo Morris. New York: Praeger.

Wattenberg, Martin P. 1986. *The Decline of American Political Parties, 1952–1984.* Cambridge: Harvard University Press.

————. 1990. *The Decline of American Political Parties, 1952–88.* Cambridge: Harvard University Press.

Weisberg, Herbert F. 1987. "The Demographics of a New Voting Gap: Marital Differences in American Voting." *Public Opinion Quarterly* 51:335–43.

————. 1989. "Some Perspectives on the 1988 Presidential Election: The Roles of Turnout and Ronald Reagan." Paper presented at the annual meeting of the American Political Science Association, Atlanta.

————. 1994. "The Motor-Voter Bill Is Desirable," in *Controversial Issues in Presidential Selection,* ed. Garry L. Rose. 2d ed. Albany: SUNY Press.

Weisberg, Herbert F., and Charles E. Smith, Jr. 1991. "The Influence of the Economy on Party Identification in the Reagan Years." *Journal of Politics* 53:1077–92.

Wells, H.G. 1927. "Democracy under Revision: A Lecture Delivered at the Sorbonne, March 15, 1927" (London: Hogarth Press), published in *The Way the World Is Going: Guesses and Forecasts of the Years Ahead* (Garden City, N.Y.: Doubleday, Doran, 1928), 51–77.

Wilcox, Clyde. 1987. "The Timing of Strategic Decisions: Candidacy Decisions in 1982 and 1984." *Legislative Studies Quarterly* 12(4):565–72.

————. 1994. "Why Was 1992 the 'Year of the Woman'? Explaining Women's Gains in 1992." In *The Year of the Woman: Myths and Realities,* ed. E. Cook, S. Thomas, and C. Wilcox. Boulder, Colo.: Westview.

Wilcox, Clyde, Clifford Brown, Jr., and Lynda Powell. 1993. "Sex and the Political Contributor: The Gender Gap among Presidential Contributors in 1988." *Political Research Quarterly* 46:355–76.

Wilcox, Clyde, Joseph Ferrara, and Dee Allsop. 1993. "Group Differences in Early Support for Military Action in the Gulf." *American Politics Quarterly* 21:343–59.

Wilcox, Clyde, Lee Sigelman, and Elizabeth Cook. 1989. "Some Like It Hot: Individual Differences in Responses to Group Feeling Thermometers." *Public Opinion Quarterly* 53:246–57.

Williams, Leonard. 1994. "Political Advertising in the Year of the Woman: Did X Mark the Spot?" in *The Year of the Woman: Myths and Realities,* ed. E. Cook, S. Thomas, and C. Wilcox. Boulder, Colo.: Westview.

Williams, Linda F. 1987. "Black Political Progress in the 1980s: The Electoral Arena." In *The New Black Politics.* 2d ed. Ed. M. Preston, L. Henderson, and P. Puryear. New York: Longman, 97–136.

Wills, Garry. 1993. "Hillary's No Eleanor Roosevelt." *Washington Post National Weekly Edition,* 1–7 November, 24.

Wolfinger, Raymond E., and Steven J. Rosenstone. 1980. *Who Votes?* New Haven: Yale University Press.

Zaller, John, with Mark Hunt. 1993. "The Rise and Fall of Candidate Perot." Paper presented at the annual meeting of the American Political Science Association, Washington, D.C.

Index

ABC/*Washington Post* poll, on appraisal of Congress, 271, 272
Abortion: as campaign issue, 96, 164; as issue among women, 213; as survey question, 151 n.7; as voter criterion, 126
Abortion rights activists, and support of Clinton, 241
Abramson, Paul, 69 n.9, 71 n.20
African Americans. *See* Black(s)
Age: as anti-Democratic force, 229–30; and black voter turnout, 186; campaign tilt of, 169; and New Deal coalition breakup, 222; and Perot support, 160; and voter turnout, 42–43, 58
Agriculture policy, as issue category, 115, 122–23, 134 n.11
Aldrich, John R., 71 n.20, 133 n.5
Alternative media, 2, 3, 4, 25; Perot's use of, 154; candidates' use of, 158. *See also* Media
Alvarez, R. Michael, 110–11 nn.14, 15
American Civil Liberties Union, 243
American Conservative Union (ACU), 297
American elections: turnout eras in, 36; voters in, 35–56. *See also* Electorate; 1992 election; 1992 presidential contest
Americans for Democratic Action (ADA), 297

Americans to Limit Congressional Terms, 290 n.3
American Voter, The, 9, 112, 113, 179, 184, 315 n.5
Analysis, 117–30; basic probit results, 117; of electoral verdict, 124–30; of partisan advantages, 117–21; of potency of predictors, 121–24
Anderson, Barbara, 69 n.9
Anderson, John, 26 n.2, 131, 153, 157, 158
Asher, Herb, 7, 17, 133 n.4
Asian Americans, 249; as campaign issue, 241
Attitude toward candidates, gender gap in, 213–15
AuCoin, Les, 312
Australian ballot, 33

Bartels, Larry M., 296
Bayesian model, 315–16 nn.10, 11; elements of, 300–301
Bayesian theory, 295–96
Bendyna, Mary E., 209
Bentsen, Lloyd, 217 n.1
Berelson, Bernard, 293–94
Best Congress Money Can Buy, The, 269, 290 n.3
Bibby, John F., 69 n.3
Big business: as associated with Bush administration, 125–26; as conservative, 247, 249

Black(s): campaign tilt of, 168; as candidates, 181–82; church attendance of, 226; in Congress, 267; as congressional candidates, 266; as Democrats, 179; gender gap in voting patterns of, 209; group loyalty of, 182–83; loyalty of, to Democratic Party, 179–80, 183; as mildly liberal, 247–48; in New Deal coalition, 220–23; 1992 vote of, 179–94; party identification of, 231, 236; political participation rates of, 184–87; structural dependence of, on Democratic Party, 180–82, 183; support of Perot, 159; voter turnout of, 41–42

Black partisanship: future of, 191–93; reexamined, 187–92

Bond, Christopher, 312

Borger, Gloria, 174

Born, Richard, 290n.5

Boxer, Barbara, 205

Box-Steffensmeier, Janet, 6, 308, 314

Boyd, Richard, 69n.7

Bradley, Bill, 16, 205, 219n.15

Breaux, John B., 266

Brown, Edmund, Jr. ("Jerry"), 2, 16, 17, 110n.12, 137, 184

Brown, Murphy, 3, 93, 226

Buchanan, Pat, 2, 110n.12, 226; primary race of, 13

Buckley, Jerry, 174

Bush, Barbara, 2, 128, 137, 138; appeal of, to traditionalists, 145, 146; vs. Hillary Clinton, 139–41, 150n.3; positive reaction to, 140

Bush, George: advantages of, 130–31, 132; black vote of, 179; as candidate, 99, 102; as conservative, 90, 162; and Dukakis, 243; effect of Perot vote on, 105–6; fundamentalist support of, 241; and Iran-*contra* affair, 5, 157; law enforcement advocates support, 241; low standing of, among blacks, 192; military support, 241; 1988 election of, 3, 19–20, 21; 1992 Electoral College votes of, 21; Perot's effect on candidacy of, 169–73; popularity of, 2; problems of candidacy of, 13–16; and Quayle, 17; signs Civil Rights Act, 191; state support of, 23; support of, as transferred to Perot, 170; thermometer ratings of, 165, 171–72; traits associated with, 102–3; unpresidential conduct of, 157; and veto of family leave, 195

Bush administration: and big business, 125–26; party identification during, 80–87; presidential approval ratings of, 85; supports traditional moral values, 226

Burden, Barry C., 128

Burnham, Walter Dean, 32

Burrell, Barbara, 197

Cable television, 4

Campaign spending, 1992 congressional races, 266

Campbell, Angus, 179, 184

Candidates, 98–108; attitudes of, 127–30; as factor in voting, 9–10; images of, 73; major party nominees, 99–103; Perot vote, 103–6

Candidates' wives, 128, 136–52; voter attention to, 24. *See also* Bush, Barbara; Clinton, Hillary; Perot, Margot

Cardinals of Capitol Hill, The, 269, 290n.3

Carter, Jimmy, 113, 125, 251; challenged in primaries, 12–13; defeat of, 3; thermometer ratings of, 99; vote percentage of, 21

Carter, Rosalynn, 137

Carville, James, 124

Casework, 11

Casey decision, 198

Cassel, Carol A., 71n.20

Catholics: church attendance of, 226; in New Deal coalition, 220, 223,

236

Caucuses, 12

CBS News/*New York Times* polls, 9, 109 nn.5, 7; 154, 156; on appraisal of Congress, 271

Census Bureau, 70 n.12; postelection survey of, 8–9

Challenger: establishing an image, 73; and long campaign, 302; spending of, and incumbent job approval, 303–4

Check overdraft scandal, 263; effect of, on incumbents, 265

Child-care spending, as survey question, 151 n.7

Chisholm, Shirley, 181

Church attendance: and New Deal coalition breakup, 222; partisanship and, 226

Citizen duty, 70 n.18; sense of, and voter turnout, 50

Civil liberties: as issue category, 115, 126; voter attitude on, 124

Civil rights, Democratic legislation promoting, 191

Civil Rights Act, 191

Clinton, Bill: abortion rights activists support, 241; advantages of, 130, 131, 132; appeal of, to Perot supporters, 156; black vote of, 179; campaign image of, 19; charges against, 2; election of, 3; Electoral College victory of, 21; emotions elicited by, 102; environmentalists support, 241; and feminist views, 196; homosexuals support, 241; lack of trust in, 5; as liberal, 89–90, 162; and New Deal coalition, 221; Perot's effect on candidacy of, 169–73; primary victories of, 17; social group support of, 243; states support, 21–23; thermometer ratings of, 165, 171–72; town hall meetings of, 3; traits associated with, 102–3; use of media of, 25; vote percentage of victory of, 20–21; women provide vic-

tory margin for, 208–9

Clinton, Hillary Rodham, 2, 128, 137, 138; vs. Barbara Bush, 139–41, 150 n.3; as electoral force, 149; influence of, 247; popularity of, 146; Republican attack on, 195, 208, 217

Closed-ended questions, 8

Cohen, Richard E., 269

Compassion issues, women's advantage on, 199

Compositional effect, 44

Confirmatory factor analysis, 257

Congress: citizens' support for, 270–72; composition of 1992, 266–68; effect of scandals on, 11; thermometer ratings of, 271. *See also* House of Representatives; Senate

Congress: America's Privileged Class, 269, 290 n.3

Congress bashing: high level of, 24; impact of, 273–88; and 1992 congressional election, 263–91; and 1994 elections, 289–90; rise of, 268–69; and voter choices, 289; and voter turnout, 285–88

Congressional candidacies, 264–66

Congressional elections, 11, 263–318; as "candidate-centered," 276–77; margins in, 273–76; outcome of, 264–68; voter behavior in, 276–78

Conover, Pamela J., 257

Conservatives: in 1992 elections, 247, 249; voting pattern of, 241; women as, 200

Constituents, aggregate perceptions of, 313. *See also* Electorate; Voters

Converse, Philip E., 32, 179, 184

Countercultural groups, 253

Cuomo, Mario, 16

D'Amato, Alfonse, 312

Dealignment, 240 n.10; defined, 25; partisan, 108; party, 256; and political volatility, 88

Debates: presidential, 19, 153, 156, 157; Perot-Gore, 174

DemLead1, 81, 85–87

DemLead2, 81, 85–87

Democratic candidates, on issue scales, 90–92

Democratic Party: advantages of, 132; broad-based appeal of, 236; as civil rights champion, 191; composition of, 231; and control of Congress, 23; factions within, 192; identification of blacks with, 182, 191; as liberal, 247, 253, 255–56; loyalty of blacks to, 179–80, 180–82, 183; and New Deal coalition, 222–26; partisanship advantage of, 75–78; proportion of women in, 231; vs. Whigs, 30. See also Democratic National Convention; Democrats

Democratic National Convention: and Perot withdrawal, 156; women nominees at, 195

Democrats: changes in partisanship of, 82; decline in election margin of, 275; drop in ratings of, 252; loyalty of, to Clinton, 160; on term limitations, 273; women as, 200

Desert Storm, Alliance victory in, 6. See also Gulf war

Dixiecrats, 153

Dixon, Alan, 315 n.8; primary defeat of, 265

Dole, Bob, 205; as Republican leader, 3

Dukakis, Michael, 89, 102; black vote of, 179, 182; Bush attack on, 243; as liberal, 250; and share of popular vote, 170

Duke, David, 2; and primary race, 13

Duncan, Phil, 71 n.22

Economic management: as criterion, 114, 115, 120, 121, 122; voter attitude on, 124

Economy: adverse, and reelection

bids, 125; as campaign issue, 4, 82, 92, 130–32, 167–68; gender difference in appraisal of, 203; as 1992 election issue, 18–19, 25; party competence survey on, 187, 191; and Perot support, 160–62

Education: campaign tilt of, 168; and Perot support, 63, 64; and voter turnout, 35, 37–39, 43–44, 59

Efficacy, campaign tilt of, 168–69

Eisenhower, Dwight D., 21, 112

Election interest, and voter turnout, 51, 64

Elections, "realigning," 32. See also American elections; Candidates

Election-specific attitudes, and voter turnout, 50–53

Electoral College, 170

Electoral verdict, 124–30; and candidates' attitudes, 127–30; and issue attitudes, 124–27

Electorate: barriers to American, 33–34; increasing volatility of, 25–26; preference of, for women candidates, 199

EMILY'S List, 4, 198, 218 n.5

Emotion(s), and candidates, 101–2

Environmentalists: as force in 1992 elections, 243, 247; support Clinton, 241, 247

Ethics Committee, investigation of, 312

Exit polls, 8; and 1992 elections, 158, 171, 197, 204–15 passim, 218 n.3

Experience, of candidates, 114, 120, 127

Exploratory factor analysis, 257

Family and Medical Leave Act, 196

"Family leave" bill, 93; Bush vetoes, 195

Family values: and candidates' wives, 145; debates on, 217; as issue, 93; Republican emphasis on, 243

Federal government: as campaign issue, 96–98; rating of, and Perot

vote, 106
Feeling thermometer, 317n.21
Feinstein, Dianne, 205, 208, 217n.1, 218n.4
Feldman, Stanley, 257
Feminists, as liberals, 247
Fenno, Richard F., Jr., 303
Fiorina, Morris, 112–13
Florio, Jim, 193
Flowers, Gennifer, 4
Foley, Tom, 110n.12
Ford, Gerald, 113, 125, 251
Foreign affairs: party competence survey on, 187, 188, 191
Foreign policy, as campaign issue, 92–93
Fowler, Wyche, Jr., 312
Franklin, Charles H., 6, 308, 314, 318n.25
Fundamentalists, white Protestant: identify with Republicans, 229, 230, 231, 237; as liberal, 247; and New Deal coalition breakup, 222; in 1992 elections, 243, 249; as political force, 222
Fund raising, importance of, 305

Gaudet, Helen, 293–94
Gay rights: as campaign issue, 168; support for, 163–64. *See also* Homosexuals
Gender: as factor in black voter turnout, 186; and New Deal coalition breakup, 222; as political issue, 143; and presidential voting, 208–16; role of, 10. *See also* Gender differences; Gender gap
Gender differences: and voter turnout, 42; in voting patterns, 218–19n.11. *See also* Gender; Gender gap
Gender gap: age and, 219n.13; in attitude toward candidates, 213–15; as campaign issue, 93; defined, 196–97; issue positions and, 212–13; in partisanship, 211–12; in party identification, 226; in support for Perot,

215–16; and voter turnout, 55
General Accounting Office, 270
General issues category: as candidate references, 114, 115, 120, 124; as source of votes, 126; voter attitudes on, 124
Gephardt, Dick, 15
Gilens, Martin, 218n.10
Glenn, John, 312
Goldwater, Barry, 20, 112, 191, 251
Gore, Al, 16; 110n.12, 134n.14, 249; Bush characterizes, 157; debates Perot, 174; pro-environment position of, 243, 247; as vice-presidential candidate, 17
Government surveys, on voter attitudes, 8
Grandy, Fred, 270
Great Depression, 25, 74
Green, Donald P., 240n.9
Greenberg and Lake, tracking polls of, 197, 209–15 passim, 218n.3
Gridlock, president–Congress, 263, 270
Group coalitions, as ideological, 242
Group support, and party coalitions, 230–36
Guinier, Lani, 192
Gulf war, as campaign issue, 82. *See also* Desert Storm
Guth, James L., 240n.9

Haar, Charlene, 205
Harding, Florence, 137
Health care, party competence survey on, 187, 188, 189, 191; as survey question, 151n.7
Heath, Josie, 205, 218n.6
Henry, H. Lon, 290n.3
Hildreth, Anne, 257
Hill, Anita, 2, 24, 136, 143, 145, 146, 148, 149–50, 195, 243, 312
Hispanics: as campaign issue, 241; in Congress, 267; as congressional candidates, 266; in House of Representatives, 23; identification of, with Democratic Party, 230; and New Deal coalition

breakup, 222; non-Cuban, 230, 237; party identification of, 231, 237; political significance of, 222; voter turnout of, 70n.12

Homosexuals: as activists in 1992 campaign, 4; as force in 1992 elections, 243, 247; as liberal, 247; rights of, as campaign issue, 94–96; support Clinton, 241; thermometer ratings for, 244–50. See also Gay Rights

House banking scandals: and thermometer ratings, 284–85; and voter turnout, 285–88

House of Representatives: check-writing scandal of, 2, 96, 263, 270, 278; Democrats control, 23; voter support for incumbents, 281–85; voting survey of, 6; women in, 196

Hunt, Mark, 155

Hutchison, Kay Bailey, 217 n.1

Ideological self-identification: gender differences in, 203; and Perot support, 159, 152–63

Immigrants, 249; as campaign issue, 241; illegal, 244, 247

Income: as campaign tilt, 168; as identifying factor with Republican Party, 229; and New Deal coalition breakup, 222; and voter turnout, 39

Incumbency, as campaign issue, 114, 120, 124, 128; importance of, 11. See also Incumbents

Incumbents: analyzing support for, 280–81; and decline in aggregate election margins, 276; electoral security of, 284; image of, 73; reasons for retirement of, 317 n.22; and redistricting, 265; reelection of, 23; retirement of, 264; return rate of, 267, 271; thermometer ratings of, 306–7; and voter ideologies, 307; women lose to, 198

Independent candidacy(ies): and access to ballot, 158; characteristics of, 157

Independents: changes in partisanship of, 82; political, and voter turnout, 48–49; support Perot, 79–80, 160, 164

Indirect effort, 133 n.6

Inflation: and Bush administration, 85–87; effects of, and unemployment, 109 n.8

Infomercials, 3, 19, 103, 154, 158

Inouye, Daniel, 312

Intelligence, as criterion for vote choice, 114, 120, 127, 129

Interest, and voter turnout, 51, 64

International involvement, as issue category, 115, 127

Iran-contra affair, 19, 74, 102, 157

Iran hostage crisis, 74

Issue(s), 89–98; attitude of voters on, 124–27; economy as, 92; as factor in 1992 elections, 72; federal goverment as, 96–98; foreign policy as, 92–93; ideological proximity, 89–92; and NES surveys, 89; social, 93–96; and third-party candidates, 10; in Wallace campaign, 106

Issue positions, gender gap in, 212–13

Jackson, Jesse, 16, 110 n.12; as loyal to Democratic Party, 183; as presidential candidate, 181–82; as vice-presidential primary candidate, 184

Jackson, John, 112

Jelen, Ted G., 218 n.7

Jews: in New Deal coalition, 220, 223, 236; party identification of, 231

Job approval, and incumbent, 308–9; and incumbent vs. challenger spending, 303–4; and incumbent standing, 302; and incumbent thermometer ratings, 306–7; in long and short campaigns, 309–13

Johnson, Lyndon, 13, 112, 251; and war on poverty, 191
Jordan, Hamilton, 17

Kassebaum, Nancy, 196, 205, 219n.15
Kasten, Robert, Jr., 312
"Keating five," 312
Keith, Bruce E., 70n.16
Kennedy, Edward, 12
Kennedy, John F., 25, 113; 1960 vote percentage of, 21
Kennedy, Robert, 13
Kerrey, Bob, 16
Kessel, John, 8, 89, 103
Key, V.O., Jr., 289
Kick the Bums Out (Americans to Limit Congressional Terms), 269, 290n.3
Kim, Jae-on, 70n.11
Kimball, David, 113
Knight, Kathleen, 257
Ku Klux Klan, 13

Labor union households: in New Deal coalition, 220, 223, 236; shift in party identification of, 231, 236–37; and voter turnout, 39–41
Lake, Celinda C., 209, 218n.3, 219n.17
Larry King Live, 3, 153, 155
Law enforcement advocates: as conservative, 247, 249; support Bush, 241
Lazarsfeld, Paul, 293–94
Leaners: effect of, on partisanship, 85; identifying, 75; as independents, 77, 79, 81; as partisans, 77, 81
Legislative elections, NES study of, 6
Liberal/conservative placement, stability of, 298–302
Liberalism, defined, 181
Liberals: in 1992 elections, 247, 249; ratings of groups, 253; voting patterns of, 242
Libertarian Party, 266

"Like-dislike" questions, 115–16
Logistic regression (logit), 70–71n.19
Long campaign: and challengers, 302; defined, 292; and Senate elections, 292–318; vs. short campaign, 308–13
"Long" seat, 219n.14
Lowess technique, smoothing approach of, 109n.6
Luskin, Robert, 71n.20
"L word" (liberal), 89, 250

McCain, John S., 312
McCarthy, Eugene, 13
McGillivray, Alice V., 71n.22
McGovern, George, 20, 99
McKelvey, Richard D., 133n.5
Macropartisanship, 80
Management, as candidate criterion, 114, 120, 127, 129
Marital gap, as campaign issue, 93–94
Marital status, and voter turnout, 47
Martin, Lynn, 205
Media: access to free (earned), 158; candidates' access to, 158; NES survey on role of, 25; Perot's use of, 154, 157
Media polls, 8, 9. *See also* ABC/*Washington Post* polls; CBS News/*New York Times* polls
Memory, concept of, and model of public opinion, 295
Mikulski, Barbara, 195
Military force, men support use of, 203
Military groups, as conservative, 247, 249; support of Bush, 241
Miller, Warren E., 179, 184, 218n.7, 257
Minorities: as congressional candidates, 266; representation of, in Congress, 23. *See also* Asian Americans; Blacks; Hispanics; Women
Mondale, Walter, 102
Morality, as campaign issue, 126
Moseley-Braun, Carol, 208, 218n.4,

267, 315 n.8

"Motor voter" bill, 34

Mughan, Anthony, 128

Multiple parties, and voter turnout, 34

Multivariate logit analysis, 221–38

Multivariate statistical procedures, 221

Munson, Richard, 290 n.3

Murray, Patty, 216; 219 n.20

NAACP convention, Perot at, 156

Nagler, Jonathan, 110–11 nn.14, 15

National Election Study (NES), on attitudes of social groups, 244–50; on candidates' wives, 150 n.4; and Congress bashing/congressional scandal, 264; on gender gap, 197, 200, 209–15 passim; on incumbent support, 280–81; and issues, 89; 1992, 6–9; and late deciders, 158; party competence survey of, 187–91; on party support, 222; postelection survey of, 109 n.7; pre- and postelection interviews of, 294; reliability of, 35

National Election Survey: See National Election Study (NES)

National Science Foundation, 6

Native southern whites: decline in support of New Deal coalition, 223; shift in party identification of, 231, 236. See also South

Natural resources, as issue category, 115, 127

Nelson, Forrest D., 133 n.5

"Neofundamentalists," 229

New Deal coalition: demise of, 220–40; reemergence of, 10; shattered nature of, 236

New Deal realignment, 25, 74

Newspaper reading, and voter turnout, 51–52

Nie, Norman H., 70 n.11, 71 n.23

Niemi, Richard G., 240 n.10, 242; 314–15 n.4

1988 presidential election, 19–20

1992 congressional elections, heritage of, 288

1992 election: black participation in, 184–87; campaign in, 18–19; importance of, 108; nominations, 12–18; social groups in, 243–50; results of, 19–23; as transition, 3–4

Nineteenth Amendment, 32

Nixon, Richard, 113; 1968 vote percentage of, 21; thermometer rating of, 99

Nonvoters: black, 185; presidential preferences of, 65; vs. voters, 65–66

North American Free Trade Agreement (NAFTA), 173, 174

Nunn, Sam, 16

Obey, David R., 290 n.2

Occupation, and voter turnout, 38–39

O'Dell, Gloria, 205

Open-ended questions, 8

"Open" seats, 266; women as candidates in, 198

Ornstein, Norman, 269

Packwood, Robert, 312

Panel studies, 6

Partisan attachments, influence of, 278–80

Partisan congruence, 278, 291 n.6

Partisan congruents, 278–80, 283–84

Partisan incongruents, 278–80

Partisan polarization, extent of, 78–79

Partisan predisposition, 314 n.3

Partisanship: effect of economy on, 25; gender difference in, 200–203; gender gap in, 211–12; inflation and, 85; measurement of, 239 n.2; religion and, 226; strength of, 70 n.15; strength of, and Perot support, 104; unemployment rates and, 85

Partisan valence, 119; value of, 120–21

Party affect, as criterion for vote choice, 114, 130

Party affinity, and support of House incumbent, 276

Party attachment, and voter turnout, 48, 59

Party coalitions, group support and, 230–36

Party identification, 74–89; and Bush administration, 80–87; and candidates' wives, 144; changes in, 75; distribution of, 72–73, 75–78; and 1992 presidential vote, 72–111; pattern of change in, 80–87; and Perot support, 159–60, 164; stability of, 74; treatment of, 9

Party support, models of, 222

Party support coalitions, 220

People in party, as criterion for vote choice, 114, 122, 130, 134n.11

People's Choice, The, 112

Perot, Margot, 150n.1

Perot, H. Ross, 26n.2; aggregate popular vote of, 170; black vote of, 179; campaign of, 153–75; campaign fluctuation of, 2; campaign issues of, 19; campaign themes of, 3, 5; characteristics of, 158–64; dynamics of campaign of, 154–58; and Electoral College vote, 170; gender differences in reaction to, 212; gender gap in support for, 215–16; image of, 73; independents as greatest supporters of, 79–80; infomercials of, 3; multivariate model of support for, 165–69; in NES survey, 7; as nonparty candidate, 256; in primary races, 17; reentry of, in contest, 156; roadblocks to 1996 candidacy of, 173–75; running mate of, 153; source of movement to, 104–5; state support of, 23; thermometer ratings of, 165, 171–72; and turnout increase, 30; use of media of, 25; vote percentage of, 23; withdrawal of,

from race, 17, 153

Perot vote, 103–6; predictors concerning, 110–11n.15

Personality, as criterion for vote choice, 114, 120, 127

Perspective differences, 257

Polarization, change in ideological, 250–52

Policy positions, gender difference in, 200–203

Political action committees (PACs), women's, 198–99

Political attitudes, long-term, and voter turnout, 47–50

Political awareness, and candidate support, 285

Political efficacy: index of, 70n.17; and voter turnout, 49, 59–62, 71n.20

Political independence: growth in, 79, 88; nature of, 75. *See also* Independents

Political parties, disaffection with, and support of Perot, 63, 64. *See also* Democratic Party; Libertarian Party; Republican Party

Political psychology approach, 11–12

Political socialization, origin of, 10

Politicians, distrust of, 4–5

Polls, and underestimation of Perot, 157–58

Polsby, Nelson W., 269

Pomper, Gerald M., 110n.14, 239n.7

Position taking, as key element, 297

Poverty, party competence survey on, 187–88, 189

Powell, G. Bingham, 33, 34

Predictors, potency of, in models, 121–24

Presentation of self, in long campaign, 297–98

Presidential approval, in Bush administration, 85, 99

Presidential election model, 113–17; independent variables in, 113–15; measurement of, 115–16; potency of predictors in, 121–24; probit analysis of,

116–17; versions of, 114
Presidential primaries, 12–13
Presidential voting, gender and, 208–16
Presidential wife, image of, 139
Probit analysis, 116–17
Proportional representation, appeal of, 34
"Proximal forces," 315 n.5
Public opinion, Bayesian model of, 313

Quayle, Dan, 110 n.12, 134 n.14; on family values, 2; and Murphy Brown, 3, 93, 226; as vice-presidential candidate, 17

Race: as campaign issue, 168; as factor in Perot support, 158–59; as factor in voting, 217
Racial groups, increase in ideological polarization of, 253
Rational-choice approach, 11
Rational-voter theories, 181
Reagan, Nancy, 137
Reagan, Ronald, 12: assaults social welfare/civil rights agenda, 192; election of, 3; as great communicator, 25; 1980 vote percentage of, 21; support of traditional moral values, 226; thermometer rating of, 99; as unpopular with blacks, 182–83
Realignment: discussion of, 74; and partisan change, 88
Recession: "double dip," 18–19; as harmful to Bush reelection campaign, 73
Record, of candidates, 114, 120, 128
Redistricting, 263–64; and increases in minority representation, 267
Religion: campaign tilt of, 168–69; and partisanship, 226
Religious denomination, and voter turnout, 46
Republican candidate, on issue scales, 90–92
Republican National Convention,

243; as antifeminist, 195, 208
Republican Party: advantages of, 132; appeal of, 94; and black vote, 183; as conservative, 247, 253, 255–56; decline in proportion of women in, 231; emphasizes family values, 243; group identification with, 226–30; movement of white men to, 200; 1994 control of Congress, 23. See also Republicans
Republicans: changes in partisanship of, 82; gain in election margins of, 275–76; party loyalty of, 160; on term limitations, 273. See also Republican Party
Residentially mobile population, 70 n.14; and voter turnout, 47
Retrospective Voting in American National Elections, 112–13
Rhodes Scholar, 4
Richards, Ann, 173
Right-to-life groups, as force in 1992 elections, 243
Riker, William H., 69 n.6
Rinehart, Sue Tolleson, 216
Rockefeller, Jay, 16
Roll-call voting: consistency in, 316 n.11; impact of, 303; as measure of position, 297
Rollins, Ed, 17, 156
Roosevelt, Eleanor, 137, 149
Roosevelt, Franklin D., 112; third-term campaign of, 294
Roosevelt, Teddy, 23
Rosenstone, Steven J., 69 n.5
Rusk, Jerrold G., 69 n.4

Sampling error, 7
Sanford, Terry, 312
Satellite feeds: candidates' use of, 158; Perot's use of, 154
Savings-and-loan crisis, 263, 288
Scammon, Richard M., 71 n.22
Scandals, effect of, 11
Schroedel, Jean, 219 n.20
Secret ballot, 33
"Selection bias" problem, 133 n.4

Senate: Democrats control, 23; election study of, 6; 1992 elections, 292–318; voting for women in, 203–8; women in, 196

Senate Election Study (SES), 294–95

Senate Judiciary Committee, 2, 24, 136, 143, 243

Senators: aggregate perceptions of, 295; developing perceptions of, 296–302; development of attitudes toward, 11

Seven-point scale, 8; questions, 89, 90

Sexual harassment, 195, 243; as campaign issue, 94; as survey topic, 151n.9

Seymour, John, 219n.14

Shelby, Richard C., 23, 312

"Short" seat, 219n.15

Short-term issue(s), as factor in voting, 9

Short-term political attitudes, and support of Perot, 64

Silver, Brian, 69n.9

Simon, Paul, 205

Smith, Charles E., Jr., 8, 80, 89, 103

Snowe, Olympia, 217n.1

Snyder, Bruce, 219n.20

Social benefits, as issue category, 115, 127

Social group differences, analysis of, 10–11; polarization of, in 1992, 241–59

Social issues: lack of gender difference in support of, 203; in 1992 campaign, 93–96

Social welfare, party competence survey on, 187–88, 189, 191

Sociodemographic groupings: and candidates' wives, 142; and voter turnout, 59

Sociodemographic traits, and voter turnout, 41–47

Socioeconomic status (SES), and voting patterns, 37–40

Sociological approach, 12

Souljah, Sister, 243

South: gender gap in, 218n.7; voter turnout in, 45–46; whites in, as part of New Deal coalition, 220, 223. *See also* Native southern whites; Southerners

Southerners, as mildly conservative, 249

Specter, Arlen, 312

Stanley, Harold W., 240n.10, 242

Stassen, Harold, 24

State legislatures, women in, 197

Stern, Philip M., 290n.3

Stevenson, Adlai, 112

Stockdale, James, 2, 156

Stokes, Donald E., 179, 184

Super Tuesday, 16–17

Supreme Court: *Casey* decision of, 198; *Webster* decision of, 195, 198

Surveys, formats used in, 7–8

Symbolism, gender-related, 216, 217

Taft, William Howard, 20

Tate, Katherine, 41

Teixeira, Ruy, 39, 46–47, 70n.14

Television talk shows: candidates' use of, 158; Perot's use of, 154

Term limitation, 263, 264, 273; enacted in states, 23

Thermometer questions, 8

Thermometer ratings: Bush, 99, 100, 165, 171–72; candidates' wives, 142–43, 150n.4; Clinton, 99–100, 165, 171–72; Democratic Party, 77–78; Perot, 99–100, 165, 171–72; Republican Party, 78; social groups, 244–50

Third-party, formation of, 181

Third-party candidacy, 108; and support of independents, 79

Third-party candidates: and access to ballot, 158; characteristics of, 157; sources of support for, 10

Thomas, Clarence, 2, 24, 136, 143, 149, 195, 217, 270, 312; Thomas-Hill hearings, 198. *See also* Hill, Anita

Three-candidate race, analysis of,

26 n.2
Thurmond, Strom, 153
Tort reform, 243
Town hall meetings, Clinton's, 3
Traditionalists: Barbara Bush's appeal
    to, 146; and Perot support, 163;
    reaction of, to candidates' wives,
    145
Traits, of candidates, 102–3
Trust: as campaign issue, 19, 20, 101;
    as criterion for vote choice, 114,
    120, 127, 128
Tsongas, Paul, 2, 16, 17, 110 n.12
Turnout facilitators, 39

Unemployment: effects of, and infla-
    tion, 109 n.8; increase in, during
    Bush administration, 85–87
United We Stand, 4. See also United
    We Stand America
United We Stand America, 173; role
    of, in special elections, 174
University of Michigan: Center for
    Political Studies of, 35; Survey
    Research Center of, 6

Verba, Sidney, 70 n.11, 71 n.23
Vietnam war, 74; and ideological
    shift, 255
Vote, overreporting of, 36
Voter ideologies, relationship of with
    incumbent, 307
Voter participation: effects of low,
    66–68; racial gap in, 185–86,
    192–93
Voter registration: as barrier, 33–34;
    effect of introduction of, 32
Voter Research and Surveys (VRS), 8,
    158; on black vote, 179; exit
    polls of, 218 n.3; on gender gap,
    197, 209–15 passim
Voters: in American elections, 35–56;
    behavior of, in congressional
    elections, 276–78; and candidate
    gender, 204–8; and candidate
    partisanship, 204–8; mood of, in
    1992, 269–73; socioeconomic
    status, and patterns of, 37–40;

women as, 195–219
Voter turnout, 30–35; calculating,
    68–69 n.2; Congress bashing
    and, 285–88; consequences of
    changes in, 65–68; factors un-
    derlying low, 34–35; joint effects
    of correlates of, 53–56; and le-
    gitimacy of winner, 66; in 1992
    congressional races, 266; in 1992
    election, 29–71; 1992 increase
    in, 23; in other democracies, 33;
    results of low black, 192–93; re-
    versing decline in, 56–62; scan-
    dal and, 285–88; and
    sociodemographic traits, 41–47.
    See also Voting turnout
Voting, framework for studying,
    9–12
Voting Rights Act of 1965, 8, 267
Voting turnout: assessment of, 24; ef-
    fect of Perot on, 10; racial differ-
    ences in, 185. See also Voter
    turnout

Wallace, George, 26 n.2; 153, 157,
    158; candidacy of, as example of
    issue voting, 106
Walsh, Lawrence, 5
Walters, Ronald, 183
War chests, of incumbents, 303–5
"Wasted vote" argument, 157
Watergate affair, 74
Webster decision, 195, 198
Weinberger, Caspar, 5, 19
Weisberg, Herbert, 80, 113,
    314–15 n.4
Welfare recipients, as mildly liberal,
    247
Whig Party, 30
White men, movement of, to Republi-
    can Party, 200
Whites: campaign tilt of, 168; drop in
    ratings of, 252; support Perot,
    159
Whitewater investigation, 21
Whitman, Christine Todd, 193, 205
Wilcox, Clyde, 218 n.7
Wilder, Doug, 16

Willkie, Wendell, 112
Wilson, Edith, 137
Wilson, Pete, 219 n.14
WISH list, 198, 218 n.5
Wlezien, Christopher, 257
Wolfinger, Raymond E., 69 n.5
"Woman's vote," composition of, 210–11
Women: anger over treatment of, 151–52 n.9; appeal of Democratic Party to, 226; in Congress, 196, 267; as congressional candidates, 266; as conservatives, 200; as Democrats, 200; fluctuating party identification of, 231; policy concerns of, 217; representation of, in Congress, 23; in state legislatures, 197; as voters, 32, 195–219, 291 n.10; and voting

for Senate seat, 203–8
Women's issues: and candidates' wives, 145, 146–48; identification of Hillary Clinton with, 143
Women's movement: as liberal, 247; in 1992 election, 243
Working class, in New Deal coalition, 220, 223
Wright, Jim, 270
Wyden, Ron, 69 n.8

Yeakel, Lynn, 208, 312
Year of the Woman, 10: in House and Senate, 197–99; women voters in, 195–219
"Years of the Woman," 195–96

Zaller, John, 155
Zavoina, William, 133 n.5

Contributors

Herb Asher is a professor of political science at The Ohio State University. He has coedited the *American Journal of Political Science*. He is author of *Presidential Elections and American Politics, Polling and the Public,* and *Causal Modeling,* and coeditor of *Theory Building and Data Analysis in the Social Sciences.* His current research focuses on labor unions' political behavior, public support for political institutions, and presidential election vote choice.

Michael K. Barr is a Ph.D. candidate in political science at The Ohio State University. His research interests include public opinion, voting behavior, political psychology, and Congress.

Paul Allen Beck is a professor of political science and chair of the department at The Ohio State University. He is the coauthor of *Party Politics in America* and *Electoral Change in Advanced Industrial Democracies.* His current research focuses on the mass media, interpersonal discussion networks, and secondary organizations as intermediaries in elections in modern democracies.

Janet M. Box-Steffensmeier is an assistant professor of political science at The Ohio State University. She has published in *Western Political Quarterly, Rationality and Society,* and *The Political Methodologist.* Her research interests include campaign finance, congressional elections, Congress, and political methodology.

Barry C. Burden is a graduate student in political science at The Ohio State University. His current interests include campaign politics, public opinion, and the role of media in politics.

Elizabeth Adell Cook is a visiting assistant professor at The American University. She is coauthor of *Between Two Absolutes: Public Opinion and the Politics of Abortion,* coeditor of *The Year of the*

Woman: Myths and Realities, and author of numerous articles on public opinion and political behavior.

Charles H. Franklin is an associate professor of political science at the University of Wisconsin, Madison. He has published articles on partisanship, statistical methodology, and the Supreme Court and public opinion. His recent articles on Senate campaigns and careers have appeared in the *American Political Science Review* and *Legislative Studies Quarterly.*

Audrey A. Haynes is a Ph.D. candidate in political science at The Ohio State University. She has published in the area of presidential nomination campaigns and has presented papers in the areas of political parties, public opinion, and comparative legislative research. Her current research focuses on the nature of the news coverage in presidential nomination campaigns.

John H. Kessel is a professor of political science at The Ohio State University. He has edited the *American Journal of Political Science* and has been president of the Midwest Political Science Association. He is the author of *The Goldwater Campaign, The Domestic Presidency, Presidential Campaign Politics,* and *Presidential Parties.*

David C. Kimball is a graduate student in political science at The Ohio State University. His areas of interest include public attitudes toward political institutions, voting behavior, and interest groups.

Jon A. Krosnick is an associate professor of psychology and political science at The Ohio State University. He is coauthor of *An Introduction to Survey Research and Data Analysis* and editor of *Thinking About Politics.* He is currently writing a book on *Designing Questionnaires Effectively.* He is a specialist in political psychology, with an emphasis on mass political behavior.

Anthony Mughan is a professor of political science at The Ohio State University. He is author of *Party and Participation in British Elections* and coeditor of *Political Leadership in Democratic Societies.* He is an expert on the politics of Western Europe, especially Great Britain.

Stephen M. Nichols is a Ph.D. candidate in political science at The Ohio State University. He studies mass political behavior, political parties, and the presidency. His research interests include third parties as well as gender and politics.

Richard G. Niemi is a professor of political science at the University of Rochester. He has written numerous books and articles in the areas of voting and socialization. Another interest is legislative districting; a coauthored article, "Expressive Harms, 'Bizarre Districts,' and Voting Rights: Evaluating Election District 'Appearance' After *Shaw,*" recently appeared in the *Michigan Law Review.*

Samuel C. Patterson is a professor of political science at The Ohio State University. He has edited the *American Journal of Political Science* and *Legislative Studies Quarterly,* and has been managing editor of the *American Political Science Review.* He has been author or editor of *The Legislative Process in the United States, Comparative Legislative Behavior, Comparing Legislatures, Handbook of Legislative Research,* and *Parliaments in the Modern World.*

Charles E. Smith, Jr., is an assistant professor of political science at the University of Mississippi. He has published articles in the *American Political Science Review* and *Journal of Politics.* His areas of interest include public opinion and voting behavior.

Harold W. Stanley is an associate professor of political science at the University of Rochester. He has published on parties and elections in the *American Political Science Review, Journal of Politics, Publius,* and other journals. His books include *Voter Mobilization and the Politics of Race* and *Senate vs. Governor, Alabama 1971.* With Niemi he edits *Vital Statistics on American Politics,* now in its fourth edition.

Katherine Tate is an associate professor of political science at The Ohio State University. She is the author of *From Protest to Politics: The New Black Voters in American Elections.* Her articles on black politics have appeared in the *American Political Science Review* and the *National Political Science Review.* She is currently working on a study of race and urban politics.

Herbert F. Weisberg is a professor of political science at The Ohio State University. He has coedited the *American Journal of Political Science* and is coeditor of *Classics in Voting Behavior* and *Controversies in Voting Behavior,* as well as *Theory-Building and Data Analysis in the Social Sciences* and *Political Science: The Science of Politics.* He has authored the monograph *Central Tendency and Variation* and has co-authored *An Introduction to Survey Research and Data Analysis.*

Clyde Wilcox is an associate professor of government at Georgetown University. He is the author of *God's Warriors: The Christian Right in 20th-Century America* and *Between Two Absolutes: Public Opinion and the Politics of Abortion,* and he has edited *Risky Business: PAC Decisionmaking in Congressional Elections.* He has coedited *The Year of the Woman: Myths and Realities,* with Elizabeth Adell Cook.